ADDICTIVE DISORDERS

MOSBY–YEAR BOOK PRIMARY CARE SERIES

SERIES EDITORS

CHARLES E. DRISCOLL, M.D.

Professor and Head
Department of Family Practice
University of Iowa College of Medicine
Iowa City, Iowa

PAUL M. FISCHER, M.D.

Associate Professor
Department of Family Medicine
Medical College of Georgia
Augusta, Georgia

JOSEPH E. SCHERGER, M.D., M.P.H.

Clinical Professor
Department of Family Practice
School of Medicine
University of California, Davis
Davis, California

Addictive Disorders

MICHAEL F. FLEMING, M.D., M.P.H.

Associate Professor
Department of Family Medicine and Practice
University of Wisconsin at Madison
Madison, Wisconsin

KRISTEN LAWTON BARRY, PH.D.

Assistant Scientist
Department of Family Medicine and Practice
University of Wisconsin at Madison
Madison, Wisconsin

Mosby
Year Book

St. Louis   Baltimore   Boston   Chicago   London   Philadelphia   Sydney   Toronto

Mosby
Year Book

Dedicated to Publishing Excellence

Sponsoring Editor: Susie Baxter
Assistant Managing Editor, Text and Reference: George Mary Gardner
Senior Production Assistant: Maria Nevinger
Proofroom Manager: Barbara Kelly

CL   MA   JG   3   4   5   6   7   8   9   0   96   95   94

Library of Congress Cataloging-in-Publication Data
Addictive disorders : a practical guide to treatment / [edited by]
  Michael F. Fleming, Kristen Barry.
      p.   cm.
    Includes bibliographical references and index.
    ISBN 0-8151-3369-3
    1. Drug abuse—Treatment.   I. Fleming, Michael F., 1948-
II. Barry, Kristen.
    [DNLM: 1. Substance Dependence—therapy.   WM 270 A2248]
  RC564.A324   1991
  618.86′06—dc20   91-30022
  DNLM/DLC   CIP
  for Library of Congress

To our families:
  Susan, Adam, Sara, and Elizabeth
  Jim, Sarah, and Joe
Thanks for your patience and love.

CONTRIBUTORS

Macaran A. Baird, M.D., M.S.
Professor and Chairman
Department of Family Medicine
SUNY Health Science Center at Syracuse
Director, Medical Education
St. Joseph's Hospital Health Center
Syracuse, New York

Kristen Lawton Barry, Ph.D.
Assistant Scientist
Department of Family Medicine and Practice
University of Wisconsin Medical School at Madison
Madison, Wisconsin

Richard L. Brown, M.D., M.P.H.
Assistant Professor
Department of Family Medicine and Practice
University of Wisconsin Medical School at Madison
Madison, Wisconsin

Delores M. Burant, M.D.
Program Director
Outpatient Recovery Services
University of Wisconsin Medical School at Madison
Madison, Wisconsin

Sandra Burge, Ph.D.
Assistant Professor
Department of Family Practice
University of Texas Health Science Center at San Antonio
San Antonio, Texas

Hope H. Ewing, M.D., M.S.Ed.
Assistant Clinical Professor of Family Medicine
University of Southern California
Los Angeles, California
Family Practice Physician
Director, The Born Free Project
Contra Costa County Health Service Department
Merrithew Memorial Hospital
Martinez, California

Patricia H. Field, Ph.D.
Chief, Toxicology Section
State Laboratory of Hygiene
University of Wisconsin at Madison
Madison, Wisconsin

James Finch, M.D.
Medical Director
Durham County Substance Abuse Services and North Carolina Governor's Institute on Alcohol and Substance Abuse
Durham, North Carolina

Michael F. Fleming, M.D., M.P.H.
Associate Professor
Department of Family Medicine and Practice
University of Wisconsin at Madison
Madison, Wisconsin

Stephen P. Flynn, M.D., M.S.P.H.
Assistant Clinical Professor
Department of Family Medicine
Case Western Reserve University
Associate Director
Department of Family Practice
Fairview General Hospital
Cleveland, Ohio

Antonnette V. Graham, Ph.D.
Assistant Professor
Department of Family Medicine
Case Western Reserve University
Director, Behavioral Science Program
Department of Family Medicine
University Hospitals of Cleveland
Cleveland, Ohio

Robert E. Gwyther, M.D., M.B.A.
Associate Professor
Department of Family Medicine
University of North Carolina
Director, Family Practice Center
Department of Family Medicine
University of North Carolina Hospitals
Chapel Hill, North Carolina

Alfred R. Hansen, Ph.D., M.D.
Associate Professor
Department of Surgery/Emergency Medicine
University of North Carolina Hospital
Chapel Hill, North Carolina

Clark J. Hudak, M.S.W., Ph.D.(cand.)
*Director, Washington Center for Pathological
    Gambling*
College Park, Maryland

Timothy J. Ives, Pharm.D., M.P.H.
Associate Professor of Pharmacy
School of Pharmacy
Clinical Associate Professor of Family Medicine
School of Medicine
University of North Carolina
Chapel Hill, North Carolina

Peter Katsufrakis, M.D.
Clinical Assistant Professor
Director of Clinical Training
*AIDS Education and Training Center of Southern
    California*
University of Southern California
Los Angeles, California

Patricia K. Kokotailo, M.D., M.P.H.
Assistant Professor
Department of Pediatrics
University of Wisconsin Medical School
Madison, Wisconsin

Thomas E. Kottke, M.D.
Associate Professor
Department of Medicine and Health Sciences Research
Mayo Clinic and Foundation
Rochester, Minnesota

Gregory L. Landry, M.D.
Associate Professor
Department of Pediatrics
Head Medical Team Physician
University of Wisconsin
Madison, Wisconsin

Patricia A. Lane, M.D.
Assistant Professor
Department of Family Practice
*University of Texas Health Science Center at San
    Antonio*
San Antonio, Texas

Michael R. Liepman, M.D.
Chief, Chemical Dependency Service
Department of Psychiatry
The Medical Center of Central Massachusetts
Associate Professor
Director, Project APT
Department of Psychiatry
University of Massachusetts Medical School
Worchester, Massachusetts
Adjunct Assistant Professor of Family Medicine

Center for Alcohol and Addiction Studies
Brown University
Providence, Rhode Island

Michael M. Miller, M.D.
Associate Clinical Professor
Department of Family Medicine and Practice
Department of Psychiatry
University of Wisconsin School of Medicine
Medical Director
NewStart Alcohol/Drug Treatment Program
Meriter Hospital
Madison, Wisconsin

Gregory Phelps, M.D., M.P.H.
Assistant Professor of Family Medicine
Mercer University School of Medicine
Director of Occupational Medicine
Department of Family Practice
Medical Center of Central Georgia
Macon, Georgia

Robert M. Politzer, M.S., Sc.D.
Director of Research
Washington Center for Pathological Gambling
College Park, Maryland

Jerome E. Schulz, M.D.
Medical Director
Family and Community Medicine
University of California
San Francisco, California

William E. Schwab, M.D.
Associate Professor
Department of Family Medicine and Practice
University of Wisconsin at Madison
Madison, Wisconsin

Jeffrey Sikkink, M.D., M.S.P.H.
Clinical Assistant Professor
Family Medicine and Practice
University of Wisconsin at Madison
Eau Claire Family Medicine Program
Eau Claire, Wisconsin

Leif I. Solberg, M.D.
Medical Director for Quality Improvement
Blue Plus/Blue Cross/Blue Shield of Minnesota
St. Paul, Minnesota

Maureen Strohm, M.D.
Associate Professor of Clinical Family Medicine
Department of Family Medicine
University of Southern California School of Medicine
Los Angeles, California

CONSULTANTS

Dana Harlow, M.S.S.A., C.A.C., L.I.S.W.
Clinical Supervisor
Lakeland Institute
North Olmsted, Ohio

James Finch, M.D.
Durham County Substance Abuse Services
Durham, North Carolina

Janis Byrd, M.D.
Department of Family Medicine and Practice
University of Wisconsin at Madison
Madison, Wisconsin

Dan Campbell, P.T./A.T.C.
Manager, Athletic Training Services
Sports Medicine Clinic
University of Wisconsin at Madison
Madison, Wisconsin

FOREWORD

Progress in the treatment of addictive disorders has been hampered by our assumptions about these patients and by our myths about their treatment. For example:

- We assume that addiction is uncommon, yet one in three patients seen in primary care has a substance abuse disorder, most commonly due to problems with alcohol, tobacco, or prescribed medications.
- We assume that the natural history of addiction is progressive. Patients eventually "hit bottom," then recover and stay "dry." In fact, for most patients the road is complex, marked by periods of problem use, abstinence, recovery, relapse, and controlled use.
- We assume that the specific addictive substance is essential in understanding a patient's problem; however, many patients use multiple substances. Furthermore, there are great similarities between "addictive personalities," regardless of the chosen substance of abuse.
- We assume that it is solely the patient's responsibility to gain control over the addiction. In fact, both the physician and the patient's family can play important roles in identifying the problem and surporting the patient's efforts to solve it.
- We assume that the quantity of the substance (e.g., alcohol, benzodiazepines, tobacco) correlates well with the level of patient's problem. In fact, there is wide variation between the quantity consumed and the degree of disruption in a person's life.
- We assume that all of a patient's problems can be traced to addiction when at least one problem is addiction. In fact, substance abuse is often intertwined with other prior psychiatric illnesses.
- We assume that addiction is easy to recognize. In fact, in most patients the problem goes undiagnosed, for example, the hypertensive patient whose blood pressure cannot be controlled because of alcohol, the patient with peptic ulcer who does not respond to H_2 blockade because of continued smoking, or the adolescent who is failing school and heavily using marijuana.

These myths have developed because much of what is written about addictive disorders has come from the "tip of the iceberg," that is, those patients who end up receiving care in specialized inpatient treatment programs. This book by Michael Fleming, M.D., and Kristen Barry, Ph.D., is a refreshing alternative because it deals with the larger spectrum of patients with addictive disorders who are seen in primary care settings.

Doctors Fleming and Barry show how care of the patient with an addictive disorder can be both straightforward and rewarding. Here are a few of the practical hints provided in this book:

Chapter 2 describes "brief interventions." These are short discussions with patients, designed to initiate their efforts to control substance abuse. Brief interventions can be done "on the run" and "in the middle" of other health care activities. This strategy has been widely studied in patients who smoke, and is now proving successful with other addictive disorders.

Chapter 3 provides protocols for the outpatient treatment of withdrawal states.

Chapter 4 describes what goes on in a typical Twelve-Step Program, and in both inpatient and outpatient treatment facilities. Did you ever wonder which type of program was optimal for your patient?

Chapter 5 describes practical ways that your office can be organized to optimize the identification and treatment of patients who smoke.

The appendix provides a dictionary of drug "street names." ("Merck" is a general term for any high-quality drug!) The appendix also provides an exhaustive list of resources available to both physicians and patients in the treatment of substance abuse disorders.

This book has been written by individuals who have struggled to identify the many faces of addiction in primary care and who treat these complex problems within the constraints of a typical 15-minute patient visit. This is an important and refreshingly new perspective on addiction.

PAUL M. FISCHER, M.D.
Associate Professor
Department of Family Medicine
Medical College of Georgia
Augusta, Georgia

FOREWORD

The problems of addiction have been present since the beginning of recorded time. However, it has not been until recent years that physicians have begun to recognize the importance of treating addicted patients. Over the past 20 years, our knowledge of the stages of addiction and the approaches needed for early identification and acute and long-term treatment have evolved significantly. As this evolution has taken place, what has been missing is a practical guide that can be easily used by physicians who have expertise as well as those physicians who have limited knowledge of the field.

Drs. Fleming and Barry have compiled an impressive group of knowledgeable practitioners to provide comprehensive information on the treatment of addictive disorders. This book provides a practical approach to treatment that can be used by physicians in their daily practice and also contains information that outlines the current and future directions for research in addiction medicine. Through the use of case examples, the physician will easily recognize cases seen in his or her own practice.

The book is designed for easy reference to the areas that will be most helpful for the physician in the treatment of addictive disorders. This practical guide will be placed on a shelf near your desk so that it can be used on a regular basis in dealing with the complex, yet common, problems of addiction.

SIDNEY H. SCHNOLL, M.D., PH.D.
Medical College of Virginia Hospitals
Chairman, Division of Substance Abuse Medicine
Professor, Medicine and Psychiatry
Richmond, Virginia

PREFACE

This book is intended to be used as a practical clinical guide. The outline format facilitates easy access to the material for use in the office. The clinical material and treatment methods presented were developed for use in busy practice settings. The material chosen was based on one overriding question: What should every health care professional know about the care of persons adversely affected by nicotine, alcohol, and other mood-altering drugs? The editors expect that primary care physicians, medical and surgical specialists, psychiatrists, and physicians with expertise in addiction medicine will find the answer to the majority of their clinical questions in at least one of the 20 chapters. Nurse practitioners, physician assistants, social workers, psychologists, alcohol and drug counselors, and pharmacists will be able to use the book as an essential reference guide. In addition, educators and students can use the material as a course syllabus for educational programs in substance abuse.

The primary goal is to provide health care professionals with a comprehensive yet practical guide. The emphasis is on detection, intervention, and treatment, although epidemiology, genetics, and basic science research are included. We have limited treatment recommendations to methods the editors and contributors have found effective in the care of their own patients. While many of the treatment recommendations presented have not been tested in randomized clinical trials, the summative clinical experience of the contributors and other experts in the field supports their use.

The ideas and approaches used in the preparation of the text were developed through a number of educational programs for physicians and other health care professionals. When preparing material for these courses we discovered that, although there is an abundance of information available in research journals and other scholarly publications, there are few practical references to assist clinicians who are not interested in becoming addiction specialists. There is a particular absence of clinical material for the management of nondependent problematic users, who represent the vast majority of patients with alcohol and drug problems who are seen in emergency departments and ambulatory care settings.

Since nicotine, alcohol, illicit drugs, and prescription drugs all are psychoactive substances with potential addictive properties, all four groups of drugs are included in most chapters. The decision to include nicotine and prescription drugs in the content of the book was based on the pharmacologic similarities of the chemicals and the presence of polysubstance use in many patients seen in clinical practice. Gambling and eating disorders also are included, because they frequently occur in patients with alcohol and drug problems. There is also an emphasis on the treatment of patients with concomitant psychiatric disorders.

The 20 chapters are grouped into four major areas of clinical care: identification and treatment of the primary disorder; management of secondary medical problems; clinical approaches to specific populations; and management of special problems, including dual diagnosis, AIDS, and compulsive disorders. The five appendixes at the end of the book include definitions, screening and diagnostic instruments, resources, an index of common street terms, and DSM-III-R criteria for major psychiatric illnesses. While the chapters have a limited number of citations, key references are included.

Part I presents an overview of addiction medicine. Chapter 1 reviews our current understanding of epidemiology, natural history, and the classification of addictive disorders. Case examples are used to define normative use, problematic use, and dependence. The authors introduce a model of dependence and recovery that illustrates the complexity and variability of the clinical course of these disorders.

Part II focuses on the identification and treatment of the primary alcohol and drug disorder. Chapter 2 reviews methods for assessment, intervention, and treatment. Included are two approaches to screening and intervention—direct and indirect—and the advantages and disadvantages of each. This chapter provides the essential strategies needed to break through the wall of denial that permeates this illness. The importance of clinician-based brief advice interventions is emphasized. Chapter 3 presents the pharmacologic treatment of withdrawal, postwithdrawal abstinence syndrome, drug maintenance, and euphoria blocking agents. As our understanding of brain-receptor mechanisms increases, there will be a number of new medications that can be used to treat these conditions effectively. Current drugs and those being tested in clinical trials are reviewed.

Chapter 4 discusses the admission criteria for inpatient and outpatient programs, a typical day in a treatment program, relapse prevention, and the role of 12-Step programs in recovery. Traditional self-help programs remain the major therapy for the treatment of chemical dependency. Chapter 5 addresses office-based smoking cessation strategies. The practice-based system established a comprehensive program to help patients quite smoking. The methods presented are based on a series of successful clinical trials.

Chapter 6 presents guidelines for the use of psychoactive drugs in chemically dependent patients. Included are drugs that can be used in recovering patients, pain management with opioids, and the clinical characterists of drug-seeking patients. Methods to prevent prescription drug abuse are given. The use of opioids in the care of patients with chronic pain syndromes is reviewed. Chapter 7 discusses the essentials of drug testing. Included are a review of laboratory methods, specimen collection techniques to minimize adulteration, and the drugs tested in medical and workplace screening programs. The role of the Medical Review Officer (MRO), federal laws and standards, and ethical and legal controversies are illustrated with case examples.

Part III presents information on the treatment of secondary medical problems. Medical complications are numerous, and account for a significant proportion of patients seen in clinical practice. Chapter 8 focuses on the management of the common adverse health effects. Some of the secondary complications reviewed include hypertension, arrhythmias, sleep problems, chronic abdominal pain, chronic diarrhea, sinusitis, and sexual dysfunction. Chapter 9 outlines methods and algorithms for diagnosis and management in patients treated in the emergency department. Topics presented include a review of the signs and symptoms of problematic alcohol and drug use, and drug-seeking behavior. The management of intoxicated patients who may have life-threatening complications is reviewed, with particular emphasis on drug-related effects.

Part IV reviews clinical approaches to specific patient populations, including family members, prenatal patients, adolescents, women, older adults, and the physically and cognitively disabled. Chapter 10 offers constructive methods that can be used to discover patients affected by another person's alcohol or drug use and ways to assist them in a recovery program. The chapter also discusses the stereotyped roles of adult children of alcoholics and the hazards of applying stereotypical roles to children and adults.

Psychoactive substance use is associated with significant health effects to mothers, infants, and their families. Pregnancy may be the first event that brings women with drug- and alcohol-related problems into the health care system. This event provides a window of opportunity for recognition, intervention, and education. Chapter 11 provides a synopsis of the effects of alcohol and other drugs on fertility and pregnancy and on the fetus, newborn, and infant. Screening questions, common responses of women in denial, specific statements for the clinician, pharmacologic treatment of newborn syndromes, and a patient handout are provided.

Chapter 12 presents approaches to treatment in adolescents. Both direct and indirect questions about substance use are presented. Questionnaires for teens and for concerned parents are provided. Health care providers also deal with children, adolescents, and adults who take part in recreational and competitive sports. The use of drugs in sports, including performance-enhancing drugs, is a rising concern in our society. Chapter 13 provides a timely synopsis of the drugs of abuse in sports, the ethical issues raised by the use of these drugs, and the provider's role in drug use by athletes.

The problematic use of alcohol, in particular, has been documented to escalate into severe consequences at a faster rate in women than in men; however, alcohol- and drug-related problems in women tend to remain underdiagnosed in ambulatory care settings. In Chapter 14 the authors provide a practical guide for when to assess women in the office for alcohol and drug problems, questions to ask, and the special needs of women in treatment, including social support, gynecologic services, violence counseling, child care, and legal assistance.

Adults over the age of 65 years take 25% of all prescribed medications, and this population is the fastest growing segment of society. Although the prevalence of alcohol and drug use decreases with age, the abuse of alcohol and of prescription and over-the-counter (OTC) medications is a common concern. Chapter 15 reviews recognition, diagnosis, and treatment options in older adults. The chapter provides a new screening questionnaire, "CHARM." This acronym was chosen to enhance clinician awareness of the need to maintain a nonthreatening approach with patients in this age group. The pharmacokinetics of benzodiazepines, maximum doses of frequently used antidepressants and neuroleptics, and specific guidelines for the use of neuroleptics also are presented.

The final chapter in this section, Chapter 16, provides a helpful overview of the medical complications of alcohol and drug disorders in patients with physical and cognitive disabilities. Health care system changes since the 1970s have increased the number of people with disabilities living in communities, which in turn has increased both access to alcohol and other drugs and the prevalence of addictive disorders in this population. Types of disabilities commonly seen in ambulatory care settings and related substance use problems are discussed. Medical care issues and the need for a team effort in intervention are stressed.

Part V covers related medical problems such as eating disorders, mental health disorders, HIV/AIDS, and gambling disorders. Eating disorders are included because they have much in common with alcohol and drug disorders. Persons with eating disorders experience denial, secretiveness, inability to discontinue the behavior, depressed feelings, and a range of physical symptoms common in addictive disorders. Chapter 17 presents an overview of anorexia nervosa and bulimia, a sample of screening questions, guidelines for assessment and referral, and the role of the ambulatory care provider in treatment.

The diagnosis and treatment of coexisting mental health and substance disorders, often called "dual diagnosis," has been a challenge to both the mental health and chemical dependency treatment communities. Chapter 18 presents a framework that can be used to assess and manage both addictive disorders and psychiatric symptoms through clinical situations.

HIV/AIDS has had a profound effect on the health care community. Health care providers are aware of the direct relationship between HIV infection and intravenous drug use. There also is a supposition that persons who are alcohol dependent are at higher risk for development of AIDS secondary to risk-taking behavior while intoxicated. Chapter 19 discusses the risks of HIV/AIDS in persons who use various types of drugs and different routes of administration. Ambulatory care providers have an opportunity to provide education and assistance to many patients at risk for AIDS. This chapter provides the practitioner with screening questions, guidelines for risk reduction counseling, and guidelines for counseling around HIV testing.

Pathologic gambling is often underdiagnosed and less frequently treated than other addictive disorders or compulsions. What distinguishes problem gamblers from others who wager on outcomes beyond their control and skill is that pathologic gambling is uncontrollable and has serious adverse consequences. Chapter 20 explains this disorder, suggests how patients with the disorder may present in an ambulatory care setting, provides screening questions for clinicians, and discusses treatment options.

We have included five appendices at the end of the book. Appendix A includes a taxonomy of terms. Appendix B includes national resources and patient education materials. Appendix C provides supplementary screening instruments for selected populations. Street names for common drugs of misuse and abuse other than alcohol are included in Appendix D. And finally, Appendix E includes DSM-III-R diagnostic criteria for selected psychiatric disorders.

There are few opportunities in clinical medicine in which we can make significant long-lasting changes in the lives of our patients. Helping a patient with an alcohol or drug disorder to recover from an often progressive illness that can lead to early death is one of these opportunities. Treatment programs that focus on recovering professionals report 5-year cure rates better than 80%. No other chronic condition is treated with such high potential cure rates. Assisting family members and friends develop realistic strategies for themselves and their alcohol- or drug-dependent loved one can relieve much pain and suffering.

MICHAEL F. FLEMING, M.D., M.P.H.
KRISTEN LAWTON BARRY, PH.D.

ACKNOWLEDGMENT

The editors wish to gratefully acknowledge the following persons, who assisted in revisions of the chapters in this book. Their time, effort, and excellent suggestions were invaluable.

John W. Beasley, M.D.
Associate Professor
Department of Family Medicine and Practice
University of Wisconsin—Madison

Sheila Blume, M.D.
South Oaks Hospital
Amityville, New York

Robert Cefalo, M.D., Ph.D.
Professor, Associate Dean
Department of Obstetrics and Gynecology
University of North Carolina—Chapel Hill

Kathleen Clark
Department of Family Medicine
University of Wisconsin—Madison

Peter Coleman, M.D.
Family Physician
Richmond, Virginia

June Dahl, Ph.D.
Professor
Department of Pharmacology
University of Wisconsin—Madison

James Robert Damos, M.D.
Associate Professor
Department of Family Medicine and Practice
University of Wisconsin—Madison

Susan Davidson, M.D., M.S.
Assistant Professor
Department of Obstetrics and Gynecology
University of Wisconsin—Madison

Raymond N. Demers, M.D.
Associate Professor
Department of Family and Community Medicine
Wayne State University
Detroit, Michigan

Charles Engel, M.D.
Addiction Medicine Specialist
Milwaukee Psychiatric Hospital
Milwaukee, Wisconsin

Marshall Fields, M.D.
Family Physician
Madison, Wisconsin

Adam Goldsmith, M.D.
Fellow in Primary Care Medicine
University of North Carolina—Chapel Hill

Frank W. Graziano, M.D.
Professor, Department of Medicine
University of Wisconsin—Madison

Myra L. Kerstitch, M.D.
Assistant Professor
Department of Family and Community Medicine
University of Arizona—Tucson

Michael Klitzner, Ph.D.
Senior Research Scientist
Pacific Institute for Research and Evaluation
Bethesda, Maryland

Stanley Livingston, M.D.
Family Physician
Madison, Wisconsin

Richard L. London, M.D.
Family Physician
Milwaukee, Wisconsin

Mary Beth Manning, C.A.D.C.
Director, McBride Center
Madison, Wisconsin

Al J. Mooney III, M.D.
Director, Willingway Hospital
Associate Clinical Professor
Department of Family Medicine
Medical College of Georgia—Augusta

Theodore Parran, M.D.
Associate Professor
Department of Medicine
Case Western Reserve University
Cleveland, Ohio

Peter Joseph Rizzolo, M.D.
Professor
Department Family Medicine
University of North Carolina—Chapel Hill

Jonathan E. Rodnick, M.D.
Chairman, Department of Family and Community
  Medicine
University of California—San Francisco

William Scheckler, M.D.
Professor and Director, Research Division
Department of Family Medicine and Practice
University of Wisconsin—Madison

Sidney Schnoll, M.D., Ph.D.
Professor
Medical College of Virginia—Richmond

Eugene Schoener, Ph.D.
Professor
Department of Family and Community Medicine
Wayne State University School of Medicine
Detroit, Michigan

Michael A. Sitorius, M.D.
Professor and Chairman
Department of Family Medicine
University of Nebraska Medical Center
Omaha, Nebraska

Douglas Smith, M.D.
Assistant Professor
Department of Family Medicine and Practice
University of Wisconsin—Madison

Narra Smith-Cox, Ph.D.
Department of Family Medicine and Practice
University of Wisconsin—Madison

John Stephenson, M.D.
Professor
Department of Pediatrics
University of Wisconsin—Madison

Michael Sweetnum, Ph.D.
Wisconsin Institute
Madison, Wisconsin

Mark Timmerman, M.D.
Department of Family Medicine and Practice
University of Wisconsin—Madison

Gregg Alan Warshaw, M.D.
Associate Professor
Department of Family Medicine
University of Cincinnati

Alan Wartenberg, M.D.
Addiction Medicine Specialist
Boston, Massachusetts

Robert Watson, M.D.
Assistant Professor
St. Luke's Hospital
University of Wisconsin—Milwaukee

We are especially indebted to Ann Runde Neis of the Department of Family Medicine at the University of Wisconsin—Madison, whose tireless editorial assistance and organization made this book possible.

MICHAEL F. FLEMING, M.D., M.P.H.
KRISTEN LAWTON BARRY, PH.D.

CONTENTS

PART ONE

Introduction

CHAPTER 1

Clinical Overview of Alcohol and Drug Disorders

Michael F. Fleming, M.D., M.P.H.

Kristen Lawton Barry, Ph.D.

The clinical management of adverse effects of alcohol and other mood-altering drugs is influenced by our understanding of the natural processes of alcohol and drug disorders. These processes include sociocultural norms of use, the clinical course of alcohol and drug disorders, and the biology of addiction. This chapter reviews our current understanding of problematic use and dependence. Although our knowledge of the natural history of these processes is limited, the material presented will provide practitioners with a foundation for the management of addictive disorders.

I. How Common are Alcohol and Drug Disorders?
   A. Prevalence and Incidence:
   1. **Importance of prevalence data to clinicians:** Clinicians who work in ambulatory care settings can expect that 15% to 20% of their adult patients have a previous history of an alcohol and/or drug disorder and that 8% to 10% have a current disorder. Practices that identify fewer patients with alcohol and drug problems may need to establish screening and case-finding procedures to detect these disorders. Identifying a history of lifetime use is important, because patients with a previous history of problematic use are at risk for relapse.
   2. **Incidence:** Incidence rates (number of new cases per unit time) are useful in estimating changing patterns of an illness. For example, the incidence of lung and breast cancer continues to increase in women, whereas the incidence of ischemic heart disease has dropped significantly. The incidence of alcohol and drug problems is more difficult to estimate, because current studies estimate the number of existing cases. We do not know the number of new cases of alcohol dependence in the United States in 1991, nor do we know if the incidence is rising or falling.

B. **Measures of Prevalence of Alcohol and Drug Use:**
  1. **Telephone survey data:** The data presented in Figure 1–1 were obtained in a series of annual telephone surveys based on national probability samples, and illustrate trends in nicotine, alcohol, and drug use between 1977 and 1990. During this time there was a dramatic decline in overall use. Although the data presented are limited to persons aged 18 to 25 years, other age groups demonstrate similar changes in use patterns (NIDA capsules, 1990). Figure 1–2 presents the changing trends in marijuana use.
  2. **Alcohol use based on tax receipts:** Alcohol sales peaked in 1981, at 2.76 gallons pure alcohol per person age ≥14 years. This is the equivalent of 33 cases of beer or 46 bottles of wine per person in a 12-month period. Figures for 1990 suggest a drop to less than 2.50 gallons per person. While these numbers suggest a decline in overall use, telephone surveys have found an increase in the numbers in two groups: abstainers (defined as fewer than 3 drinks per month) and heavy users (Seventh Report to Congress, 1990).
C. **Measures of Prevalence of Alcohol and Drug Disorders:**
  1. **Epidemiologic Catchment Area (ECA) study:** This landmark prevalence study was conducted at five sites in the early 1980s. At each site face-to-face interviews were conducted using a diagnostic interview schedule based on DSM-III (*Diagnostic and Statistical Manual of Mental Disorders,* ed 3) criteria for substance abuse or

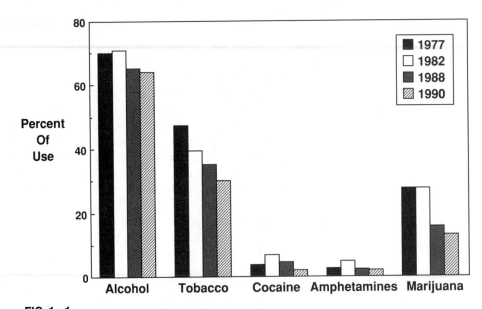

FIG 1–1.
National household survey of nicotine, alcohol, and drug use between 1977 and 1990. This figure represents any use in the past month for persons aged 18 to 25 years. Note marked decrease in prevalence of use over this 14-year period.

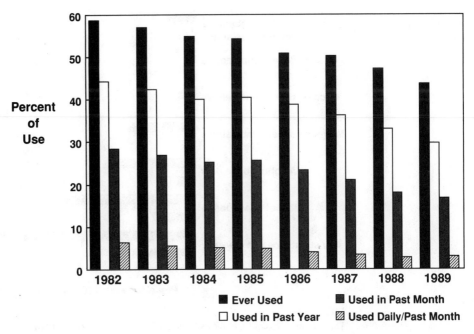

FIG 1–2.
Data obtained from the NIDA-funded "Monitoring the Future" study (*NIDA Capsules,* 1990). The figure reports changing patterns in marijuana use by high school seniors between 1982 and 1989. Although there is a significant decrease in use overall, more than 20% of respondents reported use in the past month and 4% reported daily use.

dependence. The results of this community-based sample consisting of 20,291 adults is presented in Figure 1–3.

2. **Prevalence in primary care settings:** Using methods and research instruments similar to those used in the ECA study, we studied the lifetime and 12-month prevalence of alcohol and drug disorders in five family medicine clinics located in three counties in Wisconsin in 1988 and 1989.

a. We found a lifetime prevalence of alcohol disorders of 16% to 28% in the five clinics. The 12-month prevalence in the clinics ranged between 9% and 15%. The lifetime prevalence of drug disorders was 7% to 9%. Three percent continued to experience problems with drugs in the 12 months before the study was conducted.

b. These findings likely reflect the high alcohol use rates in Wisconsin and a higher prevalence in clinical settings as compared with the community samples used in the ECA study.

II. **Definition of Alcohol and Drug Disorders**

A. **Overview of Diagnostic Problem:**

1. *Definition of a case:* The diagnosis of alcohol and drug disorders is based primarily on a history of behavioral characteristics such as

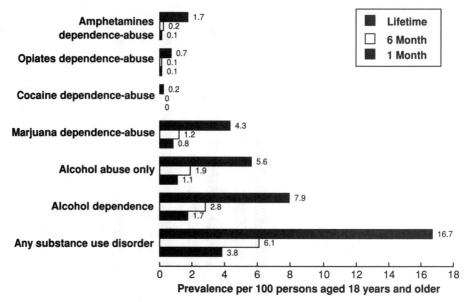

FIG 1–3.
The Epidemiological Catchment Area (ECA) study reported here was conducted in the early 1980s on a sample of more than 20,000 adults. The data obtained from this cross-sectional study report prevalence of use, abuse, and dependence in the general population. The frequency of these problems found in this study is less than that found in ambulatory care settings. The criteria for abuse and dependence are based on DSM-III criteria. A lifetime diagnosis of alcohol dependence indicates that the subjects met criteria for dependence once in their life. Persons who met criteria in the past 6 months represent a current problem with abuse or dependence.

loss of control, repeated adverse family and social consequences, and physiologic responses such as the development of abdominal pain, insomnia, blackouts, liver toxicity, tolerance, and withdrawal.

2. ***Contrast with other medical conditions:*** Unlike most other illnesses or medical problems, there is no definitive physical finding, laboratory test, or histologic technique on which to make a diagnosis of primary alcohol and drug disorders. There is no equivalent to a blood pressure measurement or a serum cholesterol level. The available tests, including those for liver function and hematologic abnormalities, detect end organ damage rather than the primary disorder. The use of these tests to diagnose alcohol disorders is similar to diagnosing hypertension on the basis of proteinuria and congestive heart failure or diabetes by the presence of retinopathy and renal casts.

B. **Limitations of terms:**
1. ***Terms:*** A number of *terms* are used in this book, and in the field of addiction medicine, to describe and define the clinical problems associated with the use of alcohol and other mood-altering drugs. The use of varying terms to describe the complex processes they represent reflects the difficulties inherent in defining these disorders.

From a clinical perspective, however, it is important for practitioners to have an understanding of the definitions of these terms and to use the same terms to describe similar clinical problems.

2. ***Terms of preference for use in clinical settings:***
   a. The term *addictive disorders* (the title of this book) is the most inclusive term used in this book and includes the clinical problems of alcohol and drug dependence, gambling compulsion, and eating disorders. While there is controversy on the inclusion of gambling and eating disorders as addictive disorders, current treatment methods use an addiction model for recovery, the clinical characteristics are similar to those of alcohol and drug problems, and these conditions frequently are noted in persons with alcohol and drug problems.
   b. *Alcohol and drug disorders* is the term used to describe the spectrum of problems and illness associated with the adverse effects of mood-altering chemicals. Drug problems include illicit drug use and prescription drug addiction. The clinical syndromes of dependence and problematic use are considered alcohol and drug disorders.
   c. *Substance dependence* is the primary clinical term used by clinicians, and is based on standard criteria, that is, those in the DSM that are used for ICD-9 (*International Classification of Diseases,* rev 9) coding. *Substance dependence* is the clinical term most frequently used for insurance reimbursement purposes. This term has been widely accepted in the medical community and insurance industry. Addiction and alcoholism are considered dependence syndromes.
   d. A term of great importance to clinicians who work primarily in ambulatory care settings is *problematic use.* This term is particularly important for clinicians working with patients who are experiencing difficulties with alcohol and drugs who either do not meet criteria for dependence or the severity of their disorder is not clear. Problematic use is categorized as mild or moderate to severe.
   e. Terms recommended for discussions of these conditions with patients, communicating with colleagues, or recording information in the records include *alcohol and drug disorder, substance dependence, addiction, mild problematic use,* and *moderate to severe problematic use.*

3. ***Terms that describe recovery:*** Because these disorders are considered lifelong problems, *alcohol dependence in remission* (or *cocaine dependence in remission*) is the preferred clinical term. In addition, the present tense of the term, "recovering," is used rather than the past tense, "recovered," because relapse may be only a drink away. Relapse with progressive disease can occur 10 to 20 years after last previous use. The use of descriptive phrases such as "former alcoholic" or "former addict" are not recommended.

4. ***Other terms:*** Additional terms commonly used in clinical medicine, developed by the American Society of Addiction Medicine, are defined in Appendix A.

5. ***Use of the terms "alcoholism" and "drug addiction":*** The terms *alcoholism, alcoholic, drug addict,* and *drug addiction* are associated with negative societal connotations. Although these terms are often used by clinicians with patients who have high levels of denial, they are powerful labels and should be used with caution. Indiscriminant use of these labels with patients, family members, and colleagues can have significant negative consequences.

C. Definitions of Use:

Patients commonly are described as "light to moderate" users or "heavy" users. While different studies vary on the definition of a "nonuser," persons who consume fewer than 3 alcoholic drinks per month and use no illicit drugs are considered nonusers. The following definitions are based on terms used in epidemiologic surveys.

1. ***Light to moderate users*** consume between 1 and 12 drinks per week, fewer than 4 drinks per occasion, and/or use other drugs once or twice a week in small quantities.

2. ***Heavy users*** drink 2 or more drinks per day, 4 or more drinks three or more times per week, exhibit binge patterns of use, and/or use illicit drugs more than twice per week.

   a. *Case examples:* Following are three case examples of nonproblematic heavy users frequently encountered in primary care settings. While these individuals are likely to remain nonproblematic users, they should be monitored for adverse health effects.

   > Irene is a 45-year-old schoolteacher who drinks two glasses of wine with dinner daily. Her use pattern has not changed in 10 years. She has had no problems with her level of use, never gets drunk, and has no history of loss of control. She has no family history of alcohol problems, and drinks because she enjoys the taste.
   >
   > Mark is a 42-year-old counselor who smokes 3 or 4 joints of marijuana per week. He began using marijuana in college. He enjoys wine, but never exceeds 3 or 4 drinks, and does not like to get drunk. He tried cocaine twice in college. He smokes after dinner to relax and unwind. He is successful and has the respect of his colleagues. He has been happily married for 15 years and has two teenage daughters.
   >
   > Joe is a 55-year-old construction worker who drinks 2 or 3 beers per day. He has no history of alcohol-related events and has not changed his use pattern in 20 years. He drank more heavily in his 20s, but rarely drinks more than 3 beers at one sitting. He has not been drunk in 5 years. His wife of 30 years does not drink, and his two sons occasionally use alcohol and marijuana with friends.

D. Definition of Problematic Use:

1. ***Problematic users:*** Problematic users have developed one or more alcohol- or drug-related problems, such as driving under the influence of alcohol (DUI), medical complications, family problems,

or other behavioral consequences. A problematic user may have experienced a single alcohol- or drug-related event or may have developed severe problems and dependency. Problems range from "minimal," for example, one or two blackouts in young adulthood, followed by family concern about the person's drinking, through "severe," including loss of work, loss of family, and withdrawal symptoms. From a clinical perspective, it is useful to classify problematic use as mild, moderate, or severe.

2. ***Why are these classifications important?*** We use these categories as a clinical guide to patient management. Persons with mild disorders frequently respond to a brief office-based intervention similar to that used by clinicians for tobacco cessation counseling. Persons with moderate to severe problems may require more intensive treatment in an alcohol treatment program. (See Chapter 2 and Fig 2–2 for a more extensive discussion of management.)

3. ***Differentiating mild, moderate, and severe problematic use:*** There is no commonly accepted number of alcohol- or drug-related events to define the three categories of problematic use. Practitioners can use both clinical judgment and DSM dependence criteria (see following section). Since denial is an important behavioral component of alcohol and drug disorders, it may be difficult to uncover the full extent of the problems until a patient has achieved abstinence and sobriety.

   a. *Case examples:* The following examples illustrate problematic use commonly encountered in clinical practice.

      (1) *Mild problematic use:*

> Mary is a 25-year-old single graduate student who drinks 4 or 5 beers two or three times per week. She recently received emergency treatment for a head injury. She reportedly slipped on a patch of ice outside of her apartment. She gets drunk about once a month, and occasionally drives herself home while intoxicated. She smokes marijuana about once a month at parties. Mary has no family history of alcohol problems, and reports no other consequences of her alcohol or drug use. She uses alcohol to be sociable, and always has been able to stop. The emergency department physician told her to limit her alcohol use to two drinks per occasion and to see her regular provider if she has any problem in cutting back.

      (2) *Moderate to severe problematic use with recovery:*

> John is a 51-year-old executive who came to the office for a physical examination. He had a drinking and tobacco problem for many years, but was able to stop using alcohol and tobacco 5 years ago. He reported that the major problems with his use were chronic abdominal pain, occasional loss of control, and two DUI arrests. While he did not want to stop his use of alcohol and tobacco, his physician, family, and employer told him that he had to stop or suffer the consequences of losing his health, his family, and his job.

He made up his mind to stop, and did so with no symptoms of withdrawal. He remains abstinent at 5 years.

Jim is a 35-year-old farmer who drank 3 to 6 beers every day after he finished his chores. His blood pressure was elevated, and he developed chronic epigastric pain that responded to ranitidine. While he did not get visibly drunk, his family complained about his heavy alcohol use and asked him to stop. Blood pressure measurements over 3 months ranged from 160/110 to 140/98. A laboratory study revealed an elevated gamma-glutamyltransferase (GGT) level. He remains abstinent 6 months after his physician and family confronted him. His blood pressure problem and epigastric pain have resolved.

E. Substance Dependence and Addiction:

1. ***Definition:*** Dependence and addiction are defined by physiologic and psychologic dependence on one or more mood-altering chemicals. Physiologic dependence is defined by the development of tolerance or of withdrawal symptoms. Psychologic dependence is demonstrated by the presence of loss of control and other progressive behavioral effects. While a patient receiving high doses of opioids for pain control may develop tolerance or withdrawal symptoms, he or she usually does not become psychologically dependent and therefore does not meet criteria for drug dependence.

2. ***UCR clinical criteria:*** The mnemonic UCR (*u*se, *c*onsequences, and *r*epetition) aids clinicians in establishing the presence of an alcohol or drug disorder. Patients who fulfill UCR criteria are likely to develop substance dependence and experience serious medical sequelae. For example, a person who continues to drink heavily after experiencing severe pancreatitis, family problems, alcohol withdrawal, or job loss is likely dependent. The most important evidence for this diagnosis is repetitive alcohol or drug use in the presence of an increasing number of alcohol-related events and consequences.

3. ***DSM-III criteria for dependence:*** Although the original DSM-III criteria have been modified (DSM-IIIR and DSM-4), they are presented here because they are easier to remember, less ambiguous, and more stringent. The dilemma with the DSM-IIIR and DSM-4 criteria is that a diagnosis of dependency is possible without evidence of physical dependence (tolerance or withdrawal symptoms). Three broad criteria must be met to establish a diagnosis of substance dependence. Persons who do not meet these three criteria are best considered problematic users rather than dependent. The symptoms for each criteria must have persisted for at least 1 month.
Criteria A: Pathologic use, e.g., loss of control, benders, making rules, repeated unsuccessful attempts to "stay stopped."
Criteria B: Repeated consequences, e.g., blackouts, health problems, family problems, financial and occupational losses.
Criteria C: Tolerance and/or withdrawal symptoms, e.g., shakes or drinking in the morning to get rid of a hangover.

a. *Case examples:* Following are two case examples of alcohol and drug dependence.

> Cindy is a 30-year-old anesthesia resident who was discovered using intravenous fentanyl while on call. She reported that she did it as a lark with her boyfriend, who was an anesthesiology attending physician. She also reported heavy alcohol and marijuana use in college, but denied blackouts or loss of control. As a result of intervention by her supervisors and family, she entered a treatment program, where her urine tested positive for cocaine, hydromorphone (Dilaudid), and diazepam. She developed significant withdrawal symptoms that required clonidine and phenobarbital therapy. After completion of the treatment program her urine drug screens remained negative for 2 years, and she remains abstinent at 5-year follow-up.

> Sheila is a 32-year-old single lawyer. In the past 2 years she has had two serious motor vehicle accidents while she was drinking. She drinks less than once a week, but becomes intoxicated on 5 or 6 drinks. Her friends have offered to drive her home, but she refuses their help. She is a hard-driving district attorney who was nominated to serve as an appellate court judge. She never drinks alone, and limits her use to parties. She has no other medical, mental health, family, or social problems. At the time of one accident she was confronted by the emergency department physician, but denied any problem. The next year, while intoxicated, the patient was involved in an accident that resulted in a fatality, and lost her license to practice law.

F. Interaction of Use and Clinical Problems:

1. ***Diagnostic categories:*** The lack of precise alcohol- or drug-related diagnostic methods adds to the difficulty of making a clinical diagnosis of an addictive disorder.

   The problem is exacerbated as clinicians attempt to understand the interrelationships of use, problematic use, and dependence. One model the authors have used to describe these interactions is presented in Figure 1–4. This model presents the relative proportions of these categories, and is not meant to provide precise estimates of the size of these groups.

2. ***Interaction model:*** The key points illustrated in Figure 1–4 are:

   a. *Frequency of mild problematic users > moderate problematic users > dependent users:* There are a significantly greater number of mild problematic users than moderate to severe or dependent users. Nondependent problematic use is the most common type of alcohol and drug disorder encountered by clinicians.

   b. *Misclassification into the wrong groups.* The shaded areas between the mild problematic users, moderate to severe users, and dependent users is included to illustrate the misclassification of many patients into the wrong groups. It is often difficult to correctly identify the extent of an alcohol and drug problem. For example patients who are initially thought to be mild users may later be diagnosed as dependent or severe problematic users. The most

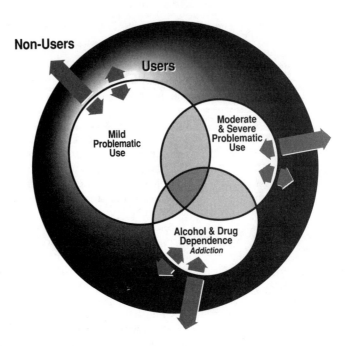

FIG 1–4.
This model was developed by Fleming and Barry to illustrate the interrelationships between use, problematic use, and dependence. The overlap between the inner circles demonstrates the difficulty in differentiating between the categories of problematic use in some patients. Although most patients will remain in a particular category, some with mild problematic use will become alcohol dependent. The *bidirectional arrows* indicate use patterns that change over time. For example, a person who is alcohol dependent may become a nonuser or user for long periods, then redevelop symptoms of dependence.

     frequent misclassification occurs between moderate to severe problematic users and dependent users.

  c. *Fluctuation between user and nonuser categories:* Problematic users and those who are addicted can move in and out of user and nonuser categories. They may attain abstinence for short periods or achieve long-term sobriety. They may try to become "controlled drinkers" before moving back into the dependence category.

  d. *Diagnostic categories:* As clinicians observe patients moving in and out of these categories, precise diagnosis can be difficult to achieve. It is our experience that a patient who has a history of problematic use or dependence always should be classified in the most severe category, even if they are having fewer problems at the time of the clinical encounter. For example, a patient who had severe problematic use in the past and is now a light drinker should be considered a severe problematic user who may be in a controlled-drinking phase.

  e. *Intervals in user and nonuser categories:* The length of time a former severe problematic user will remain in the user and nonuser categories is difficult to predict. Some may be able to maintain these levels for the rest of their lives; others return to severe problematic use. The clinical course of the illness is described in more detail in section III of this chapter.

G. Compulsive Disorders, Eating Disorders, and Gambling Compulsion:

1. *Clinical observations:* Many patients with alcohol and drug disorders develop gambling compulsions that become part of the overall addictive disorder. While it is often difficult to separate out the relative importance of the gambling compulsion, patients are more likely to resume alcohol and drug use after treatment if the gambling compulsion is not treated. There is also overlap between eating disorders and alcohol and drug addiction. It is not unusual for an alcohol-dependent woman to achieve long-term sobriety but then develop an eating disorder. The clinical problems seen with eating disorders can be life-threatening.

   a. *Case example:*

   > Joan is a 38-year-old accountant who last drank 5 years ago. She completed a 2-year outpatient program for alcohol dependence, and now reports severe episodes of bulimia that began shortly after her last drink. Her usual pattern over the past 5 years has been to binge on sugar and flour (e.g., 12 to 15 donuts in 15 minutes) followed by self-induced vomiting. This binge eating and purging will continue for 2 to 3 months, until she reaches a goal weight (140 to 145 pounds) and can no longer deal with the physical effects. She then will abstain from binge eating and purging for 2 to 3 months, until she reaches a preset weight limit of 170 pounds, after which she starts another cycle of bulimia. She has had at least 10 of these cycles in the past 5 years. She has a strong family history of depression on the maternal side and alcoholism and antisocial personality disorders on the paternal side. She feels suicidal and describes behavioral problems similar to those she had when she was drinking.

2. *Unified theory:* Clinicians and researchers have tried to develop a single theory to explain the causes of the whole spectrum of disorders that share similar clinical characteristics, but no one theory has successfully incorporated alcohol and drug problems, eating disorders, gambling compulsions, and compulsive sexual behavior. While there are clinical similarities and overlap between these problems, the causes, clinical course, and treatment suggest that a unified theory to explain the complex clinical events and course of these disorders is not likely to emerge. Treatment of each of these disorders is discussed in later chapters.

III. Clinical Models of Illness and Recovery

A. Natural Progression Model:

1. *Overview:* Traditionally, alcohol and drug disorders were thought to follow a natural progression from early signs and symptoms through

end-stage disease. The classic progression model for cocaine dependence is presented in Figure 1–5; the model for alcohol or sedative dependence is similar. Most practitioners have seen patients in withdrawal or in the emergency department who fit this model. There is gradual downward progression, with increasing severe drug-related events. When patients "hit bottom" they either die or begin the long road to recovery. The majority of patients with problems associated with alcohol and drug use do not fit this classic model of progression.

2. ***Clinical Observations:*** The clinical course of alcohol and drug disorders, as seen by most physicians, is not one of smooth progression. Often periods of problematic use are punctuated by periods of nonuse or nonproblematic use. Some persons are heavy users of alcohol throughout most of their adult lives, periodically experiencing some minor problems but never having more severe symptoms. In others the consequences involve family, work, and social situations. Some stop use of the chemical on their own and are never seen in the treatment system. Some reach treatment through family, work, or their practitioners. Most experience relapse before they achieve long-term sobriety.

B. Model of Problematic Use:

1. ***Overview:*** The model of problematic use (Fig 1–6) was developed by Fleming and Barry to depict the clinical course of alcohol and

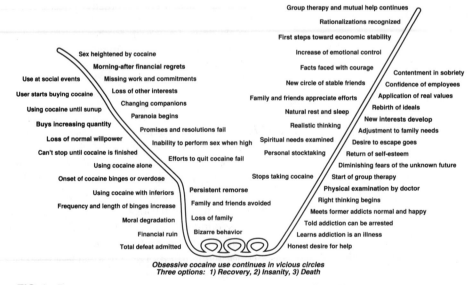

FIG 1–5.

The progressive downhill course in many patients who develop substance dependence is illustrated here. This represents a modification of the Jellnick curve for alcohol dependence. The substance-related events and recovery patterns listed are for cocaine addiction; similar patterns exist for other substances.

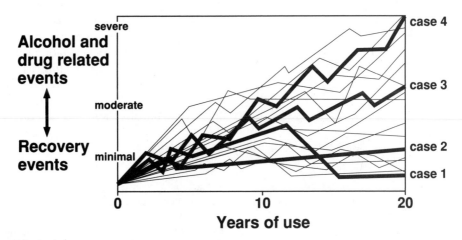

FIG 1–6.
Clinical course in 18 patients with alcohol and drug disorders. Each line represents a single patient and his or her course over 20 years. The upward deflection of each line represents a clinical event such as an episode of prolonged binge drinking, an accident, or other psychosocial problem related to alcohol or drug use. The downward deflections represent a recovery or treatment event. *Case 1* represents a patient with spontaneous recovery after 12 years of problematic use. Case 4 represents severe progressive disease culminating in death. (See p. 16 for a more extensive discussion of this model.)

    drug disorders. Each of the lines in the figure represents a single patient and the clinical course over 20 years. The upward deflection of the lines represents a clinical event, such as an episode of binge drinking, an adverse health effect, or a family problem; the downward deflection represents a recovery or treatment event. The 18 problematic or dependent users represented illustrate the wide range of clinical courses encountered by practitioners. Four case examples are included to explain the predominant patterns of the illness.

2. ***Clinical Observations:***
    a. *Complexity and variability:* The clinical course of alcohol and drug disorders and recovery is complex and variable. On one end of the spectrum are drinkers who drink heavily once or twice a year and are involved in a serious motor vehicle accident. They do not have other problems with alcohol, and often stop drinking on their own. At the other end of the spectrum are those with rapid progression of the addictive disorders, who die after 5 to 10 years of heavy use.
    b. *Continuous pattern of clinical events:* The graph (see Fig 1–6) of clinical events experienced by problematic and dependent users shows a continuous pattern of events ranging from stable, mild problematic use to rapid progression and death.
    c. *Sporadic clinical events:* The predominant clinical pattern is a series of sporadic events. In some patients the course is smooth and steadily downhill (natural progression model, see Fig 1–5). This is not so in most patients, however.

d. *Recovery events:* The clinical course is frequently interrupted by long periods of sobriety and recovery supporting events. These events may include temporary cessation of use as a result of physician advice, attending a 12-step meeting, family confrontation, legal or employment issue, or severe health problem. As with tobacco cessation, some patients stop without any external intervention. Occasionally these spontaneous recovery events will last the rest of the patient's life.

e. *Case examples* (see Fig 1–6):

Case 1: *Spontaneous recovery:*

> Marie is 45-year-old lawyer who had a history of heavy alcohol use in college but reduced her use during law school. On completion of law school she resumed her previous pattern of use and began to experiment with cocaine. She abstained completely while pregnant, but resumed her alcohol use pattern after the birth of her son. Marie's use soon escalated, and she began drinking every day and became intoxicated at least once a week. Seven years ago her family and colleagues confronted her with their concerns about her drinking. At that time she stopped drinking on her own, and has remained abstinent for 6 years.

Case 2: *Stable, mild problematic use:*

> Jim is a 45-year-old carpenter who began to use alcohol and marijuana with his friends in high school. He had a period of heavy binge use for 5 years after high school, but has maintained a daily use pattern of 2 to 3 beers after work. Except for a fight and a motor vehicle accident in his early twenties he has had no problems. Jim continues to drink about 20 beers per week and smokes a joint of marijuana once a week.

Case 3: *Unstable moderate to severe problematic use:*

> Mark is a 48-year-old salesman who started using alcohol to feel comfortable at parties when he was in his teens. He had difficulty controlling his use from the first drink. He was unable to leave a drink unfinished, and became intoxicated on most occasions when he drank. Mark drank heavily 5 nights a week. At his last company physical examination his GGT level and blood pressure were elevated. He also reported persistent abdominal pain. Twice he was arrested for driving under the influence of alcohol. His father recently died of cirrhosis. At his wife's insistence he stops drinking for periods of up to 3 months. Mark was confronted by his employer because of performance problems, and entered a treatment program.

Case 4: Dependent use with a classic pattern of progression and death:

> Joe was a 55-year-old seasonally employed construction worker who began drinking and getting high on marijuana at the age of 13

years. His father, grandfather, and two uncles drank heavily. One uncle died at age 25 in an alcohol-related auto accident. His father died in prison while Joe was still in high school. When he was in his early thirties, Joe had periods of controlled drinking and was able to maintain employment and family responsibilities. Later he began to lose construction jobs because he was unable to come to work after binge drinking on weekends. He was divorced at age 42, and did not have contact with his three children. He often drank in the morning to counteract withdrawal symptoms. He was suicidal on a number of occasions, but was always too afraid to try. He received treatment at the county detoxification unit four times, and participated in a 28-day treatment twice. He was most recently seen in the emergency department after vomiting blood and experiencing severe abdominal pain. Shortly after admission to the intensive care unit he suffered cardiopulmonary arrest and died.

C. Course of Recovery:
Recovery is complex and poorly understood. The process usually is not smooth and steady but follows a steplike series of events. Recovery is frequently associated with relapse and additional alcohol- or drug-related events before stable sobriety is attained. There are at least three patterns of recovery.
  1. *First time recovery:* Some patients enter a treatment program or attend 12-step meetings and achieve sobriety with the first treatment event. Although these individuals tend to have less severe disease, more support and resources, and fewer mental health problems, it is difficult to predict who will stay sober the first time they participate in treatment. Professionals who face licensing issues often follow this pattern of recovery and sobriety. This observation probably is related to long-term participation in a treatment program, monitoring of urine for drugs, and other required surveillance procedures.
  2. *Relapse with eventual recovery:* Other patients who participate in treatment relapse but eventually achieve sobriety. Occasional slips frequently lead to long periods of heavy, destructive drinking or drug use. Persons who are alcohol and drug dependent can attain stable recovery even after multiple treatment attempts, but the greater the number and severity of relapses the less likely they are to achieve sobriety.
  3. *Spontaneous recovery:* There is increasing evidence that problematic and occasional dependent users stop on their own and achieve long-term sobriety. They may attend a few Alcoholics Anonymous (AA) meetings, but most often receive no formal treatment. Some of these patients stopped because an important person, such as family member, friend, employer, or physician, told them they had to stop. As many as 25% of problematic and dependent users have spontaneous long-lasting recovery. Some may contend that these individuals exhibit "alcoholic behaviors" and are dry but not sober, but the evidence does not support this assumption.

IV. Alcohol and Drug Disorders: Chronic Illness Paradigm

It is useful to conceptualize the clinical course and treatment of alcohol and drug problems in the context of other chronic conditions, such as hyperlipidemia and essential hypertension. Like other chronic conditions, the difficulty in treating alcohol and drug disorders is due to the *clinical course and behavioral manifestations of a chronic illness, not because it is either the patient's or the clinician's fault.* This section reviews a number of common clinical characteristics that alcohol and drug disorders share with other chronic conditions. These characteristics include late onset of clinical symptoms, unpredictable course, causes, treatment methods, and patient-oriented treatment.

A. Late Onset of Clinical Symptoms:
   1. *Symptoms:* These conditions develop slowly, with few early symptoms. Often hypercholesterolemia is not detected until an acute vascular event occurs, such as myocardial infarction, or hypertension until the development of a hemorrhagic event such as cerebrovascular accident (CVA). Cocaine-related deaths due to cardiac arrhythmia, CVA, or suicide are a similar potentially preventable tragedy.
   2. *Detection:* In contrast to hypercholesterolemia and hypertension, where early detection through screening is standard clinical care, alcohol and drug disorders usually remain undetected until serious sequelae (e.g., motor vehicle accidents) or end organ damage (e.g., cirrhosis) develop.

B. Unpredictable Course:
   1. *Individual clinical course:* Epidemiologic studies have determined the relative risk of heart disease and stroke in patients with elevated lipid levels and hypertension. However, it is difficult to predict the clinical course in individual patients. The vast majority of patients with mild untreated essential hypertension and elevated cholesterol levels do not develop vascular disease as manifested by CVA, myocardial infarction, or renal failure.
   2. *Heavy drinkers:* Most heavy drinkers do not develop significant end organ damage. Fewer than 10% develop liver failure. This particular characteristic of the illness makes it difficult for the clinician to determine which heavy drinkers are likely to experience serious consequences of their drinking.

C. Causes:
   1. *Role of genetics:* Scientific studies have provided evidence that genetics have a role in hyperlipidemia, essential hypertension, and alcohol and drug disorders. Family pedigree and twin studies have confirmed a strong relationship between genetic effects and the development of these conditions.
   2. *Role of environment:* These conditions also can develop as a direct result of unhealthy activities (e.g., poor diet, lack of exercise, ineffective methods of dealing with stress, or excessive drinking). Societal norms, advertising, and social pressure are powerful environmental stimuli.

3. ***Interaction of genetics and environment:*** It is clear that hypertension, elevated lipid levels, and alcohol and drug disorders develop as a result of the interaction of these two factors.

D. **Treatment:**

1. ***Behavior therapy:*** The primary management of these chronic conditions includes changing long-term behavior patterns. In addition, pharmacologic treatment is much more effective when accompanied by significant changes in diet, exercise, and stress management.

2. ***Compliance:*** Problems with compliance are common with all chronic conditions. It may take months to years for many patients to change their behavior, and when necessary to take medication appropriately. Many patients never make the necessary behavior changes, and continue heavy alcohol or drug use, with associated elevated lipid levels and blood pressure.

3. ***Physician recommendations:*** It should come as no surprise when a patient with hypertension, elevated lipid levels, or an alcohol or drug disorder has difficulty complying with a clinician's recommendation to change his or her behavior. However, patients with these conditions do change their behavior patterns as a result of their physician's recommendations. *Patients in recovery from alcohol and drug disorders report physician advice as the most important factor in their ability to stop.*

E. **Patient-Oriented Treatment:**

1. ***Patient action:*** In contrast to most inpatient treatment, in which a physician treats and/or cures a problem with surgery or drugs, the management of hyperlipidemia, hypertension, and alcohol and drug disorders is totally dependent on the patient taking some action.

2. ***Behavior changes:*** *Many necessary changes are difficult to maintain.* Change often requires giving up pleasurable activities. Long-term modifications in diet, exercise, or alcohol use involve a complex series of behavior changes.

V. **Concept of "Safe" vs. "At Risk" Levels of Use**

Clinicians often are asked to provide primary preventive counseling. They are asked such questions as, "How much alcohol is safe for me to drink?," "What do you think about smoking an occasional joint?," or "What about using sedatives for sleep?"

A. **General Concept:** While any use of mood-altering drugs can result in an adverse effect, such as a motor vehicle accident or a fall-induced Colles fracture, levels of risk clearly are dose-related. The more someone uses alcohol the more likely an alcohol-related event will occur. Epidemiologic studies have shown that a person who consumes more than 20 drinks a week has an eightfold increase in alcohol-related health effects compared with one who drinks fewer than 12 drinks a week.

B. **Safe Limits of Alcohol Use:** Factors to consider when counseling patients about a safe level of use include age, family history, gender, reproductive status, previous history of use, operation of machinery, and presence of medical or mental health disorders. Research suggests that consuming fewer than 12 drinks per week and no more than three drinks at one time is associated with few health risks. The most common risks at this level of use are motor vehicle injuries and accidents.

C. Safe Levels of Illicit Drug Use: Safe limits of illicit drug use have not been determined. Illicit drug use of any quantity or frequency is associated with three major risks. (1) Drugs obtained on the street may contain toxic substances. (2) Use of illegal substances can lead to felony charges. (3) Idiosyncratic events are related even to small doses. Case studies have shown serious cardiac and central nervous system effects from very small amounts of cocaine. Patients should be advised to avoid use of all illicit drugs.

D. Safe Levels of Benzodiazepine, Sedative, and Opioid Use: The direct health risks associated with the use of psychoactive prescription medications such as benzodiazepines and opioids is limited. They are associated with limited direct organ toxicity and have a wide margin of safety. The major danger of these medications lies in their mood-altering effects and addictive characteristics. When these medications are used for short periods in limited quantities, they can provide effective therapy for a wide range of clinical problems.

The major problems seen with these medications are:

1. With prolonged use the medication may become a problem of greater magnitude than the mental health disorder or chronic pain problem for which it was originally prescribed.
2. These medications should not be prescribed alone without other treatment modalities, such as counseling, support group, or behavioral modification techniques.
3. Use of these medications in patients who have a history of substance dependence may precipitate a return to heavy drinking or drug use.

BIBLIOGRAPHY

American Society of Addiction Medicine. Syllabus for the Review Course in Addiction Medicine. Review Course Committee (Geller A, Chair), 1990.

Barnes HN, Aronson MD, Delbanco TL: *Alcoholism: A Guide for the Primary Care Physician.* New York, Springer-Verlag, 1987.

Barry KL, Fleming MF: Computerized administration of alcoholism screening tests in a primary care setting. *J Am Board Fam Pract* 1990; 3:93–98.

Diagnostic and Statistical Manual of Mental Disorders, ed 3.

Fleming MF, Barry KL: The effectiveness of alcohol screening in an ambulatory care setting. *J Stud Alcohol* 1991; 52:33–36.

Fleming MF, Barry KL: A three sample test of a masked alcohol screening questionnaire. *Alcohol Alcohol* 1991; 26:81–91.

Gordis E: Estimating the economic cost of alcohol abuse. *Alcohol Alert* 11(PH293). Department of Health and Human Services, 1991.

Herrington RE, Benzer DG, Jacobson GR, et al: Treating substance-use disorders among physicians. *JAMA* 1982; 247:2253–2257.

Institute of Medicine, Division of Mental Health and Behavioral Medicine: *Broadening the Base of Treatment for Alcohol Problems*. Washington, DC, National Academy Press, 1990.

International Classification of Diseases, rev 9, *Clinical Modification*. Washington, DC, US Department of Health and Human Services, 1981.

Kinney J, Price TRP, Bergen BJ: Impediments to alcohol education. *J Stud Alcohol* 1984; 45:453–459.

NIDA Capsules. Rockville, Md, National Institute on Drug Abuse, Cap 02-25, 1985–1987.

Seventh Special Report to the U.S. Congress on Alcohol and Health, from the Secretary of Health and Human Services. Department of Health and Human Services, January 1990.

Valliant GE: *The Natural History of Alcoholism: Causes, Patterns, and Paths to Recovery*. Cambridge, Mass, Harvard University Press, 1983.

PART TWO

Identification and Treatment
of Primary Addictions

CHAPTER 2

Identification and Office Management of Alcohol and Drug Disorders

Richard L. Brown, M.D., M.P.H.

Ten percent of ambulatory primary care patients and 25% of patients in general hospitals have primary alcohol or drug disorders. These disorders are among the most common medical disorders encountered by health care practitioners. This chapter provides a practical guide for managing alcohol and drug disorders in the context of supportive and caring practitioner-patient relationships. Specifically, it covers screening (assessing patients who seem to have no symptoms), case finding (evaluating suggestive symptoms or signs), conducting brief interventions, engaging patients in formal treatment, and preventing relapse. The emphasis of this chapter is to assist practitioners in the early identification and office-based treatment of alcohol and drug disorders.

I. Barriers to Identification and Treatment
A. Denial:
1. ***Denial by the patient:*** A major barrier to treatment is patient denial. Unconscious defenses account for much of denial. Conscious components of denial, often manifested through dishonesty, are related to drug craving and fear of living without the use of mood-altering drugs.
2. ***Denial by others:*** Family members, friends, associates, and health practitioners also deny. They may reason, "I don't like alcoholics or addicts; therefore, people I love or care about could not be alcoholics or addicts." Practitioners who have not recognized their own personal or family alcohol or drug problems are less likely to recognize these problems in others. Even if practitioners do recognize a problem, it may seem disrespectful or unkind to "accuse" a patient.

B. Attitudes:
1. Attitudes among practitioners often hinder effectiveness in diagnosis and treatment.
   a. *Pessimism:* Pessimism is an understandable result of clinical training, in which there is predominant exposure in tertiary care institutions to patients with the most chronic, severe, and refractory

alcohol and drug disorders. Treating belligerent, unkempt drunks in the emergency room who repeatedly drop out of treatment programs does not generate positive feelings toward the care of patients with alcohol disorders.

   b. *Moralism:* The belief that using mood-altering substances and that those who use them are evil is supported by many cultural norms and religious teachings. When moralism is expressed to patients, even unintentionally, their level of denial escalates.

   c. *Stereotyping:* Although practitioners usually reject stereotypic notions, they identify alcohol and drug disorders less often in patients who do not fit stereotypes, such as whites, females, and employed individuals.

   d. *Neglect:* A failure to acknowledge that alcohol and drug disorders fall within the province of medical practitioners can cause neglect. If practitioners define as their goal the prolongation of life and amelioration of suffering, these clinical problems cannot be ignored. Even those who restrict their domain to biomedical disease cannot disregard the evidence that alcohol and drug problems are at least partly genetically determined and neurochemically mediated.

II. Recognition

A. Varying Severity of Alcohol and Drug Disorders:

1. ***Range of alcohol and drug disorders:*** The symptoms and signs of alcohol and drug disorders are the negative consequences of use. There is a wide range of problematic alcohol and drug use. Constellations of symptoms and signs may be considered mild, moderate, or severe.

   a. *Mild problematic use:* Individuals with mild disorders have experienced minor consequences, such as embarrassing scenes at parties, occasional arguments with their families or friends, or legal problems.

   b. *Moderate problematic use:* Those with moderate disorders have begun to suffer more serious consequences, such as health effects, loss of control, and polydrug use.

   c. *Severe problematic use:* Individuals with severe disorders frequently have developed tolerance and physical dependence, occupational and financial problems, difficulty with relationships, and perhaps a serious illness. Classification of disorders as mild, moderate, or severe may be useful in choosing treatment options, ranging from brief intervention to prolonged inpatient treatment.

2. ***Purpose of classification scheme:*** *Classification of alcohol and drug disorders as mild, moderate, or severe problematic use is designed to help practitioners think about treatment options rather than as diagnoses for presentation to patients.* A patient who is told he or she has mild symptoms of an alcohol disorder may believe that because the problem is "mild" no changes need to be made. It is most

useful in a clinical situation to list the patient's signs and symptoms, stating that it appears that their use of alcohol or other drugs is "problematic," followed by the practitioner's recommendations for treatment.

> John, I'm concerned about your alcohol use. You are experiencing a number of problems and consequences that suggest you need to change your drinking. While I'm not sure about the severity of your alcohol problem at this time, I would like you to stop all use for the next 3 months. As we gather more information from you and your family we'll have a better idea about treatment.

3. ***Relation to treatment indications:*** Precise indications for the various treatment options are not known. This chapter provides guidelines for making those decisions.

B. Categorization of Symptoms and Signs:

The symptoms and signs of alcohol and drug disorders fall into seven categories: physical health, mental health, family, social, work or school, legal, and financial. Common symptoms and signs of mild or moderate disorders are shown in Table 2–1. Severe disorders are characterized

TABLE 2–1.

Common Manifestations of Alcohol and Drug Disorders

Biomedical

Alcohol

Gastritis, peptic ulcer, dyspepsia, vague or undiagnosed abdominal pain, diarrhea, weight gain, labile or refractory hypertension

Cocaine

Damage to nasal mucosa, coronary and other vasospasm, cardiac dysrhythmias, weight loss

Alcohol and other drugs

Trauma, sleep complaints, sexual dysfunction

Psychologic/Behavioral

Agitation, irritability, dysphoria, difficulty in coping, mood swings, hostility, violence, psychosomatic symptoms, hyperventilation, generalized anxiety, panic attacks, depression, psychosis

Family

Chronic stable family dysfunction, marital problems, behavioral problems and decline in school performance in children, anxiety and depression in family members, divorce, abuse and violence

Social

Alienation and loss of old friends, gravitation toward others with similar life-style

Work/School

Decline in performance, frequent job changes, frequent absences (especially on Mondays), requests for work excuses, initial preservation of work or school function among highly motivated groups such as professionals in practice or training.

Legal

Arrests for disturbing the peace or driving while intoxicated, stealing, drug dealing

Financial

Borrowing or owing money, selling personal or family possessions by more serious difficulties in mental health and behavior, plus the more serious biomedical consequences described in Chapter 8.

III. Data Collection and Diagnosis

A major challenge in identifying alcohol and drug disorders is to elicit information on the consequences of alcohol and drug use from patients who cannot acknowledge or who try to hide an alcohol or drug disorder. The objectives of information gathering are to establish (1) use, (2) potential negative consequences, (3) the causal link between use and consequences, and (4) the time course. The mnemonic UCR (*U*se, *C*onsequences, and *R*epetition) is a useful summary of this process.

A. Screening Interview:

1. *Timing:* It is natural to screen for alcohol and other drug disorders after taking a history on smoking, diet, or medications. An appropriate initial question that encourages honesty and does not elicit defensiveness is, "Have you drunk any alcohol or used any drugs in the past year?" A "no" response warrants a follow-up question to determine whether the patient is in recovery or has independently initiated attempts to control alcohol or drug use.

2. *CAGEAID:* If the patient admits any alcohol or drug use, ask the CAGE Questions Adapted to Include Drugs (CAGEAID; Fig 2–1). The CAGE questions (Have you ever felt you ought to *c*ut down on your drinking? Have people *a*nnoyed by criticizing your drinking? Have you ever felt bad or *g*uilty about your drinking? Have you taken an *e*ye opener?) originally were developed as a screening tool for alcohol disorders and are recommended by the U.S. Preventive Services Task Force Report of 1989. Two positive responses suggest an alcohol problem (sensitivity of 0.85 to 0.94, specificity 0.79 to 0.88). In pilot studies the CAGEAID questionnaire exhibited similar sensitivity scores. Some studies of primary care populations indicate that one positive response to the CAGE questions can signify a disorder.

3. *Pursue positive responses:* The CAGE or CAGEAID questionnaires are helpful not only for screening but also for exploring the link between alcohol or drug use and potential negative consequences. For example, in response to a patient's admission of guilt about drinking or drug use, asking, "What makes you feel guilty?" may reveal that alcohol or drugs are responsible for difficulties at home and at work. Therefore, always follow up on positive responses.

4. *Limitation:* Like screening tests for cancer (e.g., mammograms), the CAGE and CAGEAID questionnaires identify only patients who warrant further investigation; they cannot be used to make diagnoses.

B. Case Finding Interview:

Patients who screen positive or who have suggestive symptoms or signs should be examined further to determine whether they meet diagnostic criteria for alcohol or drug disorders (UCR). In assessing for alcohol or drug disorders, *the interview is the best source of information,* despite possible denial and defensiveness. This is particularly true in patients

CAGE Questions Adapted to Include Drugs (CAGEAID)

Have you felt you ought to cut down on your drinking *or drug use?*

❏ Yes   ❏ No

Have people annoyed you by criticizing your drinking *or drug use?*

❏ Yes   ❏ No

Have you felt bad or guilty about your drinking *or drug use?*

❏ Yes   ❏ No

Have you ever had a drink *or used drug*s first thing in the morning to steady your nerves or get rid of a hangover *or to get the day started?*

❏ Yes   ❏ No

FIG 2–1.
Underlined text shows the original CAGE questions; italicized text shows modifications of the CAGE questions used to screen for drug disorders. In a general population, two or more positive answers of "Sometimes," "Quite often," or "Very often" indicate a need for more in-depth assessment. Some studies of primary care populations suggest that one such response should prompt further investigation.

with minimal problems whose negative consequences are largely psychosocial. Two general approaches are used in assessment.

Approach 1

1. *Assess for quantity and frequency of alcohol and drug use.*
   a. How much alcohol did you drink in the last week? The last 24 hours?
   b. How many times in the last month did you drink more than three drinks on one occasion? Last year?
   c. How many times did you get drunk in the past month? Year?
   d. Have you ever used drugs such as marijuana or cocaine?
   e. If yes, did you use in the last year? Last month? Last week?
2. *If the content of the response raises concern* or if intonation or nonverbal cues suggest minimizing, defensiveness, or equivocation, question more closely about alcohol and drug use and how it might be exerting negative effects on life function:
   a. Has your drinking or drug use caused any problems for your

health? Your family? Your job? Your financial state? Any arrests or legal problems?

    b. Do you ever think that you've had a problem with your alcohol or drug use?

    c. Have you ever had a blackout (loss of memory for events while intoxicated)?

    d. Have you ever had an accident that was related to your alcohol or drug use?

    e. How many times in the last year did you drive after drinking?

    f. Have you ever made any rules about your drinking or drug use?

3. *Advantages and disadvantages:* This approach is direct and efficient. It establishes (1) the antecedent uses and (2) the resulting consequences. The logic of this approach, however, often does not escape patients, who on sensing that clinicians are gathering data to support an incriminating diagnosis are more apt to hide evidence of psychologic and social dysfunction.

Approach 2

1. This approach starts with a *general social history,* with focus on assessing for *potential* consequences of alcohol or drug use. The critical objective of establishing rapport with the patient is done through standard interview techniques.

    a. *Establish common ground* for the ensuing discussion, e.g., "You seem to be under a lot stress about this stomach pain, but I'm wondering if anything else is contributing."

    b. Then start with general, *open-ended questions,* e.g., "What are the stresses in your life?"

    c. *Reward on-target responses* with acknowledgement, such as eye contact, nodding, or phrases such as "Yes" or "Go on."

    d. *Paraphrase responses to convey understanding,* e.g., "Your children are certainly giving you a tough time lately."

    e. Take advantage of opportunities to *reflect the emotive content* of patients' speech back to them, e.g., "I'm sensing that you're pretty angry with your wife over this."

    f. *Make statements of empathy, respect, and partnership:* "I understand that this is a difficult time for you. I know you're trying to deal with many stresses in a constructive manner, and I'd like to help see you through this."

    g. *Building rapport* in this manner supports patient comfort and inhibits defensiveness in responses as probes become more specific and sensitive. *Nonjudgmental acceptance* of potentially embarrassing or offensive information encourages patients to reveal more.

    h. When asked in a caring manner in the context of a supportive relationship, direct questions about the fragility of family and social relationships, difficulties at work or school, legal trouble, and financial problems can uncover possible negative consequences of alcohol or drug use.

i. When such questions are asked before sufficient rapport is established or in direct relation to substance use, patients sometimes are alienated and provide little useful information. However, inadequate rapport is an unacceptable reason for not broaching the topic of alcohol or drugs with difficult patients or with patients for whom follow-up is not anticipated. It is preferable to risk alienating patients than to evade the issue of alcohol or drug problems for long periods.

2. After rapport has been established, an alcohol and drug use history is obtained using questions similar to those listed in approach 1. The last step in this strategy is to try to *establish links* between the potential consequences and substance use over time. The first three CAGE or CAGEAID questions can be helpful.

3. *Advantages and disadvantages:* Practitioners gather personal information before disclosing a threatening agenda. Only after rapport and a nonjudgmental milieu are established does the topic turn to alcohol or drug use and a possible link to consequences. At this point patients tend to be more honest with themselves and others. Thus approach 2, although indirect and less efficient, often is more effective.

C. Physical Examination

1. ***Early signs:*** The physical examination is very insensitive to mild alcohol and drug disorders. Mild symptoms of alcohol disorders may include labile and refractory hypertension and mild epigastric or right upper quadrant tenderness. Nasal mucosal damage may accompany cocaine snorting. Hypodermic marks indicate intravenous drug use. Signs of previous or current trauma can be helpful clues.

2. ***Later signs:*** Physical signs are more common in patients with severe or chronic alcohol and drug disorders (see Fig 8–1).

D. Laboratory Tests:

Blood tests may be a helpful adjunct in diagnosing alcohol abuse.

1. ***Liver function tests:*** γ-Glutamyl transferase (GGT) is the most sensitive biochemical test of heavy drinking. Aspartate aminotransferase (AST) is the second liver enzyme to increase due to alcohol, and often is present at twice the levels of alanine aminotransferase (ALT). The sensitivity of GGT for heavy drinking in ambulatory settings is 25% to 30%; therefore normal GGT levels do not exclude alcohol disorders.

2. ***Mean corpuscular volume*** (MCV): The sensitivity and specificity of elevated MCV for alcohol abuse is approximately 0.65. Macrocytosis often is found in early abusers without vitamin B_{12} or folate deficiencies, because of a direct effect of alcohol on red blood cell production.

3. ***Blood alcohol levels and urine drug screens:*** A positive blood alcohol level or the odor of alcohol on the breath at a scheduled office visit is suggestive of an alcohol disorder. However, these indicators of recent alcohol use are insensitive to alcohol disorders, be-

cause even patients who are pharmacologically dependent on alcohol can abstain for short periods and use other sedatives to prevent withdrawal symptoms. Since urine drug screens often fail to identify substance use that is quite recent, many substance abusers will have negative screens. Positive urine drug screens indicate drug use but not necessarily drug abuse, because they give no information about negative consequences of use. Surreptitiously obtained tests for alcohol and drugs may catch patients who are concealing their substance use, but can affect therapeutic relationships.

4. ***Carbohydrate deficient transferrin:*** This new test is not widely available in the United States, but may be more sensitive and specific to heavy drinking than other tests.

E. Other Sources of Information:

After interviewing, examining, and generating laboratory data, practitioners often are left with a suspicion, but no confirmation, of an alcohol or drug disorder. In this case, other sources of information can be used.

1. ***Family members:*** Practitioners can discuss with patients their concern and uncertainty about their alcohol or drug use and ask them to bring other family members to provide additional perspective.

   a. To maintain patient trust and to comply with federal confidentiality laws, it is important that practitioners not reveal information about alcohol or drugs to patients' family members without first gaining permission.

   b. With the patient present or in separate visits with family members, practitioners sometimes can induce family members to divulge information about a possible alcohol or drug disorder without bringing up the topic, by asking questions about stresses at home, their origins, and how each family member copes.

   c. In many cases, family members will not take advantage of opportunities to reveal alcohol and drug problems, because (1) they may be in denial, (2) they may feel strong allegiance to the patient, or (3) they may fear retribution or violence.

2. ***Trials:*** Practitioners can suggest trials of abstinence or of controlled use. These trials are best described as a way for patients to determine whether they have control over their drinking or drug use. Clinicians should be aware of the possibility of withdrawal during a trial, the limitations of trials, and the need to state the terms of the trial clearly.

   a. *Potential for withdrawal:* In arranging these trials, practitioners must be alert to the possibility of withdrawal, especially from alcohol and other sedatives. Patients who drink should be alerted to call their practitioner immediately if symptoms of alcohol withdrawal occur. Because seizures may be the first sign of withdrawal from other sedatives, these drugs should not be abruptly discontinued or decreased.

   b. *Limitations of trials:* Although trials can be useful, they do have limitations. Many substance abusers can exert intermittent control over their substance use. In addition, practitioners often are left to trust patient accounts of their adherence to the terms of trials. Trials can be enhanced by establishing sources of corroboration.

(1) Patients can be asked to have family members report to the practitioner at the next visit.

(2) If liver function test results were elevated before the trial, it may be useful for diagnosis and patient education to document whether a trial effects a decrease.

(3) Patients who demonstrate abstinence or controlled use for 1 month nevertheless may have an alcohol or drug disorder. Follow-up assessments for negative consequences of alcohol or drug use should be scheduled.

c. The terms of the trials must be stated clearly.

(1) In trials of abstinence, patients agree that any use of alcohol or drugs over the next month will be considered a lack of control.

(2) In trials of controlled use, patients agree to use a precise amount of alcohol or other drugs every day, no more and no less.

(3) In controlled trials of alcohol use, one or two standard drinks (Fig 2–2) per day are allowed. Patients can be asked to report

What's a standard drink?
1 standard drink =

1 can of ordinary beer or ale
° 12 oz

a single shot of spirits
whiskey, gin, vodka, etc.
1.5 oz

a glass of wine
6 oz

a small glass of sherry
4 oz

a small glass of liqueur or aperitif
4 oz

FIG 2–2.
Content of a standard alcoholic drink. There is approximately 1 oz of pure alcohol in three standard drinks. A 12-oz wine cooler is equivalent in alcohol content to a 12-oz bottle of beer.

not only on their adherence but also on changes in symptoms and function in response to limiting substance use.

(4) Failure to adhere or difficulty in adhering to the terms of the trial suggests a lack of control over substance use and a need for treatment.

3. *Referral for evaluation* by a substance abuse specialist may be suggested.

a. Patient acceptance of referrals is facilitated by confiding in the patient about the uncertainty and concern about a possible alcohol or drug problem. Explanations such as the following may be helpful: "If I were uncertain whether you had a serious heart problem, I'd certainly refer to a heart specialist for an examination. I'm concerned that you may have an alcohol or drug problem, but I just don't know. Since these problems often are fatal, I feel just as strongly about referring you to an alcohol and drug specialist for an evaluation." Practitioner demonstration of personal trust and comfort with the specialist is also helpful.

b. For best results, a consultant should receive in advance a letter citing all possible evidence of an alcohol or drug disorder. The patient's written consent to send information pertaining specifically to alcohol or drug disorders must be obtained to comply with federal confidentiality laws.

4. *Refusal:* Patient refusal of these recommendations shows a lack of readiness to accept diagnosis of an alcohol or drug disorder. Practitioners must appreciate that denial is inherent to these disorders and accept the patient's decision for the time being.

a. It is both therapeutic and conducive to a continuing therapeutic relationship for practitioners to express their concerns about substance abuse clearly and nonjudgmentally, show understanding that the patient does not wish to deal with it now, and show their desire to continue seeing the patient and their intention to continue raising the issue in the future.

b. In so doing, practitioners maintain a position to observe future negative consequences of the patient's substance use, gather additional evidence for confirming the diagnosis, and intervene when the patient may be more receptive.

F. Pitfalls:

Many practitioners avoid acting on their concerns about substance abuse until they are absolutely certain of the diagnosis. A practitioner who suspects that a patient is experiencing symptoms of an alcohol or drug disorder usually can feel confidant that the patient's use has become problematic. Due the high level of patient denial, a false positive diagnosis is rare. In addition, certainty about the diagnosis may come too late to prevent significant negative consequences. Thus practitioners must be comfortable acting on provisional diagnoses. Appropriate techniques are described in the following section.

IV. Initial Management

Having made a definite or provisional diagnosis of an alcohol or drug disorder, the practitioner should initiate treatment. The traditional, standard treatment in the United States for alcohol and drug disorders has been limited to participation in a self-help group, such as Alcoholics Anonymous, that uses the 12-step approach, or a professionally administered inpatient or outpatient program. It is now recognized that physicians and other health care professionals can promote acceptance of the diagnosis, engaging the patient in standard 12-step treatment when necessary and performing brief interventions. Brief interventions are increasingly recognized as an important treatment component, especially in mild alcohol or drug disorders. These steps, performed by the practitioner, are important aspects of treatment. These modalities are referred to as initial management.

A. Promoting acceptance of the diagnosis:

Promoting acceptance of the diagnosis often is the most critical and difficult step in treatment. Because most patients with alcohol or drug disorders will not seek specialty care before they have at least some acceptance of their problem, practitioners should become skilled at techniques for promoting acceptance.

1. ***Initial steps:*** The initial steps, discussed in a nonjudgmental, caring manner, include stating the negative consequences of the patient's substance use, expressing concern that the patient has or may be developing a problem with alcohol and/or drugs, and eliciting the patient's reaction. For example:

   > Mr. Jones, you've had this stomach problem for months now, and it's not getting any better. Your blood pressure has had many ups and downs. You're under a lot of stress at work and at home, and you say that one of the reasons that you and your wife are not getting along is your drinking. The kind of stomach and blood pressure problems you're having can be caused by alcohol, as well. I'm beginning to be concerned that you have an alcohol problem. What do you think?

2. ***Patient reaction:*** Patients' reactions can be quite varied:
   a. *Agreement:* Some patients have been waiting for their problem to be discovered, and will indicate some agreement.
   b. *Astonishment and/or embarrassment:* Some may respond with sincere astonishment and embarrassment: "Can these problems really be caused by drinking?"
   c. *Passive acceptance:* Others may indicate passive and insincere acceptance: "Thanks for your concern, Doc. I've stopped getting high before, and I can stop again. That's what I'll do. I'll take care of it. Now about my leg, . . ." It may help to draw out these patients: "You seem very accepting of your need to stop your drug use. What made you realize this?" The goal is to engage the patient in a genuine dialogue.
   d. *Denial:* Patients also can respond with straightforward denial or rationalization: "I know I drink and use a lot, but if anything,

drinking and using help me deal with my stress." For these patients, it is helpful to explore with them the positive aspects of their substance use. Once the patient believes you understand the positive aspects, he or she may be more ready to explore the negative consequences.

e. Anger: Some patients become angry, or even hostile: "That's the most ridiculous thing I've ever heard! I've been wondering about your competence all along, and now I know for sure." For these patients, it may be most productive to explore the origins of their feelings:

> PRACTITIONER: You seem angry about my raising the question of an alcohol problem.
>
> PATIENT: My father was an alcoholic through and through, never held a job, never came home, and died of cirrhosis. He was an alcoholic; I'm not!
>
> PRACTITIONER: Obviously you're unlike your father in many ways. You have a good, steady job and a loving family. But I'm beginning to be concerned that you do have in common with your father the fact that you are suffering negative consequences of drinking. This tendency can be passed down in people's genes. If you have it, it's not your fault. And I'd like to try to help you.

3. **Helpful tips:** Although there is no formula for promoting acceptance of the diagnosis, the following are some helpful tips:

a. *Always be nonjudgmental and caring.* Giving patients a reason to be angry with you allows them to shift their focus away from the matter at hand. Never be confrontational. The information and concern you convey is confrontational enough and will be more readily accepted in a package of concern and support.

b. *Avoid diagnostic pronouncements.* Startling pronouncements of definitive diagnoses can elicit defensiveness. Initially, to engage the patient in a dialogue it may help to express wondering and uncertainty about the diagnosis. This strategy is especially useful in talking to patients in whom a diagnosis is not completely substantiated.

c. *Avoid arguments with patients.* Agree to disagree when necessary.

d. *Convey medical knowledge.* Fall back on the role of medical expert whenever possible. Often you can be more certain about potential medical effects of alcohol and drugs than you can be about the psychosocial effects, as the patient chooses to reveal them. However, do not fail to express concern and engage the patient in discussion about the possible psychosocial effects of substance use. The earliest abusers often suffer only psychosocial effects of abuse.

e. *Avoid comparisons:* Do not engage in discussions comparing the patient with other alcohol or drug users.

f. *Do not express doubt* about patient reports on the quantity and frequency of substance use. Doing so only leads to additional defensiveness. Take the stand that whatever the patient is drinking or using seems to be causing harm.

g. *Avoid labeling.* Neither suggest that a patient is an "alcoholic" or "addict" nor use other pejorative labels, at least initially. In the long run, it may be useful for patients to accept and embrace these labels, but this can take time. Guide the patient up one small step at a time; don't extend your hand from a precipice.

h. *Tolerate silence* and other indications of patient discomfort in discussions about substance abuse. Don't rescue patients from awkward emotions and cognitive dissonance, which are precursors to acceptance of the diagnosis.

i. *Educate patients.* To assuage guilt, boost self-esteem, and instill optimism, inform the patient, "If you have an alcohol or drug problem, it's not your fault. This is a disease, just like cancer or diabetes, that nobody asks for. Often it is passed down in people's genes. You shouldn't blame yourself for this problem. But now that you know about it, you can get help. And treatment can be very successful."

j. *Focus on patient agendas.* For example, if patients are most concerned about their physical symptoms, express doubt that the symptoms will improve without less use of alcohol. If patients are pursuing a career goal, express doubt that the goal will be attainable if present patterns of drug use continue.

k. *Remain open* to seeing patients, regardless of their level of acceptance of the problem, but do not collude with patients to stop discussing concerns about their substance use.

l. *Recognize there is no failure in communicating your concerns* about substance abuse, even if patients become hostile or never seek follow-up. Many patients need to hear concerns from several persons before they are ready to accept the problem.

4. **Expectations:** Although the ultimate goal is patient acceptance of the diagnosis, this often takes months or years. Practitioners must be patient and understanding, because acceptance is difficult and painful. An appropriate initial goal for many patients may be to agree to a period of self-examination.

B. **Promoting Acceptance of Treatment Recommendations:**

1. **Facilitating acceptance:** Once a patient has begun to accept that his or her drinking or drug use may be a problem, it is time to make a recommendation for treatment. The more treatment options that can be presented, the better the chances that the patient will accept one. Chapter 4 presents a detailed description of current treatment options.

2. **Treatment options:** Before discussing concerns about substance abuse with a patient, practitioners should have in mind preferred

options for treatment. Inpatient programs are best for patients who are unable to achieve initial abstinence as outpatients, who have failed outpatient treatment, or who have the most severe or chronic disorders. Outpatient programs and self-help groups are appropriate entry points for most patients. For all patients, but especially those with limited financial resources, Alcoholics Anonymous, Narcotics Anonymous, and Cocaine Anonymous are important resources.

3. *Negotiating options:* Often patients prefer treatment options less intense than those that seem indicated. It is best to negotiate with these patients from the position that their long-term concerns will be best served by their getting the best treatment possible. Ultimately, however, practitioners should accept and support any treatment efforts a patient undertakes. Sometimes practitioners can elicit a commitment from patients to try more intense treatment should their initial treatment plans fail.

4. *Resistant patients:* A second level of denial is often encountered: "Yes, I may have a problem; but I can take care of it on my own."

   a. A possible response is, "Trying to manage this problem on your own is like a surgeon trying to operate on himself. Strength and willpower are not the answers to alcohol and drug problems. You've already tried many times to control this problem on your own, and it just hasn't worked. Would you consider accepting outside help now? If not, what stands in your way of accepting help?"

   b. Practitioners must accept that patients often need to learn for themselves; protracted discussion and arguing usually are counter-productive.

   c. Trials of abstinence or controlled use can be initiated, with prior agreement that patients will accept treatment if they fail the trial or if they suffer another negative consequence of their substance use.

   d. *Intervention* is a technique developed by the Johnson Institute of Minnesota to coerce patients with severe disorders into treatment. At a meeting often arranged as a surprise to the patient, caring associates, such as family members, friends, co-workers, clergy, and health care practitioners, cite first-hand evidence of the alcohol or drug problem. If the patient initially refuses treatment, the attendees make promises designed, if implemented, to devastate the patient. For example, a spouse may promise divorce, and an employer may threaten discharge. On accepting treatment, the patient is taken immediately to an inpatient setting. Intervention is risky, but usually effective if done properly. It requires substantial preparation and rehearsal and should be coordinated by a trained professional.

5. *Family treatment:* Often when the patient will not accept help, other family members will. Treating family members can indirectly help get the patient into treatment. Al-Anon, Al-A-Teen, and Al-A-Tot

are excellent resources. Chapters 4 and 10 provide more extensive discussion of family treatment.

C. Specific Components of Initial Treatment:

1. ***Treatment methods:*** There are a number of treatment methods that physicians can use in the initial management of alcohol and drug disorders, including:

   a. Brief interventions.
   b. Discussion of the diagnosis.
   c. Family interview.
   d. Use trials and contracting.
   e. Consultation with a treatment specialist.
   f. Watchful waiting.
   g. Formal Johnson Institute style of intervention.

2. ***Initial treatment flow diagram:*** Figure 2–3 presents a flow chart that offers a specific approach to initial treatment. The approaches are based on classifying alcohol and drug disorders as mild or moderate to severe disorders. This classification scheme is based on the number and severity of use-related events. Chapter 1 provides an extensive discussion on the classification of problematic use.

D. Brief Interventions:

1. Brief interventions are succinct discussions with patients aimed to initiate their efforts to control their substance use. Avoiding issues of diagnosis and treatment, they focus on providing information and modifying behavior. They consist largely of a subset of the strategies mentioned above:

   Step 1: Point out, in a nonjudgmental, caring, supportive manner, the negative consequences of the patient's drinking or drug use.

   Step 2: Express concern that the patient may be heading toward serious problems with alcohol or drugs. If possible, tie in your concern with an area of particular relevance to the patient.

   Step 3: Make a specific recommendation for cutting down or stopping alcohol and/or drug use.

   Step 4: Provide educational materials.

   Step 5: Ask the patient to return in 1 month and report his or her progress; leave open options for further recommendations.

2. Even the busiest practices can conduct brief interventions:

   PRACTITIONER: Ms. Carson, you've experienced a number of problems over the past 2 years, and I'm starting to wonder if there's a pattern here. Since your divorce 2 years ago, you've had several bouts of depression. You've been in a couple of car accidents since then, as well. You hint that you may feel guilty about your drinking, and you said that your son also has been concerned. I am concerned that alcohol may be at the root of most, if not all, of these problems, or at least making them worse. What do you think?

   PATIENT: (Long pause) Well, I guess that's possible, but I don't think I drink all that much.

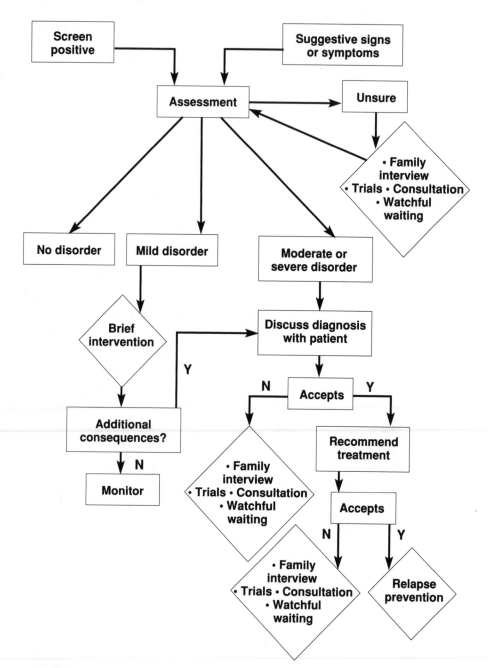

FIG 2–3.
Specific approach to the initial management in patients thought to have an alcohol or drug problem, based on classification of problematic use as mild, moderate, or severe. Family interviews, cessation trials, consultation with other specialists, or watchful waiting can help clarify the diagnosis and ameliorate patient resistance.

PRACTITIONER: Maybe so, but the amount you're drinking clearly is having bad effects on you. I know a primary concern of yours is raising your boys to the best of your ability as a single parent, and you've been very successful so far. I'm left wondering whether you will be able to continue as well as you have if your drinking continues. I'd recommend that you stop drinking altogether, or least cut down to no more than one 5-ounce glass of wine per day.

PATIENT: Well, Doctor, I suppose I can give it a try.

PRACTITIONER: Good. Would you please read this pamphlet on alcohol and problem drinking, and see me again in 1 month. If you can control your drinking, fine. If you have any difficulty, that's all right, too, and we can talk further.

PATIENT: OK.

3. ***Follow-up:*** If a patient can control drinking or drug use to the point where negative consequences do not recur, no further treatment is necessary. If follow-up in 1 month or beyond reveals that the patient is having difficulty in controlling his or her drinking or that there have been further negative consequences, additional treatment modalities can be recommended.

4. ***Abstinence:*** Abstinence should be recommended for patients who are dependent or have suffered severe or repetitive consequences. When the diagnosis is unclear or when patients have experienced only few minor consequences, brief interventions sometimes succeed at modifying behavior. Failed brief interventions may serve as leverage for engaging patients in formal treatment.

V. Relapse Prevention

A successful referral for substance abuse treatment is cause for self-congratulation, but represents only an auspicious beginning. Alcohol and drug disorders are chronic, relapsing, and remitting conditions that require ongoing care. As is true for metabolic disorders, malignancies, and collagen-vascular diseases, the therapeutic goals of treating alcohol and drug disorders are to maximize quality and quantity of life by preventing or ameliorating as many relapses as possible.

A. Early Follow-up Visits

The goals of follow-up visits soon after the patient has accepted treatment are to facilitate implementation of the treatment plan and to build a support system for recovery.

1. If patients do not follow through on recommendations, it may be necessary to reassess their acceptance of their need for treatment.

2. If patients find their treatment program or self-help group objectionable, and if explanations and negotiations fail to reengage them, the practitioner should attempt to negotiate alternative treatment plans.

3. Once the patient is enrolled in treatment, it is important to ensure that plans for ongoing monitoring are in place. Often health care practitioners are the best persons to negotiate and assist patients in implementing these plans, because they will continue to see patients

if they choose to discontinue treatment. Aspects of this plan should include:

   a. Having patients develop a contingency plan for when they sense an impending relapse, such as phoning their AA sponsor, treatment specialist, or practitioner and attending extra treatment sessions or self-help group meetings.

   b. Identifying an individual, often the health care practitioner, as a center of an information network about the patient's recovery. Sources of such information may include the patient's treatment program, 12-step program sponsor, family, friends, and employer. The practitioner asks the patient to encourage these sources to contact the practitioner should concerns about the patient's recovery arise. In this role, the practitioner does not provide treatment but monitors the patient for risk of relapse and negotiates additional measures for relapse prevention and treatment as needed.

4. ***Random urine specimens:*** For patients recovering from problems with drugs other than alcohol, practitioners should seek agreement to submit observed urine specimens at arbitrarily selected future office visits.

   a. In negotiating permission for urine drug screens, practitioners may need to stress that this measure does not reflect lack of trust of the patient so much as recognition that denial is an inherent component of drug problems. Patients often have as little control over their ability to be honest about their drug problems as they do over their use of drugs.

   b. Urine drug screens are a simple, nonpunitive mechanism for identifying relapse and returning a patient to treatment as early as possible, and it is hoped, before serious adverse effects of renewed drug use occur. Patients recovering from drug abuse and dependence report that the prospect of drug screens help them resist cravings for drugs.

5. Patients should be counseled that relapses are common. Relapses should be viewed not as failure but as opportunities for learning to achieve longer and stronger recovery. When patients understand that their practitioners will respond to relapses in a nonjudgmental manner, they will be more likely to report relapses and accept additional treatment.

B. Later Follow-up Visits:

The goals of later follow-up visits are maintenance of the recovery support system and early identification of relapses.

1. Follow-up visits should be scheduled every 2 weeks initially, and once every 2 months for 1 to 2 years of relapse-free recovery.

2. If it is not being addressed in ongoing treatment, practitioners should monitor patients for conditions that place them at risk for relapse, such as stress or social situations that predispose them to alcohol or drug use. The goal is to help patients formulate and implement coping strategies.

3. Practitioners should observe these patients for mental agitation or dysphoria and for disruptions in physical or mental health, family problems, problems with friends, problems at work or school, legal problems, or financial problems, which may lead to or stem from relapse.

4. Lack of adherence to the treatment plan recommended by a treatment specialist is a major predictor of relapse. Patients in early recovery are at risk for relapse after starting to regain a sense of control over their lives. At this time, called the "honeymoon period," patients are prone to minimize their previous difficulties and believe that they can use alcohol or drugs in a controlled fashion. Patients should be warned about the dangers of early recovery.

5. If the practitioner recognizes impending or current relapse, the patient should be presented with the evidence in a nonjudgmental, concerned fashion.

   a. Practitioners should negotiate with patients for additional commitment to recovery.

   b. Increased 12-step meeting attendance and more intensive treatment are possible recommendations.

   c. The final responsibility for choosing treatment, again, rests with the patient.

   d. The practitioner should support any additional commitment to treatment and negotiate a contract for follow-up, including contingencies for future relapse.

   e. Practitioners must realize that many patients must suffer relapses to learn what it will take for an enduring, rewarding recovery.

BIBLIOGRAPHY

Brown RL, Carter WB, Gordon MJ: Diagnosis of alcoholism in a simulated patient encounter by primary care physicians. *J Fam Pract* 1987; 25:259–264.

Clark WD: Alcoholism: Blocks to diagnosis and treatment. *Am J Med* 1981; 71:275–281.

Ewing JA: Detecting alcoholism: the CAGE questionnaire. *JAMA* 1984; 252:1905–1907.

Holt S, Skinner HA, Israel Y: Early identification of alcohol abuse. 2: Clinical and laboratory indicators. *Can Med Assoc J* 1981; 124:1279–1294.

Institute of Medicine: "The community role" identification, brief intervention, and referral, in *Broadening the Base of Treatment for Alcohol Problems.* Washington, DC, National Academy Press, 1990, pp 211–241.

Moore RD, Bone LR, Geller G, et al: Prevalence, detection, and treatment of alcoholism in hospitalized patients. *JAMA* 1989; 261:403–407.

Skinner HA, Holt S: Early intervention for alcohol problems. *J R Coll Gen Pract* 1983; 33:787–791.

Skinner HA, Holt S, Israel Y: Early identification of alcohol abuse: Critical issues and psychosocial indicators for a composite index. *Can Med Assoc J* 1981; 124:1141–1152.

Weinberg JR: Interview techniques for diagnosing alcoholism. *Am Fam Physician* 1974; 9:107–115.

Whitfield CL: Outpatient management of the alcoholic patient. *Psychiatric Annals* 1982; 12:447–457.

CHAPTER 3

Pharmacologic Management of Nicotine, Alcohol, and Other Drug Dependence

Michael F. Fleming, M.D., M.P.H.

The pharmacologic treatment of nicotine, alcohol, and drug dependence by physicians has been limited traditionally to the management of withdrawal symptoms, medical complications, and in some cases aversion therapy with disulfiram (Antabuse). However, recent clinical and neuropharmacologic advances are expected to expand dramatically the role of the physician in the treatment of the primary addictive disorder. This chapter primarily reviews the clinical management of alcohol and drug withdrawal and discusses pharmacologic treatment of postwithdrawal abstinence symptoms and drug maintenance.

I. **Overview of Pharmacologic Treatment of Drug Dependence**
   Pharmacologic treatment involves the management of several clinical problems related to nicotine, alcohol, and drug dependence.
   A. **Drug Withdrawal:**
      The primary drugs for which pharmacologic intervention may be needed are alcohol, sedatives, stimulants, and opioids. Although other mood-altering drugs, such as cannabinoids, phencyclidine HCl (PCP), hallucinogens, inhalants, and anabolic steroids, seldom are associated with withdrawal symptoms, some patients who use these drugs may benefit from pharmacotherapy after cessation of drug use.
   B. **Postwithdrawal Craving and Abstinence Syndromes:**
      There are several clinical syndromes in the late, or "protracted," withdrawal phase of treatment in which pharmacologic intervention may help in reducing the high rate of relapse associated with drug dependence. While these physiologic and psychologic responses to abstinence are not well understood, they are distinct from sleep disorders, mood changes, anxiety, and memory problems that occur in the postwithdrawal period. In contrast to these chronic effects, abstinence syndromes are acute and frequently occur in response to cues or environmental stimuli associated with previous use.
   C. **Drug Maintenance:**
      Drug agonists or cross-tolerant drugs often are used in opioid-

dependent patients in an attempt to substitute a less harmful drug for the primary drug. An example is the use of methadone in narcotic addiction.

D. Drugs Used to Block Desired Mood-Altering Effects:
The opioid receptor naltrexone (Trexan) blocks the effects of heroin and other opioids. It is used after the acute withdrawal phase as an adjunct to treatment. Disulfiram is used in the postwithdrawal period to reinforce sobriety.

E. Pharmacologic Treatment of Health Effects:
Chapter 8 presents treatment of other medical complications. Chapter 9 discusses the pharmacologic treatment of drug intoxication, overdose, and drug-related emergencies. Chapter 18 reviews the treatment of mental health disorders associated with addiction.

II. General Comments on Management of Withdrawal
  A. Principles of Management of Drug Withdrawal:
    1. *Early treatment: Early* pharmacologic treatment can reduce the frequency and magnitude of drug withdrawal complications.
    2. *Outpatient treatment:* For most patients identified in a primary care setting detoxification can be carried out safely in an outpatient setting.
    3. *Medical assessment:* Patients with clinical symptoms of drug withdrawal should undergo a comprehensive medical assessment, including blood alcohol level and blood and urine drug screens.
    4. *Supportive care:* Supportive, empathetic care is an essential component of acute withdrawal management.
    5. *Role of medication:* Pharmacologic treatment is only one component of a comprehensive treatment plan and should never be used as the sole treatment.
    6. *Relapse:* Recurrent episodes of drug withdrawal are associated with increased severity of withdrawal and potentially fatal complications.

  B. Guidelines for Determining Outpatient vs. Inpatient Treatment of Drug Withdrawal
Mood-altering drugs likely to require inpatient treatment are alcohol, barbiturates, all benzodiazepines, cocaine, methamphetamine, and opioids. The following factors are important when planning detoxification in an outpatient setting. These criteria are meant to serve as guidelines, not as strict rules.
    1. *Medical criteria:*
      a. *Severity of withdrawal:* The development of mild tremor, anxiety, and tachycardia is common when patients dependent on alcohol, barbiturates, or tranquilizers reduce or stop use of these mood-altering drugs. Patients with a history of mild withdrawal likely will develop a similar withdrawal syndrome the next time they become abstinent. However, patients who have previously developed withdrawal seizures, delirium, or psychosis are likely to

have significant withdrawal symptoms and should be admitted for observation and probable pharmacologic treatment.

b. *Tolerance:* Patients with a high tolerance who are taking the equivalent of more than 60 mg diazepam (Valium) per day are not candidates for outpatient treatment. Equivalent doses for other benzodiazepines are 300 mg chlordiazepoxide (Librium), 12 mg lorazepam (Ativan), and 5 mg alprazolam (Xanax).

c. *Medical contraindications* for outpatient treatment include:

(1) CNS: History of a recent head trauma, cerebrovascular accident (CVA).

(2) GI: Acute abdominal pain, unstable liver function.

(3) Infections: pneumonia, sepsis, acquired immune deficiency syndrome (AIDS).

(4) Cardiovascular: Arrhythmias, angina or recent history of ischemic heart disease, hypertension.

(5) Severe respiratory disease.

(6) Age: Older than 65 years.

2. **Abstinence criteria:**

a. *Patient contract:* Patients must agree to remain abstinent from *all* mood-altering agents. A clear commitment not to use drugs is important. Patients who have ambivalent feelings and indicate they will use "if things get too rough" are not likely to benefit from an outpatient withdrawal protocol.

b. *Participation in a treatment program:* Patients should agree to take part in a treatment program. The program they choose will depend on personal finances and community resources. However, patients need to commit to getting "some professional help." Patients who will not agree to treatment but say, "I can do it on my own," likely will not recover from their drug dependence. These patients likely have high levels of denial, which is difficult to overcome. It may be appropriate for physicians to refuse outpatient pharmacotherapy for symptoms of drug withdrawal to patients who do not meet abstinence criteria.

c. *Treatment plan:* Patients *must* agree to the treatment plan, including frequency of physician visits, avoidance of taverns, random alcohol or drug testing, and medication guidelines.

3. **Social support:**

a. *Role of family members:* Patients who live alone or do not have drug-free support systems are not candidates for outpatient treatment. A sober and responsible family member or friend is an integral part of outpatient medical detoxification. This person will assist the patient (and physician) get through the first few days of treatment. The family member or friend can aid specifically in the medical detoxification plan by:

(1) Encouraging and assisting the patient to attend Alcoholics Anonymous (AA) or Narcotics Anonymous (NA).

  (2) Providing a safe, quiet, loving environment.

  (3) Watching for serious withdrawal symptoms.

  (4) Assisting with medications.

  (5) Providing massages and hot baths for muscle cramps and anxiety.

  (6) Driving the patient to and from the physician's office.

  (7) Minimizing risk of relapse by keeping the patient away from situations that may lead to relapse.

  (8) Disposing of drugs that may be in the home environment.

  (9) Facilitating participation in a treatment program.

 b. *Family contract:* It is important to discuss each of these tasks with the helping family member. Write specific tasks on a prescription pad to improve the likelihood of the family member following through with assignments.

 c. *Family treatment:* Participating in the treatment plan also may have therapeutic value for the family member. Repeated contacts with a physician and a treatment program may initiate their participation in a family program for themselves and other family members.

4. ***Physician factors:***

 a. *Relationships:* A trusting physician-patient relationship is a powerful therapeutic tool and can help break through the impregnable denial. If this physician also is knowledgeable about the treatment of drug withdrawal, an outpatient treatment plan is more likely to work.

 b. *Daily contact:* Patients should be evaluated *daily* until the risk of withdrawal is minimal and the patient has started a treatment rehabilitation program. This may be 3 days for alcohol abuse or as long as 10 days for long-acting benzodiazepines, methamphetamine, opioids, and even cocaine. Weekend contacts are extremely important, because the risk of relapse is greater on Saturday and Sunday.

C. **Nonpharmacologic Treatment of Drug Withdrawal**

The rate of relapse may be lower in patients who are detoxified without the use of psychoactive drugs such as benzodiazepines, barbiturates, or methadone. This is related to the severity of the chemical dependence and the degree of physical dependence. Supportive care to reduce the use of psychoactive medication for detoxification is likely to reduce the frequency of relapse.

1. ***Supportive care:*** *R*eality orientation, *R*eassurance, and *R*espect.

2. ***Key components of supportive care:***

 a. Reduce environmental stimuli by providing a quiet room with controlled lighting and limiting the number of care givers and visitors.

 b. Encourage physical comfort by changing or supporting the patient's body position with pillows and blankets. Engage in quiet conversation only if initiated by the patient, and allow the patient to sleep between assessments.

    c. Orient the patient to time, place, and person when conducting clinical assessments.

    d. Offer reassurance and encouragement, and focus questions or comments on taking "one day at time."

    e. Minimize the use of stimulants such as coffee, candy, and tobacco.

  3. *Negative factors:* Detrimental environmental effects include dark rooms with shadows, abrupt loud noises such as cardiac monitor sounds, physical restraints such as intravenous lines, Poseys, or hospital gowns, and hostility, negativism, or anger on the part of the care giver.

III. Alcohol and Sedative Drug Withdrawal

A. Sedative Drugs Associated With Physical Dependence and Withdrawal

Although any of the drugs in this class can produce physical dependence if used long enough or in high enough doses, certain agents seem to have a greater propensity for doing so.

  1. *Sedative drugs associated with withdrawal include:*

    a. Alcohol.

    b. Short-acting benzodiazepines such as lorazepam (Ativan), alprazolam (Xanax), and triazolam (Halcion).

    c. Long-acting benzodiazepines such as diazepam (Valium) and chlordiazepoxide (Librium).

    d. Barbiturates such as secobarbital, pentobarbital, or butalbital (a component of Fiorinal).

    e. Quaalude (no longer marketed legally in the United States), glutethimide (Doriden), meprobamate (Equanil).

B. Pathophysiology of Sedative Drug Withdrawal

  1. *CNS depression:* Sedatives are mood-altering drugs that depress the level of CNS arousal. While sedatives have disinhibiting properties at *low* dosages, their primary effect is to inhibit a number of CNS functions.

  2. *GABA neurotransmitters:* All sedative drug action appears to be associated with the γ-aminobutyric acid (GABA) chloride channel receptor complex on neurons in the CNS. GABA receptor complexes are primary inhibitory sites located on synaptic membranes throughout the brain. GABA released in the synaptic cleft binds to the receptor and opens chloride channels, which hyperpolarize the membranes and thereby lower cell excitability.

  3. *Receptors:* Specific receptors for benzodiazepines and barbiturates are associated with GABA receptor chloride channel complexes. Alcohol does not appear to have a specific receptor, but affects the GABA complexes through a less selective membrane mechanism.

  4. *Receptor activation:* Activation of these "drug" receptors with

barbiturates or benzodiazepines leads to similar effects as the activation of GABA receptors by the transmitter. Drug receptor activation shows some cooperative interaction and can potentiate the effects of GABA or have a direct effect on the chloride channels.

5. *GABA release:* Long-term sedative use alters the function of the GABA complexes by depleting the amount of GABA available for release into the synaptic spaces.

6. *Inhibitory/excitatory:* Many clinical signs of withdrawal are thought to be a direct result of change in the balance of the inhibitory/excitatory systems.

C. **Risk Factors of Sedative Withdrawal**

1. Several risk factors are associated with a higher probability for the development of withdrawal symptoms. I have found this list of risk factors helpful in determining which patients may require pharmacotherapy and inpatient treatment:
   a. Age more than 40 years.
   b. Male gender.
   c. Daily consumption more than a fifth of liquor.
   d. Drinking around the clock to maintain a steady blood alcohol level.
   e. Excessive drinking over 10 years.
   f. Development of tremulousness and anxiety within 6 to 8 hours of cessation.
   g. History of seizures, hallucinations, delusions with alcohol withdrawal.
   h. Presence of an acute medical problem, such as pneumonia.
   i. Alcohol level ≥250 mg/dL on admission.

2. Presence of these risk factors is scored as follows:
   a. 0–2 factors: low risk for severe withdrawal.
   b. 3–6 factors: moderate risk.
   c. 7–9 factors: high risk.

D. **Clinical Characteristics of Sedative Withdrawal**

1. *Withdrawal syndromes:*

   Withdrawal from sedative drugs can be separated into three distinct clinical syndromes. Alcohol withdrawal is the prototype for all sedatives, and is discussed below, followed by unique features of barbiturate, alprazolam, and diazepam withdrawal.

   a. *Stage 1, minor withdrawal:*
      (1) Characterized by restlessness, anxiety, sleeping problems, agitation, and tremor. Tachycardia, low-grade fever, or diaphoresis also may develop, as well as elevated systolic and diastolic blood pressure.

   b. *Stage 2, major withdrawal:*
      (1) Characterized by signs and symptoms of stage 1 withdrawal plus *visual or auditory hallucinations.* Visual hallucinations are more common than auditory. The hallucinations occur in

the presence of a clear sensorium; the patient may be aware he or she is hallucinating. Hallucinations occur more often at night.

(2) Patients are increasingly agitated and frightened. Tremors may involve the whole body rather than a simple coarse tremor of the hands. The pulse often is >100, diastolic pressure >100, and diaphoresis more pronounced. Vomiting may occur.

c. *Stage 3, delirium tremens:*

(1) The major diagnostic criterion for stage 3 withdrawal is the presence of delirium. Patients are confused and disoriented. The delirium in alcohol withdrawal commonly manifests itself by disorientation to time, place, and person, as well as global confusion and inability to recognize familiar objects or persons.

(2) The clinical signs and symptoms usually are severe. Diastolic pressure of 110 is not unusual. Vomiting may be severe, and patients often need intravenous fluids. In the absence of other medical problems, a temperature >38.5° C (>100° F) is a serious prognostic sign. A patient in delirium tremens may or may not have hallucinations.

(3) All patients with stage 3 withdrawal should be hospitalized and should not be treated in free-standing treatment units.

(4) Alcohol withdrawal delirium is a medical emergency, and the patient should be examined thoroughly for other problems. Associated medical problems include embolism, infection, meningitis, pancreatitis, and water and electrolyte imbalance. Mortality ranges from 2% to 5% and often is associated with respiratory failure or cardiovascular collapse.

2. **Withdrawal seizures:**
Alcohol withdrawal seizures occur 12 to 48 hours after the last drink. Withdrawal seizures typically are grand mal, last <5 minutes, and are singular. Twenty percent occur in salvos of two or three. Status epilepticus is not associated with withdrawal, but indicates another problem. Seizures from barbiturates, alprazolam, and cocaine are similar and usually occur within 72 hours of the last use.

3. **Time course for sedative withdrawal** (Fig 3–1):
Stage 1 withdrawal symptoms usually begin 5 to 8 hours after the last drink of alcohol. Withdrawal seizures develop within 12 to 48 hours. Seizures may be seen in any of the three stages, but are most likely in stage 2. Symptoms of stage 2 withdrawal may begin as soon as 24 hours after the last drink or be delayed for 72 hours. Symptoms of stage 3 withdrawal have been reported as early as 48 hours or as late as 10 days after the last drink or drug use.

4. **Unusual presentations of sedative withdrawal:**
a. Most patients have several clinical components, but an occasional

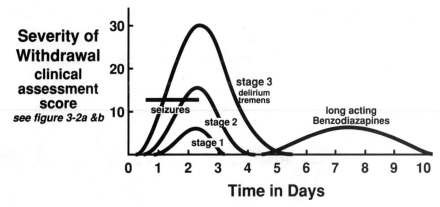

FIG 3–1.
Time course of alcohol and sedative withdrawal. Stage 3 of alcohol withdrawal may last up to 5 days. Long-acting sedatives, such as diazepam, may produce moderate withdrawal symptoms lasting 10 days.

patient may present with a single isolated event, such as a seizure, cardiac arrhythmia, delirium, or hallucinations. Because these symptoms may be delayed for 7 to 10 days, diagnosis may be difficult.

b. An unusual presentation is hallucinatory delusional syndrome. This is an isolated well-organized psychotic picture, with none of the other signs of sedative withdrawal.

5. *Clinical characteristics of barbiturate withdrawal:*

a. Before the discovery of benzodiazepines in the early 1950s, barbiturate withdrawal was a common and serious medical problem. Barbiturate withdrawal is similar to alcohol withdrawal, with clinical findings of fever, delirium, and seizures. Barbiturate seizures can occur in the absence of other signs of withdrawal. Onset and duration depend on the half-life of the barbiturate, but these drugs typically have a later onset than alcohol does. The drug of choice for the treatment of barbiturate withdrawal is controversial. I prefer to use phenobarbital; diazepam and carbamazepine (Tegretol) are alternative drugs for the treatment of barbiturate withdrawal.

6. *Clinical characteristics of alprazolam withdrawal:*

a. Alprazolam (Xanax) has become one of the common drugs associated with severe withdrawal. All patients who take 1 mg or more per day for more than 3 months develop varying degrees of physical dependence and are at risk for sedative withdrawal.

b. As the most commonly prescribed drug for panic disorders and anxiety, treatment centers have encountered increasing numbers of alcoholics and addicts with severe physical dependence on alprazolam.

c. Clinical characteristics include rapid onset of withdrawal symptoms, including seizures and delirium. I prefer to use phenobarbital to treat alprazolam withdrawal; diazepam and carbamazepine are alternative drugs used in many centers.

7. ***Clinical characteristics of diazepam withdrawal:***

   a. Patients withdrawing from diazepam (Valium) appear to be hypochondriacal and have difficulty concentrating for 2 to 3 weeks. Typical symptoms include hypersensitivity to sensory modalities, including hyperacusis, tinnitus, and perceptual changes. Muscle

Identification of Stages of Alcohol Withdrawal (Note: Absence of Symptoms - 0)			
SYMPTOMS	1 POINT: STAGE 1	2 POINTS: STAGE 2	3 POINTS: STAGE 3
ONSET	5-8 Hours After Last Drink	1-3 Days After Last Drink	72-96 Hours After last Drink
TEMPERATURE	Slight increase: 37.2-37.7	37.7 - 39.1	39.1 - 40.5
PULSE	Tachycardia: 100-120	Tachycardia: 12-140.	Above 140. May become irregular.
RESPIRATIONS	20-24	24-30	30 & Over
BLOOD PRESSURE	Fluctuating and/or elevated: SBP>160 DBP>100	Both systolic & diastolic Elevated: SBP>160 DBP>100.	**Severe Hypertension:** SBP>180; DBP>120. **Severe Hypotension:** SBP<100; DPB<60
ANXIETY	"Inner Anxiety", Nervous	Irritable - Tearful - Fearful	Emotionally out of control.
AGITATION	Restless. Loss of Concentration. Easily Disturbed. Reactive.	Fidgety. Can't Sit Still. Picking. May Pace.	Hyperactive: can't contain.
TREMOR	**Mild** (may not be visible; tough fingers; note tongue-eye movement)	**Visible and/arm:** have patient extend upper extremities. Tongue tremor. Constant eyeball movement.	**Exaggerated;** May be total body movement
DIAPHORESIS	Palms/forehead damp - slight diaphoresis.	Beads of sweat - obvious.	Drenching sweat.
EATING DISTURBANCE	Not hungry, however, picks & eats over 50%	Eats less than 50% with encouragement.	Eats less than 10%
GI DISTRESS	Mild N-V-D: (any of these symptoms or all).	Moderate N-V-D.	Severe N-V-D: (may be incontinent of stool).
SLEEP DISTURBANCE	Difficult settling. Up 1-3 times during the night.	Awake half of the night.	Completely sleepless.
CLOUDING SENSORIUM	Can't do serial 7 subtraction. Knows correct date but not sure. Generally coherent.	Disoriented to time by 2 days. Confusion. Harder to reorient.	Can't identify significant others. Disoriented to time & place.
HALLUCINATIONS	**Not** present	**Mild** auditory/visual.	**Auditory/visual:** (may be fused or nonfused).
CONVULSIONS	**Usually not present:** (occur 12-36 hours after last drink	**"Rum Fits"** 5 minutes & subside **Grand Mal Seizure.** Tonic Spasms/ Clonic Jerking **PRECEDE** DELIRIUM TREMENS BY 24 HOURS.	**Severe** reoccurring convulsions.

KEY POINTS

1. IDENTIFICATION OF POTENTIAL ALCOHOL WITHDRAWAL IN THE HOSPITALIZED PATIENT IS VITA IN PREVENTION AND DEPENDS ON NURSING INTERVIEW AND ASSESSMENT SKILLS IN THE MAJORITY OF INSTANCES.

2. WITHDRAWAL FROM ALCOHOL IS A CRITICAL MEDICAL EMERGENCY.

3. IF MEDICATED ADEQUATELY, MOST WITHDRAWAL STOPS AT STAGE 1!

4. QUESTIONS. CALL:_____

NURSING INTERVENTIONS		
STAGE 1	**STAGE 2**	**STAGE 3**
Assess/Document S/S. Notify MD if score > 5. Medicate according to protocol & Physician orders. Heparin well secured. **Diffuse agitation & anxiety:** walk/talk; be supportive; be firm; allow patient some control to useenergy. **Treat symptomatically:** fluids; orange juice for K+; antiemetics. **Review lab results:** Blood Alcohol Level; CBC; Lytes; LFT's (hepatitis); Drug Screen; Mixed Abuse; Ammonia Level; Magnesium; Glucose; Protime.	**Access/Document S/S.** Notify MD if score > 10. Notify house staff of protocol. Medicate as required for all symptoms. **SYMPATHETIC STORM:** requires sympathetic care. Talk down-quiet-orient; be nonjudgemental & reassuring; may require a sitter; pad side rails; use restrains only if necessary to prevent injury - **not** for convenience; try posey or light restraints before leathers. **DECREASE VISUAL - AUDITORY STIMULATION:** Quite room; avoid TV. Well lighted room; decrease shadows/fear. Limit activity & numbers of people. **PROVIDE CALM CARE.** Support & educate family. Frequent Vital Signs Q 15-30 minutes as ordered.	**Access/Document S/S. ONCE DT's OCCUR - LITTLE CAN BE DONE TO ALTER THEM!** Acute Stage: Notify MD; Push ICU bed for initial onset of STAGE 3! Medicate: sedation. **Monitor:** Temp; to use B/P; pulse; Resp. **Have Available:** Oxygen; Suction; Cooling Blanket; 1:1 Nursing Care; Restraints/Padded Rails. **Maintain patient dignity:** foley/rectal tube. **Family:** support/reassure. **SYMPTOMATIC TREATMENT:** Assess for potential complications: **SHOCK; STROKE; ALKALOSIS; ARRHYTHMIAS, HEART ATTACK, FLUID/ELECTROLYTE IMBALANCE; AND/OR SUDDEN DEATH FROM CARDIAC/ RESPIRATORY FAILURE.** Notify MD of complications and treat as ordered.

FIG 3-2.

Clinical assessment protocol for use by nurses and physicians in patients receiving therapy for drug withdrawal.

Signature of Provider: _____

23 - 07 _____

Date: _____   07 - 15 _____

Unit: _____   15 - 23 _____

SCORING FOR STAGE IDENTIFICATION (see reverse)												
Time												
Temperature*												
Pulse*												
Respirations												
Blood Pressure*												
*Record actual VS in Shaded Area												
Anxiety												
Agitation												
Tremor												
Diaphoresis												
Eating Disturbance												
GI Distress: N-V-D												
Sleep Disturbance												
Clouding Sensorium												
Hallucinations												
Convulsions												
TOTALS:												

TOTAL POINTS INDICATING STAGE
(Number System & Stage Identification: See Reverse)

1 - 10: Stage 1 Withdrawal
10 - 20: Stage 2 Withdrawal
20 - >20: Stage 3 Wighdrawal

PROVIDER INTERVENTIONS: _____

_____
_____
_____
_____
_____
_____
_____
_____
_____
_____
_____

FIG 3-2 (cont.).

cramping may be a prominent symptom. Patients have been
known to have severe abdominal pain that may mimic acute abdomen.

b. Withdrawal symptoms from long-acting benzodiazepines may not
develop for 5 to 10 days after cessation of the drug. Phenobarbital and carbamazepine are the drugs of choice for diazepam
withdrawal.

E. General Management Protocol

1. The clinical assessment protocol shown in Figure 3–2 is a modification of the CIWA developed by Shaw (1981).
   a. The guidelines used at the University of Wisconsin include the 11 most common signs and symptoms of sedative withdrawal. The severity score of each characteristic can vary from 1 to 3 points. Scores up to 10 are classified as stage 1; 10 to 20, stage 2; >20, stage 3. The assessment is done at least twice in each 8-hour shift during the active phase of withdrawal.
   b. Using a standard assessment instrument provides a structured format for the nurses and physicians to monitor the clinical course of sedative withdrawal. This instrument also eases communication between providers and aids in the use of medication. It is an excellent educational tool for medical students and student nurses.

2. *Protocol:*
   a. Clinical assessment (see Fig 3–2).
   b. No restriction of fluid intake or food, with the exception of stimulants such as coffee, tea, or cola. Patients should be given a high-calorie, high-carbohydrate diet.
   c. Intravenous fluids (5% dextrose–0.5N saline solution) should be administered to all patients with stage 3 sedative withdrawal. Potassium and magnesium may need to be replaced.
   d. Complete blood cell count, liver function tests, electrolytes, magnesium, prothrombin time (PT), chest radiograph, electrocardiogram, serum creatinine concentration, blood alcohol level, and urine drug screen in all patients at risk for drug withdrawal.
   e. Restraints need to be available at the bedside for any patient who is at high risk for stage 2 or 3 sedative withdrawal. Patients with stage 2 or 3 withdrawal need close observation by a family member and/or nursing staff. A soft cloth restraint (e.g., Posey) usually is adequate.

F. Principles of Pharmacotherapy of Sedative Withdrawal

1. *Cross-tolerant drugs:* Pharmacologic treatment of sedative-hypnotic withdrawal is based on administration of a cross-dependent drug, such as diazepam or phenobarbital, in progressively decreasing doses. Carbamazepine and clonazepam are alternative drugs used in some programs.

2. *Treatment goals:*
   a. Relieve symptoms (e.g., tremulousness, agitation, anxiety, sleep disturbances, manifestations of autonomic hyperactivity).
   b. Prevent stage 2 or 3 withdrawal syndrome.
   c. Prevent seizures.
   d. Minimize the chance of new dependency on the medication used for withdrawal.

   e. Minimize the toxicity of medication used for detoxification (e.g., respiratory depression, aspiration pneumonia).

3. *Variation in tolerance:* The most difficult problem in the management of alcohol withdrawal for physicians who are unfamiliar with this problem is the large variation in the amount of medication needed in patients who have a high tolerance for sedatives. Although the detoxification protocol provides specific dosage recommendations, medication needs of different patients may vary by 10-fold.

4. *Benzodiazepines:* The medications most widely used for the treatment of alcohol withdrawal are the benzodiazepines. Of the treatments used before the development of the benzodiazepines, such as chloral hydrate, paraldehyde, and alcohol, only phenobarbital is used with any frequency.

5. *Prevention of stage 3 withdrawal:* Clinical trials have shown that all of the benzodiazepines are more effective than placebo or no drug therapy in decreasing anxiety, restlessness, tremor, and seizure and in prevention of stage 2 or 3 withdrawal. However, phenobarbital for detoxification has several advantages over benzodiazepines, particularly in polydrug abuse, hepatic dysfunction, and potential seizure.

6. *Front-end treatment:* The major principle in the use of these medications is to use sufficient dosage in the first 24 to 48 hours. Benzodiazepines can be administered with a high loading dose at the outset. Tapering is unnecessary for the long-acting benzodiazepines. Medication is much less effective once major withdrawal symptoms have developed!

7. *Complications:* Complications of treatment with high doses of benzodiazepines primarily occur in patients with respiratory or cardiac disease. Complications frequently occur 3 to 5 days after initial treatment, as the long-acting metabolites are released. Methods that minimize the development of respiratory complications include the following:

   a. Try to limit the dose to 200 mg diazepam or 1,000 mg chlordiazepoxide.

   b. Supplement with a short-acting drug such as lorazepam.

   c. Avoid the use of tapering doses of long-acting benzodiazepines.

   d. Haloperidol should be used with some caution, because it can lower the seizure threshold. Administer haloperidol to treat agitation and psychotic symptoms in patients whose symptoms are not well controlled with appropriate doses of benzodiazepines, phenobarbital, or carbamazepine.

G. **Medication Protocols for Sedative Withdrawal**

   1. *Protocol*

      a. *Multivitamins,* 1 tab/day.

b. *B complex vitamins 1 mL and thiamine HCl 100 mg,* IM qd × 3 days.
c. *Magnesium Plus,* 2 tabs tid, or magnesium sulfate 1 gm IM q6h × 4 doses if (1) history of withdrawal seizure, (2) high risk for stage 2 withdrawal, (3) initial serum Mg^{2+} <1.5, or (4) carpopedal spasms.
d. *Atenolol* 50 mg PO bid × 4 days if no contraindications present.
e. *Antiemetics:* Hydroxyzine (Vistaril) 50 mg q4h IM prn to treat nausea.
f. *Seizure treatment:*
   (1) Patients already receiving an anticonvulsant should be maintained on that drug.
   (2) Diazepam and carbamazepine are the drugs of choice for seizures.
   (3) Prophylactic use of *carbamazepine* may reduce the risk of seizures. Patients with a history of withdrawal seizures may benefit from a loading dose of 100 mg/hr × 4 hours, then 200 mg q6h × 7 days.
g. Stage 1 withdrawal: Loading dose of 10–20 mg diazepam PO q2h × three doses or until patient is sedated but arousable.
   (1) Most inpatients will require a total loading dose of 60 mg, outpatients 40 mg.
   (2) Because of the long half-life of diazepam, most patients who receive early treatment will not need additional diazepam.
h. Stage 2 or 3 withdrawal:
   (1) Administer 10–20 mg diazepam PO/IV q30min until symptoms are controlled.
   (2) Patients who need >150 mg diazepam for control of symptoms should receive supplemental lorazepam and/or haloperidol (Haldol).
i. For patients whose symptoms are not controlled by diazepam or who have end-stage liver disease:
   (1) Administer lorazepam (Ativan) 4–6 mg IV/IM q30min until symptoms subside.
j. Treatment of agitation and psychotic symptoms:
   (1) Haloperidol 2–10 mg IM/IV q2h.
   (2) Benztropine mesylate (Cogentin) seldom is necessary unless haloperidol is needed for more than 72 hours.
   (3) Haloperidol 20 mg in a 24-hour period may be necessary; however, it increases the risk for withdrawal seizures.

2. **Vitamins and thiamine:**
   a. Alcoholics often are depleted of B complex vitamins. Multivitamins are commonly given, although their value is unproved. Thiamine IM is recommended before any IV glucose is administered.

3. *Magnesium sulfate:*
   a. Total body stores of magnesium usually are depleted in alcoholics. A 1,000 mg depletion of magnesium is not unusual. Although the clinical importance of this observation is unclear, replacement may decrease the risk for withdrawal seizures and the development of delirium tremens. Low magnesium levels also are associated with carpopedal spasms.
   b. A new oral form of magnesium (a protein complex) is available. It is not associated with diarrhea and can rapidly raise serum magnesium levels. Two tablets tid is equivalent to 1 ampule parenteral magnesium sulfate.
   c. For a patient with seizures and low magnesium levels, 4–6 ampules magnesium sulfate can be given in the first 24 hours. The IM injection is painful, but is safer and much less costly than the IV route. The major problem with IV infusion of magnesium sulfate is hypotension; however, inasmuch as most patients with withdrawal are hypertensive, this rarely is a problem.

4. *Hydration:*
   a. Most alcoholic patients are overhydrated secondary to alterations in the vasopressin system. Most patients in withdrawal should not be hydrated with IV fluids. An occasional patient with protracted vomiting in stage 3 withdrawal may need IV fluids. Overhydration with the use of IV fluids can develop, and is associated with cardiac failure and cerebral edema. Fluid and electrolyte status need to be monitored closely in stage 3 withdrawal.

5. *Antiemetics:*
   a. Hydroxyzine (Vistaril) is the antiemetic of choice. Promethazine (Phenergan) or prochlorperazine (Compazine) are not recommended, because phenothiazines lower the seizure threshold. They are contraindicated in patients with a history of withdrawal seizures.

6. *β-Blockers*
   a. β-Blockers (Atenolol) may be used to decrease tremor, cardiac arrhythmias, and other adrenergic symptoms. They are particularly useful in older patients or those with a history of ischemic heart disease. Contraindications include diabetes-prone hypoglycemia, congestive heart failure, chronic obstructive lung disease, and Wolff-Parkinson-White syndrome. The major drawback to the use of β-blockers is that they may mask early signs of stage 3 withdrawal. Patients need to be carefully monitored for development of hallucinations and delirium.
   b. β-Blockers should never be used without benzodiazepines or phenobarbital, because they do not prevent psychomotor symptoms or delirium tremens.

7. *Benzodiazepines:*
   a. Diazepam and lorazepam are used as the prototype benzodiaz-

epines, but chlordiazepoxide (Librium) and oxazepam (Serax) also are used as warranted by individual circumstances.

b. A loading dose of diazepam is the prefered method: 40–60 mg diazepam is given over 6 hours, after the onset of withdrawal, usually within 24 hours of the patient's last drink.

c. Diazepam and chlordiazepoxide are not absorbed when given IM, and *never* should be given IM, but are limited to PO and IV administration. Lorazepam is rapidly absorbed IM, SQ, IV, and PO.

d. The dose equivalent of 10 mg diazepam is 50 mg chlordiazepoxide, 2 mg lorazepam, or 40–60 mg oxazepam. There are controversies regarding dose equivalents, particularly with oxazepam.

e. Diazepam should be started immediately after a patient begins to develop signs of withdrawal. A loading dose of diazepam simplifies treatment and is as effective as the usual method of administering benzodiazepines, q4–6h for 72–96 hours.

f. Benzodiazepines should not be used prophylactically. The Clinical Assessment Protocol (see Fig 3–2) may be used to monitor the severity of withdrawal symptoms and to assist in the decision of when pharmacotherapy should be started. At the onset of withdrawal symptoms or when the total score (see Fig 3–2) exceeds 5, administer 20 mg diazepam PO. Two additional doses of 10–20 mg diazepam are administered at 2-hour intervals for a total dose of 40–60 mg.

g. Patients should be able to sit up and drink a glass of juice before the second and third loading doses are given.

h. Outpatients should receive the first dose of diazepam in the physician's office and be observed for 60 minutes. The second and third doses may be given at home in the presence of a family member.

i. Lorazepam may be used instead of diazepam in patients with cirrhosis. However, because of its short half-life, lorazepam must be given more often and is more difficult to use. Patients withdrawing with lorazepam may break through the medication, with resurgence of symptoms, including seizures and delirium. Lorazepam has no anticonvulsant properties.

j. An alternative dosing schedule is the 3-day taper. When signs of withdrawal develop, give diazepam 20 mg PO (Librium 100 mg) q6h for the first 24 hours, then diazepam 20 mg q8h for the second 24 hours, then diazepam 20 mg q12h on the third day.

8. ***Phenobarbital:***

a. Phenobarbital has many useful pharmacologic properties that make it preferable to benzodiazepines for treatment of polydrug abuse and in patients at high risk for seizures:

(1) Excellent anticonvulsant properties.

(2) Direct excretion (about 5%) unchanged in urine.

(3) Not dependent on hepatic transformation.

(4) Low abuse potential.

(5) Excellent absorption with IM administration.

b. There are two methods to determine the initial dose of pheno-
the second dose of pentobarbital, the patient has marked
tolerance, and 480 mg should be given in the first 24
barbital. The first is to use a standard protocol and adjust the
dose depending on patient response. The second is to estimate
the dose required based on the pentobarbital challenge test.

(1) *Method 1:*

    (a) Administer 120 mg phenobarbital IM and give 30 mg PO
q8h.

    (b) If the patient responds appropriately, reduce the PO
dose of phenobarbital by 10%/day × 10 days.

    (c) If necessary, administer two additional IM doses of phe-
nobarbital, to a total of 360 mg IM/24 hr.

(2) *Method 2:*

    (a) Calculate the amount needed in the first 24 hours by
using the pentobarbital challenge (see 9, below).

    (b) Administer half the calculated amount IM and half PO in
three divided doses in the first 24 hours.

    (c) Total maximum dose of phenobarbital over 24 hours is
600 mg. Respiratory depression is likely at this dose.

c. ***Pentobarbital tolerance test:***

The pentobarbital tolerance test was developed for use in patients who are polydrug abusers of sedative-hypnotic drugs and
in alcoholic patients in whom risk for withdrawal is unclear. The
goal of the challenge is to estimate sedative tolerance and calculate the dose of phenobarbital needed to safely detoxify the patient. *This test should be used only in asymptomatic patients who
are not experiencing withdrawal symptoms.* The test is administered as follows:

(1) Give 200 mg pentobarbital PO.

(2) After 1 hour, assess level of consciousness and toxicity (i.e.,
arousability, speech, gait, nystagmus).

(3) Calculate phenobarbital needed in the first 24 hours by classifying tolerance, as follows:

    (a) *Minimum tolerance:* Patient is asleep, sedated, and diffi-
cult to arouse. Significant withdrawal is unlikely, and
medication is not called for.

    (b) *Moderate tolerance:* Patient is only mildly sedated;
speech is moderately slurred; moderate ataxia and
coarse nystagmus are present. These findings suggest
tolerance. Estimated 24-hour phenobarbital requirement
for the first 24 hours is 120–240 mg.

(c) *Severe tolerance:* Patient is comfortable and not sedated. The only sign of intoxication is a fine lateral nystagmus. Administer a second dose of pentobarbital 200 mg. If slurred speech, ataxia, and nystagmus develop, give 240–360 mg in the first 24 hours. If there is no effect with the second dose of pentobarbital, the patient has marked tolerance, and 480 mg should be given in the first 24 hours.

9. *Tegretol:*
   a. Tegretol has become the drug of choice for polysedative abuse in some centers. It is particularly effective with drugs such as alprazolam, which are associated with a high prevalence of withdrawal seizures.
   b. Advantages include the absence of respiratory depression, excellent anticonvulsant properties, and that the medication can be started in the presence of blood alcohol/drug levels before the onset of symptoms. The latter advantage is important in persons who have a history of rapid onset of withdrawal seizures.
   c. Administer a loading dose of 100 mg qh × four doses, then 200 mg q6h until a therapeutic level is obtained. The drug may be stopped in 10–14 days for short-acting drugs such as lorazepam, or 4–8 weeks for alprazolam and diazepam.

H. **Medical Complications of Alcohol and Sedative Withdrawal**
The most frequent complications of withdrawal are seizures, psychosis, delirium, and violent behavior. More serious complications include aspiration pneumonia, respiratory arrest, and cardiovascular collapse.

1. *Treatment of withdrawal seizures:*
   a. Many clinicians give the first dose of diazepam or phenobarbital as soon as a history of withdrawal seizures is obtained. As with the development of hallucinations and delirium, the sooner the medication is given the more likely the medication will prevent complications.
   b. If the patient is receiving adequate doses of diazepam, a single seizure may not necessitate additional medication.
   c. In patients with multiple seizures a computed tomography (CT) scan should be obtained to rule out intracranial disease.
   d. Carbamazepine is preferred over phenytoin (Dilantin) for treatment of these seizures. Carbamazepine may be considered for prophylactic treatment if the patient is currently receiving an anticonvulsant or has a history of epilepsy or of alcohol withdrawal seizures.

2. *Treatment of agitation with physical restraints:*
   a. Patients with alcohol withdrawal are anxious and easily misinterpret their environment. The beeping of a cardiac monitor, the noise of an oxygen mask or respirator, or the general noise level of the hospital can be upsetting to someone in withdrawal, often resulting in severe agitation. Although sometimes necessary, re-

straints may increase agitation. Patients recovering from withdrawal report that restraints are the most frightening aspect of treatment.

b. Alcohol treatment centers rarely, if ever, use physical restraints to control the agitated patient in withdrawal. This is in sharp contrast to general medical or surgical services, where physical restraints often are necessary to prevent injury to the patient, staff, and other patients.

c. Reasons for this difference include nursing staff experienced in "talking patients down," smaller patient-staff ratios, a quiet peaceful environment, locked units in which patients can wander, and absence of patients with other medical or surgical problems. The environment of an alcohol treatment facility cannot be duplicated in the intensive care unit or in medical or surgical wards, but some of these techniques can be used to minimize the need for restraints.

3. ***Respiratory failure and aspiration:***

a. A major potential side effect of treatment with long-acting benzodiazepines is delayed sedative effect as long-acting metabolites of diazepam are released. This effect is observed most often in patients who continue to receive high doses after 48 hours of the onset of withdrawal. Respiratory status should be monitored carefully if high doses are used for 3 to 4 days, to prevent development of atelectasis, aspiration, and hypoxemia.

I. Polydrug Withdrawal

Patients addicted to sedatives and opioids are at much greater risk for stage 3 withdrawal. The safest way to manage withdrawal in these patients is to withdraw opioids first and continue with a sedative. After 2 to 3 weeks sedative withdrawal can be initiated using a phenobarbital protocol.

J. Experimental Pharmacotherapy

Clonidine has been tested alone and in combination with benzodiazepines, and ameliorates many hyperadrenergic effects of withdrawal. However, it does not prevent stage 2 or 3 withdrawal and probably should not be used alone. It also has no anticonvulsant properties. Some clinicians use clonidine to treat persistent hypertension and other adrenergic symptoms. As discussed, carbamazepine has been used in doses of 200 mg qid for 5 to 7 days with encouraging results. Valproic acid 400–500 mg/day is being tested in clinical trials. Other experimental drugs include γ-hydroxybutyric acid and carbamazepine derivatives.

IV. Stimulant Withdrawal

Most stimulants affect the CNS by increasing the release of neurotransmitters (dopamine, norepinephrine, serotonin). Cocaine (particularly crack), amphetamines (methamphetamine, or ice), and nicotine are the primary drugs in this class.

A. Pathophysiology of Stimulant Withdrawal

1. *Dopamine:* Cocaine primarily affects reuptake of dopamine and norepinephrine. Chronic cocaine use alters receptor sensitivities in the limbic system and other parts of the brain. These research findings correlate with the clinical observation that patients undergoing cocaine withdrawal develop a parkinsonism-like tremor. As a result of these observations, dopamine agonist drugs such as bromocriptine (Parlodel) have been used to reduce the symptoms of cocaine withdrawal. Although clinical trials suggest a reduction in withdrawal symptoms, most clinicians have had limited success with bromocriptine.

2. *Norepinephrine:* Amphetamines are related chemically to naturally occurring catecholamines. The euphoria experienced is related to enhanced release of dopamine and norepinephrine.

3. *Nicotine receptors:* Nicotine cholinergic and perhaps nicotine receptors in the brain are associated with central stimulation, peripheral muscle relaxation, and complex neuroendocrine effects. Patients can develop physical dependence in 7 to 10 days with continuous heavy tobacco use.

B. Risk Factors of Stimulant Withdrawal

1. *Severity of withdrawal* from stimulants depends on tolerance to alcohol and other sedatives, drug potency, duration of use, and route of administration. Many of these patients markedly underestimate their alcohol and sedative use. High-risk drugs include cocaine and methamphetamines. High-risk forms of administration are parenteral and smoking. Other stimulants (e.g., caffeine, diet aids) can be associated with physical symptoms, such as tremor, nausea, and agitation, but these seldom require pharmacologic treatment.

C. Clinical Characteristics of Stimulant Withdrawal

Depression, hyperinsomnia, fatigue, headache, irritability, poor concentration, and restlessness are common symptoms of stimulant withdrawal. REM (rapid eye movement) sleep may be increased for weeks after last use. Patients often experience an intense drug craving. In severe cases depression with suicidal attempts are not uncommon.

1. *Cocaine withdrawal:* Symptoms unique to cocaine withdrawal include paranoia, acute psychosis, intense craving and drug-seeking behavior, severe anhedonia, depression, and suicide ideation that may last up to 6 months. These symptoms most often are observed with smoking of crack (e.g., freebasing) and IV injections.

2. *Amphetamine withdrawal:* Symptoms are similar to those of cocaine withdrawal except that amphetamine psychosis may persist after the period of intoxication. Symptoms include feelings of persecution, paranoia, compulsive behavior, and visual or auditory hallucinations. These symptoms usually are associated with active, high doses or long-term abuse. The drug-induced psychosis may persist

in the withdrawal period, and can be difficult to separate from an organic illness.

3. ***Tobacco withdrawal:*** Effects of tobacco withdrawal may persist for months, and include increased appetite and intense craving and drug-seeking behavior. Short-term effects of tobacco cessation include irritability, difficulty with concentration, and easy fatigability. Physical dependence on nicotine has become increasingly recognized as an important clinical syndrome. Recovering alcoholics who also have stopped smoking often report nicotine withdrawal and craving more severe than alcohol withdrawal.

D. **Pharmacotherapy of Stimulant Withdrawal**

1. ***Generalized symptoms:***

   Treatment is based on the specific symptoms. The primary symptoms treated with medication include paranoia, depression, and panic attacks. These symptoms can develop with any of the stimulant drugs. Specific recommendations for cocaine, amphetamines, and nicotine are discussed in subsequent sections.

   a. *Paranoia:* Paranoia can be a significant symptom that can place a patient at risk for dangerous behavior to themselves and others. Antipsychotic agents such as haloperidol (Haldol) and thioridazine (Mellaril) are the primary drugs of choice

      (1) Haloperidol 5 mg PO/IV; may repeat q4–6h, to 20 mg/day.

      (2) Thioridazine 25–50 mg q8h, to 150 mg/day.

   b. *Depression:* Depression can be severe, placing patients at risk for suicide. Antidepressants are particularly useful for persistent affective symptoms, and should be continued for 3 to 6 months. They appear to enhance the activity of norepinephrine receptors.

      (1) Desipramine (Norpramin) 50 mg once per day for the first 5 days of withdrawal; then increase to 100 mg/day for the next 10 days. If possible, increase to 150 mg/day within 14 days of last stimulant use. Antidepressants frequently are used in patients who have attempted suicide; therefore patients should be given no more than a week's supply.

   c. *Panic attacks:* Acute anxiety problems and panic attacks most often are seen in inexperienced users or those who use crack or ice. These problems usually are seen with active use, but can persist in the withdrawal period. Treatment of panic attacks includes the use of tricyclics, phenobarbital, or lorazepam (Ativan).

   d. *Generalized withdrawal symptoms:* Adrenergic agonists and calcium channel blockers are being tested in clinical trials for general symptoms of cocaine, amphetamine, and tobacco withdrawal, such as irritability and craving.

2. ***Cocaine Withdrawal:***

   Experimental detoxification involves the use of antiparkinsonian agents. The early enthusiasm for these drugs has been tempered by equivocal clinical trials and drug side effects. These drugs are used primarily in the acute withdrawal period. Many clinicians limit use of bromocriptine to those patients with severe craving. Adverse effects of these drugs include dizziness, difficulty in concentrating, delirium, hallucinations, leg edema, and orthostatic hypotension.

    (1) Bromocriptine 2.5 mg bid × 5–7 days.

    (2) Desipramine may be useful in the treatment of cocaine withdrawal. Start at 50 mg/day, and increase by 50 mg/day, to 150 mg/day.

3. ***Amphetamine Withdrawal:***

There are no specific pharmacologic treatment recommendations for amphetamine withdrawal other than those discussed earlier. Clonidine is being tested in clinical trials. Future drugs are expected to focus on blocking the adrenergic and dopaminergic effects of amphetamine withdrawal in the specific areas of the CNS responsible for withdrawal.

4. ***Tobacco Withdrawal:***

Several drugs are being tested in clinical trials to ameliorate the symptoms of nicotine withdrawal and post-withdrawal craving. These include nicotine, clonidine, and other α_2-agonists. Nicorette gum is the only currently approved medication for the pharmacologic treatment of tobacco withdrawal.

  a. *Nicotine:*

    (1) The primary stimulant drug in tobacco, nicotine, has been incorporated into a polycrilex gum (Nicorette) and topical skin patches.

    (2) Nicorette contains 2 mg nicotine, and about 1 mg is released if the gum is used properly. Although the average cigarette contains 8 mg nicotine, only 1 mg enters the bloodstream. One piece of Nicorette gum produces a stable nicotine level for approximately 60 minutes.

    (3) To receive the maximum benefit, patients should use the gum as follows. The gum is chewed for 1–2 minutes, then is placed between the teeth and cheek. The gum should not be swallowed.

    (4) Nicorette has been effective in reducing the severity of withdrawal. It is unclear whether patients who use Nicorette are more likely to remain abstinent than those who do not use this treatment adjunct.

  b. *Clonidine:*

Although not approved for use, clonidine commonly is used in the topical form. A No. 1 or No. 2 patch is applied q7d × 3 weeks, as an adjunct to other therapies. Initial results suggest clonidine may reduce the high rate of relapse seen with nicotine dependence.

V. Opioid Withdrawal

   A. Pathophysiology of Opioid Withdrawal:
   The cause of opioid withdrawal is not understood. Investigators suspect it is related to changes in the function of transmitters under tonic control of endogenous opioid peptides (e.g., norepinephrine).

   B. Clinical Characteristics of Opioid Withdrawal
   The clinical syndrome of opioid withdrawal is prototypic for the pure agonist drugs in this class. The mixed agonist-antagonists, such as pentazocine, may produce a different clinical withdrawal picture. A mild or partial abstinence syndrome and physical dependence can develop after a few days of regular opioid use. Patients who receive high doses of opioids for postoperative care may develop a mild abstinence syndrome. However, the full syndrome develops only after months of continuous heavy use.

   1. *Symptoms of withdrawal:*
      a. Drug craving and intense drug-seeking behavior is the sine qua non of opioid withdrawal. Patients demand, plead, complain, and manipulate providers for psychoactive drugs to relieve their symptoms of withdrawal.
      b. Patients often complain of an intense skin crawling sensation, which can last for weeks with long-acting opioids such as methadone. They have gooseflesh, diaphoresis, and rhinorrhea. They are anxious, scared, and have difficulty sleeping.
      c. Patients may experience diffuse pain in the back, joints, and abdomen. Muscle cramps are a prominent symptom. Nausea and diarrhea may develop, with severe abdominal pain and cramps.

   2. *Physical signs of withdrawal:*
      a. Physical examination reveals the patient to be agitated and diaphoretic. Pulse rate, respiratory rate, and systolic blood pressure are elevated, but less so than with sedative withdrawal. There is evidence of piloerection (gooseflesh), rhinorrhea, and dilated pupils.
      b. Patients are not febrile unless there is concomitant infection. Seizures, hallucinations, and delirium do not occur with opioid withdrawal, and if present, suggest polydrug use with a sedative-hypnotic drug, such as alcohol.

   3. *Grading scheme for opioid withdrawal:* One method to grade the severity of withdrawal is to categorize withdrawal symptoms into four categories:
      Grade 0: Drug craving, anxiety, drug-seeking behavior.
      Grade 1: Yawning, sweating, lacrimation, rhinorrhea.
      Grade 2: Mydriasis, gooseflesh, muscle twitching, anorexia.
      Grade 3: Insomnia; increased pulse rate, respiratory rate, and blood pressure; abdominal cramps, vomiting, diarrhea, weakness.

a. Patients with only grade 0 symptoms in the first 24 hours of withdrawal have limited physical dependence, and probably can be treated as outpatients with little or no pharmacotherapy.

b. Patients with grade 1 or 2 symptoms in the first 24 hours of withdrawal will need inpatient treatment and medication.

c. Patients with grade 3 symptoms are likely to have severe withdrawal symptoms, and require methadone or clonidine therapy.

C. **Risk Factors of Opioid Withdrawal**

1. *Severity of withdrawal:* The agonist and mixed agonist-antagonist opioids are associated with the development of physical dependence and clinical withdrawal. Duration and severity depend on drug potency, tolerance, and duration of action of opioids.

2. *Higher risk drugs:* Drugs highly likely to produce dependence include oxycodone (Percodan), methadone, heroin, morphine, hydromorphone (Dilaudid), and meperidine (Demerol). Patients using short-acting drugs such as fentanyl IV are likely to have severe physical dependence.

3. *Lower risk drugs:* Propoxyphene (Darvon), codeine (Tylenol No. 3), and pentazocine (Talwin) have the lowest prevalence of withdrawal.

4. *Interaction of cocaine and opioids:* Patients using cocaine usually have a milder withdrawal from opioids, because of the action of cocaine on α-adrenergic activity on the locus ceruleus.

D. **Pharmacotherapy of Opioid Withdrawal**

The four approaches to the pharmacologic treatment of narcotic withdrawal include the use of methadone, clonidine, buprenorphine, and symptom-specific medication. Methadone is associated with a higher rate of relapse and promotes drug-seeking behavior. Primary care physicians who choose to use methadone for withdrawal should consult a physician with expertise in addiction medicine. Some states require a special license to use methadone for withdrawal. Clonidine and buprenorphine are the preferred drugs for use in opioid detoxification.

1. *Clonidine:* Clonidine is effective for reducing the intensity of drug craving, sweating, piloerection, skin-crawling sensation, anxiety, and agitation. It does not ameliorate insomnia, muscle cramps, joint pain, or nausea, vomiting, and diarrhea.

a. The standard protocol is to administer clonidine 0.2 mg PO tid × 5 days. If systolic pressure <96, cannot be maintained, the dose may be reduced or therapy changed to buprenorphine. In addition to PO clonidine, a No. 2 clonidine topical patch for 14 days will provide even withdrawal. Note that the patch needs to be replaced every 7 days. (Clonidine patch No. 2 delivers the equivalent of 0.2 mg bid × 7 days). The patch is used as a supplement to maintain the equivalent of 1 mg clonidine/24 hours in the first 5 days.

b. Some clinicians use higher doses (e.g., 0.3–0.4 mg q6h) for severe withdrawal, and do not use topical clonidine.

c. Patients who have been taking high doses (>30 mg/day) of methadone may have withdrawal symptoms for as long as 6 weeks. Because symptoms become refractory to the effects of clonidine after 3 weeks, methadone should be reduced to 30 mg/day before using clonidine for withdrawal.

d. *Treatment of specific symptoms:*

(1) *Nausea and vomiting:* Promethazine 25 mg IM q4h or hydroxyzine 25 mg PO.

(2) *Insomnia:* Lorazepam or temazepam (Restoril) are the drugs of choice. Some clinicians use chloral hydrate 1–2 tabs q4h.

(3) *Anxiety and agitation:* Phenobarbital 30–60 mg PO q6h prn.

(4) *Muscle cramps and joint pain:* Methocarbamol (Robaxin) is the drug of choice. Alternative agents include chlorzoxazone (Parafon Forte) 1–2 tabs q4h prn or ibuprofen 800 mg q8h prn.

2. ***Buprenorphine:***

Although this partial mu receptor agonist has been promoted widely for postoperative pain relief, it also is effective for use in opioid withdrawal. It has a number of useful pharmacologic properties that make it a versatile medication. It is more potent than meperidine and has a longer half-life, and is not widely abused. The following protocol for detoxification was developed by researchers at the National Institute of Drug Abuse. Buprenorphine (Buprex) is used primarily in patients who have failed detoxification with clonidine or methadone. Clinical trials are under way at the Yale Center for Alcohol and Drug Studies to determine if relapse rates are lower with buprenorphine.

a. Buprenorphine is administered subcutaneously q4h. The dose needed to suppress symptoms of opioid withdrawal are estimated by determining the heroin equivalent, with 10 mg heroin being equivalent to 0.3 mg buprenorphine. A patient using 100 mg morphine per day will require a total of 3.0 mg buprenorphine administered in six divided doses in the first 24 hours. Doses over 0.5 mg should be limited, because nausea frequently develops at that dose.

b. Once the dose needed to suppress the physical signs of opioid withdrawal is determined, buprenorphine dosage is reduced by half every 48 hours, tapering to zero by the eighth day.

3. Methadone:

a. Methadone maintenance therapy should be withdrawn by decreasing the dosage by 2–3 mg/day, down to 30 mg and then 1–2 mg/day. In theory, patients receiving 40 mg methadone per day can be detoxified in 20 days. However, withdrawal symptoms may persist for months, and slow taper may result in a lower rate of relapse. Some centers reduce methadone dosage by 3% to 5% per week.

b. Patients dependent on other opioids should be detoxified by starting with 10 mg methadone as an initial dose. If the withdrawal symptoms persist after 60 minutes, give an additional 10 mg. Methadone may be given q12h for the first 2 days. The average dose needed in the first 24 hours is 20–30 mg. Patients need to be carefully monitored for respiratory depression.

c. When methadone is used for detoxification, the dosage should be tapered in 7–10 days. If methadone is continued past 10 days, patients frequently become physically dependent on methadone, and very slow taper is required to detoxify them from methadone.

d. The major clinical problem in determining methadone dosage needed is the drug-seeking behavior that accompanies withdrawal. The patient should show objective clinical signs (gooseflesh, sweating, tachycardia, mydriasis) before exceeding 30 mg in the first 24 hours.

VI. Withdrawal from Cannabinoids, Phencyclidine, Hallucinogens, and Anabolic Steroids

The prevalence of withdrawal symptoms from these drugs has not been well-defined. These drugs do not appear to cause classic physical dependence, with the possible exception of anabolic steroids. Case reports suggest that a typical hyperadrenergic syndrome develops with long-term anabolic steroid use. However, most of these patients were dependent on other mood-altering drugs at the time. It is difficult to separate the effects of a single drug in the presence of polydrug abuse. Although supportive care is enough for most patients who develop symptoms following abstinence, an occasional patient may need pharmacotherapy for symptomatic relief.

A. Cannabinoids
Like amphetamines, there is no specific pharmacotherapy for marijuana. The most distressing symptoms of withdrawal are chronic (amotivational syndrome) rather than acute, and are best treated by Narcotics Anonymous, group therapy, and psychotherapy. These problems are not amenable to pharmacotherapy.

B. Phencyclidine
PCP appears to stimulate catecholamine receptors and block acetylcholine receptors. Haloperidine, a dopamine antagonist, is useful in the treatment of paranoia and psychotic symptoms. Desipramine may be valuable in the post-use period.

C. Hallucinogens
The primary action of these drugs is through an increase in activity of serotonergic neurons. Flashbacks and hallucinations usually resolve with supportive care. Severe agitation may respond to lorazepam.

D. Anabolic Steroids

It has been postulated that long-term exposure to high doses of androgenic steroids may lead to acute hyperadrenergic withdrawal symptoms with abrupt cessation of these drugs. Clinical observations have yet to confirm the prevalence of withdrawal symptoms, but the drug-seeking behavior and other long-term effects, such as depression and anhedonia, suggest physical dependence.

VII. Post-Withdrawal Abstinence Symptoms

A. Overview of Clinical Observations

1. ***Definition:*** Post-withdrawal abstinence symptoms (e.g., changes in pulse rate or blood pressure, tremor, nausea, diarrhea, panic attacks, diaphoresis, headache, mood changes) are defined as acute, short-lived physiologic-psychologic responses that occur after medical detoxification. These responses most often occur in the first 6 months of abstinence, but have been reported as late as 2 years after withdrawal. These events occur in response to environmental stimuli and internal cues that lead to craving.

2. ***Chronic recovery problems:*** It is important to separate acute and subacute abstinence symptoms from chronic recovery problems, such as sleep disorders, changes in appetite, chronic diarrhea, affective disorders, and memory loss. Although there may be different sets of abstinence symptoms for different drugs, these drug-specific "syndromes" have not been well-delineated.

3. ***Relationship to relapse:*** Considering the importance of these symptoms and their relationship with craving and relapse, little is known about these physiologic and psychologic conditions. Understanding these responses may help in development of medications to reduce the acute effects and in turn prevent relapse.

4. ***Research:*** Abstinence symptoms have been observed in laboratory and clinical settings. Research on heroin users has demonstrated hyperthermia, tachycardia, and increased catecholamine excretion for 6 months after last use. A cluster of intense symptoms 1 to 3 months after drinking cessation is associated with the "dry drunk" experience reported by many recovering alcoholics. These symptoms may fluctuate with periods of intense symptoms for 1 to 3 weeks, followed by alternating periods of minimal symptoms.

B. Nonpharmacologic Treatment

Nonpharmacologic treatment includes increasing exercise and decreasing the use of caffeine, nicotine, and sugar.

C. Pharmacological Treatment

1. ***Sedative abstinence symptoms:***

   a. There are no drugs that can be safely used to prevent or treat post-withdrawal abstinence symptoms from sedative drugs.

   b. Benzodiazepines continue to be used to treat both acute effects such as panic attacks and more chronic problems such as generalized anxiety and sleep disorders; however, these drugs should not be used in patients with chemical dependency disorders, because they may lead to relapse. Buspirone (BuSpar) has been promoted as a nonaddicting drug for the treatment of panic attacks; however there is limited clinical experience with this drug in recovering persons.

c. Fluoxetine (Prozac), desipramine, and lithium may be useful in recovering alcoholics and addicts for specific chronic problems (e.g., persistent affective symptoms), but do not appear to ameliorate post-withdrawal abstinence syndromes and cravings. Several clinical trials are under way, primarily with drugs such as fluoxetine and buspirone.

2. ***Stimulant abstinence symptoms:***

a. Desipramine is the only accepted medication that appears to reduce craving in patients addicted to stimulants, and may reduce the chance of relapse in the post-withdrawal phase of treatment. The antidepressant should be used in standard doses for up to 6 months.

b. Experimental drugs being tested to reduce craving include mazindol (an inhibitor of dopamine reuptake), fluoxetine, buprenorphine, and carbamazepine. There is also a new injectable long-acting tricyclic agent that may be of clinical use.

3. ***Opioid abstinence syndromes:***

a. Clonidine may suppress craving, but the effects appear limited to 3 to 4 weeks. Mixed agonists-antagonist such as buprenorphine are being tested in clinical trials. Methadone and newer drugs such as LAAM (L-acetyl, α-methadol) may increase the severity of post-withdrawal craving.

D. **"Ideal Drug":** An ideal drug that would prevent post-withdrawal symptoms would:

a. Act at specific receptor sites for a single class of drugs.

b. Prevent, or at least reduce, the intensity of craving and abstinence syndromes.

c. Have no mood-altering effects or addictive properties.

d. Elicit a low incidence of side effects.

E. **Future Therapy:** Several drugs are being used and tested to treat post-withdrawal abstinence symptoms, but none of them fulfill the four criteria.

VIII. **Drug Maintenance**

A. **Overview**

1. ***Drug substitution:*** Drug agonists or cross-dependent drugs often are used in alcoholics and addicts in an attempt to substitute a less harmful drug for the primary drug.

2. ***Duration of use:*** Because the goal is maintenance for a specific drug class, these medications are generally used for long periods.

3. ***Role in recovering alcoholics:*** Of special interest is the inde-

pendent treatment for dual diagnosis. For example, it is not clear what the role of methadone maintenance is in abstinence-oriented treatment. Patients can become abstinent from alcohol, yet continue methadone.

4. ***Rationale:*** The rationale for maintenance is based on the clinical observation that there is a group of addicts who are unable to stay drug-free. Clinicians assume that these persons have irreversible changes in their CNS or mental health disorders that do not respond to current methods.

5. ***Prolongation of life:*** Maintenance is not the ideal treatment, but it does significantly improve life function and can reduce the health consequences of continued use, particularly AIDS. However patients need to be closely observed and their use critically examined.

B. Opioid Maintenance

1. ***Methadone:***

   a. The current requirement for methadone maintenance therapy is physical dependence on opioids, as defined by a physician. The requirements have become less stringent and are primarily left to the discretion of the physician with a program license.

   b. Methadone maintenance dosage varies, but most patients are given 30–80 mg/day. In the occasional patient who rapidly metabolizes the drug, higher dosage may be needed. Studies suggest that patients have fewer relapses with the higher doses. The dosage in pregnancy is controversial, but should be ≤30 mg/day to minimize the severity of neonatal withdrawal. Methadone withdrawal should not be done during pregnancy.

   c. Federal law requires that during the first month of treatment patients must get methadone from the clinic seven days a week. If their urine samples remain clean after 60 days, they may be allowed to attend the clinic every other day. After 90 days they are allowed to pick up their weekend dose on Friday. After 1 year they attend the clinic twice a week.

   d. Methadone can be used by any physician who has a Drug Enforcement Agency number for detoxification, chronic pain, and temporary maintenance therapy for up to 21 days in an inpatient setting. Methadone cannot be used for opioid maintenance for more than 21 days unless the physician has a special methadone program license.

2. ***Experimental opioid agonists:***
   LAAM, a long-acting opioid agonist, has been tested in clinical trials and may reduce the frequency of use to every 3 days. Other agonists currently being tested that may be less addicting than methadone are metakephid and buprenorphine.

C. Alcohol/Sedative Maintenance

The benzodiazepines continue to be used for their agonist properties, yet they are not helpful in alcoholics or addicts. Their use is often associated with relapse, and is contraindicated in recovering persons.

D. Cocaine Maintenance

No specific cocaine agonists have been discovered, but several drugs are being tested as cocaine replacements to reduce craving. These include the dopaminergic drugs, such as bromocriptine. Carbamazepine, buprenorphine, desipramine, and methylphenidate (Ritalin) currently are being tested in clinical trials. Initial results have demonstrated no benefit.

IX. Medications Used to Alter Desired Effects

A. Alcohol Metabolic Inhibitors

1. *Disulfiram:*

   a. Disulfiram (Antabuse) inhibits several enzyme systems, including an aldehyde dehydrogenase (ADH) and dopamine β-hydroxylase. It is absorbed slowly over 12 hours, and accumulates in fat stores; 20% remains after 7 days. Adverse reactions can occur for 5 to 7 days after the last dose if any alcohol is ingested.

   b. The usual dose is 250 mg/day; however, I usually prescribe 100 mg to minimize the risk of a serious reaction. Higher doses (500 mg) have been used in aversive therapy programs. An occasional parole officer may ask that a high dose be used in someone on probation. It is difficult to justify high doses, because of the risk of life-threatening effects.

   c. The reaction to disulfiram occurs within 15 minutes of alcohol ingestion. Common symptoms include cutaneous flushing, headache, nausea, and vomiting. More severe symptoms are chest pain, hypotension, and syncope. ECG changes may include ST depression, T wave flattening, and prolongation of the QT interval. Serious morbidity is secondary to myocardial infarction, seizures, arrhythmias, and congestive heart failure. Because of these effects, disulfiram is contraindicated in patients with a history of cardiovascular disease, suicide ideation, or hypothyroidism and in patients receiving monoamine oxidase inhibitors or antihypertensive drugs.

   d. Although normally 2 to 3 drinks are required to produce a reaction to disulfiram, patients who have inadvertently taken 15 mL cough syrup with 50% alcohol have reported symptoms. Rubbing alcohol, mouthwash, and alcohol fumes in poorly ventilated areas have been implicated in mild reactions. Severe reactions should be treated with oxygen, fluids, pressors and antiarrhythmic agents. Prostaglandin inhibitors (aspirin) and histamine$_2$ blockers (ranitidine) may reduce the flushing response.

   e. Common side effects of disulfiram include sedation, weakness, a metallic taste, and impotence. An elevated cholesterol level may occur, but is responsive to pyridoxine. Liver failure has been reported; therefore liver function should be monitored. More severe reactions include optic neuritis, polyneuropathy, acute psychosis, and fetal limb abnormalities if used in pregnancy.

f. Disulfiram inhibits the metabolism of a number of drugs that include isoniazid (ataxia and psychosis), warfarin sodium (Coumadin; prolonged prothrombin time), phenytoin (Dilantin; increased levels), or caffeine (tremors, tachycardia).

g. Disulfiram should be used as one component of a treatment program. Patients need to understand the adverse effects of this medication and its usefulness as a recovery tool, not a cure. Some patients who "cheat" find that they can have 1 or 2 drinks without a reaction, especially with the lower doses currently used.

h. Although a recent Veterans Administration trial found disulfiram therapy no better than counseling alone, there are a number of reasons why it should be of help to reduce relapse. The decision not to drink has to be made only once a day. The impulse to drink must be deferred at least 5 to 7 days. Discontinuation of the drug without the advice of a physician is a clear sign of impending relapse and may allow the patient to get help before taking a drink. Its greatest clinical use may be in patients who repeatedly relapse.

2. *Calcium carbamide*

a. Like disulfiram, calcium carbamide (Temposil) inhibits ADH. However, it does not suppress the enzyme dopamine β-hydroxylase, as disulfiram does, and thus has fewer adverse effects. There are fewer adrenergic effects when patients drink alcohol after taking calcium carbamide.

b. Calcium carbamide is not available in the United States. However, clinical trials suggest it is a strong psychologic deterrent and may reduce the rates of relapse. Its primary role may be in schizophrenic patients who become alcohol dependent. Disulfiram is contraindicated in this population because it inhibits dopamine β-hydroxylase activity.

3. *Nitrefazole:*

a. Nitrefazole, a longer acting ADH inhibitor, is being tested in clinical trials in Europe, and may have important advantages over disulfiram.

B. Cocaine Euphoria Blocking Drugs

Several drugs are being tested that may block the sought after mood-altering effects. Nifedipine and buphrenorphine are in clinical trials. Diltiazem, verapamil, penfluridol (possible cocaine antagonist), and sulpride are being tested in animals.

C. Opioid Euphoria Blocking Drugs

Naltrexone is an important deterrent for patients with severe physical dependence on opioids. It is used most often as one component of a comprehensive treatment program that includes random urine drug screening and an intensive aftercare treatment program. This pure opioid receptor antagonist blocks the pleasurable mood-altering effects of any externally administered opioids. The usual dose is 50 mg/day. A depot or patch form of naltrexone is expected to be available soon.

BIBLIOGRAPHY

Alling C, Balldin J, Bokstrom K, et al: Studies on duration of a late recovery period after chronic abuse of ethanol. *Acta Psychiatr Scand* 1982; 66:384–397.

Benfordo J: *Alcohol and Other Drug Abuse Manual* (unpublished). Madison, University of Wisconsin Hospital and Clinics, 1981.

Bickel WK, Stitzer ML, Bigelow GE, et al: A clinical trial of buprenorphine: Comparison with methadone in the detoxification of heroin addicts. *Clin Pharmacol Ther* 1988; 43:72–78.

Busto U, Sellers E, Naranjo C, et al: Withdrawal reaction after long-term therapeutic use of benzodiazepines. *N Engl J Med* 1986; 315:854–859.

Devenyi P, Harrison M: Prevention of alcohol withdrawal seizures with oral diazepam loading. *Can Med Assoc J* 1985; 132:798–800.

Femino J, Lewis D: *Clinical Pharmacology and Therapeutics of the Alcohol Withdrawal Syndrome.* Bethesda, Md, National Institute on Alcoholism and Alcohol Abuse, 1982.

Foy A, March S, Drinkwater V: Use of an objective clinical scale in the assessment and management of alcohol withdrawal in a large general hospital. *Alcoholism Clin Exp Res* 1988; 12:360–364.

Gawin FH, Allen D, Humblestone B: Outpatient treatment of "crack" cocaine smoking with flupenthixol decanoate: A preliminary report. *Arch Gen Psychiatry,* 1989; 46:322–325.

Gawin FH, Kleber HD: Abstinence symptomatology and psychiatric diagnoses in cocaine abusers. *Arch Gen Psychiatry* 1986; 43:107–113.

Glassman A, Stetner J, Walsh BT, et al: Heavy smokers, smoking cessation and clonidine. *JAMA* 1988; 259:2863–2866.

Gordon E: *Alcohol Withdrawal Syndrome.* Bethesda, Md, National Institute of Alcohol and Alcohol Abuse, No 5 PH 270, 1989.

Isbell H, Fraser H, Wikler A, et al: An experimental study of the cause of "rum fits" and delirium tremens, in Isbell H, Wikler A, et al (eds):

Kleber H, et al: Clonidine and naltrexone in the outpatient treatment of heroin withdrawal. *Am J Drug Alcohol Abuse* 1987; 13:1–17.

Kraus M, Gottlieb L, Horwitz R, et al: Randomized clinical trial of atenolol in patients with alcohol withdrawal. *N Engl J Med* 1985; 313:218–222.

Little H, Dolin S, Halsey M: Calcium channel antagonists decrease the ethanol withdrawal syndrome. *Life Sci* 1986; 39:2059–2065.

Meyer RE: Prospects for a rational pharmacotherapy of alcoholism. *J Clin Psychiatry* 1989; 50:403–412.

Ng S, Hauser W, Brust J, et al: Alcohol consumption and withdrawal in new-onset seizures. *N Engl J Med* 1988; 319:666–673.

Rosenbloom A: Optimizing drug treatment of alcohol withdrawal. *Am J Med* 1986; 81:901–903.

Sellers E, Kalant H: Alcohol intoxication and withdrawal. *N Engl J Med* 1976; 294:201–206.

Sellers E, Naranjo C, Harrison M, et al: Diazepam loading: Simplified treatment of alcohol withdrawal. *Clin Pharmacol Ther* 1983; 34:822–826.

Shaw: CIWA. 1981.

CHAPTER 4

Alcohol and Drug Treatment and Role of 12-Step Programs

Jerome Schulz, MD

Kristen Barry, Ph.D.

The successful treatment of alcohol and drug dependence began in 1935 with the development of Alcoholics Anonymous (AA), the beginning of 12-Step self-help groups. It may be a stretch to compare the discovery of penicillin to the discovery of 12-Step groups, yet millions of persons who have maintained sobriety and health through AA would argue that the comparison is appropriate. Before the appearance of AA with its 12-Step approach, there was minimal success with psychiatric-based psychotherapy, community support systems, or incarceration for drug addicts. Although other treatment approaches are being tested, the AA-based treatment philosophy remains the standard in the United States. As the most successful therapeutic method available for the treatment of alcohol and drug dependence, physicians need a thorough understanding of what chemical dependency treatment is, how it works, and how to refer patients for treatment. The goal of this chapter is to provide readers with a comprehensive practical review of this treatment approach.

I. **Overview of Standard Chemical Dependency Treatment**
 A. **Which Patients Who use Mood-Altering Drugs are Best Treated Using a Chemical Dependency Treatment Program and a 12-Step Approach?**
 Who benefits from treatment? Any patient who has experienced significant consequences from alcohol or drug abuse (e.g., family problems, arrest for driving while intoxicated [DWI], work problems, health problems) and has continued to use alcohol and/or drugs will benefit from a 12-Step program and/or treatment program. Even patients who stop using drugs and alcohol on their own often benefit from participation in a treatment program.
 B. **What are the Underlying Assumptions for Standard Treatment of Alcohol and Drug Dependence?**
 1. Alcohol and drug dependence is a treatable disease.

2. Alcohol and drug dependence is a progressive, incurable disease.
3. Effective treatment includes treatment for the family as well as the individual's psychologic, physical, social, and vocational needs.
4. 12-step programs, such as AA, Narcotics Anonymous (NA), and Al-Anon are an essential component of a long-term treatment plan.

Name _____ Date ___/___/___ Site _____

Age _____ ❑ M ❑ F DOB ___/___/___ Education (years) _____

Primary Physician _____

Chemical Dependency History
Drug of Choice _____

	Use more than 5 times in life		Frequency	Amount	Last Use
Alcohol	Yes	No	_____	_____	_____
Tranquilizers	Yes	No	_____	_____	_____
Marijuana	Yes	No	_____	_____	_____
Cocaine	Yes	No	_____	_____	_____
Tobacco	Yes	No	_____	_____	_____
Amphetamines	Yes	No	_____	_____	_____
Narcotics	Yes	No	_____	_____	_____

Substance Problems (lifetime history)
- ❑ Larger amts than intended
- ❑ Drug Seeking
- ❑ Gave up important activities
- ❑ Marked tolerance
- ❑ Substance taken to relieve withdrawal
- ❑ Persistent desire despite attempts to cut down
- ❑ Frequent intoxication despite obligations
- ❑ Cont. use despite knowledge of problems
- ❑ Withdrawal Symptoms

Substance significantly interferes with (lifetime history):
Work ❑ Yes ❑ No   School ❑ Yes ❑ No   Outside Interests ❑ Yes ❑ No
Health ❑ Yes ❑ No   Family ❑ Yes ❑ No   Friendship ❑ Yes ❑ No

Psychiatric Disorders (lifetime history):
Depression ❑ Yes ❑ No   Suicide Thoughts ❑ Yes ❑ No   Eating Disorders ❑ Yes ❑ No
Psychosis ❑ Yes ❑ No   Violent Behavior ❑ Yes ❑ No   Mood Swings ❑ Yes ❑ No
Anxiety ❑ Yes ❑ No   Sleep Disorder ❑ Yes ❑ No   Gambling Compulsion ❑ Yes ❑ No

Medical History (lifetime history):
Seizures ❑ Yes ❑ No   Legal Problems ❑ Yes ❑ No   Physical Abuse ❑ Yes ❑ No
Blackouts ❑ Yes ❑ No   DWI's ❑ Yes ❑ No   FH of Chem. Depend. ❑ Yes ❑ No

Past Medical History   Date   Location

Hosp _____ _____ _____
_____ _____ _____

Surg _____ _____ _____
_____ _____ _____

Chem Dep. _____ _____ _____
Treatment _____ _____ _____
_____ _____ _____

Illness _____ _____ _____
_____ _____ _____

Injury _____ _____ _____
_____ _____ _____

FIG 4–1.
History and physical assessment protocal, which can be used for outpatient or inpatient treatment of alcohol and drug disorders. The history includes major DSM-III-R criteria for dependence. The physical checklist includes the primary physical findings in addictive disorders.

Many other step-oriented help groups also exist and are beneficial in relieving the need for substance use.

5. The primary goals of treatment are abstinence and reintegration into the community.

6. There is no lifetime cure for alcoholism, and relapse can occur at any time after cessation of alcohol and drug use.

Medications _____

_____

STD/AIDS Risk factors _____   _____

_____   _____

Physical (check boxes for abnormalities, Explain at bottom of page)

Ht. _____   Wt. _____   BP ___/___   P _____   RR _____   Temp. _____

Gen _____

Mental Status	❑ Orientation x 3	❑ Serial 7's	❑ 3 objects
Neuro	❑ Tremor	❑ Fine/Gross Motor	❑ Cerebellar Testing	❑ Neuropathy ❑ Asterixis
Skin	❑ Spiders	❑ Rhinophyma	❑ Jaundice	❑ Palmar Erythema
HEENT	❑ Teeth	❑ Gingiva	❑ Nasal Septum	❑ Pupils
Nodes	❑ Cervical	❑ Axillary	❑ Inguinal	
Resp	❑ Wheezing	❑ Rales		
CV	❑ Arrhythmia	❑ LVH	❑ Pedal pulses	
ABD	❑ Ascites	❑ Liver Enlargement	❑ Prominent Ven. Pattern	
GU	❑ Warts	❑ Vagina	❑ Cervix	❑ Adnexa
Rectal	❑ Pruritis ani	❑ Bleeding		

Lab Data (Date)   PPD _____   Hepatitis _____   HIV _____

GGT _____   Cholesterol _____   Drug Screen _____

Physical Finding: _____

_____

_____

Assessment: _____

_____

Plan: _____

signed _____

FIG 4-1 (cont.).

7. Recovery is a *process,* not a single event. Relapse is common, and repeated participation in a treatment program may be required to achieve long-term sobriety.

8. Comprehensive treatment programs that include the use of the 12-Step philosophy and meetings remain the best method available for the treatment of alcohol and drug dependence.

9. Psychotherapy and medication (e.g., disulfiram [Antabuse], antidepressants, naloxone, clonidine) may be useful adjuncts to a standard treatment program, but should never be used alone.

C. **What is the Physician's Role in the Treatment of Patients who are Alcohol and Drug Dependent?**

1. Once the physician has identified an alcohol or drug problem (see Chapter 2) and the patient agrees to participate in a treatment program, the next step is referral for examination by a health care professional with expertise in conducting alcohol and other drug assessments. A physician may want to participate in medical assessment and/or detoxification of a patient before entry into a treatment program. An example of a history and physical assessment protocol for patients receiving treatment for chemical dependence is presented in Figure 4–1.

2. The physician can encourage family members to participate in a family program and Al-Anon meetings.

3. Recovering persons need a strong aftercare program in addition to a 12-Step program (which should be lifelong) for at least 24 months after cessation of alcohol and drug use. The primary care physician can monitor patients for symptoms of relapse, and if necessary provide prompt referral into a treatment program.

D. **Does Treatment Work?**

1. **Sobriety rates:** Five-year sobriety rates for recovering physicians and other professional groups who receive standard treatment exceeds 80%. Sobriety rates for other groups are lower. End-stage alcoholics have 5-year sobriety rates of 10% to 20%. An exception is alcoholics who have had liver transplants; this group has been found to have 2-year sobriety rates exceeding 85%. There is no research to date indicating that any one treatment method is clearly superior to all others for *all* patients.

2. **Matching patients to resources:** There is an attempt by treatment specialists to "match" individuals to the best available treatment option for them based on:

    a. Available resources in the community.

    b. Patient variables such as coexisting medical or psychiatric problems, available social supports (current living arrangement, family relationships, employment), amount of structure the person requires, previous treatment attempts, time available, age, and social/cultural background. (NOTE: Some treatment programs have separate programs for women.)

3. ***Factors associated with improved prognosis:***
   a. Job and family support remains intact.
   b. Health and cognitive functioning are intact.
   c. Patients are motivated and have minimal denial.
   d. A crisis brings them to treatment (e.g., DWI arrest, job problems, family intervention).
   e. Resources to participate in a treatment program are present.
   f. Early diagnosis of chemical dependency.
   g. Active participation in a 12-step program.

II. Review of Treatment Methods and Programs

A. Overview of Treatment Methods Used by Treatment Programs

This section presents a brief overview of the different treatment programs (Table 4–1). While there is variation in the services provided, the basic structure of these programs is the same throughout the United States. The basic services are as follows:

1. ***Detoxification:*** Detoxification is necessary before patients can participate in treatment. Some patients may need to be hospitalized for withdrawal from mood-altering drugs; others can go through with-

TABLE 4–1.

Overview of Treatment Programs

Inpatient

Hospital-based inpatient program: Intensive program in which the patient spends 24 hours a day in a hospital. Indications for hospitalization include (1) detoxification, (2) coexisting mental health disorders, and (3) serious health problems that may complicate treatment.

Residential Treatment: Often called *inpatient treatment,* although most residential treatment programs are not in a hospital setting. Some are not certified to perform detoxification or administer medications. Patients may be given day or overnight passes toward the end of the treatment program.

Outpatient

Day/outpatient treatment: Intensive program for approximately 4 weeks followed by a 6- to 24-month aftercare program. Many outpatient programs have both daytime and evening programs to allow their clients to maintain their usual occupation.

Family

Family treatment: Most treatment facilities have a special program for family members of chemically dependent persons. Specific programs of education, counseling, and group therapy are provided for families of patients in the facility.

Other Community-Based Programs

Halfway houses: Community-based facilities that provide long-term care for recovering persons. Many clients work during the day and sleep at the halfway house at night and on weekends. Many communities have separate facilities for men, women, adolescents, and pregnant women. 12-Step and group meetings usually are included in halfway house programs.

12-Step programs: These programs are based on the approach developed by Alcoholics Anonymous (AA), and include AA, Narcotics Anonymous (NA), Cocaine Anonymous (CA), Overeaters Anonymous (OA), and Gamblers Anonymous (GA). The only requirement for attending an AA meeting is a *desire to stop drinking.* Patients do not have to be sober to attend AA.

12-Step programs for persons adversely affected by another's addiction: These programs are also based on the AA model, and include Al-Anon, Alateen, and Adult Children of Alcoholics (ACOA). Anyone may attend; the only requirement is a desire to get help.

---

drawal as an outpatient under physician supervision. Outpatient detoxification is discussed in Chapter 3.

2. ***Group therapy:*** Group therapy is an essential component of treatment. The therapist uses different techniques to aid the recovery process, including discussion of specific topics, role plays, group confrontation of individual members, and sculpturing. Group sessions help patients understand the consequences of their use, and help them break through the denial process.

3. ***Educational programs:*** Educational programs consist of lectures by treatment professionals, videotape reviews, and discussions of assigned reading material.

4. ***Psychotherapy:*** One-to-one supportive psychotherapy is a helpful adjunct to the other treatment modalities. *Intensive psychoanalysis is not helpful in early recovery, and may precipitate a relapse.*

5. ***Role of providers:*** Providers need to review medical problems, mental health issues, and the recovery process, and are an important component of treatment. Physicians usually focus on the admission history, physical examination, and detoxification, and have a unique opportunity to emphasize and explain any medical complications patients may have.

6. ***Role of 12-Step meetings:*** 12-Step meetings are an essential component of treatment. These meetings may take place at the treatment facility or in the community.

7. ***Daily journal:*** Each patient in a treatment program may be required to write a daily journal. Writings include thoughts for the day, problems, feelings, and coping strategies for continued sobriety. Patients are encouraged to continue this journal during aftercare.

8. ***Family programs:*** Family treatment is an important part of most programs. Programs often are designed for two types of family members:
   a. Family education and therapy for family members of a patient *receiving treatment* in the program.
   b. Programs for family members of individuals who are alcohol and/or drug abusers (past or present) but are *not* in treatment.

B. **Inpatient Treatment** (Hospital-Based and Residential Treatment Centers)
   1. ***Admission criteria:***
      a. Health problems.
      b. Failure to maintain sobriety after appropriate outpatient treatment.
      c. Major unstable psychiatric illness.
      d. Absent social support.
   2. ***Purpose*** of inpatient treatment: The purpose of inpatient treatment is to provide an intensive *beginning* toward long-term recovery. Programs offer drug- and alcohol-free environments to begin the process of recovery.
      a. The initial phase of treatment is completed.

b. The duration of inpatient treatment is 7 to 30 days, depending on the severity of the problem and insurance benefits available.

3. ***Goals:*** Treatment goals generally include:

   a. Detoxification and abstinence from mood-altering drugs and alcohol.

   b. Assessment of problems in all areas of life (e.g., intellectual, physical, emotional, spiritual, social, educational, recreational, vocational).

   c. Education regarding the disease of chemical dependency.

   d. Assist the patient in identifying behaviors and attitudes that may inhibit the recovery process.

   e. Acquaint the patient with support systems such as AA and NA as an integral part of recovery.

   f. Assist the patient in adapting new coping skills when dealing with stressful situations that previously would be handled with drugs or alcohol.

   g. Assist the patient in recognizing that the need for recovery is a life-long process.

   h. Assist the patient in returning to home and work.

   i. Help affected family members with problems resulting from the patient's chemical abuse (see Chapter 10 for more information).

4. ***Inpatient treatment structure:*** Treatment programs structure each day with the following activities (see Appendix 4–1 for an example of the daily treatment structure):

   a. *Daily* group meetings, during which the patient hears other patients talk about their problems with alcohol and drugs and can identify similar patterns. When the patient has been in the group long enough to gain some degree of comfort, he or she is encouraged to share the problems that alcohol and drugs have caused in his or her life.

   b. *Daily* lectures to learn about the medical, emotional, and interpersonal consequences of chemical dependency.

   c. *Daily* individual counseling with a chemical dependency specialist who works with the patient through the inpatient phase of the treatment and recovery process and observes the patient in the aftercare program. Individual counseling provides the patient with the opportunity to deal with any special needs and issues particular to his or her situation.

   d. *Family therapy sessions* are held on a regular basis and are a key aspect in recovery. Research indicates that alcoholic patients who have family involvement and support in the treatment and recovery process are most likely to experience successful recovery.

   e. *Daily* activity therapy in which patients are introduced to alternatives for spending leisure time (e.g., exercise, recreation, games, hobbies). These activities can help patients develop new skills and expose them to enjoyable experiences unrelated to chemicals.

f. *Daily 12-Step meetings.* Most treatment programs encourage patients to go to 12-Step meetings as part of the treatment process. Restructuring friendships may be necessary if old friends also were involved in the use and abuse of chemicals. Groups such as AA often serve this function for recovering individuals.

g. Generally, at least *once per week,* patients, spouses, and families take part in a family group session. The focus of this group is on issues of family dysfunction related to chemical abuse and dependency. These sessions generally include a time to share and an educational component, often a lecture on a specific topic related to family functioning, such as family roles, family similarities, and healthy coping mechanisms for the family.

h. *Meditation* often is used in the morning to start the day, and again in the evening to end the day. This is a quiet time when patients may use the *Twenty-Four Hours a Day* book, which includes readings and meditations based on AA principles. This is designed to help the patient relax and experience "serenity." It focuses on the positive aspects of recovery.

C. **Outpatient Treatment**
1. *Admission criteria:*
   a. Absence of serious health or psychiatric problems.
   b. Drug withdrawal completed.
   c. Social support system available.
   d. Ability to abstain from mood-altering drugs and alcohol.
2. *Purpose of treatment:* The purpose of outpatient recovery programs is to provide extra support during initial abstinence, along with information and education about the disease of addiction. It also helps the patient identify the consequences of chemical dependency in his or her life and thus to break through denial. These programs help individuals apply recovery techniques to their own problems and life situation.
3. *Abstinence model:* The abstinence orientation involves taking "one day at a time." When individuals addicted to chemicals think about spending the rest of their lives without their drug(s) of choice, it can be overwhelming, and they can relapse.
4. *Outpatient treatment structure:* The structure of outpatient treatment is similar to inpatient treatment, and includes group sessions, lectures, videos, and individual counseling.
5. *Family involvement.* Outpatients are expected to include their family and/or significant others, if possible, in some aspects of treatment (usually a family lecture series and family group sessions).
6. *Urine drug screening:* Outpatients are expected to abstain from the use of all mood-altering chemicals and alcohol while in treatment. To ensure this, some programs expect patients to participate in random urine screening.
7. *Meeting times:* Outpatient programs frequently meet in the

evening, allowing patients to work and maintain daily routines. These programs usually last 4 to 8 weeks.

D. Family Treatment

If your patient has family members who are willing to be involved, an essential part of the treatment process can be helping family members to see the effect of the chemical dependency on their lives, even if they do not use chemicals themselves. Many programs have special groups for family members (with or without the patient) to help family members begin to identify and heal the damage caused by chemical dependency in the family. Family members are encouraged to attend Al-Anon, Alateen, or ACOA meetings for support. (See Chapter 10 for a more detailed discussion.)

E. Extended Care Treatment

Halfway Houses or 3/4's Way Houses are sober environments that offer recovering chemically dependent patients a gradual transition from inpatient treatment to the "real" world. Patients appropriate for these facilities include those with multiple previous treatment failures, poor social support systems, complicating medical or psychiatric problems, and adolescents. Duration of the program may vary from 3 to 12 months. Patients are expected to maintain abstinence while living in the facility. Programs include group meetings, 12-Step meetings, and work release time in the community.

F. Community-Based Treatment

Many communities have programs for people arrested for drunk driving. Some counties have certified chemical dependency counselors to aid physicians in evaluating patients with possible drug or alcohol problems.

G. Treatment Resource Worksheet (Fig 4–2)

Easy access to information regarding community treatment resources simplifies the referral process. A physician or member of a treatment staff may contact agencies, self-help groups, and treatment centers in the community to complete this worksheet. Yearly updating may be necessary. The worksheet includes the following information:

1. *AA information number:* Most communities have many AA meetings, and listings of available times and meeting places generally are available on request. In addition, the staff at the AA information office can answer specific patient questions regarding the organization in a particular community.
2. *Al-Anon information number:* Most communities have 12-Step meetings for family members of alcoholics. Both the provider and the family member can obtain information regarding meetings from this source.
3. *Narcotics Anonymous information number:* Not all communities have a separate 12-Step program for individuals who are primarily drug abusers. Treatment centers in the community can provide information on services.

Treatment Resource Worksheet

1. AA information number: _____

2. Al-Anon information number: _____

3. Narcotics Anonymous information number: _____

4. Community mental health substance abuse services:

    Name _____ Phone _____

    Address _____ Hours _____

    Contact Person _____

    Services available (circle) Counseling: alcohol/other drugs
                                 Detoxification: alcohol/other drugs
                                 Half-way house: men/women
                                 Methadone program
                                 Adolescent program/family program
                                 Other _____

5. Fee-for-service treatment programs:

    Name _____ Phone _____

    Hours _____ Contact Person _____

    Type of facility (circle)   Residential/outpatient/evening
                                     Adolescent/adult

    Payment accepted: Insurance/sliding scale/indigent care

6. Individual therapist knowledgeable regarding substance abuse:

    Name _____ Phone _____

    Services (circle):   Individual/families/interventions

    Name _____ Phone _____

    Services (circle):   Individual/families/interventions

7. AA Member Contracts

    Name _____ Phone _____

    Name _____ Phone _____

    Name _____ Phone _____

FIG 4–2.
The Treatment Resource Worksheet is a useful office guide when referring a patient for treatment. Completion of the worksheet may be facilitated by calling the local AA chapter and the community mental health center.

4. ***Community mental health substance abuse services:***
Community-sponsored substance abuse services for individuals with limited resources are available in many communities. Knowledge of a contact person and the range of services can aid in the referral process for patients.

5. ***Fee-for-services treatment programs:*** Some communities have one or more fee-for-service treatment programs, both outpatient and inpatient. Obtaining information about these programs is particularly important because they may work with specific insurance companies. Referral is easiest when the provider can match the patient to the appropriate program.

6. ***Individual therapist knowledgeable about substance abuse:*** Because some patients may have coexisting emotional, psychiatric, or family problems, finding one or more therapists in the community who have a strong awareness of alcohol and drug problems is important.

III. **Community Support Programs**
   A. **How Can 12-Step Support Groups Help?**
   1. ***Feelings of isolation:*** 12-Step support groups can break the feelings of uniqueness and isolation that people with alcohol and drug addiction, and those close to them, often experience. When patients attend support groups they often report that, for the first time in their lives, they do not feel alone, that finally someone understands what they have been feeling for so many years.

   2. ***Education:*** Support groups educate people about the disease of alcohol and drug addiction.

   3. ***Hope for recovery:*** Support groups show the patient that there is hope for recovery. By hearing other people share what they have experienced and learned in recovery, they can see that recovery has been possible for others, no matter how bad the situation.

   4. ***Socialization skills:*** Groups can teach basic socialization skills. Many people affected by alcohol and drug addiction become isolated and self-focused. Groups give newcomers unconditional support as they struggle through early recovery.

   5. ***Feedback to patient:*** Groups can provide a reality base for patients in recovery. When people think they are unique and begin to isolate themselves, they have no source of feedback on what they are doing and the potential consequences of their behavior.

   6. ***Setbacks:*** Groups provide assistance when patients experience setbacks in recovery.

   7. ***Use of time:*** Groups help fill the time that is freed up in recovery when patients stop drinking and using chemicals. This can be a major problem for people in early recovery who have spent most of their time drinking or using drugs. Going to a meeting provides a positive way for people to constructively use excess time.

   B. **12-Step Support Groups:** Alcoholics Anonymous As A Model

(See Appendix 4–2 for a glossary of terms.) AA is the prototype of many other support groups and the one with the longest history. AA was co-founded in 1935 by two alcoholics, Bill W. and Dr. Bob. All other 12-Step groups, including Narcotics Anonymous (NA), Cocaine Anonymous (CA), Overeaters Anonymous (OA), and Gamblers Anonymous (GA) use the same approach and format.

The preamble of AA, frequently read at the beginning of AA meetings, points out important facts about AA and how the group works:

Alcoholics Anonymous is a fellowship of men and women who share their experience, strength, and hope with each other, that they may solve their common problem and help others to recover from alcoholism. The only requirement for membership is a desire to stop drinking. There are no dues or fees for AA membership; we are self-supporting through our own contributions. AA is not allied with any sect, denomination, politics, organization, or institution; does not wish to engage in any controversy; neither endorses nor opposes any causes. Our primary purpose is to stay sober and help other alcoholics to achieve sobriety.*

1. **12-Step Model:** AA is a spiritual program based on the *12 Steps* (see Appendix 4–3) and *12 Traditions* (Appendix 4–4), which alcoholics apply to their lives so that they may recover from alcoholism. The 12-Steps are the spiritual basis for AA and the backbone of recovery for AA members. It is important to point out that AA is considered a *spiritual program* and is *not identified with a particular religion.* AA literature indicates that "God" is not used in the religious sense and is not connected with any religious belief.

2. **Higher power:** The AA *Higher Power* is a source of strength to the alcoholic. The Higher Power can be the person's AA group or any Higher Power outside of himself or herself. There are many atheists and agnostics in AA, and this can be helpful information for patients who are reluctant to go to AA because of their discomfort with the concept of God.
   a. **The Big Book:** The basic AA text, titled *Alcoholics Anonymous* and called The Big Book has a chapter entitled, "We Agnostics" to help people overcome this obstacle.

3. **12 Traditions:** The 12 Traditions are the guidelines that help AA groups function smoothly.

4. **Open meetings:** The two main types of AA meetings are open and closed meetings. Anyone may attend an open meeting. There are several types of open meetings:
   a. *Speaker meeting:* A speaker usually gives the classic AA talk about how it was, what happened to him or her, and how it is now. Speakers often talk for up to an hour and almost never use notes

*The Preamble reprinted from the AA *Grapevine.* New York, Alcoholics Anonymous World Services. Used by permission.

or scripts. AA speakers feel this helps them "talk from the heart and not the head."

b. *Topic meeting:* One participant may choose an issue to address, such as anger and sobriety. The chairperson will share his or her views on the topic, then encourage other group members to share their ideas and experiences.

c. *Step meeting:* One of the 12 steps is discussed. The step meeting helps members learn the steps and how to use them in their own recovery. Members may read a section in a book called the *Twelve Steps and Twelve Traditions* on the step they are discussing. Each member then shares how it relates to his or her recovery.

d. *Big Book meeting:* Study of the Big Book. This type of meeting is helpful for beginners in the 12-Step program.

e. *Orientation meeting:* Designed to explain AA to newcomers and others interested in AA. The meeting is open to anyone (including *physicians*), and can be an excellent resource to expose patients to the principles of AA. Persons other than the speaker or speakers usually do not share at orientation meetings.

5. ***Closed meetings:*** A closed 12-Step meeting is limited to persons who have a desire to stop drinking. Sometimes, if asked, closed groups will allow physicians and clergy who are not alcoholics to observe a closed meeting. They do this to better help the professional understand what happens at an AA meeting.

a. Closed AA meetings usually start with the Serenity Prayer. Then each person introduces himself or herself by saying, "Hi, My name is_____, and I'm an alcoholic." Many groups have a brief business meeting, which takes less than 10 minutes.

b. Several types of closed AA meetings are similar to open meetings. Often people are afraid to go to an AA meeting because they do not want to talk or share. This can be easily remedied by saying, "I pass."

c. AA meetings also can be classified by *who attends* the meeting. This is important to understand when a patient says they cannot find a meeting with anyone like themselves. Special groups include women, professionals (e.g., nurses, physicians, lawyers, clergy), young adults, senior citizens, nonsmokers, agnostics, gays and lesbians, blacks, and Hispanics. Not all cities and towns have all groups. It will be useful to contact your local AA organization to get information regarding local AA meetings. You may record the phone number of your local source of AA information in the Treatment Resource Worksheet (see Fig 4–2).

IV. **Relapse Prevention**

A. **Recovery Process**

See Appendix 4–5 for tips in avoiding relapse.

1. ***Recovery as a life-long process:*** Recovery is a life-long process requiring long-term group involvement by the patient. Like other

chronic diseases, such as diabetes and chronic heart disease, patients, particularly when under stress, are tempted to return to their old patterns of behavior. It is important for physicians to remember that chemical dependency is a chronic relapsing disease. The physician plays a key role in helping patients prevent relapses and in supporting them if they should relapse, so that they can reestablish abstinence.

2. ***High-risk situations:*** An important part of relapse prevention is the recognition by the patient, family, and aftercare providers of high-risk situations (e.g., ball game, bowling), behaviors (e.g., argument with spouse), and times (e.g., holidays, hospitalization).

3. ***Some prescribed medications can jeopardize recovery:*** Some needed medical and dental procedures often require medications that can jeopardize sobriety and precipitate relapse. Medical and dental care requiring medications other than antibiotics should be monitored by a physician with addiction expertise.

B. Symptoms of Relapse
1. ***Clues to relapse:*** Clues to potential relapse that patients, families, physicians, and aftercare providers need to heed include:
   a. Isolation.
   b. Irritability and anger.
   c. Request for mood-altering drugs.
   d. Excessive euphoria early in sobriety.
   e. "I can control it" attitude.
   f. Unwillingness to discuss the recovery program.
   g. Unwillingness to talk about feelings.

2. ***Special relapse programs:*** Many treatment programs now have special relapse programs for individuals who have been treated for chemical dependency and return to the use of alcohol and/or drugs. The program will provide active support for a specific period of time (e.g., 6 weeks), including group therapy and individual counseling two or more times per week. These are usually individualized programs because they are designed to help the patient identify and handle behaviors and attitudes that lead to relapse. Halfway houses also are a resource for chronic relapsing patients.

C. What can the Physician do to Help the Recovering Person?
1. *Strongly* emphasize the need to attend an aftercare program.
2. Encourage frequent contact with sponsor.
3. Encourage frequent attendance at 12-Step meetings (at least once a week, and more frequently in times of increased stress).
4. *Do not prescribe sleeping pills or minor tranquilizers.*
5. Label the patient's chart signifying that he or she is in recovery, so that mood-altering chemicals are not prescribed.
6. Show the patient your support and caring in his or her recovery program by acknowledging "dry dates" and anniversaries in recovery.
7. Look for clues of potential or early relapse and help the patient reverse this process early.

V. Other Issues
A. Confidentiality
Treatment programs are sensitive to the confidential nature of the treatment process and will not give information about any patient in treatment without informed patient consent. Federal regulations protect a patient's right to confidentiality. Employers may ask patients to sign a record release form so they can monitor the employee's progress.
B. Insurance Coverage for Drug and Alcohol Treatment
Most insurance companies understand the importance of providing resources for treatment of alcohol and drug dependence. The amount of resources provided by most insurance plans was drastically reduced in 1984 and in 1990. Outpatient treatment is provided by most insurance plans. Many have limits that severely restrict the duration of treatment. Inpatient treatment may be severely limited in the absence of serious medical and mental health problems. Many communities also have services for patients who are uninsured. County mental health programs usually provide assessment services and outpatient treatment programs.

BIBLIOGRAPHY

Alcoholics Anonymous: The Story of How Many Thousands of Men and Women Have Recovered From Alcoholism, ed 3. New York, Alcoholics Anonymous World Services, 1976.

Bean MH: Alcoholics Anonymous: Principles and methods. *Psychiatr Ann* 1975; 5:5–13.

Bjorklund P: *What is Spirituality?* Center City, Minn, Hazelden Foundation, 1983.

Blondell R: *12-Step programs.* University of Louisville, Department of Family Practice. Project SAEFP (Substance Abuse Education for Family Physicians) Workshop Materials, Society for Teachers of Family Medicine, 1990.

Donovan DM: Assessment of addictive behaviors: Implications of an emerging biopsychosocial model, in Donovan DM, Marlatt GA (eds): *Assessment of Addictive Behaviors.* New York, *Guilford Press,* 1988.

Finch J. Elements of treatment. Project SAEFP (Substance Abuse Education for Family Physicians) Workshop Materials, Society for Teachers of Family Medicine, 1990.

Gawin FH, Ellinwood EH. Cocaine and other stimulants: Actions, abuse and treatment. *N Engl J Med* 1988; 318:1173–1182.

Gitlow SE, Peyser HS: *Alcoholism: A Practical Treatment Guide.* New York, Grune & Stratton, 1980.

Marlatt GA: Matching clients to treatment: Treatment models and stages of change, in Donovan DM, Marlatt GA (eds): *Assessment of Addictive Behaviors.* New York, *Guilford Press,* 1988.

Miller WR, Hester RK: Inpatient alcoholism treatment: Who benefits? *Am Psychol* 1986; July:794–805.

Pattison EM: A Multivariate-Multimoral Model for Alcoholism, in Pattison EM (ed): *Selection of Treatment for Alcoholics.* Rutgers, NJ, Rutgers Center of Alcohol Studies.

Twelve Steps and Twelve Traditions. New York, Alcoholics Anonymous World Services.

Whitfield CL, et al: *Alcoholism in Principles of Ambulatory Medicine.* Baltimore, Williams & Wilkins, 1986.

APPENDIXES

Patient Education Handouts

APPENDIX 4−1.

Daily Schedule for Typical Inpatient or Residential Treatment Program*

Time	Activity
6:30 AM	Wake-up
7:00	Physical therapy (exercise)
7:30	Meditation
8:00	Breakfast
8:30	Blood pressure check and room inspection (patients are responsible for cleaning their own rooms)
9:00	Community meeting (gives patients a voice in the program, a place to have input into the schedule and activities, etc.)
10:00	Group therapy
11:30	Free time
12:00 PM	Lunch
1:00	Individual counseling and/or group session
3:00	Free time (quiet time to complete reading and worksheet assignments, write letters; *no TV*)
3:30	Physical activity (sometimes away from the facility, e.g., bowling, YMCA)
5:00	Lecture
6:00	Dinner
7:00	Free time
7:30	AA/NA
9:30	Free time
10:00	Serenity hour (meditation, quiet time to write thoughts for the day in a journal)
11:00	Free time
11:30	Lights out

*Courtesy of DePaul Madison Family Institute, Madison, Wis, 1990.

APPENDIX 4–2.

12-Step Glossary of Terms*

Alcoholics Anonymous	Group of individuals who admit that they are powerless over alcohol. These groups were co-founded by Bill W. and Dr. Bob. AA members conduct "meetings" to share their experience, strength, and hope, to solve their common problems. The only requirement for membership is a desire to stop drinking. The AA program is based on 12 Steps applied to their lives in order that they may recover from alcoholism.
Al-Anon	12-Step program for relatives and friends of alcoholics. These groups were founded by Lois and Ann, the wives of the co-founders of AA. Some groups deal with issues of the Adult Children of Alcoholics (ACOA).
Alateen	12-Step Al-Anon program for teenage children of alcoholics.
The Big Book	Basic text for AA. Includes the philosophy of AA, how it works, and stories about the lives of some early members of AA.
Closed meeting	12-Step meeting that is closed to the public; attendance is limited to alcoholics.
Discussion meeting	12-Step meeting with focus on a specific topic. All group members have an opportunity to share their ideas on the topic.
Institutional meeting	12-Step meeting held in a hospital, treatment center, etc.
Meeting directory	Booklet published by the local chapter that lists the time, place, and type of meetings available in the local area.
Narcotics Anonymous	Variation of AA for drug addicts.
Nar-Anon	Variation of Al-Anon for relatives and friends of drug addicts.
Sponsor	Specific person (of the same sex and usually with at least 1 year of sobriety) whom the new AA member chooses to be a mentor and role model.

*From Blondell R: Project SAEFP, 1990. Used by permission.

APPENDIX 4–3.

Twelve Steps*

1. We admitted we were powerless over alcohol, that our lives had become unmanageable.
2. Came to believe that a Power greater than ourselves could restore us to sanity.
3. Made a decision to turn our will and our lives over to the care of God as we understood Him.
4. Made a searching and fearless moral inventory of ourselves.
5. Admitted to God, to ourselves, and to another human being the exact nature of our wrongs.
6. Were entirely ready to have God remove all these defects of character.
7. Humbly asked him to remove our shortcomings.
8. Made a list of all persons we had harmed, and became willing to make amends to them all.
9. Made direct amends to such people wherever possible, except when to do so would injure them or others.
10. Continued to take personal inventory, and when we were wrong promptly admitted it.
11. Sought through prayer and meditation to improve our conscious contact with God as we understood Him, praying only for knowledge of His will for us and the power to carry that out.
12. Having had a spiritual awakening as the result of these steps, we tried to carry this message to alcoholics and to practice these principles in all our affairs.

*The Twelve Steps are reprinted with permission of Alcoholics Anonymous World Services, Inc. Permission to reprint this material does not mean that AA has reviewed or approved the contents of this publication, nor that AA agrees with the views expressed herein. AA is a program of recovery from alcoholism. Use of the Twelve Steps in connection with programs and activities patterned after AA but that address other problems does not imply otherwise.

APPENDIX 4–4.

Twelve Traditions*

1. Our common welfare should come first; personal recovery depends on AA unity.
2. For our group purpose there is but one ultimate authority, a loving God as He may express Himself in our group conscience. Our leaders are but trusted servants; they do not govern.
3. The only requirement for AA membership is a desire to stop drinking.
4. Each group should be autonomous except in matters affecting other groups or AA as a whole.
5. Each group has but one primary purpose, to carry its message to the alcoholic who still suffers.
6. An AA group ought never endorse, finance, or lend the AA name to any related facility or outside enterprise, lest problems of money, property, and prestige divert us from our primary purpose.
7. Every AA group ought to be fully self-supporting, declining outside contributions.
8. AA should remain forever nonprofessional, but our service centers may employ special workers.
9. AA, as such, ought never be organized; but we may create service boards or committees directly responsible to those they serve.
10. AA has no opinion on outside issues; hence the AA name ought never be drawn into public controversy.
11. Our public relations policy is based on attraction rather than promotion; we need always maintain personal anonymity at the level of press, radio, and films.
12. Anonymity is the spiritual foundation of all our Traditions, ever reminding us to place principles before personalities.

*The Twelve Traditions are reprinted with permission of Alcoholics Anonymous World Services, Inc. Permission to reprint this material does not mean that AA has reviewed or approved the contents of this publication, nor that AA agrees with the views expressed herein. AA is a program of recovery from alcoholism. Use of the Twelve Traditions in connection with programs and activities patterned after AA but that address other problems does not imply otherwise.

APPENDIX 4–5.
Tips to Avoid Relapse

To avoid relapse, chemically dependent persons need to:

1. Attend 12-Step meetings *at least weekly*.
2. Identify and learn to handle high-risk situations (e.g., the person who drank every time he or she went bowling may need to stop bowling for a while until the situation can be dealt with sobriety.)
3. Identify and learn to handle urges and cravings to use alcohol and drugs.
4. Identify and handle social pressures (e.g., This may mean the avoidance of social situations with "drinking buddies." If the extended family drinks at holiday gatherings, the dependent person and significant others may choose either to avoid holiday get-togethers until comfortable, or to come early to the gathering, eat with the family, and leave immediately after dinner). Social pressures vary with the individual.
5. Learn anger management. Often there is a great deal of underlying anger attached to giving up the chemical.
6. Creatively use leisure time in sobriety.
7. Learn to balance life-style so that previous pressures and "triggers" are not overwhelming.

CHAPTER 5

Smoking Cessation Strategies

Leif I. Solberg, M.D.

Thomas E. Kottke, M.D.

Use of tobacco is not commonly regarded as substance abuse in the same sense as abuse of other substances. It should be.

1. Any use is abuse. Tobacco is the only substance in common use that, even when used correctly and in moderation, likely will produce disease and death.
2. Harmful effects of tobacco on Americans are much greater than those of all other abused substances combined, even considering all the indirect harmful effects of alcohol abuse such as traffic injuries, homicide, and suicide. It is not just the chief preventable cause of disease and death, the 435,000 U.S. deaths per year attributable to tobacco exceed all other preventable causes combined.

About 45 million Americans, 28% of the adult population, use tobacco. It is particularly worrisome that this rate is 20% to 60% higher in certain segments of the population, especially persons with less education and some ethnic minorities (Native Americans, Hispanics, and African-Americans). Teenagers and women are another source for concern, because smoking prevalence has fallen at a much lower rate in these groups. The hopeful news is that so many users have quit and that quitters rapidly lose most of their increased health risks. Even long-term us-ers will benefit substantially from quitting.

The methods presented are applicable to all forms of tobacco use, including chewing tobacco, snuff, cigars, cigarettes, and pipe smoking.

I. Intervention: What Works and What Doesn't
A. What We've Learned from Patients
1. ***People quit:*** Users do quit successfully. There are approximately as many former tobacco users in the U.S. as current users.
2. ***Knowledge is not the problem:*** Current tobacco users already know that the habit is dangerous to their health; therefore further efforts to dramatize or individualize these facts may be needless or even counterproductive.

3. *People want to quit:* Most current tobacco users already want to quit, and have tried it at least once. As many as 50% may try each year. Therefore it may be better to assume that the tobacco user will have at least some interest in quitting and not spend as much time trying to convince.
4. *Repeated attempts are necessary:* Of those who have quit using tobacco, 95% did so unassisted by any formal program or pharmacologic-psychologic aid; however, success was achieved only after an average of 3 or 4 attempts. Encourage those who have failed in their attempt by reassuring them that this is common and should be viewed as a learning opportunity, not a failure.
5. *Importance of physician advice:* When asked what would be the most motivating stimulus to a quit attempt, most current smokers say that advice from their physicians would be most important by far. Most smokers also report that no physician has ever asked them to quit, and few quitters cite physician advice as a significant factor in their quitting.
6. *Physician effectiveness:* Two things appear to impress smokers that their physician really wants them to quit.
   a. Quitting is brought up during every office visit by both the physician and other office staff.
   b. Quitting always is discussed in a helpful, friendly, and nondemanding way that emphasizes specific plans and assistance rather than harassment, scare tactics or preaching.
7. *Summary of studies:* A quantitative review by Kottke of all of the controlled smoking trials conducted in medical practices concluded that no single intervention strategy is particularly more effective than others. Instead, success rates increase in direct relation to:
   a. Number of times an intervention is made.
   b. Duration of time during which interventions are attempted.
   c. Variety of approaches used.
   d. Variety of people involved in the intervention (e.g., physicians, nurses, receptionists).

This evidence strongly suggests that assisting smoking cessation is done by behavior shaping rather than by health beliefs or cognitive reasoning.

B. **Why Physicians Have Not Been Successful in Helping Patients to Quit Smoking**
1. They do not know which of their patients use tobacco.
2. They are most aware of and act on those patients most resistant to quitting.
3. They have no reminder to raise the topic during office visits.
4. They do not have easy access to information about previous interventions that could help them build on previous discussions and attempts.
5. They usually overemphasize dangers (scare tactics).
6. They offer little specific help.

7. They do not provide the post-cessation reinforcement that is critical to success.

8. They become discouraged because they feel they rarely identify successful quitters and often encounter resistant smokers.

C. **How to Solve These Problems**

Although some of these problems can be improved by education, most call for a change in the office environment. For such a change to be acceptable in busy practices, it must be:

1. Efficient of both physician and staff time.

2. Economical.

3. Facilitative of discussion at each office visit and follow-up as needed.

4. Seen by patients as helpful rather than confrontative.

The only known way to accomplish these goals is to build and maintain an *office system* that involves all staff and physicians in an efficient, constructive, and integrated way.

II. **Critical Office System Components**

A. **System Development**

The office system described here and in Figure 5–1 was developed, tested, and modified in one urban family practice clinic when it became clear that good intentions, knowledge, and average memory were not enough to practice successful office smoking cessation. This system has stood the test of 5 years of continuous use and has been widely replicated in a variety of practice and residency settings. It also has become the backbone of the American Academy of Family Physicians (AAFP) Stop-Smoking Kit (see Appendix B, Resources) and a part of the National Cancer Institute manual and training program for physicians.

Some would argue that the system is too complex and requires too much effort and change in office procedures. Although we wish we could simply suggest changing one's personal approach to the smoking patient and using chart labels, there is evidence that this is not enough. Unless the office support is there for all of the tasks described, physicians will continue to be relatively ineffective in helping their patients to quit using tobacco.

B. **Screening and Labeling**

1. *Case finding:* Every office patient older than 15 years whose chart is not labeled for tobacco use status must be asked whether tobacco is used. This should be done when the vital signs are taken by the office nurse or assistant.

2. *Label chart:* When tobacco use status is determined, an appropriate label should be attached in a visible location on the medical chart:

   a. Nonuser: *green dot.* These charts should be labeled so that the patient is not asked unnecessarily at each visit.

   b. Current, regular user of tobacco: *black dot.*

   c. Recent quitter: *green plus black dot* (e.g., beside each other) or *red dot.*

3. *Reassess smoking status:* At each subsequent visit, each patient who is either a current user or a recent quitter must be asked again

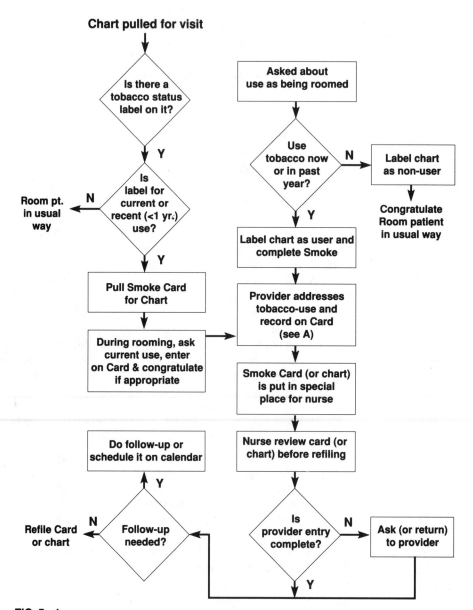

FIG 5–1.
Flow chart outlines an approach for patients in ambulatory care settings. The approach provides clinicians with an office-based system to identify, treat, and follow-up use of tobacco products. The key points are the use of a smoking reminder card and office staff for implementation and maintenance of the system.

whether and how much tobacco he or she is using, and the label changed if indicated.

4. ***Change label to green dot:*** Once a quitter has abstained long enough to be unlikely to return to use (e.g., 1 year), the label should be changed to reflect this (e.g., cover the user label with a nonuser label).

C. Physician Reminders

1. ***Visible reminder:*** Because the patient's reason for the visit must dominate the physician's attention, it is important to have a visible reminder for the physician to bring up the topic of tobacco use. A label as noted above is unlikely to accomplish this, because it likely will be covered by a fee slip or other papers.

2. ***Smoke Card:*** A special progress record or Smoke Card (Fig 5–2) that can be attached to the outside of the chart serves to remind the physician about actual current use as well as about previous discussions and plans about quitting. During the current visit the physician can build on that information.

   a. The Smoke Card can be kept in the record, but ideally is kept in a separate file outside the medical record, for the following reasons.

      (1) Keeping the card in the chart means that it likely will become buried under other papers and not serve its reminder function.

W Winner	S Stop on own	H Stop with help	L Later	N No	O Omitted

NAME_____ PHONE (H)_____ (W) _____

ADDRESS_____ BIRTH YEAR_____ SEX_____

TOBACCO HIST. TYPE_____; YRS_____; # QUITS_____; LONGEST QUIT_____; LATEST QUIT____

COMMENTS_____

Staff Completion				Provider Completion		
DATE	AMT. USED/DAY	PROVIDER	HISTORY	CAT.*	PLAN	FOLLOW-UP

* Category = User quit attitude (see symbols at top of card)

FIG 5–2.

"Doctors Helping Smokers" reminder card is an easy manual system that any office practice can implement and maintain with minimal effort. This card has been used and tested in a large number of practices, and has been effective in the establishment of a practice-based smoking cessation program.

(2) In large medical organizations, changes in chart contents may require a difficult and time-consuming process.

(3) If the Smoke Card is separate, it can be more easily used as a communication device between the physician and whoever is to do desired follow-up.

(4) It will be easier to find the Smoke Card for follow-up telephone calls in a file, rather than searching for the entire chart.

(5) Keeping Smoke Cards together makes auditing and evaluating the system much simpler.

b. A Smoke Card is begun by the nurse or medical assistant whenever a current or recent tobacco user is first identified. This person completes the upper part of the card (see Fig 5–2). The date, amount, and initials of the provider are entered on a new line of the card.

c. The physician should enter the user category (Table 5–1), significant plans, and follow-up on the card. The history portion may be used if there are any important new facts or events (e.g., attempt to quit, special problems in quitting).

D. Physician Message

1. *Presentation of message:* It is best to bring up smoking cessation after the patient's presenting problem has been taken care of. The overall tone should be friendly, helpful, and specific.

2. *Use of time:* Since most users want to quit, most of the time should be spent on making plans and arranging any needed help and follow-up rather than on the dangers of tobacco use. The physician should be able to complete this discussion in less than 2–3 minutes.

TABLE 5–1.

Blue Plus Doctors Helping Smokers: Office Smoking Cessation Program Physician Guidelines*

Category	Explanation	Plan	Follow-up
W	*Winner.* Previous daily use but not in past day.	Congratulate! Ask if help needed.	Arrange office phone follow-up if patient has quit in past month.
S	Willing to set quit date in 1–4 weeks but prefers to stop by *Self.*	Congratulate! Set quit date, provide self-help materials.	Arrange office phone follow-up 3–7 days after quit date.
H	Willing to quit within next month but wants *Help.*	Congratulate! Provide self-help materials.	Set appointment with office counselor or MD
L	Interested in quitting, but not now *(Later).*	Advise of your desire to help when ready.	If patient gives a date for readiness, arrange office phone follow-up at that time.
N	*No.* Not interested in quitting.	Advise of your desire to help when they change their mind.	Don't ask again at routine visits for 6–12 months.
O	*Omit.* No provider discussion of tobacco use because of inadequate time, inappropriate, or forgot.		Be sure to bring up at next office visit.

*Modified from Selberg L: *Med Times* 1988; 116:123.

3. ***Reinforcement issues:*** It is reinforcement at each contact, rather than any single discussion, that is important to success. If more than 3 minutes is spent on this problem, it is unlikely that this important reinforcement will occur with every smoker.

4. ***Smoker reaction:*** Direction of the discussion will depend on the patient's reaction to the physician's question about whether he or she is ready to quit smoking (Fig 5–3). Possible smoker reactions are summarized in Table 5–1, along with recommendations on how to respond to each of them. Because it is important for the physician to

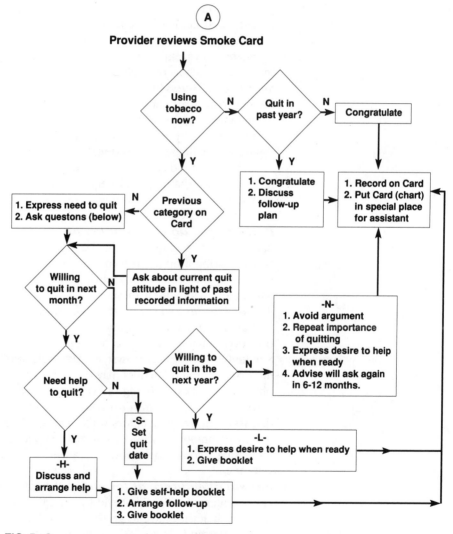

FIG 5–3.
Provider/patient tobacco intervention flow chart. Note that except for brief, clear advice, all actions depend on the response of the tobacco user.

enter a category on the Smoke Card at every visit, an O (omit) category is included as well for those inevitable occasions when no quit discussion took place.

5. ***Keep the discussion brief:*** A brief discussion can be possible if:
    a. A well-documented Smoke Card is present, so that smoking history and previous quit discussions are quickly viewable.
    b. Little time is spent trying to persuade users that they should quit.
    c. Efforts to solve complex quitting problems are deferred to a later "quit visit."
    d. A Smoke Card is present to minimize time required to record the discussion.
    e. The physician is willing to accept (for now) a user's lack of interest in quitting. This does not mean accepting tobacco use.

6. ***Format:*** Ask questions rather than making declarations or commands, as much as possible.

7. ***Sequence discussion:*** The basic outline of a brief discussion for the majority of patients who are interested in quitting should be something like this:
    "I believe that it is very important for you to quit!"
    "Are you willing to try to quit?"
    "Will you set a date to quit? When?"
    "Do you need any special help with quitting?"
    "Would it be all right for my nurse to call you 3 to 7 days after your quit date to see whether you need any help?"

8. ***Patients who do not want to quit:*** Tell those few patients who have no interest in quitting that you can accept that for now but that you will bring it up again some time in the future because you really believe it's important and because you want to be able to help them when they change their mind.

9. ***Avoid debate:*** Remember that even a few helpful words at each visit are better than an argument or a long discussion that happens only occasionally. The key to doing this briefly lies in using the Smoke Card and category system. Although some discussion of patient concerns and barriers may be useful if it can be kept brief, the physician must avoid being drawn into either arguments or efforts to solve complex problems during that visit. One 10-minute tobacco discussion in five encounters with a smoker is not only less helpful than five 2-minute discussions, it may produce the opposite effect, increasing smoking behavior.

E. **Assistance**
    1. ***Patient attendance at formal quit programs:*** Few tobacco users are interested or will attend formal quit programs or counseling, particularly if they have to go to another place for them. However counseling can help some, so users interested in that approach should be encouraged to attend.
    2. ***Financial savings:*** Quitting tobacco use immediately saves sub-

stantial amounts of money ($30–$120/mo), so even poor people can afford to pay for reasonably priced quitting assistance (even though most third parties do not cover this service).

3. *Self-help booklets:* Self-help booklets are useful and should be given to every user with interest in quitting. For those with trouble quitting, simply giving a booklet is unlikely to be enough.

4. *Problem solving:* Personalized problem solving (ideally involving other family members as well) can be more helpful than written materials alone, and should be offered to any patient who has experienced trouble in quitting. Although some physicians may wish to perform this counseling themselves (at a scheduled follow-up visit), there are good reasons to have another person (ideally, a nurse) do it:

   a. Cost is less.
   b. Nurses have been trained to provide education and problem solving around problems of daily life and probably are better at it than most physicians.
   c. Nurses usually enjoy counseling, so they will feel better about their work and help to see that the rest of the system works well.

5. *Family involvement:* Since social support for quitting and the daily milieu are critical aspects of major habit changes, try to involve a spouse or significant others in these sessions (whether they smoke or not).

6. *Number of counseling sessions:* Although a single counseling session may be all that is needed by some, most patients will benefit from a series of three to five sessions. A package charge that is less than if the visits were separately arranged may help to motivate attendance.

7. *Use of nicotine gum:* Other forms of assistance (e.g., nicotine gum or other pharmacologic aids) are likely to be beneficial only if they are combined with counseling and a structured program. It is a disfavor to prescribe nicotine gum over the phone or without instruction and follow-up. (See section IV, B for a more detailed description of these issues).

8. *Counselor Training*
   a. *Selection of staff:* The main requirement of a smoking cessation counselor is the ability to conduct one-on-one health education and facilitation of self problem solving. Most graduate RNs and various other health professionals have the inclination and background for this.
   b. *Education of staff counselor:* Smoking cessation counselors should attain knowledge about tobacco abuse and quitting. Most information can come from reading this chapter and various self-help quitting guides (see section F, below). Attending a smoking cessation program such as those run by the American Lung Association (ALA) is an added benefit. Some of the larger ALA chapters

may have leadership training sessions, which also would be helpful.

  c. **Development of counseling program:** An outline of specific
     tasks for each counseling session is essential. Our program is sum-
     marized in Figure 5–4. We encourage those needing help to at-
     tend four sessions, although one session may help some. You may

---

Smoking Cessation Visits

First Visit: 30 minutes

❑ Complete smoking history including family information.

❑ Assess motivation, reasons for quitting, barriers, support.

❑ Present options for quitting: (1) on own; (2) referral to community program; (3)
    individual plan with our nurse ($30/30 min/visit); (4) prepay package of four sessions with our
    nurse ($75 for one 30 min visit and three 20 min visits).

❑ Encourage family involvement, including quitting together and/or attending together.

❑ Advise about nicotine gum.

❑ Set a quit date and develop a plan for approaching it.

❑ Suggest patient start a tally of smoking patterns.

❑ Arrange follow up.

Second Visit: 20 minutes (at or around quit date)

❑ Review progress and tally.

❑ Reassess motivation and confidence.

❑ Review tips for quit day and thereafter.

❑ Teach relaxation if appropriate.

❑ Encourage enlisting help of a support person.

Third Visit: 20 minutes (1 week after quit date; call if no-show)

❑ Congratulate!

❑ Review progress.

❑ Set another quit date if patient restarted.

❑ Review difficult behaviors and plan alternate action.

❑ Teach good eating habits and low-calorie food if appropriate.

❑ Teach imagery and affirmation of self as nonsmoker.

Fourth Visit: 20 minutes (3–5 weeks after quit)

❑ Congratulate!

❑ Review progress.

❑ Reinforce new behaviors.

❑ Review techniques (e.g., relaxation and imagery, affirmation, low-calorie foods, deep breathing).

❑ Plan for problem times when patient may return to smoking and what to do if they restart.

FIG 5–4.
Recommended approach for persons who need counseling assistance to quit smoking. Although
only a minority of quitting smokers need and want this help, it is important to have it available
from nurses or physicians.

introduce a reduced fee (paid in advance) to include all four sessions; this may enhance the likelihood that patients will continue the counseling.

F. Follow-up

1. ***Focus on recent quitters who have relapsed:*** As many as 50% of tobacco users make quit attempts in a year; thus more may be accomplished by reinforcing attempts that you are aware of than by trying to stimulate new attempts.

2. ***Friendliness:*** Friendly efforts to support quit attempts almost invariably will be welcomed and will strengthen the desired impression that the physician really believes it is important for them to quit.

3. ***Follow-up phone call by nurse:*** The most helpful support is a telephone call during that critical first week after a quit attempt. Fifty percent of quit attempts end within 2 days, and 75% within 1 week. This phone call can be made easily and effectively by an office nurse. Remember to include follow-up calls for those patients who have already quit on their own within the preceding few weeks.

4. ***Follow-up post card:*** An alternative to phone calls is a postcard, although this is less personal and therefore probably less reinforcing. However, a postcard is recommended for patients without phones or who cannot be reached after three or four tries. A mailed reinforcement is preferable to none at all.

5. ***Use of Smoke Card for follow-up:*** Using Smoke Cards simplifies any follow-up arrangements:
   a. The Smoke Card can be left where follow-up information can be noted by the nurse before it is refiled.
   b. The name of the person to be followed-up can be written on a special calendar on the approximate date the call should be placed.
   c. The Smoke Card should be pulled at the time of the follow-up, and any findings or plans should be noted on a new line, as done for the previous tobacco discussion.

G. Supportive Environment

To emphasize your commitment to smoking cessation and to avoid giving mixed messages about it, there are several office environment considerations.

1. ***Smoke-free office:*** A no-smoking policy is not just for patients but for staff and physicians. If this is not already in effect, it may be wise to do so before initiating the rest of this program. Otherwise, employees may blame the program for the policy change. It is also wise to involve some smokers in the plans for change, and to execute it in a respectful way.

2. ***Signs and posters:*** Visual aids posted in appropriate locations can help to make patients aware of your interest and ability to help them quit.

3. ***Smoking advertising in waiting room reading materials:***

Magazines in the waiting room or examination rooms send a message about practice attitudes as well. Select those free from tobacco ads.

III. Critical Components in Establishing and Maintaining the System

No formal system for any procedure has ever been established in an organization without significant effort and support. This fact is particularly important for medical offices, which often are not systematic about accomplishing clinical purposes. Although the aspects of starting and maintaining the system may appear imposing, they are critically important, and most tasks can be delegated to the staff coordinator. The material is set up in a table format, and you may want to check off each item as it is completed.

A. Policy Establishment

The practice policy-making body needs to provide clear support for establishing the system. The following steps are important:

❑ Formally decide to make the system a part of normal practice operations.

❑ Identify coordinators with authority and responsibility for implementing it.

❑ Assure that both physicians and staff will support the system

❑ Establish or approve a strategy and timetable.

❑ Make follow-up reports on the system's status part of future management meetings.

B. Coordination of New System

❑ A staff coordinator is needed who has the authority and interest to develop and carry out a plan for implementing and maintaining the system.

❑ A physician coordinator is needed to work with the staff coordinator and provide legitimacy and follow-up with the other physicians.

❑ In larger clinics it may be prudent to have a work group or committee that occasionally meets with the coordinators for planning and evaluation.

C. Questions to Answer When Developing an Implementation Plan

❑ Exactly how will each of the components of the system be implemented in your office? Are there special problems or needs that will require unique modification?

❑ What are each of the tasks that will need to be done in order for the system to work?

❑ Who will be responsible for each of the tasks? What is the role of the physician?

❑ Will the system be established as a trial in one functional area of a larger clinic before expanding to the rest?

D. Orientation and Training

❑ First, everyone must be oriented to the need for the system.

❑ Each person needs orientation and training in the tasks expected of him or her.

❑ After the system has been established, new personnel will need orientation, original personnel will need reinforcement and perhaps retraining.

E. **Resources Needed to Implement System**
   - ❏ Charts labels, Smoke Cards, files, etc.
   - ❏ Self-help booklets stocked in places convenient for distribution during visits.
   - ❏ Posters, signs.
   - ❏ Community smoking cessation program information for those few smokers who would like to try that approach.

F. **Audit**
   Use the audit to verify that the system is operating as desired and accomplishing the desired effects. It is important to have a means to measure function and outcomes. If the Smoke Cards are kept in a central file, it is easy to audit them quickly for the above purposes. Forms and descriptions for doing this are available from the authors. Other aspects of the system can be audited even more easily by checking a random sample of charts of patients seen since the system was started.

G. **Maintenance Support**
   Unless special efforts are made to keep a newly started system going until it becomes a habit (probably 12 to 18 months), it is likely to deteriorate after the initial enthusiasm wanes. Give feedback of audit results to the whole group, emphasizing the positive results and making adjustments in the system. You may also need to give feedback to individuals, retraining or motivating as needed, as well as training and orienting new personnel to the system. Hold "spirit building" events (e.g., a party, recognition, public relations activities). Recognize that having this program can be a big plus for community recognition as well as building morale of clinic staff.

IV. **Special Quitting Problems**
   A. **Resistant Smoker**
      1. ***Low prevalence:*** There are fewer resistant smokers than you'd think, usually no more than 5% to 15%. Some of these will quit soon, although they just told you never to bother them about the topic again. Many of them will quit eventually.
      2. ***Scare tactics:*** Efforts to overwhelm resistance or to change resistance by scare tactics or intimidation will have harmful effects.
         a. Patients will become more convinced of their need to continue smoking.
         b. They will learn never to bring up the topic or to expect help from you in the future.
         c. They will associate tobacco intervention with frustration.
      3. Accept patients' right to make this decision for themselves, but say, "I'll bring this up again in the future, because I think it's important and to see if you've changed your mind."
   B. **Addicted Smoker**
      Although tobacco is clearly a substance that can fulfill all the criteria for

addiction, most smokers do not seem to have a physiologic dependence on tobacco that is strong enough to be a major problem with quitting. This idea is supported by the 35 million successful quitters who did so on their own. For this majority, the main problems are psychologic, social, and habit, in some combination unique to each person.

1. ***Identify the addicted minority:*** History is the best guide. The most useful question for a smoker who has tried to quit is to ask him or her whether *withdrawal symptoms* were the most important factor that led them to return to tobacco use in the first 2 weeks of quitting.
   a. The primary withdrawal symptoms are tobacco craving, restlessness, increased appetite, impatience, anxiety, and irritability.
   b. There is evidence that the strength of addiction can be adequately assessed by determining whether tobacco is used within 30 minutes of getting up in the morning. This question is part of the Fagerstrom Nicotine Dependency Test (Fig 5–5).
2. ***Help the highly dependent smoker attempt to quit:*** Assisting

---

Fagerstrom Nicotine Dependency Test

Question	Score
1. How soon after you wake up do you smoke your first cigarette?	1 if within 30 minutes
2. Do you find it difficult to refrain from smoking in places where it's forbidden?	1 if Yes
3. Which of all the cigarettes you smoke in a day is the most satisfying?	1 if it's the first
4. How many cigarettes a day do you smoke?	1 if 16–25, 2 if >25
5. Do you smoke more during the morning than during the rest of the day?	1 if Yes
6. Do you smoke when you are so ill that you are in bed most of the day?	1 if Yes
7. Does the brand you smoke have a low, medium, or high nicotine content?	1 if medium, 2 if high
8. How often do you inhale?	1 if sometimes, 2 if always

FIG 5–5.
Fagerstrom Nicotine Dependency Test. Scores of 7 to 10 reflect high dependence and are associated with more withdrawal symptoms. However, studies of the predictive value of this test for cessation success have not been conclusive.

patients by reducing their withdrawal symptoms is critical in this group. Craving, withdrawal, and drug-seeking behavior can be severe and can precipitate relapse. The following methods to conduct a brief intervention can be effective:

a. Reassure the patient that these symptoms will disappear, the worst ones within 1 week and all symptoms within 2–3 weeks.

b. Suggest selecting a quit date when other factors (e.g., other stress or proximity to other people) will not aggravate withdrawal symptoms or make their effects more damaging.

c. Make use of stress management techniques (see 4, below).

d. Involve family and colleagues for support.

e. Consider offering nicotine replacement therapy.

3. ***Nicotine replacement therapy:*** The theoretical basis for nicotine replacement therapy is to delay withdrawal symptoms until after habit and psychologic and social issues have been resolved. Although addiction continues, the nicotine is delivered as a single substance, free from the carcinogenic and other dangers to be found in the other 4,000 chemical agents in tobacco. Although other routes of administration are being investigated, nicotine polyacrilex (Nicorette gum) is the only form available at this time.

a. Never begin or maintain replacement therapy by telephone.

b. Require that tobacco use be completely stopped while using the replacement. Do not use them together!

c. Provide at least 10 minutes of instruction and written information about proper use.

d. Require that users take part in a behavior modification program, either group or individual, either in the practice or elsewhere (see II E).

e. Insist on periodic visits (perhaps as part of the above-noted program) to reassess use before further refills are provided.

f. Plan to use the replacement for at least 1, and up to 6, months, with gradual withdrawal.

g. Patient selection includes consideration for the contraindications of pregnancy, breast-feeding, angina, arrhythmias, temporomandibular joint disease, dental problems, and such. However, if you are convinced that the patient will continue to use tobacco unless the replacement is prescribed, consider whether his or her health will be better or worse with the replacement, even though the contraindications are present (and get written informed consent).

h. *Guidelines for use of nicotine gum:*

   (1) Enough replacement per day to minimize withdrawal symptoms (about 1 stick for every 2 cigarettes).

   (2) Regular dosage rather than prn.

   (3) Only chew enough initially to break the surface, then maintain the gum against the cheek lining except to move it from time to time.

(4) Frequent chewing aggravates dental and jaw problems and releases nicotine to be swallowed, causing nausea.

(5) Avoid liquids while chewing the gum.

(6) Rinse mouth with water before inserting the gum.

4. **Other aids:** A wide variety of pharmacologic aids have been tried over the years; nearly all lack evidence of effectiveness.

   a. *Psychotropic medications:* Stimulants or relaxing-tranquilizing agents have been tried on the theory that they would replace the "beneficial" effects of nicotine (e.g., boredom, stress) or minimize withdrawal symptoms. There is no scientific evidence that these agents are effective in enhancement of quitting unless there are significant clinical problems requiring those medications.

   b. *Clonidine:* This adrenergic blocker has been reported effective in anecdotal and small case reports. However, a recent randomized controlled trial among family practice patients showed no effect on short-term quit rates.

   c. *Hypnosis and acupuncture:* These techniques may be helpful to some individuals, although they lack scientific proof of benefit. Nevertheless, practitioners with these skills may want to try them for the occasional patient unresponsive to other approaches. A major problem is that some smokers look to these therapies as a "magical" cure that will work despite their own low level of motivation to change. Such attitudes should be screened carefully before agreeing to try such approaches.

C. **Weight Control**

1. **Fear of weight gain:** A common reason for patients to put off quitting is fear that quitting tobacco will lead to weight gain. Women in particular are concerned about gaining weight, and it is not helpful to try to convince them otherwise. However, the physician should clarify the small amount of weight usually gained, the health effects of even a large weight gain vs. that of tobacco use, and the potential to minimize weight gain.

2. **Weight loss and tobacco cessation:** Do *not* advise those concerned with weight gain to avoid dealing with both weight and tobacco issues at the same time. Evidence supports that this is feasible. Such advice may only convince smokers that they should not quit.

3. **Normal weight gain:** Do tell them that a small weight gain often does occur; however, it can be controlled. Some reasons for weight gain are reduced metabolism after cessation of smoking and increased food intake secondary to improved taste function after quitting, using food to provide substitute oral gratification, and using food to deal with stress or withdrawal symptoms.

4. **Methods to minimize weight gain:** Reassure patients that most of the weight gain is usually gone within 6 to 12 months. A number of strategies will reduce the expected weight gain: monitoring food intake, using low-calorie substitutes for the oral habit (e.g., carrots, cel-

ery), starting an exercise program, and working with your nurse or some other simultaneous program of weight control.

D. Stress Management

As with weight control, you will need some acceptable response to those who have used tobacco as a way of coping with stress or who fear the stress associated with quitting. Responses that can be used include:

1. Reassurance that the stress of withdrawal should not last longer than 2 to 3 weeks.
2. Starting an exercise program at the same time has been helpful for many.
3. Your nurse (or other program) can teach relaxation exercises that may be as effective in calming stress.

E. Family and Social Issues

The use of tobacco by those around the patient and the degree of support for quitting by family and significant others are the most powerful aids or barriers to quitting. This issue is generally overlooked by physicians and formal smoking cessation programs. Support has been found to be the key to prolonged cessation. Strongly encourage quitters to involve those at home in whatever way is most helpful to quitting. If you or your staff are going to provide the problem-solving counseling needed by some quitters, include family members in at least some of these sessions.

V. Conclusion

A. Expected Results

If your system succeeds in delivering a supportive message to tobacco-using patients on at least 75% of their encounters with your practice, you should expect at least a 10% quit rate for those who have had at least two encounters over a 1-year period. At our pilot clinic site in Minnesota, the rate was 24%.

B. Effort Required

1. Remember that children and elderly have much lower tobacco use rates. Only one of every five to seven patients you see will be a current or recent user. At 2 to 3 minutes per patient and 25 patients per day, this program requires only about 10 minutes a day.
2. All tasks involved with starting and recording on Smoke Cards, pulling and refiling them, noting follow-up, and making phone calls should not take more than the same 10 minutes per day. Counseling will add time to this, but should be reimbursable at a rate sufficient to cover the rest of the system costs.
3. Once a practice has made the effort to set up and maintain this system, it is relatively easy to adapt it to other preventive services. (Contact the authors for ways to implement these ideas.)

C. Everybody's Doing It.

The National Cancer Institute and the American Cancer Society have formed a partnership to establish a Train-the-Trainer seminar that is being repeated all over the United States in hopes of multiplying the impact and getting as many physicians as possible to become systematic in addressing this problem. The American Academy of Family Physicians, some health care insurance carriers, and other organizations have similar programs. It has become clear that physicians and their office staffs are the most important people in this prevention campaign.

REFERENCES

Fielding JE: Smoking: Health effects and control. *N Engl J Med* 1985; 313:491–498, 555–561.

Fielding JE, Phenow KJ: Health effects of involuntary smoking. *N Engl J Med* 1988; 319:1452–1460.

Fiore MC, Novotny TE, Pierce JP: Methods used to quit smoking in the United States. *JAMA* 1990; 263:2760–2765.

US Preventive Services Task Force: Recommendations for smoking cessation counseling. *JAMA* 1988; 259:2882.

Gritz ER: Cigarette smoking: The need for action by health professionals. *Cancer* 1988; 38:194–212.

Kottke TE, Battista RN, DeFriese GH, et al: Attributes of successful smoking cessation interventions in medical practice. *JAMA* 1988; 259:2883–2889.

Kottke TE, Solberg LI, Brekke ML: Initiation and maintenance of patient behavioral change: What is the role of the physician? *J Gen Int Med* 1990; 5(S):562–567.

Solberg LI: Implementing a tobacco cessation program in clinical practice. *Med Times* 1988; 116:119–124.

Solberg LI, Maxwell PL, Kottke TE, et al: A systematic primary care office-based smoking cessation program. *J Fam Pract* 1990; 30:647–654.

CHAPTER 6

Prescription Drug Abuse and Chemically Dependent Patient

Timothy J. Ives, Pharm.D., M.P.H.

Psychoactive medications are one of the most frequently prescribed classes of prescription drugs. Clinicians use these medications for a wide range of clinical problems. Like other medications, they have an extensive array of adverse effects, which may include dependence and drug-seeking behavior. These drugs are particularly of potential harm to individuals who are at risk for or already have alcohol or drug disorders. The goals of this chapter are to:

1. Present guidelines for the use of psychoactive drugs in chemically dependent patients.
2. Increase the clinical awareness of practitioners regarding drug-seeking behavior.
3. Provide clinical guidelines for the appropriate use of these medications.

I. Use of Psychoactive Drugs in Chemically Dependent Persons

All the following medications or drugs have mood-altering effects and are considered hazardous to the maintenance of sobriety. Over-the-counter (OTC) combination products are of particular concern. For example, many OTC cold preparations contain alcohol or antihistamines. Therefore, when prescribing cough-cold remedies, specify single-agent products that contain no psychoactive drugs (e.g., acetaminophen or ibuprofen for pain, pseudoephedrine for congestion).

A. Alcohol

1. Sources of alcohol such as shaving lotion, cologne, mouthwash, and cough syrup may be used by alcoholic patients when the usual forms of alcohol are not available. Many drug products (e.g., elixirs, tinctures, syrups) may contain alcohol. Recovering patients should be advised to *check the label* of all OTC products for any mood-altering compounds such as alcohol or antihistamines.

B. Opioids

1. **Dextromethorphan,** found in various cough-control products (e.g., Robitussin DM, Formula 44, NyQuil) has been subject to abuse. The typical abuser is an adolescent.

2. *Propoxyphene* (e.g., Darvon, Darvocet) has abuse potential despite having a poor analgesic effect equivalent to only 650 mg aspirin or 400 mg ibuprofen. The strong mood-altering effects of this drug often are underestimated.

3. *Opioids* in combination with sedatives are of particular concern. For example, carisoprodol (Soma), a centrally acting muscle relaxant, in combination with codeine ("Soma Coma") is used on the streets as a substitute for heroin ("poor man's heroin") or other opioids when these are not available.

4. *Codeine* can be obtained without a prescription as a Schedule V combination product (e.g., Dimetane DC, Naldecon CX, Novahistine DH, Robitussin AC, other generic preparations). (See Table 6–1 for a description of drug schedules.) This may be problematic in the management of patients dependent on opioid agents.

C. **Antihistamines**

1. *Clinical effects:* Antihistamines with anticholinergic activity (e.g., chlorpheniramine, diphenhydramine) and anticholinergic agents such as benztropine (Cogentin) and trihexyphenidyl (Artane) may produce a mild euphoria, or at high doses a toxic psychosis characterized by confusion, disorientation, and hallucinations. At the least, antihistamines and benztropine can provide a sedative effect.

2. *Synergistic effects:* Patients who abuse or are chemically dependent on alcohol, barbiturates, cannabinoids, or opioids are at risk for relapse if they use drugs with anticholinergic properties. In addition to containing alcohol in many liquid preparations, many OTC cough-cold medications (e.g., Nytol, Sominex, Contac, Dristan,

TABLE 6–1.

Schedule of Controlled Substances

Schedule I	High abuse potential; no approved medical use		Heroin, LSD, THC, mescaline
Schedule II	High abuse potential; severe psychologic and/or physical dependence	Written prescription; no refill; 34-day supply; warning label	Opioid analgesics, amphetamines, methylphenidate, amobarbital, pentobarbital
Schedule III	Less abuse potential than drugs in Schedules I and II; moderate or low psychologic and/or physical dependence	Written or oral prescription; 6-month supply; 5 refills	Certain barbiturates, opioid preparations, and anabolic steroids
Schedule IV	Less abuse potential than Schedule III drugs	Same as Schedule III.	Benzodiazepines, phenobarbital
Schedule V	Very low abuse potential	OTC	Antitussive* and antidiarrheal preparations, buprenorphine

*There is abuse of codeine-containing cough syrups. As a result, some states have made these prescription drugs. Because the scheduling of a drug can take several years, the Comprehensive Crime Control Act of 1984 gave the US Attorney General emergency scheduling authority. A drug can be designated a controlled substance within 30 days after it has been determined that it is a hazard to the public health. As of Feb. 27, 1991, anabolic steroids have been reclassified as Schedule III controlled substances.
LSD = lysergic acid diethylamide, THC = tetrahydrocannabinol.

NyQuil) contain antihistamines with anticholinergic properties.

3. ***Withdrawal:*** Anticholinergic agents are associated with withdrawal. Symptoms may include anxiety, hallucinations, gastrointestinal discomfort, diaphoresis, or myalgias.

D. Stimulants

1. ***Clinical effects:*** Prescription or OTC medications used for weight control, nasal congestion, or colds can contain pseudoephedrine, phenylpropanolamine, ephedrine, or caffeine. These agents can cause stimulation, euphoria, paranoid psychosis, anxiety, and hypertensive crises.

2. **Fluoxetine** (Prozac): This newer antidepressant has a mild intrinsic stimulant effect in some patients. Its use should be avoided in chemically dependent patients until it has been properly evaluated in this population.

E. Sedatives

1. ***Controversial indications:*** Barbiturates, benzodiazepines, and synthetic sedatives have strong sedative and therefore mood-altering properties. While this class of drugs should be contraindicated in persons who are dependent or addicted, others would argue that they can be safely used to treat anxiety, acute stress reactions, panic attacks, and sleep disorders, but only when using a clear, time-limited contract.

2. ***Usefulness:*** The only clear indication for sedative drugs in this group is the management of acute withdrawal syndromes. Sedatives also should be stopped as soon as possible after detoxification, and never used for the treatment of post-withdrawal abstinence syndromes (see Chapter 3).

3. ***Absence of effectiveness in dependent persons:*** While the research findings on the effectiveness of sedatives for the treatment of anxiety, panic disorders, and sleep problems in chemically dependent persons is unclear, many of the contributors in this book have made the clinical observation that these drugs are ineffective in this population. *Sedatives often make sleep disorders worse, increase anxiety and panic disorders, and are associated with development of severe depression.*

4. ***Specific effects:*** The following sedative agents should be used with extreme caution in dependent or recovering persons, including those patients in full remission who may have stopped using alcohol or other drugs years earlier.

   a. **Barbiturates:** Phenobarbital, pentobarbital (Nembutal), secobarbital (Seconal), amobarbital (Amytal), and combination products containing butalbital (Fiorinal) or phenobarbital (Donnatal). Alcohol-dependent patients with a history of seizures may be at risk for relapse if phenobarbital is used, especially phenobarbital elixir (13.5% alcohol = 27 proof).

   b. **Benzodiazepines:** Alprazolam (Xanax), chlordiazepoxide (Librium), diazepam (Valium), flurazepam (Dalmane), lorazepam (Ativan), oxazepam (Serax), quazepam (Doral), temazepam (Restoril), estazolam (ProSom), and triazolam (Halcion). Alprazolam is one of the most common drugs used by dependent patients who enter treatment programs, and is associated with severe withdrawal reactions, including seizures.

c. **Synthetic sedatives:** Chloral hydrate (Noctec), ethylchlorvynol (Placidyl), glutethamide (Doriden), and methylprylon (Norludar). While these drugs are rarely seen in the drug screens of patients who enter treatment programs, there are few clinical indications for their use.

F. Drugs That Can Be Used in Recovering Patients

1. **Treatment methods:** Table 6–2 lists common medications that do not appear to have mood-altering properties, and nonpharmacologic approaches to treatment. These methods can be used with relative confidence and are not a threat to a recovering person's sobriety. As discussed in other chapters, nonpharmacologic approaches are underutilized in the treatment of headache, musculoskeletal problems, insomnia, anxiety, and depression. Exercise, in particular, is an effective therapy for many of these problems. Other adjuncts, such as acupuncture, biofeedback, or massage, should be considered.

2. **Recovery:** Recovering persons are anxious, irritable, and depressed in the early phases of recovery. While it is important for clinicians to recognize these symptoms and attempt to relieve these problems, nonpharmacologic methods are the preferred techniques for symptom relief. In addition, increasing the frequency of attendance at a 12-step program may be a most beneficial approach to management of these clinical issues.

II. Pain Management with Opioid Agents

There are a large number of indications for the use of opioids in clinical medicine. Opioids can block pain effectively, with few direct adverse effects. The use of morphine drips and self-administered methods have allowed patients in severe pain to be comfortable. However, these drugs are associated with physical dependence, and occasionally with addiction. This section presents clinical guidelines to minimize the development of opioid dependence.

A. General Guidelines for Care

1. **Physical dependence:** Many patients recovering from surgical procedures and those with metastatic disease may become physically dependent on opioid agents. Most, however, do not become addicted. Patients can develop physical dependence on opioids without becoming psychologically addicted.

2. **Placebos:** Placebos usually are not helpful in assessing pain, because many patients can obtain temporary relief from a placebo.

3. **Tapering dosage:** Be aware of the potential for the development

TABLE 6–2.

Management of Common Medical Problems

Cough

Benzonatate (Tessalon)

Dextromethorphan (in select cases)

Headache/musculoskeletal pain

Aspirin, acetaminophen, ibuprofen

Physical therapy: Application of heat or cold, or TENS (transcutaneous electrical nerve stimulation) units

If chronic pain occurs, the addition of a tricyclic antidepressant agent with a low degree of sedation (e.g., desipramine)

Hypertension

Calcium channel blockers (diltiazem, nicardipine, nifedipine, verapamil)

Hydrophilic β-blockers (e.g., atenolol)

Diuretics

Angiotensin converting enzyme (ACE) inhibitors (captopril, enalapril, fosinopril, lisinopril, or ramipril)

Prazosin

Insomnia

Meditation

Relaxation

Massage

Allergies/upper respiratory tract infection

Terfenadine (Seldane)

Astemizole (Hismanal)

Beclomethasone (Beconase or Vancenase Nasal Inhaler)

Gastrointestinal tract disorders

Antacids

Sucralfate (Carafate)

Ranitidine (Zantac)

Arthritis/pain (e.g., motor vehicle accident, myocardial infarction, surgery)

Acetaminophen

Aspirin

Ibuprofen or any nonsteroidal anti-inflammatory agent (Advil, Motrin)

If an opioid agent is indicated for moderate pain, use codeine, because of its lower potential for dependence

Morphine may be indicated for more severe pain

Direct discussion with the patient about concerns about the use of these agents is strongly encouraged

Anxiety

Buspirone (BuSpar)

Depression

Bupropion (Wellbutrin), desipramine (Norpramin), Fluoxetine (Prozac)

of physical dependence. Tapering the dose of the drug slowly will help prevent the onset of withdrawal symptoms and drug-seeking behavior. Rapid tapering may lead to increased use and visits to emergency departments.

4. ***Alternative therapies:*** Although opioid agents can be used in treatment of chronic pain, alternative analgesics and adjunctive agents (e.g., nonsteroidal anti-inflammatory drugs [NSAIDs], antide-

pressants, anticonvulsants) should be given a full therapeutic trial first.

5. ***Terminal patients:*** In the management of patients with terminal disease, the risk for developing tolerance is less problematic and should be an accepted as a consequence of patient care, both in a medical and societal context. Patients who are dying have a right to comfort and minimal pain even when physical dependence develops.

6. ***Pain control in an opioid-dependent patient:*** In the treatment of acute pain (e.g., dental procedures) in a chemically dependent or recovering person, a full assessment of the patient's analgesic needs based on the severity of symptoms is essential before prescribing any agent. The use of opioid analgesics must be carefully handled by monitoring the patient through periodic encounters and by communication with family members. Because of increased tolerance to opioids, the patient who is opioid dependent may require higher amounts of opioid analgesia to control acute pain.

B. **General Guidelines for Pharmacologic Treatment of Pain**

The following general guidelines should be followed in chemically dependent or recovering patients in pain:

1. ***Determine cause of pain:*** If possible, initially determine the cause of the pain, and have a clear goal when using opioid agents for the management of pain (e.g., intermittent use for acute exacerbation of chronic pain).

2. ***Individualize dosage:*** Select the route of administration that most appropriately matches the patient's condition. In most patients, the oral route is an acceptable route of administration.

3. ***Schedule:*** Administer analgesics on a regular schedule if pain persists throughout the day and night.

4. ***Pharmacology:*** Become familiar with the dosage range, pharmacokinetics, and duration of action of the most commonly prescribed opioid agents and NSAIDs.

5. ***Avoid mixing agents:*** In patients exhibiting tolerance, avoid using mixed agonist-antagonist agents (e.g., pentazocine [Talwin], butorphanol [Stadol], or buprenorphine [Buprenex]), which may induce withdrawal.

6. ***Opioid Craving:*** *Any* opioid agent (pure agonist or agonist-antagonist) has the capacity to induce opioid craving.

7. **Avoid long-term use of meperidine.** Accumulation of normeperidine, a metabolite of meperidine, may cause central nervous system stimulant actions (e.g., seizures, myoclonus, tremors).

8. ***Adverse effects:*** The most common adverse effects of the opioid agents are sedation, constipation, nausea, vomiting, and respiratory depression.

9. ***Drug combinations:*** Drugs that enhance analgesia through differ-

ent mechanisms of action are recommended. An example of this combination is use of an opioid agent (central site of action) with an NSAID (peripheral site of action).

10. *Antidepressants:* Consider the use of tricyclic antidepressants (e.g., amitriptyline, nortriptyline, imipramine, or desipramine) or anticonvulsants (e.g., phenytoin, carbamazepine, sodium valproate, or clonazepam) as adjuncts for neurologic pain.

C. **Use of Opioid Agents in Persons Known or Suspected of Having a Current Alcohol or Drug Problem**

1. *Drug history:* No treatment, apart from emergency pharmacotherapy, should be given without first finding out what drugs the patient previously had taken or is currently receiving from other physicians.

2. *Confirm diagnosis:* A diagnosis of alcohol or drug dependence should be confirmed by an appropriate history and physical examination, a review of available medical records, and a Breathalizer or screening test drug. A family member may be very helpful in sorting out the extent of the patient's dependence.

3. *Opioid agents for pain relief:* When opioid agents are prescribed for pain relief, only one physician should prescribe. The prescription should be filled at a single pharmacy known to the physician.

4. *Chart labels:* Labeling charts of all chemically dependent or recovering patients may be helpful for other clinicians or emergency department personnel not familiar with the patient. A discrete red sticker placed on an inside corner of the chart may be useful.

5. *Physician alert:* Patients need to be encouraged to tell physicians, dentists, pharmacists, or any other pertinent health care providers that they are chemically dependent.

III. **Methods to Minimize Development of Drug Dependence**

A. **Prescription Drug Abuse**

1. *Health issues:* Prescription medications have been involved in approximately 60% of drug-related emergency department visits and 70% of all drug-related deaths. In 1987, eight of the 20 most frequently noted drugs associated with drug abuse and dependence were commonly prescribed medications. These include diazepam (Valium), alprazolam (Xanax), codeine (Tylenol with Codeine), propoxyphene (Darvon, Darvocet), and triazolam (Halcion).

B. **Physician Recognition of Drug-Seeking Behavior**

1. *Patient behavior:* Recognizing drug-seeking and other manipulative behavior by patients is a challenge. Examples of drug-seeking behaviors include frequently switching pharmacies, falsifying the amounts of drugs taken, or going to several different physicians for the purpose of obtaining drugs. Drug-seeking may stem from causes ranging from emotional dependence to drug dealing.

2. *Family member interview:* Methods to recognize drug-seeking behavior include asking family members or caretakers to confirm

suspicions about the use of psychoactive medications or illicit drugs.

3. ***Street-wise knowledge:*** One of the best "educators" for prescribers on the subject of chemical dependency and drug-seeking behavior is a recovering patient. Recovering patients in the community can provide invaluable insight into local drug procurement and current popular drugs.

C. **Clinical Characteristics of Drug-Seeking Patients**

1. ***Mental health issues:*** Patients may have evidence of poor impulse control (e.g., eating, gambling, sex), personality disorders, or chronic medical or psychiatric disorders.

2. ***Lack of response:*** The treatment course may be marked by a poor response to standard therapies or unexpected improvement, exacerbations, and fluctuations.

3. ***Prescription loss:*** Patients may use an excessive amount of drugs, necessitating earlier return visits to the prescriber, or frequently report losing the prescription vial.

4. ***New patients:*** Patients may "Doctor shop," especially those patients with multiple complaints. Care needs to be taken in prescribing psychoactive drugs for new patients. Old prescription vials with different physicians or pharmacies in different cities may be a tip-off.

5. ***Requests for specific drug:*** Patients, either well known or unknown, may request a specific psychoactive drug by name. These patients also attempt to eliminate all other forms of treatment that do not include psychoactive agents.

6. ***Friday phone calls:*** Patients may call for medication refills, especially controlled substances, late on Friday afternoon or on weekends, when a colleague who is unfamiliar with the patient is on call.

7. ***Clinical presentation:*** Specific clinical complaints that should make a practitioner cautious include:
   a. Chronic disabilities, especially chronic pain syndrome.
   b. Insomnia, anxiety, or depression.
   c. Self-induced or self-inflicted illness (e.g., multiple cigarette burns, purging). Careful examination of a patient's forearms for signs of self-abuse is important.
   d. History of chronic nephrolithiasis in the absence of radiologic diagnosis.
   e. Atypical headache.
   f. Unexplained tremor, elevated blood pressure, tachycardia, weight loss.
   g. Perceived change in personality.
   h. Sudden and unexplained memory loss or mental confusion.
   i. Deterioration of level of function (particularly in elderly).
   j. Family concern about a change in the patient's behavior.

D. **Working with Drug-Seeking Patients**

1. ***Patient health:*** Ultimately, practitioners will be required to assertively adhere to what they believe is the best interest of the patient,

despite demands. Patients who demand and plead for increasing doses of benzodiazepines or opioids may need to taper off all psychoactive medications, even if it means the patient may choose to leave the practice. In addition to the risk of addiction, patients can, and do, overdose on drugs they received from well-intentioned clinicians.

2. ***Balancing act:*** The practitioner must balance the patient's distress (or apparent distress) with safe prescribing. For example, patients who become dependent on propoxyphene (Darvon) for management of chronic work-related myalgias may need to continue taking the drug to financially support themselves. If their dependence increases, a decision may then need to be made regarding withdrawal and abstinence.

3. ***Underlying problems:*** Patient distress may provide an indication of the importance of the drug itself to those patients. Confronting patients with this information may motivate them to look at their drug use and obtain appropriate counseling. While drug dependence is the most frequent cause, family dysfunction, physical abuse or other extreme environmental stresses may be present.

4. ***Telephone policy:*** The development of a policy that includes not prescribing controlled substances by telephone, especially after normal clinic hours, is useful. Sometimes it may be necessary to refuse the patient's request.

E. **General Guidelines for Prescribing Psychoactive Drugs in New Patients**

1. ***Assessment:*** Examine the patient, make a diagnosis, and determine if pharmacotherapy is appropriate. Determine who has been caring for this patient previously, and find out what has been prescribed or used in treatment in the past and for what indication(s). Contract or request records with written consent. Find out what drugs, either prescribed or illicit, the patient is taking or has taken, either recently or in the distant past (including OTC, particularly in the elderly).

2. ***Prescriptions for new patients:*** In emergency situations, prescribe no more than 1 day's supply of a drug and arrange for a return visit. This will allow time to gather more information. Validate a new patient's identity by requesting proper identification, such as a driver's license containing a photograph. If possible, consider alternate medications with little or no psychoactive properties and addiction potential (see Table 6–1). If psychoactive drugs are prescribed for a new patient in a nonemergency situation, no more than 1 week's supply, with no refills, should be written.

3. ***Treatment goals:*** Set realistic therapeutic goals in a plan that is agreed to and understood by both the patient and the physician (e.g., reasons for medication, expected duration of use and/or indications for stopping.)

IV. Medication History Skills

The following steps can be covered when evaluating medication or illicit drug use in any patient. Specific alcohol and illicit drug questions are not included here, but in other chapters. While most clinicians will not have the time to conduct the comprehensive medication history discussed here, they may choose to focus on a specific set of questions for a given patient. Another strategy is to identify one of their clinical staff to conduct the interview.

A. Prescription Medications Currently Being Taken
1. What *prescription* drugs currently (i.e., within the last 2 weeks) are being taken, and for what purpose?
2. Review the dosage and the specific dosage regimen.
3. Review the duration of time the patient has been taking the medication.
4. Assess patient knowledge and compliance. Some medications, especially antihypertensive agents (e.g., clonidine, propranolol, atenolol, labetalol), and sedatives are used blunt the withdrawal syndrome seen with the abuse of drugs such as alcohol or opioid agents.

B. Over-the-Counter Medication
1. Questions about OTC drug use can be based on specific organ systems or symptoms.
2. One approach includes starting at the head and working downward. The questions may focus on cough-cold preparations, which can include antihistamines, sympathomimetic agents, opioids, and alcohol (in the vehicle). Example of specific questions are:
   a. Do you ever use anything for a cold, cough, upset stomach, pain?
   b. Which products do you use?
   c. How often do you use these products?
3. Ask about prescription (or OTC) agents *previously* used.

C. Home Remedies
1. One of the primary ingredients in most home remedies is alcohol. Questions include *why, how often,* and *in what quantities* these remedies are used.

V. Guidelines For Prescribing

A. Reducing Risk
1. *Storage issues:* Practitioners can take any or all the following measures to reduce the risk of being targeted as a source of illicitly obtained drugs of abuse.
   a. If opioid agents are administered in the office, patients should not know where these agents are stored, to avoid potential problems with theft.
   b. Do not stock large quantities of drugs of potential abuse, especially samples from pharmaceutical companies.
   c. Do not store abusable drugs near sinks, toilets, or bathrooms where they can be taken without staff or provider knowledge.

B. Prescriptions
1. *Refills:* All prescriptions should indicate whether, how often, and

for how long it may be refilled. Medication refills should be authorized by only one prescriber on a predetermined schedule, based on guidelines set by both the physician and the patient. By law, Schedule II prescriptions (e.g., Percodan) cannot be refilled.

2. ***Limited quantity:*** No greater quantity of a controlled substance should be prescribed than is needed until the next scheduled office visit.

   a. All prescriptions should be written so as to prevent any potential alterations by the patient or others. When indicating the prescribed amounts of the drug, always use both written and numerical notations, for example, "Dispense 10 (ten) tablets," rather than, "Dispense 10 tablets," which can be altered to read: "100 tablets."

   b. Have the patient *return to the office* for additional prescriptions. Telephone orders do not allow the physician to (re)assess the patient's present need for the medication.

3. ***Prescription blanks:*** Prescription pads and forms should be kept locked up and out of sight. Preprinted prescription pads with the name of a proprietary (trade brand) product should be avoided. Presigned prescription blanks or those with the prescriber's DEA registration number printed on them should not be used. Also, when preprinted institutional (hospital) prescription blanks are used, the prescriber should print his or her name, address, and DEA registration number on each one.

4. ***Duplicate prescriptions:*** Frequently patients receive duplicate prescriptions, and one prescriber does not know what another has written. A call to the pharmacy where the patient's medications are filled provides a method for determining if other prescriptions are being filled for the same drugs from other physicians.

   a. With the advent of computerized patient records in many pharmacies, pharmacists are alert for polypharmacy and multiple-physician utilization.

   b. If there is any doubt, pharmacists should routinely confirm all Schedule II prescriptions, especially hydromorphone (Dilaudid), with the prescribing physician.

5. ***Prescription components:*** When prescribing for a chemically dependent or recovering patient, the major components of concern are as follows:

   a. ***Date:*** Especially important for prescribing Schedule II medications, which must be filled within 72 hours after writing. Schedule III and IV medications cannot be filled or refilled 6 months after the date the prescription was written.

   b. ***Patient name and address:*** Required on all Schedule II prescriptions. More important, this will avoid potential confusion, especially in families with several people taking medications.

   c. ***Refill information:*** Should be noted on every prescription written. Schedule II drugs *cannot* be refilled. Schedule III and IV prescriptions cannot be refilled more than five times within 6 months. Unless you wish to specify refills, always circle or write "Do Not Refill," to prevent forgeries for extra refills.

d. ***Signature:*** The practitioner's personal signature (last name in full) is required, preferably in ink, as well as the DEA registration number and practice address. It is possible to have the DEA registration number and practice address preprinted on the prescription blank.

BIBLIOGRAPHY

Bewley TH: Prescribing psychoactive drugs to addicts. *Br Med J* 1980; 281:497–498.

Mulry JT, Stockhoff J: Drug use in the chemically dependent. *Postgrad Med* 1988; 83:279–290.

Ogar B: Prescription drug abuse and dependence in clinical practice. *South Med J* 1987; 80:1153–1159.

Principles of Analgesic Use in the Treatment of Acute Pain and Chronic Cancer Pain, ed 2. Skokie, Ill, American Pain Society, 1989.

Stock CJ: Safe use of codeine in the recovering alcoholic or addict. *DICP Ann Pharmacother* 1991; 25:49–53.

Wesson DR, Smith DE: Prescription drug abuse: Patient, physician, and cultural responsibilities. *West J Med* 1990; 152:613–616.

Wilford BB: Abuse of prescription drugs. *West J Med* 1990; 152:609–612.

CHAPTER 7

Drug Testing: Clinical and Workplace Issues

Greg Phelps, M.D., M.P.H.

Patricia Field, Ph.D.

Drug testing has become an acknowledged component in the prevention and treatment of alcohol and drug disorders. Physicians are recognizing the value of drug testing for confirmation of substance use in both outpatient and inpatient medical settings to overcome the frequent underreporting of drug use. Drug testing also has become an essential therapeutic component of aftercare programs, especially with recovering persons who work in settings where their drug use may be hazardous to the public. Many industries have implemented pre-employment and random employee screening to increase productivity and decrease liability associated with problematic employee drug use. Screening for illicit drug use is practiced in more than 80% of Fortune 500 companies.

Physicians who may have limited training in drug testing often are asked to supervise these programs, particularly in smaller industries that do not maintain their own medical departments. Although not all physicians will supervise drug testing, they will probably treat patients employed in industries that use drug screening. The goal of this chapter is to (1) review the essentials of drug testing, (2) inform providers about drug testing procedures, (3) provide information on specimen collection and testing procedures, and (4) discuss technical legal and medical issues associated with drug testing.

I. Drug Testing
   A. Role of Drug Testing in Clinical Medicine
      Drug tests are used for the detection of psychoactive substances in many clinical situations. Testing includes screening and diagnosis in outpatient clinics, acute care settings, and inpatient treatment.
      1. *Use in clinical care:* Although ethical and legal issues limit the use of drug testing for screening purposes, the procedure is being used increasingly where benefits outweigh the risk. An example is the use of drug testing in pregnant women. The rationale for drug testing is based on the potential effect of unrecognized drug use on

maternal and fetal well-being. This information can be used to confront a patient and assist her in maintaining sobriety. Drug testing also is an essential part of the care of patients managed in acute care settings, such as emergency departments or intensive care units. Common clinical problems in which drug testing is helpful include:

a. Altered mental status.

b. Acute psychotic symptoms, especially paranoia and hallucinations.

c. Seizures.

d. Cardiac arrhythmias.

e. Chest pain.

f. Evidence of withdrawal.

g. Signs and symptoms of drug intoxication.

h. Suspected drug overdose.

i. Serious traumatic injuries.

j. Unexplained injury in the workplace.

2. ***Routine admission orders:*** Some argue that a urine drug screen should be performed in all patients admitted to a hospital. Others recommend at least a blood alcohol test in patients admitted because of burns, falls, and accidents, because these injuries are highly associated with alcohol use. Since many patients who currently enter treatment programs are polydrug users, drug testing often reveals drug use that has not been reported by the patient.

B. Accuracy of Current Tests

The predictive value of a single test or multiple tests depends on the sensitivity and specificity of the test and on the prevalence of the drug in the population being tested. While the accuracy of a screening test by thin-layer chromatography or immunoassay may exceed 80%, combined screening and confirmatory testing, using appropriately selected test methods, can correctly yield true positive results more than 99% of the time. Achieving the highest accuracy and specificity requires a confirmation test using a different technology than the screening test. Confirmatory tests impose additional expense.

1. ***Class specificity of tests:*** Many screening tests (e.g., radioimmunoassay [RIA] and electroimmunoassay [EIA]) are *class* specific rather than *compound* specific. It is recommended that any positive tests be confirmed on the same sample using another method, to identify the specific drug (e.g., codeine vs. morphine vs. hydrocodone). Immunoassay tests should not be confirmed by the same or another type of immunoassay but by a test using a different analytical principle. The most accurate confirmation testing is performed by gas chromatography with mass spectroscopy (GC-MS).

2. ***Reasons for false negative results:*** The high false negative rate reported for drug testing is not a reflection of the tests themselves but of multiple other factors, which can include adulteration of the urine specimen by the subject, high cutoff points set by the laboratory or regulatory agencies, and the short half-life of most illicit drugs.

3. All drug testing must meet the following criteria using the mnemonic *"able"*:

a. Verif*able:* The specimen belongs to the patient and is not adulterated.

b. Confirm*able:* Positive screening test results have been confirmed using a different method of analysis (e.g., immunoassay confirmed by chromatography, not by a different brand of immunoassay).

c. Reli*able:* The technology of each test is reliable and valid.

C. Limitations of Drug Testing

Several issues restrict the usefulness of urine drug testing. Detection of different substances depends on the amount used, the time since last use, and the pharmacokinetics of the drug. For example, cocaine has a very short half-life, often disappearing from detection in as little as 2 days. On the other hand, daily marijuana smokers may have a positive test up to several weeks after the last dose. Other issues include the selection of threshold or cutoff points for a positive test.

1. ***Threshold:*** Threshold is the minimum concentration a laboratory agrees to report as positive.

a. None of these tests simply screen for the presence or absence of a drug. They are designed to give a quantitative or semiquantitative result based on specific cutoff values or concentrations.

b. A high threshold is acceptable for drug overdose admissions and in testing for severe chronic drug abuse. A moderate threshold has been set for federal employee drug testing programs, to have uniform standards nationwide and to reduce claims of passive exposure. A sensitive threshold should be chosen for those interested in detecting any drug use (e.g., drug-abuse treatment programs, prison work-release programs).

c. To minimize the chance of a false positive result, the cutoff levels may allow a large proportion of patients who have detectable levels to be reported as negative. For example, the federal employee drug testing cutoff value for marijuana of 100 ng/dL will fail to report 40% of those who have measurable urine levels of marijuana. This high cutoff effectively eliminates the detection of passive or secondary inhalation.

D. Laboratory Test Selection

It is important to have a clear understanding of which drugs are included in a laboratory's testing procedures and to select a test "menu" that includes the drugs of interest in the population being tested.

1. ***Drugs usually not included:*** Several important drugs, including alcohol, LSD, methadone, meperidine, fentanyl, benzodiazepines, and barbiturates, are not included in many standard urine drug "screens."

2. ***Drugs mandated in federal programs:*** Federal employee drug testing programs, on which many employee drug testing programs are based, are limited to testing for amphetamines, cocaine, cannabinoids, phencyclidine (PCP), and opioids. The rationale is that these drugs almost always are "illicit" and that to test for other drugs that

have legitimate uses could be considered an invasion of privacy, which could jeopardize the whole testing program. However, it is important to note that these five classes of drug are not necessarily those most likely to be abused by many segments of the working population.

3. ***Sociocultural variation in drug use:*** Reported patterns of drug use and abuse vary by socioeconomic status. Upper- and middle-class professionals and managers are more likely to abuse alcohol, cocaine, and benzodiazepines rather than PCP and intravenous opioids.

4. ***Variation by geographic region:*** Drug abuse patterns vary by geographic region. In 1990, methamphetamine was becoming more prevalent than cocaine on the West Coast but was still uncommon in the Midwest. PCP was more common in northern Virginia and southern California than in other areas of the United States. Abuse of solvents and inhalants was more common in the Southwest (e.g., Texas) than in other areas.

5. ***Variation by accessibility and habit:*** It is important to be aware of drug use among professional groups. For example, health professionals have access to narcotic analgesics (e.g., meperidine). Anesthesiologists who become drug dependent may choose drugs such as fentanyl. Dentists have access to and may habituate to gases used for dental anesthesia, such as nitrous oxide. None of these commonly are part of drug-testing panels.

E. **Screening Tests**

Screening tests are designed to be either simple, inexpensive, sensitive, and suitable for detecting a wide range of abused drugs (e.g., TLC; see section II B, below) or selective for a *class* of such drugs (e.g., immunoassay; see section II A, below).

F. **Confirmatory Tests**

1. ***Confirmation with a test using a different analytical principle:*** Since the predictive value of any simple test is too low for the certainty needed for drug tests, it is *essential* that positive screening test results be confirmed by a more specific test using a different analytical process. This is a basic principle of forensic toxicology and is essential for creating a record that will stand up to scrutiny (e.g., for legal purposes). Confirmation also is necessary to identify a specific drug. For example, two different compounds that might cross react with the same antibody in *any* immunoassay should be further examined with a chromatographic procedure (e.g., gas chromatography).

a. *Case examples:*

A patient admitted to the emergency room with symptoms of opiate overdose responds to naloxone (Narcan) treatment. An immunoassay for opiates in the urine is positive and confirms the clinical impression. If identification and quantification of the specific opiate is not requested by the treating physician, and if the result is not likely to be of interest to an employer, police agency, or insurance company (i.e., if no accident or arrest has occurred), then the screening test alone may be sufficient.

A patient is being counseled for drug abuse in an inpatient drug-free program. Her urine drug screening test is positive for cocaine. She admits cocaine use. If this information is kept confidential between the patient and treatment staff and is used only within the treatment setting, there is no need for a confirmatory test. The patient's admission of drug use "confirms" the test results.

A patient has a history of amphetamine abuse. An immunoassay screening test for the class amphetamines is positive. The patient insists he inadvertently took only a single dose of an over-the-counter cold medication containing pseudoephedrine. A confirmatory test is essential to determine which drug is present. It is possible that a quantitative, confirmatory test will give information that will help to answer the question of whether the amount present is consistent with one dose of cold medication. However, interpretation based on urine drug concentrations generally is discouraged because urine drug concentrations give little or no information about how much drug was used or when.

II. Testing Methods
A. Immunoassays

Immunoassays are based on antibody recognition of drugs or drug classes (e.g., opioids, amphetamines) and are designed for a specific purpose, such as therapeutic drug monitoring.

1. ***Overview of general immunoassay methods:*** These tests are based on antibody recognition of drugs or chemical substances. Immunoassays designed for specific purposes, such as therapeutic drug monitoring, can be compound specific and provide quantitative results. Immunoassays designed for "screening" generally are class specific (e.g., opioids, amphetamines, cannabinoids). This means that members of a class (e.g., morphine, codeine, dextromethorphan) may cross react with different affinities for the antibody. Therefore results are only semiquantitative, and confirmation is essential to identify the specific member of the class and to rule out unrelated compounds that may cross react to interfere with the immunoassay.

   a. *Advantages:* Immunoassay is inexpensive, convenient, and sensitive.

   b. *Disadvantages:* Problems are primarily related to interference of substances that can produce false positive results (e.g., poppy seeds, diet pills, cold medications). Adulteration techniques can be used by subjects to produce false positive or false negative tests (e.g., adding bleach to urine).

2. ***Radioimmunoassay (RIA):*** This was the first type of immunoassay developed. An antibody to a specific drug or drug class is mixed with a small quantity of a radiolabeled drug and with a small portion of the specimen. If the specimen is drug free, all of the radiolabeled drug binds with the antibody and little or no radioactivity stays in the supernatant fluid (after centrifugation, filtration, or binding to an

antibody-coated tube). If the drug is present in the patient specimen, it competes with the radiolabeled drug for antibody binding sites. Thus radioactivity is increased in the supernatant and decreased in the precipitate or coated tube. The amount of radioactivity in either the supernatant or precipitate can be counted with a gamma counter.

   a. ***Advantages:*** Radioimmunoassays are available for a wide variety of drugs and drug classes. The method is readily adaptable to automation for processing large quantities of drug tests.

   b. ***Disadvantages:*** The principal drawbacks are equipment costs, licensing, and disposal of radioactive materials.

3. ***Enzyme Multiplied Immunoassay Techniques (EIA or EMIT*):*** EMIT tests use an enzyme rather than a radiolabel on the drug moiety, which competes with any drug present in the patient sample for antibody binding sites. Enzyme molecules that are antibody bound are sterically hindered from reacting. Enzyme molecules that are free, due to drugs in the patient's specimen competing for the antibody binding sites, are able to react with indicator molecules, causing absorbancy changes that are readily measured in a spectrophotometer.

   a. ***Advantages:*** No centrifugation or separation step is necessary. No radioactive materials are used. EMIT tests are available for a wide variety of drugs. The test is convenient to use and only requires equipment readily available in clinical laboratories. EMIT technology can also be automated for medium and large numbers of samples.

   b. ***Disadvantages:*** The system is more susceptible to interference and deliberate tampering than other methods. There have been problems with cross-reactivity.

4. ***Fluorescence polarization immunoassay tests (FPIA):*** FPIA uses a fluorescent label on the drug moiety that competes with any drug present in the patient sample for antibody binding sites. Labeled molecules that are antibody bound are sterically hindered from freely rotating in the light path and are more readily detectable in plane-polarized light. The test results are semiquantitative.

   a. ***Advantages:*** FPIA requires less specimen manipulation than EIA or RIA. The specialized equipment needed is usually available from the manufacturer on a "reagent rental" (no capital outlay) basis. It is very convenient for small workloads.

   b. ***Disadvantages:*** FPIA tends to be more costly than RIA or EIA. FPIA requires specialized equipment available only from the reagent manufacturer (Abbott Laboratories, North Chicago, Ill.). The manufacturer requires that FPIA instrument operators take a 1-week training course in Texas. FPIA is less readily automated than RIA and EIA for large workloads.

---

*EMIT is a trademark of SYVA Corp.

B. Chromatographic Techniques

1. ***Thin-Layer Chromatography (TLC):*** This method is more cost effective than immunoassay for broad-spectrum drug screening (e.g., emergency departments, drug use detection and treatment programs), because it can detect many drugs in one test. Immunoassay requires a series of drug-specific or drug class tests, and no immunoassay methods are available for some drugs detectable by TLC. Unlike immunoassays, TLC does not rely on antigen-antibody functioning. Rather, a pH-dependent extract is purified, then separated by chromatographic procedures. Drugs are qualitatively evaluated by visual comparison with standards after being sprayed with dyes or chemical reagents.

   a. ***Advantages:*** The test is less costly than the battery of immunoassays required to cover a comparable range of drugs. Numerous drugs can be tested simultaneously. Adulterants are less likely to interfere with the test.

   b. ***Disadvantages:*** Subjective analysis of the results must be performed by trained technicians. Turnaround time for emergencies can be as slow as 3 to 4 hours. For many drugs, TLC is not as reliable as immunoassays.

2. ***Gas Chromatography (GC):*** This technology uses a heated, absorbent column to separate specimen components flowing under pressure in a gas. A flame ionization or nitrogen phosphorus–sensitive detector at the end of the column records the presence of eluting drugs. The drug is identified by its unique retention time on the column. The peak area can give very accurate quantitative information.

   a. ***Advantages:*** Toxicology screening performed competently on GC can detect far more drugs in a single test than any immunoassay or TLC. For some confirmations, the GC retention time provides more information about the drug identification than mass spectrometry. GC also is an excellent quantitative method.

   b. ***Disadvantages:*** GC requires considerable investment in equipment, personnel, and training. Therefore it is more costly and is not used often for routine screening.

3. **Liquid Chromatography** *(HPLC):* HPLC is similar to GC, but uses flowing solvents as a propellant at normal or moderately elevated temperatures.

   a. ***Advantages:*** HPLC is preferable for thermolabile compounds.

   b. ***Disadvantages:*** HPLC is more expensive and time consuming than GC.

C. Gas Chromatography–Mass Spectrometry

Mass spectrometry (GC-MS) is known as the "gold standard" because of its capability to identify a molecule based on its fragments. This is the only test acceptable for confirmation in federal employee drug testing programs. This technology is essentially two tests in one: a gas chromatograph separates the components based on retention time, then the mass spectrometer identifies the individual ionic forms.

1. *Advantages:* In any drug testing likely to be challenged in court, this is the preferred confirmatory test. In a review of defensibility of testing technology, Hoyt and colleagues found EIA plus GC-MS or RIA plus GC-MS to be the best test combinations.
2. *Disadvantages:* The test is not suitable for screening specimens (except possibly in overdose or emergency situations) because of its greater cost and time required per specimen. The equipment is costly and requires highly trained technologists.

D. New Technologies

1. *Hair analysis:* Hair analysis currently is not accepted in the forensic community for drug abuse screening (e.g., pre-employment testing), but there is growing interest regarding its medical value (e.g., use during pregnancy).
2. *Meconium:* Drug testing in newborn meconium has been used increasingly by many centers to detect illicit drug use in perinatal patients.
   a. Testing is done by the Meconium Testing Center, in Detroit. Currently the Center tests for cocaine, opioids, cannabinoids, and amphetamines using EMIT. Clinicians can call 313-745-4331 for information about sending specimens.
   b. A number of studies have been conducted at Wayne State University in Detroit, that suggest meconium assay is 4 to 10 times as sensitive as urine drug testing. The prevalence of positive drug screens at Hutzel Hospital (Detroit) ranges from 8% to 10% by urine screening and 30% to 40% by meconium screening. One unreported study in a suburban hospital reported a 1% prevalence by urine and a 10% prevalence by meconium.
   c. Current studies also are studying the differences in meconium positivity on days 1, 2, or 3 after birth. It is likely that day 1 meconium reflects drug use in an earlier point in time than meconium expelled on day 3. This test may give us information on drug use as far back as 2 months prior to delivery in the third trimester.

E. Specimens: Drugs Normally Tested for When a Drug Screen is Ordered; Limitations and Problems with Specific Drugs and Drug Classes

1. *Tests performed on blood or serum:*
   a. Blood tests are used primarily in acute care settings (e.g., emergency room, intensive care unit). In cases of intoxication, overdose, or accident, tests for alcohol, CNS depressants, and stimulants are valuable as an adjunct to treatment and provide useful information regarding any observed impairment.
   b. Quantitative blood drug concentrations can help in evaluating prognosis, particularly if performed sequentially over the first several hours or days after admission. Blood drug concentrations provide useful information on the issue of whether a person may have been impaired at a particular time.
   c. Blood drug concentrations are especially useful when testing "for

cause" (e.g., after an accident or other incident). However, rapid clearance of most psychoactive drugs makes blood less useful than urine for the detection of chronic or intermittent drug use or abuse.

2. ***Tests commonly performed on urine or blood:***
   a. *Sedatives:*
      (1) *Alcohol:* Enzyme and colorimetric tests specific for ethanol are readily available. GC separates, identifies, and quantitates the various alcohols.
      (2) *Benzodiazepines:* Immunoassays do not distinguish among the benzodiazepines. GC methods are capable of detecting, identifying, and quantitating the benzodiazepines.
      (3) *Barbiturates:* Immunoassay screening tests are commonly available but do not distinguish short-acting from long-acting barbiturates. GC or LC methods are used to detect, identify, and quantitate barbiturates.
   b. *Stimulants:* Immunoassay, TLC, and GS-MS commonly are used to detect these classes of drugs.
      (1) *Cocaine, crack, freebase:* Immunoassays for cocaine are specific. Tests do not distinguish among the various forms of cocaine once it has been used. GC-MS is used for confirmation and quantitation.
      (2) *Amphetamines:* Many substances (e.g., cold medications, diet medications) are capable of causing false positive amphetamine immunoassay results. The need for a confirmatory test is especially important. Care must be used with confirmatory tests. Ephedrine can cause a false positive GC-MS result under certain circumstances. For phentermine, the GC retention time is more important than the GC-MS fragmentation pattern in differentiating it from methamphetamine.
   c. *Opioids and synthetic narcotic analogs:* Immunoassay or TLC is used to screen, and GC or GC-MS to confirm results.
      (1) *Methadone:* Requires a specific immunoassay.
      (2) *Heroin, morphine, codeine:* Readily cross react with the common "opioid" assays.
      (3) *Propoxyphene* (Darvon): Cross reacts with the common "opioid" assays only if present in very high concentrations.
      (4) *Meperidine* (Demerol): Cross reacts with the common "opioid" assays only if present in very high concentrations.
      (5) *Fentanyl and fentanyl analogs:* Requires a specific immunoassay; difficult to confirm.
   d. *Designer drugs:* Designer drugs are, by definition, often one step ahead of drug detection systems. Immunoassays seldom are available. Broad-spectrum GC and GC-MS techniques are more likely to detect designer drugs.
   e. *Hallucinogens:* Immunoassay, TLC, and GC-MS commonly are used to detect these drugs.

(1) *Cannabinoids:* Immunoassays for cannabinoids are quite specific. TLC and GC-MS are useful for confirmation.

(2) *Phencyclidine* (PCP): Immunoassay is specific. GC or GC-MS are used to confirm.

(3) *LSD:* Requires a specific assay not commonly available. Confirmation is difficult.

(4) *Mescaline:* No immunoassay available. Difficult to detect by chromatographic techniques.

   f. *Inhalants:* Headspace GC is used for analysis. Confirmation may be difficult. For the best chance of detection of volatile substance abuse, a blood specimen should be analyzed shortly after collection and collected to fill or nearly fill a tightly sealed container shortly after use.

   g. *Anabolic steroids:* GC-MS is used for screening and for confirmation. The detection and interpretation of steroid abuse is difficult and complex.

F. Duration and Cutoff Limits for Urine Testing

Table 7–1 summarizes National Institute of Drug Abuse (NIDA) federal employee drug screening levels, confirmation levels, and the duration the drug can be expected to appear after last use in the urine at these concentrations (Council on Scientific Affairs, 1987; McCunney, 1989; Osterloth and Becker, 1990; Schwartz, 1988).

G. Positive Results for Reasons Other Than Drug Abuse

1. ***Poppy seeds:*** Poppy seeds may give a false positive test for opioids. A confirmatory test for a key metabolite of heroin, 6-O-acetylmorphine can rule out heroin abuse.

2. ***Vicks TGB:*** Vicks Inhaler contains trace amounts of an isomer of methamphetamine that may yield a positive, *confirmed* amphetamine test. The GC-MS profiles of both isomers are identical.

TABLE 7–1.

Parameters for Urine Drug Screening*

Drug	NIDA Cutoff Screen (ng/mL)	√ Confirmation	Duration in Urine (days)
Marijuana:		√	
Single Use	100	15	<.7
Chronic Use	100	15	<30
Cocaine	300	150	<3
Opiates	300	300	<2
PCP	25	25	<7
Amphetamines	1000	500	<2
Alcohol			<1
Barbiturates			<2
Phenobarbital			<7
Methadone			<4
Methaqualone			<7

*Values represent drug level cutoffs, as described by NIDA. Individual physicians or laboratories may choose to use different cutoff levels. Cutoff levels have not been established for alcohol, barbiturates, methadone, and methaqualone.

3. ***Diet aids:*** Phentermine, available over the counter as a diet aid, gives false positive immunoassay results for amphetamines. It is important to look at the GC retention time to discriminate phentermine from methamphetamine, because the GC-MS profiles are identical.
4. ***Medical indications:*** Cocaine still is used therapeutically in medical and dental settings for ear, nose, and throat procedures and occasionally as a local anesthetic for repairing lacerations. It is important to question patients about prescription and OTC medications as well as recent procedures.

H. **Proficiency Testing and Laboratory Certification Programs**
1. ***Proficiency testing programs*** for a wide variety of drugs in blood, serum, and urine specimens are available from the College of American Pathologists, the American Association for Clinical Chemistry, and other regulatory and voluntary agencies, such as the State of New York and the California Association of Toxicologists. Clients wishing assurance of laboratory competence should ask the laboratory for evidence of successful participation in external proficiency testing programs covering the drugs of interest to the client.
2. ***Certification programs:*** The two national urine drug testing laboratory certification programs have several unique features. The National Laboratory Certification Program (NLCP) was created under the auspices of the National Institute of Drug Abuse to regulate laboratories performing drug tests in federal employees. The College of American Pathologists and American Association for Clinical Chemistry Forensic Urine Drug Testing (FUDT) program is similar.

III. **Drug Testing in Ambulatory Care Setting**
A. **General Legal Guidelines**
1. ***Consent procedures:*** When performing a drug test, carefully record the method used to obtain informed consent from the patient. If consent is not obtained, document the rationale in the patient's medical record. For example, if parents request a drug test in a minor without the adolescent's knowledge, the parents must sign a consent form. Providers need to determine a method to record and file the information consistent with state and employer regulations.
2. ***Medical vs. legal indications:*** If performing the test for a medical reason without a patient's consent, documentation may help if there is any legal action taken by the patient or if a judge requests the information for some action against the patient. Situations in which drug tests are ordered for medical reasons include:
   a. Concern about drug withdrawal in a patient with altered mental status.
   b. Comatose emergency room patient who may have overdosed on alcohol or other drugs.
   c. Patient with exacerbation of a major psychiatric disorder.

B. **Guidelines for Collecting Urine Samples for Drug Testing**
1. ***Direct observation:*** The most tamper-resistant method is one in which the patient voids while being observed.

2. ***Voiding problems:*** Some patients find themselves unable to void in the presence of an observer; "shy bladder" syndrome is remarkably prevalent. Schedule patients at least 2 hours before the clinic closing time. The patient should not be permitted to leave the clinic and have the opportunity to void elsewhere during this time.

3. ***Unobserved collection:*** Many programs prefer unobserved specimen collection in a room with no plumbing and with "dress precautions" (e.g., strip to a gown) to prevent specimens being carried in. In these programs, an observed specimen collection occurs only if there is reason to believe that the individual has tampered with a previous specimen. Keep toilet water dyed blue with a commercial sanitizing agent to discourage diluting specimens with toilet water.

4. ***Sink precautions:*** If a sink is present in the room where the urine is collected, have a plumber disconnect the hot tap water or have someone stay in the bathroom to observe, to prevent dilution of the specimen with warm water.

5. ***Chain of custody:*** Maintaining a proper "paper trail" (chain of custody) also is important. This trail should not only confirm the person of origin but should be designed to negate claims of specimen tampering. Urine containers should not be passed through window slots, but should be carried out by the patient and handed to the staff. While in the patient's presence the staff member should draw out the required volume, approximately 60 mL, and place the urine in the container. The container should then be sealed with a tamper-proof seal. The seal should contain the patient's name and signature. The person receiving the specimen also should sign his or her name on the seal, certifying that proper procedures were followed.

6. ***Testing for adulteration:*** The remainder of the sample should be tested for adulteration. There are a number of recommended programs to ensure an undiluted or unadulterated specimen. Table 7–2 lists the pH, relative density, and appearance of urines that have been adulterated. These include:

   a. Evaluation of temperature. The specimen should be within 2° of body temperature immediately after voiding; specimens carried next to the skin (armpit, between the legs, in socks) will not pass this test.

   b. Specific gravity should be >1.010. Urine foaming tests are advisable to rule out certain contaminants (e.g., soaps).

   c. Color and odor of the specimen should be appropriate. Many adulterants can be readily detected by their characteristic odor (e.g., vinegar, bleach).

C. Methods Patients Use to Fool Drug Testing Procedure

1. Sending a look-alike family member to take the test.
2. Hiding vials of "clean urine" in places such as the vagina or rectum.
3. Hiding bottles of urine in clothing, such as socks.
4. Instilling someone else's urine into the bladder.

TABLE 7–2.
pH, Relative Density, and Appearance of Adulterated Urine*

Adulterant	pH	Relative Density	Appearance
Unadulterated urine	5–7	1.005–1.030	
NaCl			
25–75 gm/L	5.5	1.035	
Liquid Drano			
12–23 mL/L	6–7	1.018–1.019	
42–125 mL/L	8–11	1.020–1.028	
Liquid hand soap			
12–42 mL/L	6–7	1.018–1.021	Cloudy to turbid
107 mL/L	8	1.033	Cloudy to turbid
Visine			
107–125 mL/L	7	1.016–1.018	
Vinegar			
125 mL/L	4	1.018	
Golden Seal tea			
15–30 g/L	6	1.022–1.024	
Water		<1005	
Temperature			
°C	32.5–37.5		
°F	90.5–99.8		

*From Mikkelson SL, Ash KO: *Clin Chem* 1988; 34:2333–2336.

    5. Adulterants for immunoassay tests include: lemon juice, vinegar, chlorine bleach, Golden Seal tea, table salt, Liquid Drano, Visine eyedrops, soap containing lemon juice
    6. Diluting the urine by drinking large amounts of water.
    7. Ingesting diuretics such as furosemide.

IV. Workplace Drug Testing
A. Background
1. ***Prevalence of alcohol problems:*** Lewis and Cooper (1989) showed in a study of 173 occupationally related deaths in Texas that the principal drug involved in fatal worksite accidents was alcohol. At autopsy, 23 (13.3%) of the decedents had detectable amounts of alcohol; only one had traces of illicit drugs. The average smoker costs his or her employer $500 to $3,000 in lost time secondary to smoking-related illness each year. As workplaces become drug-free and employers begin to request that their employees not smoke during working hours, testing for the nicotine metabolite cotinine may become part of the drug testing procedure.

B. Three Common Employee Testing Procedures
1. ***Pre-employment screening:***
    a. Most lawyers believe pre-employment screening involves the least legal hazard, because if the applicant fails, he or she is not being discharged from a job already held.
2. ***Probable cause:***
    a. Involves injury or unusual behavior at the place of employment.

b. A chronic problem seen in these cases is the "wrong person" getting tested. For example, in a forklift accident the forklift operator is the one most likely to be impaired and cause the accident; the person hit, however, is the one most likely to be tested.

c. Probable cause may also include staggering, slurring of speech, or bizarre behavior.

d. The concept of probable cause for drug testing must be applied carefully. If there is evidence of race or gender discrimination or no well-reasoned arguable cause for testing, the employee may sue for wrongful discharge.

3. *Random testing:*

a. Random testing must be truly random, not falling repeatedly on suspected users.

b. Random testing must be unannounced to be effective. Employees should be selected early in the day and immediately sent for testing.

c. Once approached, employees should not be allowed to leave or return the next day, pleading lateness of hour or lack of urine.

C. **Does Drug Testing in the Workplace Reduce Alcohol and Drug Use?**

Needleman and Romberg have demonstrated a measurable drop in positive urine samples as the duration of a testing program increases. In two separate studies in which urine was tested, in which the employer was not informed of the results, there was no correlation between a positive test and the likelihood of being dismissed within the first year. The rate of positive drug tests in the military has dropped dramatically since random drug testing was instituted. While it is difficult to assess whether legal drugs, such as alcohol, simply were substituted for illicit drugs, these programs do have an effect on illicit drug use.

V. **Legal Issues: Legal Precedents and Consent Issues**

A. **Background**

1. *Importance to clinicians:* Drug testing has been challenged on many legal fronts. Because the specimen may be the single piece of evidence in adversarial proceedings, it is imperative that the practicing physician have a clear understanding of the legal issues, including negligence, invasion of privacy, defamation, battery, and emotional distress. Most legal arguments involve the Fourth Amendment (unreasonable search) and the Fifth Amendment (right not to incriminate oneself). Other constitutional arguments have revolved around implied rights to privacy and equal nondiscriminatory protection of the Fourteenth Amendment.

2. *Justification for random testing programs:* In general, safety issues have justified random drug testing of public employees, particularly those in safety-sensitive positions, such as railroad engineers and air traffic controllers. Private industry has greater testing leeway, unless barred by local statute.

3. *Accuracy issues:* Although drug testing must be accurate beyond a

reasonable doubt, the law does not require the tests to be perfect (California vs. Trombetta; in Osterloth and Becker, 1990). Generally the courts have asked that confirmatory tests have 95% or better accuracy and that they have general scientific acceptance (Frye vs. United States; in Osterloth and Becker, 1990).

4. ***Tests determine use only:*** It must be remembered that a urine drug test is merely a test for a specific substance in the urine. It is an index of exposure. A positive urine test says nothing about impairment, addiction, or intoxication (except alcohol) or whether the chemical found is appropriate for the patient. Blood specimens are preferred if impairment (on the job, in an accident, or as a cause of emergency room admission) is an issue. The courts generally have upheld urine drug testing programs when it can be shown that:

   a. The drug testing program is appropriate for the workplace.

   b. In either random testing or for an articulated cause, selection of an individual to be tested is fair and impartial.

B. Consent Procedures in Workplace

1. ***Guidelines:*** The cornerstone to any industrial drug testing procedure is a well-considered, well-publicized policy in place before the first specimen is acquired. The policy should be nondiscriminatory and clearly state procedures and consequences. Confidentiality is imperative. The issue of pre-employment screening should be discussed before the employee has accepted the position. In random or "for cause" testing, the policy must be spelled out well before the need arises.

2. ***Records:*** Employees being tested should sign a consent for urine drug testing as well as permission for the laboratory and medical review officer to communicate with the employer. It is essential to retain all records. Positive specimens should be frozen and retained. Record keeping in the area of substance abuse is under the most stringent federal guidelines.

3. ***Labeling of specimen:*** Specimens should be clearly labeled with the date and patient identification and secured with a tamper-resistant seal at the time of collection. The seal should not be broken until the specimen is analyzed. A clear and written chain of custody should accompany every specimen to and from the laboratory. Failure to seal the specimen and document a chain of custody raises doubts about the specimen's integrity. This will invalidate results in the federal employee drug testing program and in the view of many courts of law.

C. Consent Procedures in Medical Settings

1. ***Informed consent:*** In medical practice (except for the emergency room) consent is problematic. The practitioner is asking for permission to test for a drug that the patient may deny having used. Experts are split on the issue. Two recent articles in *Western Journal of Medicine* clearly demonstrate this split.

   a. Jessup (1990) states, "Legal experts in addiction medicine advocate that urine testing of pregnant women should become a consensual procedure."

    b. Hogerman and colleagues (1990) state, "Physicians should not feel obligated to obtain any special consent from pregnant patients for doing urine toxicology beyond their usual general consent for diagnosis and treatment."

2. ***Legal vs. medical consent:*** Blood alcohol and other drug tests in emergency rooms may be ordered for medical or legal purposes. Some laboratories ask clients to designate whether specimens are "legal," implying a written consent with chain of custody and documentation, or "medical," implying routine collection and handling, which allows the possibility of legal "impeachment" or nonusability of the results for legal purposes. For legal specimens, the tamper-resistant seal and chain of custody forms are recommended. For medical specimens, the simple use of a tamper-resistant seal will circumvent many questions if the result is later needed by the courts. *Failure to use a seal or document the chain is not a protection from courts, attorneys, or subpoenas.*

3. ***Unexpected issues:*** Drug screens in patients who are injured on the job can provide useful information, but can also complicate Worker's Compensation claims. For example, in one memorable case an employee was found unconscious on the workroom floor. A standard medical workup for the person who has lost consciousness was undertaken. Four illicit substances were detected in an otherwise normal evaluation. The employer refused to allow the employee to return to work until a diagnosis was given. The patient refused to allow disclosure. The lack of policy dealing with workplace drug abuse by the industry formed a major part of a very uncomfortable standoff.

D. Federal Laws

As a result of a spectacular train wreck in which urine tests of the engineer and crew were positive for marijuana, the federal government adopted a series of regulations. These regulations constitute the first federal standards for drug testing, with mandated cutoff levels. Some of these regulations include the following programs.

1. ***Federal workers:*** All transportation workers must undergo pre-employment and random employee drug testing.

2. ***Laboratory standardization:*** Laboratories undertaking Department of Transportation urine testing must be inspected and approved by the National Laboratory Certification Program of NIDA.

3. ***Medical review officer:*** The role of the medical review officer (MRO) was established. At present this officer is required to be a licensed physician experienced in the field of substance abuse. MROs serve as a buffer between the laboratory and the employer. They evaluate the accuracy of negative and, more important, positive results. Figure 7–1 presents a flow chart used by the MRO to determine the appropriate action when a positive test is reported.

4. ***Drugs tested for:*** The NIDA mandates testing for five specific

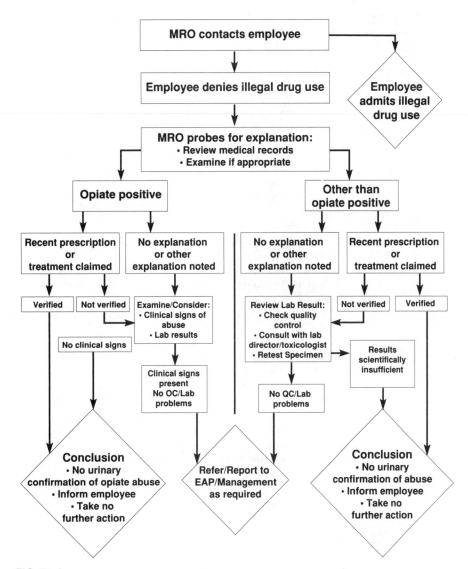

FIG 7–1.
The primary responsibility of the medical care review officer (MRO) is to review and interpret positive test results obtained in drug testing programs. A positive result does not automatically identify an employee as an illegal drug user. This flow chart describes a method MROs can use to determine appropriate action. (From National Institute on Drug Abuse: *Medical Review Officer Manual: A Guide to Evaluating Urine Drug Analysis.* Washington, DC, Department of Health and Human Services, 1988.)

classes of drugs: PCP, marijuana, cocaine, opiates, and amphetamines. NIDA also mandates that specimens be collected in such fashion as to assure their validity. This is a particular and unique problem for the MRO in that it forces him or her into the unfamiliar role of supervisor and enforcer.

REFERENCES

Bailey DN: Drug screening in an unconventional matrix: Hair analysis. *JAMA* 1989; 262:3331.

Council on Scientific Affairs: Scientific issues in drug testing. *JAMA* 1987; 257:3110–3114.

Hawks RL, Chiang CN (eds): Urine testing for drugs of abuse. NIDA Research Monograph 73, 121 pp. DHHS Publication (ADDM) 84-1481. Superintendent of Documents, Washington, DC, US Government Printing Office, 1986.

Hogerman G, Wilson CA, et al: *West J Med* 1990; May:559–564.

Jessup M: The treatment of perinatal addiction: Identification, intervention and advocacy. *West J Med* 1990; May:554–558.

Lewis RJ, Cooper S: Alcohol, other drugs, and fatal work-related injuries. *J Occup Med* 1989; Jan: 23–28.

McCunney RJ: Drug testing: Technical complications of a complex social issue. *Am J Ind Med* 1989; 15:589–600.

Mikkelson SL, Ash KO: Adulterants causing false negatives in illicit drug testing. *Clin Chem* 1988; 34:2333–2336.

Morland J, Bugge A, Skuterud B, et al: Cannabinoids in blood and urine after passive inhalation of *Cannabis* smoke. *J Forensic Sci* 1985; 30:997–1002.

National Institute on Drug Abuse: *Medical Review Officer Manual: A Guide to Evaluating Urine Drug Analysis.* Washington, DC, Department of Health and Human Services, 1988.

Needleman SB, Romberg RW: Comparison of drug abuse in different military populations. *J Forensic Sci* 1989; 34:848–857.

Osterloth JD, Becker CE: Chemical dependency and drug abuse in the workplace. *West J Med* 1990; May:506–513.

Ritz D: Expert testimony and urine drug screening. Addiction Medicine: State of the Art, San Diego, Nov 9–11, 1989.

Schuckit MA: Drug testing: What it can and cannot do. *Drug Abuse Alcoholism Newsletter* 1990; 19:1–3.

Schwartz RH: Urine testing in the detection of drugs of abuse. *Arch Intern Med* 1988; 148:2407–2412.

Schwartz RH, Hawks RL: Laboratory detection of marijuana use. *JAMA* 1985; 254:788–792.

Walsh JM, Yohay SC: Drug and alcohol abuse in the workplace: A guide to the issues. Washington, DC, National Foundation for the Study of Equal Employment Policy, 1987, 149 pp.

PART THREE

Treatment of Medical Problems Associated With Alcohol and Drug Disorders

Adverse Health Effects and Medical Complications of Alcohol, Nicotine, and Drug Use

Jeffrey Sikkink, M.D., M.S.P.H.

Michael Fleming, M.D., M.P.H.

The medical complications of alcohol, nicotine, and illicit drug abuse are numerous and account for a significant proportion of a clinician's practice. Chronic tobacco use is the primary cause of adult respiratory problems and is an important cause for the clinical syndromes associated with atherosclerotic disease of the coronary, cerebral, and peripheral vessels. It has been clearly demonstrated that multiple types of cancer are strongly associated with tobacco use. Heavy alcohol use is the most common cause of secondary hypertension. Suicide attempts with prescription drugs are increasing, and intravenous drug abuse is an important risk factor for human immunodeficiency virus (HIV) infection.

The number of deaths each year that can be attributed to tobacco, alcohol, or drug abuse exceeds 500,000. Tobacco use is associated with an estimated 380,000 deaths per year (>1,000/day); of this number, about 115,000 are due to coronary heart disease, 27,000 to cerebrovascular accident (CVA) 136,000 to cancer, 60,000 to chronic obstructive pulmonary disease, and 50,000 to other causes. Alcohol abuse accounts for approximately 98,000 deaths annually. Motor vehicle accidents, alcohol-related homicides, alcoholic cirrhosis, suicide, and non−motor vehicle accidents account for most of these deaths. The mortality from drug use continues to escalate with the acquired immune deficiency syndrome (AIDS) epidemic, trauma, acute vascular events, and suicide.

This chapter discusses the adverse health effects of alcohol, tobacco, and illicit drugs, with focus on the management of the common medical complications associated with these drugs. The chapter is not a comprehensive review of all the medical problems, but presents common clinical effects encountered in ambulatory care settings. Additional sources of clinical information are listed in the Appendix.

I. Alcohol

The medical effects of alcohol include hypertension, arrhythmias, cardiomyopathy, chronic abdominal pain, chronic diarrhea, liver dysfunction, sexual problems, hematopoietic changes, and central nervous system effects. Figure 8–1 illustrates the prevalence of medical effects attributable to excess alcohol consumption.

A. Cardiovascular System
    1. *Hypertension:*
        a. *Overview:* In the last decade, studies have demonstrated that heavy alcohol use is related to increased blood pressure and is the most common form of secondary hypertension. While some heavy drinkers have a pattern of labile hypertension associated with acute withdrawal, the majority of heavy drinkers with hypertension have a 24-hour diurnal pattern of blood pressure elevation similar to those with non-alcohol-induced hypertension. Nine cross-sectional and six prospective studies document this association. Overall results suggest that alcohol consumption of three or more drinks per day is associated with increased blood pressure. However, some studies have demonstrated increased risk for hypertension with as little as one drink per day.
        b. *Prevalence:* Studies suggest that the prevalence of hypertension attributable to excess alcohol consumption varies from 5% to 11%. The prevalence is probably higher in men than in women, because of increased alcohol consumption in men.
        c. *Mechanism:* Two hypotheses for the mechanism of alcohol-induced hypertension have been tested. The first suggests that in some hypertensive alcoholic patients acute withdrawal develops as

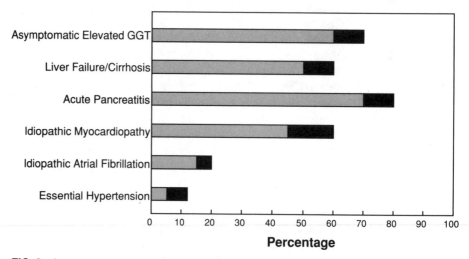

FIG 8–1.
Black bars represent frequency of alcohol use as a causative factor in six conditions. Data were obtained from multiple sources, including discussion with a number of clinicians with expertise in addiction medicine, and standard reference texts, and represent a best estimate; precise figures are not known.

the blood alcohol level falls. Since many patients try to abstain before they see their physician, blood pressure is temporarily elevated in the physician's office. The second proposes a direct pressor effect of alcohol through an unknown mechanism. Studies that have examined levels of renin, angiotensin, norepinephrine, and cortisol have been inconclusive.

d. *Alcohol reduction in heavy drinkers with hypertension:* Several small uncontrolled studies have shown that reduced alcohol consumption in hypertensive patients can lower blood pressure in a relatively short time. Reduction or cessation of alcohol use in heavy drinkers (more than three drinks per day) may reduce the need for antihypertensive medication or reduce the blood pressure to the normal range. A therapeutic trial of abstinence may help to determine which heavy drinkers will benefit from cessation of alcohol use. This maneuver also may serve to directly educate the patient that alcohol reduction can help to control blood pressure.

e. *Alcohol reduction in light drinkers with hypertension:* The amount of alcohol that is safe in hypertensive patients who are light drinkers (one to two drinks per occasion, less than 12 per week) has not been determined. Factors to consider are a personal history of ischemic heart disease, a history of binge drinking, or a family history of CVA. Patients with any of these risk factors should abstain from alcohol use.

2. ***Cardiac arrhythmias:***
   a. *Atrial arrhythmias* associated with chronic alcohol use include supraventricular tachycardia, atrial fibrillation, and atrial flutter. Fifteen percent to 20% of idiopathic cases of atrial fibrillation may be induced by chronic alcohol use.
   b. *Ventricular tachycardia* has not been widely reported. However, there is an increased incidence of unexplained sudden death in alcoholics, which may be due to ventricular arrhythmias.
   c. *Treatment:* In the presence of continued alcohol use, treatment of these arrhythmias may be more resistant to cardioversion, digitalis, or calcium channel blocking agents. Patients with recurrent or refractory atrial arrhythmias should be carefully questioned about alcohol use.

3. ***Ischemic heart disease:***
   a. *Epidemiology:* Multiple epidemiologic studies have demonstrated a U-shaped relationship between alcohol use and ischemic heart disease (IHD). Abstainers have a rate of IHD similar to that of heavy drinkers. Persons who drink one to two drinks per day have significantly lower rates. A major methodologic problem with these studies, however, is the inclusion of recovering alcoholics in the abstinent group.
   b. *Mechanism:* The mechanism of this protective effect is unknown,

but may be related to elevated high-density lipoprotein (HDL_2), apolipoprotein A1 levels, and clotting changes seen in heavy drinkers. The amount of alcohol needed to elevate lipoprotein levels has not been determined.

   c. *Protective effect:* There have been no clinical trials to test the possible protective effect of daily alcohol use. The potential risk of daily alcohol use outweighs any potential reduction in rates of IHD.

4. ***Cardiomyopathy:***

   a. *Toxicity:* Alcohol is known to have toxic effects on both skeletal and cardiac muscle; the association is dose related. Numerous studies have shown that alcohol can depress cardiac contractility and lead to cardiomyopathy. Approximately half of all patients with idiopathic cardiomyopathy are alcohol dependent.

   b. *Recovery:* Although the clinical signs and symptoms of idiopathic and alcohol-induced cardiomyopathy are similar, alcohol-induced cardiopathy has a better prognosis if patients are able to stop drinking. About 30% of alcohol-induced cardiomyopathy is reversible with abstinence.

5. ***Hemorrhagic stroke:***

   a. Ongoing clinical studies indicate a higher than normal incidence of hemorrhagic CVA and intracranial bleeding among heavy users of alcohol. Many cases occur after prolonged binge drinking, especially in younger patients.

   b. *Mechanisms:* The primary hypotheses for the cause of alcohol-associated CVA are direct blood pressure and coagulation effects. Patients who reduce their alcohol intake have been found to have a lower risk of hemorrhagic stroke.

B. Gastrointestinal System

Alcohol abuse is associated with esophagitis, undifferentiated abdominal pain, gastritis, hepatitis, pancreatitis, and chronic diarrhea. It is important to consider occult alcohol use in the differential diagnosis in every patient with abdominal pain. Alcohol-induced effects on the upper intestinal tract are a frequent cause of undifferentiated abdominal pain.

1. ***Esophageal dysfunction:***

   a. *Clinical problems:* Alcohol frequently is either the primary etiologic factor or is one of multiple causal factors associated with esophageal dysfunction. This drug is associated with the development of esophageal reflux, Barrett's esophagus, traumatic rupture of the esophagus, and Mallory-Weiss tears. Compared with nonalcoholic nonsmokers, alcohol-dependent patients who smoke have a 10-fold risk for cancer of the esophagus.

   b. *Level of use:* There is little change in esophageal function at lower blood alcohol concentrations. At higher blood alcohol concentrations there is decreased peristalsis and decreased lower esophageal sphincter pressure.

2. ***Gastric and duodenal effects:***
   a. *Clinical issues:* Heavy alcohol use can disrupt the gastric mucosal barrier and cause acute gastritis. While these effects are most often seen in chronic heavy drinkers, they can occur after moderate or short-term alcohol use. Clinical symptoms include acute epigastric pain that is relieved with antacids. The diagnosis may not be clear, since many patients have normal endoscopic examinations and upper gastrointestinal radiographs. Significant bleeding is uncommon, and the stool usually is negative for occult blood. The diagnosis is made by excluding other diagnoses, such as ulcer, esophageal dysfunction, pancreatitis, cholecystitis, and hepatitis.
   b. *Peptic ulcer disease:* Alcohol is not thought to play a role in the pathogenesis of peptic ulcer disease. Unlike acute and chronic gastritis, peptic ulcer disease is not more common in alcoholics. Nevertheless, alcohol exacerbates the clinical course and severity of ulcer symptoms.
   c. *Treatment:* The treatment of gastrointestinal disease is similar across alcohol-dependent and nonalcoholic groups, with one added provision. Alcohol-dependent patients may try to minimize the connection between gastrointestinal ailments and alcohol intake. Pointing out the association between gastrointestinal disease and alcohol ingestion can greatly increase the likelihood of abstinence.

3. ***Pancreatitis:***
   a. *Prevalence:* Alcohol abuse is the most common cause of both acute and chronic pancreatitis in the United States. While pancreatitis has been known to occur after a single episode of heavy alcohol use, prolonged heavy drinking is common in most cases. Approximately 5% of alcohol-dependent patients will develop pancreatitis.
   b. *Clinical characteristics:*
      (1) *Acute alcoholic pancreatitis:* Acute alcoholic pancreatitis is characterized by the abrupt onset of abdominal pain, nausea, vomiting, and increased levels of serum or urine pancreatic enzymes. While most attacks are not fatal, hemorrhagic pancreatitis can develop and lead to shock, renal failure, respiratory failure, and death. The mortality rate in hemorrhagic pancreatitis exceeds 50%. Two thirds of patients with recurrent alcoholic pancreatitis develop chronic pancreatitis.
      (2) *Chronic alcoholic pancreatitis:* Chronic pancreatitis is characterized by recurrent or persistent abdominal pain and evidence of functional pancreatic insufficiency. Steatorrhea and diabetes are the most common findings. Cessation of drinking will slow but not necessarily stop the development of chronic pancreatitis or pseudocyst formation.
   c. *Treatment:*
      (1) *Acute pancreatitis:*

(a) Management usually involves intravenous fluid replacement; bowel rest, often with nasogastric suction; and narcotic pain medication.

(b) Outpatient management may be possible in very mild cases without severe pain, vomiting, and dehydration. No reported clinical trials have examined the effectiveness and safety of outpatient treatment.

(c) Patients should be informed that the only successful treatment for alcoholic pancreatitis is complete abstinence from alcohol.

(2) *Chronic pancreatitis:* Chronic pancreatitis is treated by replacing those endocrine and exocrine deficiencies that result from pancreatic insufficiency.

(a) Patients in whom diabetes develops are given insulin. Pancreatic enzyme supplements may be necessary to treat malabsorption. Pancreatic enzyme capsules contain lipase, amylase, and proteases. The average lipase dose is 4,000 to 24,000 U with each meal and snack.

(b) Patients should be monitored for the development of pancreatic pseudocyst. Patients with pseudocyst who develop infection, ascites, or pleural effusions may benefit from surgical drainage.

(c) Nonnarcotic methods for pain relief, such as anti-inflammatory drugs, tricyclic antidepressants, exercise, relaxation techniques, and self-hypnosis, are the preferred methods. Chapter 6 provides guidelines on the use of opioids in alcohol-dependent patients.

(d) Endoscopic retrograde pancreatography may be indicated in patients with unremitting pain. Patients with proximal stenotic lesions may be candidates for sphincteroplasty. Dilated ducts may be treated with a pancreatojejunostomy. Patients with nontreatable lesions and chronic pain may be considered for a pancreatic resection.

4. ***Chronic diarrhea and malabsorption:***

a. *Symptoms:* Many alcoholics have chronic diarrhea as a result of malabsorption in the small intestine. The major symptoms are frequent loose stools. Fatty stools or the presence of mucus does not occur unless chronic pancreatitis or other gastrointestinal diseases have developed. The rectal fissures and pruritis ani frequently associated with heavy drinking probably are related to the chronic diarrhea.

b. *Mechanism:* The mechanism is related to structural and functional changes in the small intestine. The intestinal mucosa has flattened villi, and digestive enzymes often are decreased. These changes often are reversible after a period of abstinence. Patients with severe malnutrition may require either total parenteral nutrition or very slow increments of tube feedings so that the intestine can be reacclimated to normal absorption.

c. *Clinical evaluation:* Assessment includes evaluation for infectious agents (e.g., *Shigella, Salmonella, Campylobacter, Giardia,* and other parasites) and food intolerance (e.g., lactose intolerance). A small bowel follow-through examination and colonoscopy are indicated to exclude other diagnoses. Patients should be evaluated for severity of nutritional deprivation (albumin, total protein, hemoglobin, folate, magnesium).

d. *Treatment:* Treatment is based on replacing essential vitamins and electrolytes, slowing transit time with loperamide (Imodium) or diphenoxylate (Lomotil), and abstinence from all alcoholic beverages.

(1) Folate is replaced with 1 mg/day orally for 4 to 5 weeks.

(2) Magnesium (Mg^{2+}) replacement often is necessary in malnourished alcohol-dependent patients. Magnesium deficiency manifests itself as muscle weakness, CNS depression, confusion, and convulsions. Ventricular arrhythmias have been reported in Mg^{2+}-deficient patients.

(3) Patients with severe magnesium deficiency (serum magnesium <1.0 mEq/L) or symptoms (positive Chvostek sign or asterixis) should receive replacement therapy with 1 gm (2 mL) magnesium sulfate intravenously or intramuscularly every 4 hours until the serum magnesium level is greater than 1.0 mEg/L. Patients should be monitored carefully during the replacement phase for signs of toxicity (decreased deep tendon reflexes).

(4) Less severe deficiencies may be replaced with oral magnesium. Magnesium Plus is a new magnesium protein complex that is not associated with diarrhea and rapidly replaces deficient magnesium stores.

5. ***Liver disease:***

At least three distinct clinical patterns of liver problems are associated with chronic alcohol use. Since the majority of heavy drinkers have no symptoms when seen in ambulatory care settings, the traditional categories of liver problems based on histologic changes are not useful. The categories discussed are based on clinical observations. Group 1 is composed of patients who have elevated liver function but no symptoms. Group 2 comprises patients with abnormal liver function, elevated bilirubin levels, and enlarged tender liver. Group 3 includes patients with symptoms of liver failure likely to progress to liver failure and death. Table 8–1 summarizes the characteristics of alcohol-related liver disease.

a. *Asymptomatic dysfunction:* The clinical symptom is elevated

TABLE 8–1.

Characteristics of Alcohol-Related Liver Disease

Disease	Characteristics	Significance
Asymptomatic dysfunction	Elevated GGT (rarely more than 3 times normal); other liver function tests usually normal	Resolves to normal within 3 mo if drinking stopped
Alcoholic hepatitis	Elevated liver function tests; AST usually higher than ALT; present in 15%–20% of heavy drinkers	Probable precursor of cirrhosis
Cirrhosis	Clinical picture of liver failure—encephalopathy, edema; ascites, decreased albumin; increased bilirubin, prolonged PT; occurs in 8%–10% of heavy drinkers	Increased risk of death from liver failure or related complications; stopping drinking helps prognosis

ALT = alanine aminotransferase, AST = aspartate aminotransferase, GGT = γ-glutamyltransferase, PT = prothrombin time.

γ-glutamyltransferase (GGT) in the absence of other clinical signs. GGT rarely is more than three times normal in this category. The liver may be palpable and enlarged but usually is nontender. Twenty percent to 30% of heavy drinkers (three or more drinks per day) have elevated GGT levels. The mechanism of hepatocellular injury is unknown.

(1) Patients who have elevated liver function should not use alcohol. The elevated GGT should return to normal levels in 3 months. While persistent elevation is not uncommon, other etiologic factors should be considered if the elevation persists beyond 6 months. These factors include viral hepatitis, drug reactions, Wilson's disease, hemachromatosis, liver tumors, and liver abscess. Minimal examination includes abdominal ultrasound, viral antibody tests (A, B, and C), and determination ceruloplasmin and ferritin levels.

b. *Alcoholic hepatitis:* Hepatitis occurs in 15% to 20% of heavy drinkers. The clinical picture includes elevated liver function, right upper quadrant tenderness, and hepatomegaly. The bilirubin level usually is elevated. This is a severe problem, and liver failure frequently develops if alcohol use continues. Supportive treatment, fluids, and rest are helpful in debilitated patients. Abstinent patients should have liver enzyme levels observed over time to document improvement.

c. *Liver failure and alcoholic cirrhosis:* The clinical symptoms are those of liver failure, and include encephalopathy, peripheral edema, ascites, hypoalbuminemia, hyperbilirubinemia, anemia, and hypothrombinemia. The disease has a wide variation in its clinical course. It is difficult to predict liver disease progression in an individual patient. Clinical and laboratory findings do not always predict the severity of the pathologic findings. The disease progresses in some patients despite abstinence.

(1) *Epidemiology:* In the United States, cirrhosis is the ninth most common cause of death. Mortality rates have fallen over the past three decades to 12 in 100,000 persons. Rates in eastern Europe have doubled over the past four decades, and exceed 30 in 100,000 persons. Alcoholic cirrhosis occurs in about 8% to 10% of chronic heavy drinkers.

(2) *Threshold:* The minimal amount of alcohol needed to induce liver failure may be as low as three drinks per day in susceptible individuals. Women with a family history of alcoholic cirrhosis may be at greatest risk. Heavy drinkers do not have to meet criteria for alcohol dependence to develop cirrhosis. The variability in susceptibility is not yet understood, but probably is a result of genetic and nutritional differences.

(3) *Mechanism:* Multiple hypotheses have been proposed to explain the development of alcoholic cirrhosis. First, alcohol alters cell membrane function and phospholipid metabolism. Second, acetaldehyde, a major metabolite of ethanol, may be present in higher concentrations in alcohol-dependent patients who develop liver disease. Third, ethanol can exert toxic effects on the liver by means of nutritional deprivation. Deficiency of essential vitamins, trace metals, proteins, and energy are thought to increase susceptibility to liver damage.

(4) *Management:* Liver biopsy is the gold standard for confirming the diagnosis and determining the severity of the condition. Liver biopsy is recommended when the enzyme pattern is not typical for alcoholic liver disease or there is rapid deterioration in health. The most important goal in the treatment of alcoholic cirrhosis is to encourage the patient to maintain abstinence. Without abstinence all other forms of treatment are doomed to fail and disease progression is a certainty. A number of centers are using liver transplantation for end-stage disease. Two-year survival exceeds 75% and is similar to that in patients who receive transplants for viral-induced cirrhosis.

(5) *Pharmacotherapy:* Medical therapy for the treatment of alcoholic cirrhosis includes the following guidelines.

(a) Well-balanced diet and vitamin supplementation with thiamine (50–100 mg/day) and folate (1 mg/day).

(b) While there is no evidence that steroids can improve the clinical course or prolong survival in mild to moderately ill patients, severely ill patients experienced lower mortality rates when given high doses of prednisone (Diehl, 1989).

(c) Anabolic steroids, free radical scavengers, insulin and glucagon infusions, D-penicillamine, and amino acid mixtures all have been found of no benefit or limited benefit in the treatment of alcoholic liver disease.

(d) Colchicine may improve long-term survival in patients with stable alcoholic liver disease. The proposed mechanism is related to its antifibrotic activity. The study protocol dose for colchicine was 1 mg five times per week (Kersherobich, 1988). Propylthiouracil and calcium channel blockers are being tested in clinical trials.

(6) *Pharmacotherapy for ascites:* Treatment of ascites should include bed rest, minimal dietary sodium (2–4 gm/day), fluid restriction (1.5–2 L/day), spironolactone (50–200 mg/day in four divided doses with a maximum diuresis of 1 L/day as an end point). Peritoneovenous shunting procedures are useful in patients who have failed standard treatment.

(7) *Encephalopathy:* Treatment remains focused on reducing the nitrogen load in the portal system. Current treatment is based on dietary reductions in protein (<40 gm/day) and therapy with neomycin and lactulose.

(8) *Gastrointestinal hemorrhage:* Bleeding resulting from portal hypertension is a common life-threatening complication of end-stage liver disease. The primary therapy includes sclerosal therapy for esophageal varices, H_2 blockers (ranitidine), and β-blockers, which have been shown in some studies to decrease the risk of recurrent bleeding. Portal shunting procedures can be considered in selected patients.

C. Cancer

Alcohol is closely associated with the development of four cancers: esophageal, liver, nasopharyngeal, and laryngeal. The relationship appears to be causal. There also is evidence to suggest a mildly elevated risk for breast, prostrate, and gastric cancer. Nicotine use potentiates the carcinogenic activity of alcohol. In addition, nitrosamines found in alcoholic beverages may be important carcinogenic agents. The mechanism probably is related to altered T cell function, and may be a direct effect of alcohol metabolites.

1. *Esophageal cancer:*
   Weight loss and dysphagia are the most frequently reported symptoms. Most patients in whom esophageal cancer is diagnosed at this point have 5-year survival rates of less than 10%. Smokers who consume large amounts of alcohol should be carefully questioned for any symptoms consistent with esophageal cancer. Minimal evaluation would include an esophagram. Since smaller lesions can be missed by this technique, patients who have persistent symptoms should be considered for esophagoscopy and biopsy.

2. *Liver cancer:*
   An enlarged irregular liver edge is a common clinical finding. Patients with persistent elevation of liver function should be further examined. Fifteen percent to 20% of patients with alcohol-induced

cirrhosis will develop a hepatoma. All patients with cirrhosis should be monitored with a liver-imaging method, such as radionucleotide scan, ultrasound, or computed tomography (CT).

3. *Nasopharyngeal cancer:*

   Heavy alcohol use is reported by approximately three fourths of all patients with head and neck cancers. There is a strong association with tobacco use. The two agents are thought to act synergistically in the oncogenesis of nasopharyngeal cancers. Symptoms may include pain, hoarseness, and dysphagia; however, these symptoms often are late manifestations. Patients at high risk should be questioned carefully about minor pain or chronic irritation of the upper airway and should receive careful ear, nose, and throat examinations.

D. Sexual Dysfunction

Despite the widespread belief that drugs and alcohol can enhance sexual activities, the opposite effect is more often noted. Many drugs of abuse, including alcohol, have disinhibiting capabilities that may lead initially to increased libido but with excessive long-term use often lead to deterioration of sexual function. While alcohol cessation may reverse many sexual problems, patients with significant gonadal atrophy (pole-to-pole measurement <2.5 cm) are less likely to respond to treatment.

1. *Male sexual dysfunction:*

   a. *Clinical issues:* Alcohol can lead to impotence in the male, with both acute and chronic use. It has been found that increased blood alcohol concentrations lead to decreased sexual arousal, increased ejaculatory latency, and decreased orgasmic pleasure. The incidence of impotence may be as high as 50% in patients with chronic alcoholism. In addition, many alcoholic men develop testicular atrophy and decreased fertility.

   b. *Mechanism:* The mechanism is complex, and likely results from a direct alcohol toxicity to the Leydig cells and altered hypothalamic function. While testosterone levels may be depressed, recent studies have demonstrated that many men who are alcohol dependent can have normal testosterone and estrogen levels.

2. *Female sexual dysfunction*

   a. *Clinical issues:* Sexual function in the female alcoholic is less clearly understood. Many female alcoholics complain of decreased libido, decreased vaginal lubrication, and menstrual cycle abnormalities. Ovaries often are small and without follicular development. Some data suggest that fertility rates are lower in women with alcohol disorders.

   b. *Eating disorder effect:* The presence of anorexia nervosa or bulimia aggravates the problem. Amenorrhea, anorexia, weight loss, and infertility are associated with anorexia nervosa.

E. Nervous System Effects

The nervous system effects included in this section were chosen because of their frequent appearance in primary care practices. They include headaches, sleep disorders, memory impairment, and peripheral neuropathy. Other clinical problems less frequently seen by primary care providers can be reviewed in neurology textbooks. Examples of these include Wernicke encephalopathy, Korsakov psychosis, and cerebellar degeneration.

1. *Headache:*
   a. *Clinical issues:* Chronic headaches are extremely common in heavy drinkers and alcohol-dependent patients. All patients with chronic undefined headaches, especially those who request specific medications, should have careful alcohol and drug histories taken. The clinical picture can be a combination of vascular, intracranial, and tension symptoms. A complete neurologic examination and a CT scan may be necessary to exclude other processes, such as subdural hematomas, that are more commonly seen in alcohol-dependent patients.
   b. *Migraine headaches:* Any alcohol use can precipitate vascular headaches in patients who have migraine headaches.
   c. *Management:* Treatment of alcohol-induced headaches with opiates or sedatives often exacerbates the problem in alcohol-dependent patients. This paradoxical effect is not well understood, but is a common clinical observation. The use of psychoactive drugs for alcohol-induced headaches can lead to increased alcohol and drug use, and has been linked to affective disorders. Nonsteroidals, nonpharmacologic treatment, and abstinence are the primary methods found to be effective.

2. *Sleep disorders:*
   a. *Clinical issues:* Patients who are alcohol dependent have abnormal sleep patterns, which may persist for as long as 2 years after complete abstinence. A large number of patients with chronic sleep problems are using alcohol and other mood-altering drugs. In many of these patients the alcohol or drug use is the underlying cause of the sleep disorder.
   b. *Management:* Mood-altering drugs such as benzodiazepines or other sedatives do not help, and often exacerbate symptoms. Treatment should focus on nonpharmacologic treatments, such as alcohol and drug abstinence, exercise, relaxation techniques, self-hypnosis, warm milk, and cessation of all caffeine use. Reassurance that the sleep patterns will improve over the first year of treatment may be helpful.

3. *Memory impairment:*
   a. *Recognition:* Short-term memory often is affected. Subtle short-term memory deficits may be extremely difficult to diagnose in the outpatient setting. One half to three fourths of chronically alcohol-dependent patients demonstrate deficits in cognition and memory.
   b. *Testing:* The size of the third ventricle on CT scan may directly correlate with the cognitive defects. Autopsy studies have demonstrated that structural brain lesions affect centers of memory and

learning. In addition, alcohol may have direct toxic effects on acetylcholine receptors in the frontal cortex.

  c. *Management:* The reversibility of memory loss is uncertain. Many
cognitive deficits are irreversible and do not improve with abstinence. Severely malnourished patients should receive thiamine
before oral nutrition or intravenous fluids are given, to prevent
Wernicke encephalopathy.

4. ***Peripheral neuropathy:***

  a. *Clinical issues:* Alcoholic peripheral neuropathy is toxic impairment of peripheral nerve function, initially occurring in the distal
sensory nerves. It closely resembles diabetic neuropathy. When
this syndrome becomes more severe, it also may affect the motor
nerves. Muscle wasting and decreased deep tendon reflexes may
become apparent. The most common symptom is burning pain in
a symmetric glove and stocking distribution.

  b. *Vitamin deficiencies:* Alcoholic neuropathy is thought to be associated with nutritional deficits, although it rarely occurs in the absence of alcohol exposure. Multiple deficiencies have been in-
voked, including deficits of thiamin, biotin, pantothenic acid, and
pyridoxine.

  c. *Treatment and recovery:* Patients with peripheral neuropathy often
make a significant recovery with alcohol abstinence and adequate
nutrition. Thiamine should be supplied initially at 100 mg/day.
While multivitamins also are given, they are not essential in patients receiving well-balanced diets. Severe cases may require
physical therapy.

F. Hematologic Effects

Alcohol has direct effects on all hemologic cell lines as well as the production of clotting factors in the liver.

1. ***Platelets:***

Alcohol-dependent patients often exhibit thrombocytopenia, which is
reversible, often within a few days of abstinence. Platelet counts of
30,000 to 50,000 are not unusual and apparently are caused by both a
toxic effect on the megakaryocytes and the trapping of platelets in the
spleen. Thrombocytopenia also can be seen in severe folate deficiency associated with alcohol dependence.

2. ***Red cell line:***

Alcohol may act directly by inhibiting the folate system and the production of DNA. Increased mean corpuscular volume (MCV) and serum folate level monitoring are helpful in early detection of the disease process. However, it should be noted that alcohol may also
cause an increased MCV without folate or B_{12} deficiency. Anemia may
occur secondary to iron deficiency and often is a result of gastrointestinal bleeding.

3. ***Specific infectious disease predilection:***

  a. *Acute effects:*

    (1) Alcohol intoxication decreases the gag reflex and ciliary clear-

ance and thus increases susceptibility to aspiration pneumonia.

(2) Alcohol-dependent patients are more susceptible to gram-negative pneumonia and pneumococcal pneumonia. The normal flora of the mouth may be altered by the presence of gram-negative bacteria.

(3) Alcohol use may lead to occult basilar skull fractures and subsequent meningitis.

b. *Chronic effects:*

(1) Patients with cirrhosis often have coexisting splenomegaly. They have several immune problems as a result of increased sequestration of neutrophils. In many cases, neutrophil counts may remain normal, whereas the marrow reserves are significantly depleated.

(2) Liver and spleen congestion markedly decreases the fixed macrophage phagocytic capacity.

(3) There is an observed tendency toward life-threatening sepsis, particularly with *Pneumococcus.*

(4) Folate deficiency may predispose to decreased white blood cell production. Ascitic fluid predisposes patients to infection (spontaneous bacterial peritonitis).

(5) Leg edema predisposes patients to group A streptococcal cellulitis.

G. Teratogenic Effects

1. ***Fetal alcohol syndrome:***

Alcohol is teratogenic when ingested on a regular basis by women who are pregnant. As little as three drinks per day may have major deforming effects on the developing fetus. National prevalence is one to two cases in 1,000 live births, but rises in areas where maternal alcohol consumption is above the norm.

a. *Syndrome characteristics:* Fetal alcohol syndrome (FAS) includes growth retardation, craniofacial anomalies, CNS dysfunction, and major organ system malformations. Facial changes include a short palpebral fissure, hypoplastic upper lip with a thin vermillion border, small or absent philtrum, and microcephaly (see Fig 11–1). Other associated anomalies include cardiac and ocular abnormalities as well as minor limb and joint abnormalities. The most significant reported problems are delayed development and moderate to severe mental retardation.

b. *Mechanism:* The mechanism is unknown, but five potential mechanisms are being studied: placental dysfunction, nutritional deficiency, acetaldehyde toxicity, fetal hypoxia, and the role of prostaglandins. It is likely that more than one of these mechanisms explains the teratogenicity. The teratogenicity of alcohol is greatest in the first 6 weeks of pregnancy. Since many alcohol-dependent women have irregular cycles, it is likely that heavy drinking and fetal damage can occur even before the woman is aware she is pregnant.

c. *Treatment:* Prevention is the most important form of treatment. All pregnant women should be informed about the risks of alcohol consumption. Preconception counseling is ideal, but not always possible. Detection often is a major problem, because pregnant women are reluctant to admit heavy alcohol consumption.

2. ***Fetal alcohol effects:***
The term fetal alcohol effects (FAE) is used when only some of the criteria for FAS are met. A milder condition, FAE may be even more common and more difficult to diagnose than FAS. The mechanism likely is similar to FAS, but the amount of alcohol consumed may be substantially less. Since no safe level of alcohol ingestion during pregnancy has been determined, pregnant women should be advised to abstain from alcohol consumption altogether.

II. Tobacco Abuse

Tobacco smoking accounts for more morbidity and mortality than all other psychoactive drugs combined. The addictive potential of nicotine is similar to that of other stimulants. First users can become dependent within weeks of initial use. Negative health consequences are largely a result of other ingredients in cigarette smoke. These ingredients are carcinogenic, atherogenic, and cause injury to the respiratory and gastrointestinal systems.

A. Respiratory Effects

1. ***Chronic Obstructive Pulmonary Disease:*** Tobacco use leads to numerous changes in the respiratory system, including increased mucus production, inflammation, ulceration, squamous metaplasia, fibrosis, and decreased ciliary function, that predispose smokers to pulmonary disease. Chronic obstructive pulmonary disease (COPD) would be rare if there were no cigarette smokers (80% to 90% of cases are related to smoking). Although the symptoms of COPD can be ameliorated with medications, progression can be arrested only by cessation of smoking. Early diagnosis, patient education, and physician intervention are essential.

2. ***Pneumonia:*** Smoking predisposes patients to pneumonias. Smokers are more susceptible to gram-negative infections, especially *Haemophilus influenzae* and *Klebsiella pneumoniae.* Smokers are more likely to require hospitalization because of coexisting pulmonary disease and reduced ability to clear secretions.

3. ***Asthma:*** Because tobacco smoke is a potent airway irritant and leads to increased bronchospasm, smoking is particularly hazardous in patients with asthma. Chronic exposure to tobacco smoke exacerbates the symptoms of asthma. Long-term use of bronchodilators, steroids, and antibiotics often is necessary. Smoking cessation can be advised as an alternative to increasing the numbers of asthma medications. In addition, some patients with asthma may develop bronchospasm

from passive smoking. A careful history may reveal otherwise unsuspected aggravation by smoke exposure.

4. ***Passive smoking:*** Children chronically exposed to smoke inhalation have higher rates of otitis media and respiratory illness. A recent study (Janerich et al., 1990) estimated that 17% of lung cancer in nonsmokers could be the result of passive smoke exposure during childhood and adolescence. Miscarriage, stillbirth, and low birth weight are more likely in women chronically exposed to cigarette smoke. Parents who smoke should be encouraged to smoke outside the house or in an area not occupied by children. All health professionals should work to promote a smoke-free environment in clinics, hospitals, and workplaces (see Chapter 5 for details).

B. Gastrointestinal Tract

1. ***Clinical issues:*** Although smoking has multiple adverse gastrointestinal effects, it is particularly known to aggravate reflux esophagitis and peptic ulcer disease. Smoking decreases lower esophageal sphincter pressure, which causes increased problems with reflux esophagitis, particularly when patients smoke immediately before bedtime. Smoking is associated with a higher incidence of peptic ulcer disease (especially duodenal ulcer). There appears to be a dose-response relationship between smoking and ulcer disease. It is also known that ulcers heal more slowly in patients who smoke.

C. Vascular Disease

1. ***Ischemic heart disease:*** Approximately 30% of all ischemic heart disease (IHD) is attributable to tobacco use. Smokers are twice as likely to develop IHD as nonsmokers are. However, smoking cessation will decrease individual risk. After 10 years, former smokers (<1 pack/day) have the same risk as nonsmokers. The mechanism of development is related to increased platelet aggregation and coronary vasoconstriction. Smoking is more closely associated with acute events (myocardial infarction, sudden death) than it is in the genesis of the atheromatous process itself.

2. ***Cerebrovascular accident:*** Although the association is not so strong as for IHD, smoking is estimated to account for 27,000 deaths/year from cerebrovascular accident (CVA). Smoking cessation reduces both the risk of ischemic stroke and subarachnoid hemorrhage. Relative risks return to normal after 5 to 15 years of cessation.

3. ***Peripheral vascular disease*** is strongly associated with tobacco use. Smoking cessation substantially reduces the risk of peripheral vascular disease. Smoking cessation improves exercise tolerance and decreases the risk for amputation.

D. Pregnancy Effects

1. ***Epidemiology:*** Numerous studies have documented an association between smoking and lower birth weight. Compared with nonsmokers, women who smoke have twice the risk of having a low birth weight infant (<2500 gm). The effect is dose related.

2. *Clinical issues:* Cigarette smoking is associated with increased rates of miscarriage, stillbirth, placental abruption, placenta previa, bleeding in pregnancy, and preterm rupture of membranes. A 1977 study estimated that approximately 4,600 infants die each year as a result of maternal smoking.

3. *Mechanism:* The mechanism of action is uncertain, but may arise from the carbon monoxide–induced impairment of maternal and fetal hemoglobin or from placental vasoconstriction.

4. *Treatment:* All pregnant women should be advised to stop smoking. Cutting back is no longer an advisable alternative. It has been demonstrated that women who stop smoking before or early in a pregnancy substantially reduce their risk of having a low birth weight infant.

E. **Cancer**

1. *Type:* Oral, pharyngeal, laryngeal, esophageal, pancreatic, bladder, and kidney cancers are strongly associated with tobacco exposure. An estimated 30% of all cancer deaths are due to smoking. In 1982, the Surgeon General's Report stated that cigarette smoking is the major single cause of cancer mortality in the United States.

2. *Lung cancer:* Lung cancer is 10 times more likely in smokers than in nonsmokers. The 5-year survival rate from lung cancer is less than 10%. Only one third of lung cancers are thought to be resectable at the time of diagnosis, and only one third of patients are still alive 5 years after resection.

F. **Benefits of Smoking Cessation**

1. A 1990 report from the Surgeon General summarized the major benefits of smoking cessation:

   a. Smoking cessation has significant immediate and long-term benefits for all smokers whether or not they have a smoking-related illness.

   b. Smokers who quit can be expected to live longer than those who continue.

   c. The risk for cancer, coronary artery disease, CVA, and COPD decreases in those who stop smoking.

   d. If a woman stops smoking before pregnancy or in the first trimester, she can reduce the risk of having a low birth weight infant to that in a nonsmoker.

   e. The health benefits of quitting far outweigh the risks of the average 5 lb weight gain associated with smoking cessation.

III. **Cocaine**

A. **Psychiatric Effects**

1. *Clinical issues:* The aftereffects of acute intoxication include depression, irritability, restlessness, and generalized discomfort. Anxiety may progress to panic attacks. Patients may have acute psychosis, which resolves in 12 to 24 hours. They may experience hallucinations ("snow lights," "coke bugs"). The most important long-term psychiat-

ric effect of cocaine use is paranoia; when combined with acute intoxication, this is termed "armed paranoia." Paranoid patients are prone to violent behavior.

2. ***Management:*** Acute psychiatric reactions are best treated in a quiet, supportive environment. Valium 5-10 mg PO or IV can be administered to extremely anxious patients.

B. Cardiac Effects

1. ***Chest pain:*** Chest pain, often similar to angina pectoris, is reported in as many as one half to three fourths of cocaine users. True myocardial infarction, usually subendocardial infarction, also can occur. The proposed mechanism suggests that there is increased norepinephrine release (causing increased blood pressure and pulse) and vasospasm, which result in decreased myocardial oxygen supply.

   a. Treatment is similar to that for angina and myocardial infarction due to atherosclerotic disease. In addition, phentolamine 3 to 5 mg every 5 to 10 minutes may be useful to reduce pulse and blood pressure in patients with extreme toxicity. Propranolol 1 mg IV every minute (up to five doses) is also useful.

2. ***Heart failure:*** Congestive heart failure can be seen in chronic cocaine users. This may be due to repeated subendocardial myocardial infarction or to contracture bands in the myocardium. Furosemide (Lasix) and digoxin are the primary drugs of choice.

3. ***Arrhythmia:*** The most common arrhythmia associated with cocaine use is sinus tachycardia. Occasionally ventricular fibrillation may be terminal in acidotic or hypoxic patients. Verapamil 5 to 10 mg IV over 2 minutes has been recommended in ventricular fibrillation caused by cocaine use.

4. ***Cardiovascular collapse:*** Cocaine users after a prolonged binge can experience cardiovascular collapse. This event may be preceded by sense of impending doom.

C. Central Nervous System Effects

1. ***Seizures:*** Seizures are the most common CNS effect. Cocaine causes a decreased seizure threshold and increased body temperature. Seizures can be terminal, and should be treated with intravenous diazepam 10 mg IV over 2 minutes, or lorazepam 4 mg IV.

2. ***Cerebrovascular accident:*** CVA has been caused by cocaine abuse, probably as a result of vasospasm. Subarachnoid hemorrhage has been reported in patients with arteriovenous malformation or berry aneurysm.

3. ***Other symptoms:*** Headache is a frequent complaint of cocaine users.

D. Pulmonary Effects

1. ***Clinical issues:*** Pulmonary effects are related to smoking freebase (crack) cocaine. Black sputum, cough, and dyspnea are associated with frequent freebasing. Spontaneous pneumothorax (Valsalva is used to increase absorption) occasionally is seen in crack cocaine users. Noncardiac pulmonary edema is an acute hypersensitivity reac-

tion to crack cocaine; the syndrome consists of infiltrates, fever, bronchospasm, increased eosinophil counts, and pruritis.

E. Obstetric Effects

1. *Clinical issues:* Abruption occurs at a higher rate in cocaine abusers, probably as a result of vasospasm in the placental vascular system. Stillbirth and miscarriage are more common in cocaine users. Cocaine use can predispose to preterm labor. Babies born to cocaine-addicted mothers may experience a withdrawal syndrome characterized by irritability, tremulousness, and poor feeding.

F. Ear, Nose, and Throat Effects

1. *Clinical issues:* Chronic sinusitis with marked inflammation is the most common symptom seen in ambulatory care settings. An important tipoff of cocaine abuse is the presence of unilateral nasal edema. Nasal septal perforations and abscessed teeth are common in chronic heavy cocaine snorters.

G. Treatment

1. Treatment of cocaine use is similar to treatment of other dependencies. Patients who are heavy users are candidates for inpatient programs. Persons who are cocaine dependent may need extended care or a "halfway house," so they can adjust to an abstinent life-style. Patients with good social support and a stable job may be successfully treated as outpatients.

IV. Marijuana

A. Epidemiology

Sixty percent of high school seniors have tried marijuana at least once; one in eight of these students will progress to regular use. Many of those who try marijuana will also experiment with other drugs. Occasional marijuana use often, but not invariably, progresses to regular use, in a predictable way. The heavy user often enters into a life-style that is centered around the use of the drug, that is, *Cannabis dependence syndrome.*

B. Acute and Chronic Effects

1. *Acute clinical effects:* Acute effects are variable, and often reflect the user's expectation as well as the pharmacologic effects of the drug. Common initial effects include a sense of relaxation and euphoria. However, some individuals also experience negative symptoms, including excessive excitement, confusion, disturbing hallucinations, panic reactions, and paranoia. Because marijuana alters concentration and reflex response, it is dangerous to operate a motor while under the influence of this substance.

2. *Chronic complications:* Amotivational syndrome is one of the most commonly seen chronic effects of marijuana use. It is characterized by seven components:
   a. Loss of interest in usual activities.
   b. Loss of desire to work.
   c. Loss of energy.
   d. Mood swings and easy frustration.

    e. Impaired concentration and decreased learning potential.

    f. Decreased attention to personal grooming.

    g. Increased time spent in acquiring and using drugs.

  3. ***Respiratory tract symptoms*** include a persistent dry cough and upper airway irritation. Marijuana contains more carcinogens and tar than tobacco smoke does. The smoke is in contact with the respiratory epithelium longer, because users often take more time per inhalation and draw more deeply than do tobacco smokers. Heavy marijuana smokers have been shown to have functional impairment of the airways. Pathologic samples demonstrate a diffuse infiltrate of mononuclear leukocytes in the lung tissues. There also is a strong possibility that chronic marijuana smoking is associated with respiratory tract cancer and COPD.

C. Treatment

Heavy users may require an organized chemical dependency treatment program. Patients with lesser degrees of dependence and good social support may respond to a trial of abstinence with individual and/or family counseling. Social reintegration is a key element of treatment.

V. Other Drugs

A. Hallucinogens

  1. ***General comments:*** Various substances, including lysergic acid diethylamide (LSD), psilocybin, psilocin, dimethyltryptamine (DMT), mescaline, and 2,5-dimethoxy-4-methyamphetamine (STP) cause marked alteration in the user's perception of reality. The popularity of these drugs has declined since the 1970s; nevertheless, because LSD is relatively easy to produce in a laboratory, it continues to be widely available.

  2. ***Tolerance:*** The chronic use of these drugs is not generally thought to induce withdrawal on cessation. However, there is evidence that tolerance will disappear rapidly with short periods of abstinence.

  3. ***Acute clinical effects:*** Hallucinogens are capable of producing a wide variety of effects, which can vary from mild relaxation and euphoria to an uncontrollable psychotic reaction. The dosage, setting, and psychologic profile of the user may be important determinants of effect. In addition, the same dose of the same drug can produce widely varying effects in the same individual. Terrifying visions and extreme paranoia ("bad trips") can occur. Hallucinogens also produce an alteration of sensorium associated with accidental death and suicide in some users.

  4. ***Chronic flashbacks:*** Chronic use of these drugs has been reported to result in "flashbacks" (unpleasant hallucinations) even after drug use has ceased. Little is known about the cause and appropriate treatment of flashbacks. Care should be taken to rule out an underlying psychopathologic condition.

  5. ***Treatment:*** Inpatient programs are suggested for patients with heavy use patterns and significant interruption of social interactions.

Patients with "bad trips" are treated supportively in a nonthreatening environment, with one-to-one contact. Benzodiazepines may be useful for short-term sedation. If flashbacks are associated with other significant repetitive psychiatric symptoms (e.g., depression, delusions, paranoia), treatment with antidepressants or antipsychotics may be useful.

B. Phencyclidine

1. *Pharmacology:* Phencyclidine (PCP) is known as a dissociative anesthetic, and sometimes is grouped with the hallucinogens. The pharmacologic properties of PCP make it distinct from all other classes of drugs of abuse. It has depressant, hallucinogenic, and analgesic properties.

2. *Prevalence:* Six percent of high school students admit to having used PCP. Many more may have used it inadvertently, because it sometimes is marketed as "superpot" (PCP-laced marijuana or parsley).

3. *Acute clinical issues:* Acute PCP intoxication causes ataxia, dysarthria, nystagmus, diaphoresis, increased salivation, and analgesia. Subjectively, users may experience a state of relaxation, which can progress to severe emotional lability and feelings of grandiosity. There are many reports of violent behavior, accidents, and suicide in patients under the influence of PCP. Convulsions, coma, respiratory depression, and cardiac collapse may occur with increasing toxicity.

4. *Long-term effects:* Chronic PCP abuse leads to progressively severe psychiatric side effects, and eventually may result in severe depression or a psychotic state resembling schizophrenia. These effects can last for months.

5. *Management:* Treatment of mild PCP intoxication is supportive. Severe intoxication necessitates close monitoring in an intensive care unit. Frequent monitoring of vital signs is required. Severe hypertension has been reported, and is treated with phentolamine 3 to 5 mg IV. Acidification of the urine theoretically can increase excretion. Seizures due to PCP intoxication may be treated with lorazepam or diazepam. Further treatment is outlined in Chapter 3.

C. Inhalants

1. *Overview:* The use of inhalants is most common in junior high and high school students. Inhalants are cheap and readily available. Nitrous oxide cartridges can be ordered through the mail. Usage pattern may vary from occasional use to daily use. Inhalants are commonly used in groups. The average users are 14 to 15 years old and male.

2. *Types:* The three main types of inhalants are hydrocarbons, volatile nitrates, and nitrous oxide. Common examples are gasoline, kerosene, chloroform, isopropyl alcohol, airplane glue, lacquer thinner, acetone, benzene, naphtha, carbon tetrachloride, fluoride sprays, metallic paints, and typewriter correction fluid. They may be inhaled

TABLE 8–2.

Medication Used in Treating Complications of Alcohol and Drug Abuse

Drug	Indication	Dosage/Route	Interval	Comments/Precautions
Diazepam (Valium)	Withdrawal Seizures Agitation Panic reaction	2–10 mg IV/PO IV rate <2 mg/min Withdrawal loading 20 mg PO q2h × 3	q5–10 min to symptom relief or max 30 mg	Larger doses may be required in selected patients; monitor respirations carefully
Lorazepam (Ativan)	Withdrawal Seizures Agitation Panic reaction	2 mg IV/IM/PO IV rate 2 mg/min (Lorazepam 1 mg equal to diazepam 5 mg)	q5–10 min to symptom relief or max 6 mg	Larger doses may be required in selected patients; monitor respirations carefully
Haloperidol (Haldol)	Hallucinations Severe agitation Psychotic reactions	2–5 mg IM/PO	qh to symptom relief	Hold if systolic BP <90; watch for distonic reactions
Phentolamine (Regitine)	Hypertension in conjunction with cocaine or amphetamine abuse	3–5 mg IV/IM	May repeat in 5–10 min prn	Watch for tachycardia and hypotension
Propranolol (Inderal)	Hypertension and tachycardia in withdrawal Panic reactions	1–3 mg IV (Test 0.2 mg IV) 10–40 mg PO	May repeat in 2 min tid–qid	Avoid in CHF and patients with history of bronchospasm
Naloxone (Narcan)	Narcotic overdose Unexplained coma	0.4–0.8 mg IV, then 2 mg in 5 min	Continue 2 mg IV q20–60 min	Watch for recurrence of comatose state
Magnesium (Magnesium Plus)	Hypomagnesemia	1–2 gm IM/IV (max IV rate 150 mg/min + max 20% solution)	q4–6h until serum Mg normalizes	Caution in patients with renal impairment; monitor respirations and deep tendon reflexes
Magnesium chloride	Hypomagnesemia	133 elemental mg PO	bid–qid	Caution in patients with renal impairment
Folic acid	Folate deficiency	1 mg PO	qd	
Thiamine	Thiamine deficiency Prevention of Wernicke-Korsakoff syndrome	100 mg PO/IM × 3 days; may then reduce to 25 mg	qd; total 3 wk	Give to malnourished alcoholics prior to IV fluids or significant PO intake
Desipramine		50–150 mg PO	hs or in divided doses	

from a saturated cloth, in containers such as bags or balloons, or directly from a tank, can, or bottle.

3. **Clinical issues:** Inhalants are rapidly absorbed into the brain and stored in body fat. The primary effects are on the central nervous system and peripheral nerves. The sought-after effect is a euphoric sensation. However, this pleasurable effect frequently is followed by nausea, headache, and amnesia. Heavy use can lead to hypoxia, multiple organ system damage, and death.

4. **Effects** of inhalants include:
   a. *Acute organic brain syndrome,* characterized by dizziness, amnesia, confusion, unsteady gait, and slurred speech.
   b. *Acute psychotic reactions* may be seen, with delusions, feelings of omnipotence, and hallucinations (both visual and auditory).
   c. *Nitrous oxide* can cause airway freezing and/or laryngospasm.

    d. *Laboratory abnormalities* may include depressed red and white blood cell counts, elevated liver or kidney function tests.

    e. *Chronic effects,* such as confusion and disorientation, occasionally have been reported to last for months.

    f. *Peripheral neuropathy* causing painful extremities for 12 months or more is an effect of airplane glue inhalation.

    g. *Chronic pulmonary irritation, anemia, neurologic problems, and lead poisoning* result from inhaling gasoline fumes.

5. ***Recognition:*** Symptoms of abuse include decreased school performance; loss of interest in extracurricular, family, and social activities; and onset of legal problems.

6. ***Management:*** Treatment should be tailored to the individual. Traditional chemical dependency treatment programs often are needed. Adolescent 12-Step groups are especially useful, and family involvement and counseling are essential.

VI. Medications Used in Treating Complications of Alcohol and Drug Abuse

Drug treatment of the health effects of alcohol and illicit drugs is summarized in Table 8–2. This list complements pharmacologic treatment (discussed in other chapters).

BIBLIOGRAPHY

Acute reactions to drugs of abuse. *Med Lett* 1990; 32:92–94.

Alcohol and Health. Rockville, Md, National Institute of Alcohol Abuse and Alcoholism, 1987.

Barnes HN, Aronson MD, Delbanco TL (eds): *Alcoholism: A Guide for the Primary Care Physician.* New York, Springer-Verlag, 1987.

Burbige E, Lewis D, Halsted C: Alcohol and the gastrointestinal tract. *Med Clin North Am* 1984; 68:77–89.

Cocores J, Miller N, Pottash A, et al: Sexual dysfunction in abusers of cocaine and alcohol. *Am J Drug Alcohol Abuse* 1988; 14:169–173.

Collini FJ, Brener B: Portal hypertension. *Surg Gynecol Obstet* 1990; 170:177–192.

Diehl A: Alcoholic liver disease. *Med Clin North Am* 1989; 73:815–830.

Facts on Alcoholism and Alcohol-Related Problems. National Council on Alcoholism, New York, 1986.

Friedman G, Siegelaub A, Seltzer C: Cigarettes, alcohol, coffee and peptic ulcer. *N Engl J Med* 1974; 290:128–135.

Geokas M, et al: Ethanol, the liver, and the gastrointestinal tract. *Ann Intern Med* 1981; 95:198–211.

Gitlow S, Dziedzic L, Dziedzic S: Alcohol and hypertension: Implications from research for clinical practice. *J Substance Abuse Treatment* 1986; 3:121–129.

Iber F: *Alcohol and Drug Abuse.* Boca Raton, Fla, CRC Press, 1991.

Janerich D, Thompson W, Varela L: Lung cancer and exposure to tobacco smoke in the household. *N Engl J Med* 1990; 323:632–636.

Johnson C, Reeves KO, Jackson D, et al: Alcohol and sex, heart, and lung. *Urol Clin North Am* 1983; 12:93–97.

Kershenobich D, Vargas F, Garcia-Tsao G, et al: Colchine in the treatment of cirrhosis of the liver. *N Engl J Med* 1988; 318:1709–1713.

MacMahon S: Alcohol consumption and hypertension. *Hypertension* 1987; 9:111–121.

Mayer E, Grabowski C, Fisher R: Effects of graded doses of alcohol upon esophageal motor function. *Gastroenterology* 1978; 75:1133–1136.

Riggs S, Cyr M: Complications and comorbidities of substance use. Project ADEPT. Providence, RI, Brown University, 1988.

Rubin E, Lieber C: Fatty liver, alcoholic hepatitis, and cirrhosis produced by alcohol in primates. *N Engl J Med* 1974; 290:128–135.

Singh M, Simsek H: Ethanol and the pancreas: Current status. *Gastroenterology* 1990; 98:1051–1062.

Steere M: Classification and pathogenesis of pancreatitis. *Surg Clin North Am* 1989; 98:1051–1062.

Tarr JE, Macklin M: Cocaine. *Pediatr Clin North Am* 1987; 34:319–331.

US Department of Health and Human Services: Clinical opportunities for smoking intervention. Public Health Service, National Institute of Health, NIH Publication No 86:2178, August 1986.

US Department of Health and Human Services: Smoking, tobacco and health: A fact book. Public Health Service, CDC, Center for Disease Prevention and Health Promotion, Office on Smoking and Health, DHHS Public No (CDC)87-8397 (rev 10/89).

US Department of Health and Human Services: The health benefits of smoking cessation. Public Health Service, CDC, Center for Chronic Disease Prevention, Office of Smoking and Health, DHHS Publication No (CDC)90-8416, 1990.

Wein A, Van Arsdalen K: (1988). Drug induced male sexual dysfunction. *Urol Clin North Am* 1988; 15:23–31.

CHAPTER 9

Emergency Department Management of Alcohol and Drug Disorders

Robert E. Gwyther, M.D.

Alfred R. Hansen, M.D., Ph.D.

This chapter focuses on the management of alcohol and drug disorders in the emergency department (ED). Management of the inebriated patient involved in a serious traumatic event can be a complex clinical problem. The care of patients with alcohol and drug problems who come to the ED traditionally has been limited to the treatment of medical complications. The role of the ED treatment team is expanding to include the identification of problematic users whose primary disorder has been unrecognized or untreated. This chapter provides an outline of methods and algorithms for diagnosis and management of the medical complications as well as for treatment of the primary addictive disorder.

I. Overview
A. Alcohol Abuse
While illicit drugs have received increasing attention, alcohol use is still the most serious drug problem in emergency departments.

1. *Prevalence:* It is estimated that between 13% and 40% of all patients seen in the ED have been using alcohol. In addition to alcohol intoxication, patients also present to the ED with a myriad of alcohol-related medical complications, including cardiomyopathy, cirrhosis, gastrointestinal bleeding, pancreatitis, seizure disorders, encephalopathies, neuropathies, myopathies, hematopoietic disorders, and a variety of metabolic disturbances.

2. *Alcohol-related injuries:* The drinking driver has long been implicated in nearly half of all motor vehicle fatalities. Similarly, in 50% to 80% of homicides and 25% to 50% of suicides, drownings, falls, and industrial accidents, alcohol is implicated as a primary factor. It has been estimated that heavy drinkers are twice as likely to die of injury as are nondrinkers. Alcohol often is a factor in family violence, and should be suspected in cases of child abuse, spouse battering, and various forms of sexual abuse.

3. ***Role of the physician:*** A recent article by Lowenstein (1990) indicates that ED physicians tend to focus on the medical or surgical problems of the alcoholic patient and seriously neglect the primary problem. Physicians working in the ED have a responsibility to manage not only the medical sequelae but the primary alcohol and drug disorder. This is particularly important in light of evidence that an ED visit can be a powerful motivator for the patient to acknowledge a primary addictive disorder and seek definitive treatment.

B. **Illicit Drugs**

1. ***Medical problems:*** As in alcoholic patients, victims of illicit drug use present to the ED with acute intoxication and various medical and surgical complications. Clinicians in the ED must be alert to the potential for drug-induced causes for everything from acute psychosis to sudden death.

2. ***Specific problems:*** Cocaine should be considered in new cases of seizure, as well as in cerebrovascular accident (CVA) and acute myocardial infarction in the relatively young. Drug ingestion is always part of the differential diagnosis for altered mental status, and has been increasingly associated with injury, particularly penetrating trauma.

3. ***Infections:*** Septic complications of needle sharing have caused epidemics of hepatitis. Endocarditis also is a frequent complication. Needle sharing has been a major factor in the spread of acquired immune deficiency syndrome (AIDS), particularly in the Northeast. Growing parenteral use of illicit drugs has caused an increase in septic complications at injection sites or by blood-borne organisms.

II. **Diagnosis of Problematic Use in the Emergency Department**

A. **Signs and Symptoms of Problematic Use**

Alcohol and drugs often are part of a more complex spectrum of health care problems. Patients may present with problems that are either direct effects, withdrawal effects, or end organ damage effects of substance abuse. The alcohol and drug disorder may be the problem of the patient or of a member of the patient's family (e.g., alcoholism in the parent of a child who presents with a fracture following a beating).

1. ***Medical problems associated with alcohol and other drug use*** include the following:

a. *Trauma:*
(1) Assault victim.
(2) Drowning.
(3) Falls.
(4) Industrial accident.
(5) Motor vehicle crash.

b. *Medical:*
(1) Acute abdominal pain.
(2) AIDS.

      (3) Aspiration pneumonia.

      (4) Cardiac arrhythmias.

      (5) Cardiomyopathy.

      (6) Cellulitis.

      (7) Chest pain.

      (8) Cirrhosis/ascites.

      (9) Early myocardial infarction.

      (10) Encephalopathy.

      (11) GI bleeding.

      (12) Hyperventilation.

      (13) Pancreatitis.

      (14) Poisoning.

      (15) Seizure.

      (16) Sepsis.

      (17) Soft tissue infections.

      (18) Subacute bacterial endocarditis.

  c. *Behavioral/psychiatric:*

      (1) Acute psychosis.

      (2) Anxiety.

      (3) Child abuse/neglect.

      (4) Delirium.

      (5) Depression.

      (6) Mania.

      (7) Panic attacks.

      (8) Suicide attempt.

2. ***Going beyond the obvious:*** The alert clinician is diligent in searching for medical or surgical complications in the apparently "inebriated" patient. One should never conclude, for example, that the obtunded patient with alcohol on his or her breath is merely drunk until a thorough evaluation is completed and the patient seems to be recovering as expected. Likewise, the patient injured in a motor vehicle crash or an industrial accident should be screened for alcohol and substance abuse so that potential underlying causes of the injury can be addressed. Patients with anxiety disorders, acute confusion, seizures, hypertension, arrhythmias, gastrointestinal bleeding, abdominal pain, or chest pain should be thoroughly screened for chemical causes of the medical or psychiatric disorder.

3. ***Opportunity knocks:*** The ED visit should be exploited to make a diagnosis of alcohol or drug abuse or dependence. Such diagnoses may be easy to make in the ED because:

  a. Alcohol and drug disorders may be obvious because of how the patient presents to the ED (e.g., heroin overdose).

  b. Patients may feel more vulnerable in the ED and, in an effort to help themselves, readily confess to consuming substances.

  c. Family cooperation may be forthcoming in an ED if a patient's health is perceived to be at stake.

    d. Families might consider the visit to be the patient's last straw, providing the impetus to seek treatment.

    e. The primary provider may be made aware of the patient's status by ED personnel.

4. ***First contact problems:*** To the physician having a first contact with a patient in the ED, the diagnosis of an alcohol or drug disorder may be more difficult because:

    a. Patients do not have preexisting rapport with ED personnel and may not be comfortable confiding their drug and alcohol problems.

    b. Patients may fear legal reprisal and not volunteer their use of substances.

    c. To diagnose everyone in the ED who has alcohol on the breath or in the blood would lead to many false positive diagnoses.

B. Drug-Seeking Behavior in the Emergency Department

Patients who are alcohol or drug dependent often use EDs to obtain drugs. Many can recite sophisticated medical histories or feign diagnoses they know are difficult to dispute, hoping the unwary physician will prescribe their drug of choice. Likely scenarios include patients with low back pain, migraine headache, and renal colic.

1. ***Low back pain:*** The presence of a drug disorder should be considered in patients with low back pain, especially if they have had recurrent ED visits requiring repeated, extended courses of narcotic agents in the past or a history inconsistent with objective physical findings.

2. ***Migraine headache:*** Concern centers on patients with frequent ED visits requiring narcotic treatment with an absence of evaluation or adequate follow-up and those who refuse treatment with nonnarcotic drugs such as prochlorperazine (Compazine).

3. ***Renal colic:*** Attention should be focused on patients who bring in their own urine specimens containing blood, those refusing to provide a urine specimen under direct observation, or patients with suspected self-inflicted urethral injury.

4. ***Specific drug requests:*** Focus on patients who request specific, narcotic "drugs that work," such as oxycodone (Percodan) or meperidine (Demerol), when other commonly efficacious management plans are refused.

5. ***Lost prescriptions:*** Suspect a drug disorder in patients who have "lost their prescriptions." Local pharmacies should be called to determine frequency of refills and number of physicians who have provided prescriptions.

6. ***The traveler:*** Consider drug-seeking behavior in patients requesting refills for opiates or sedatives who report that they left their prescription drugs at a distant home.

7. ***The negotiator:*** Suspect drug-seeking behavior in patients who request pain relief, but who then request hypnotics when the physician expresses concern about administering opioids.

C. **Taking the Drug and/or Alcohol History in the Emergency Department**

1. *Information source:* The ED clinician must obtain a history from the best available sources (e.g., patient, family members, witnesses to an accident, paramedics, police). The interview should be conducted using the general techniques and guidelines discussed in Chapter 2.

2. *Confidentiality:* If queried about confidentiality, the physician should convey that the information will be part of a confidential medical record but is not exempt from subpoena. He or she should emphasize that good medical care requires the best knowledge possible regarding substances in the patient's body.

D. **Physical Findings**

Physical examination is an important part of the diagnosis of alcohol and drug disorders. Findings can be obvious, subtle, or confusing. The body reacts directly to the effects of drugs, and has homeostatic mechanisms that counter these effects. Under the influence of drugs patients may manifest one set of findings, whereas the opposite findings may be present during withdrawal. In addition, patients often abuse several drugs at the same time, and the findings may present a mixed picture. The clinician should complete a general physical examination soon after the patient arrives in the ED. Particular attention should be paid to the following:

1. *Cranium:* Inspect for contusions, lacerations, or depressed fractures. Check for Battle's sign.

2. *Ears:* Inspect for hemotypanium or otorrhea.

3. *Eyes/pupils:* Check size and reactivity, conjugate gaze, extraocular movement.

4. *Nose and throat:* Assess patency of airway and gag reflex, septal perforation.

5. *Chest:* Check breath sounds for equality, rales, and consolidation.

6. *Heart:* Rate, rhythm, gallop, or significant murmurs.

7. *Abdomen:* Bowel sounds, tenderness or rigidity; assess for GI bleeding by stool guaiac test.

8. *Skin and extremities:* Needle tracks, phlebitis, or significant injuries.

9. *Neurologic:* Thorough general physical neurologic examination, including mental status; cranial nerves; cerebellar, motor, and sensory signs; deep tendon reflexes; Babinski sign, station, and gait.

E. **Laboratory Tests and Screens**

Nearly all patients with signs or symptoms of intoxication should be assessed for the presence of alcohol or other psychoactive substances.

1. *Blood alcohol level:* A "medical" blood alcohol level is not drawn to establish a diagnosis of intoxication in the criminal sense. Rather, it is obtained to give further credence to the clinical diagnosis of alcohol intoxication. A single drink will raise the blood alcohol level 15 to 25 mg/dL, depending on sex, size, and stomach contents.

The greater the body mass the more alcohol it takes to raise the blood alcohol level. A level of 300 mg/dL in a man suggests ingestion of 15 to 20 drinks. As indicated in the following list, blood levels should correlate roughly with the patient's condition, and are especially helpful in management:

a. 50 mg/dL Some loss of cognition, judgment, and coordination.
b. 80 mg/dL Driving impaired even in the tolerant drinker.
c. 100 mg/dL Legally intoxicated in most states.
d. 200–300 mg/dL Markedly impaired.
e. 400–600 mg/dL Toxic in all; respiratory depression, coma, and death in inexperienced drinkers.

2. ***Alcohol levels are dynamic:*** Alcohol in the gut continues to be absorbed. Alcohol is metabolized by zero-order kinetics, and blood levels fall at the rate of approximately 20 mg/dL, or about one alcoholic drink per hour. Alcoholics are able to tolerate much higher blood alcohol levels than nondrinkers can; this is thought to be due to increased cellular tolerance rather than increased metabolic rate. Thus an adolescent who has overdosed may have acute toxicity with a blood alcohol level that is easily tolerated by an alcohol-dependent adult. An absence of significant blood alcohol concentration in a patient exhibiting confusion, obtundation, or ataxia should spur a further aggressive search for cause.

3. ***Toxicology screens:*** Routine serum or urine toxicology screens are of little value in the emergency management of the obtunded patient. Although such screens usually are broad in scope and screen for a large number of substances of abuse, they are not available within a time frame necessary to guide acute intervention. Nevertheless, toxicology screens can be of benefit in follow-up counseling or in patients who deny substance abuse.

4. ***Laboratory tests:*** Specific toxicology laboratory tests of use in emergency situations include the following:

a. *Arterial blood gases* are particularly useful in assessing respiratory distress, evaluation and management of shock, or alerting the physician to a metabolic acidosis.
b. *Electrolytes, blood urea nitrogen, creatinine, and glucose:* The presence of anion gap acidosis causes the clinician to consider alcohols, salicylates, and ethylene glycol in the differential diagnosis of coma. They are also of value in patients with hyper- or hypoglycemia, renal failure, or severe electrolyte imbalance.
c. *Salicylate levels* should be requested in any patient with a history of aspirin ingestion or significant anion gap acidosis.
d. Although the utility of routine *acetaminophen levels* is controversial, they may be of use in evaluating polysubstance ingestion or ingestions associated with self-destructive behaviors.
e. *Carboxyhemoglobin levels* should be obtained in any alcohol-

dependent patients rescued from a fire or found obtunded in a closed, heated space.

f.   *Barbiturate levels* are helpful in the diagnosis and management of any comatose patient suspected of barbiturate intoxication. Levels of many of the barbiturates and anticonvulsants can be obtained stat in many hospital toxicology laboratories, because the labs provide levels for monitoring therapeutic effects.

g.   The remainder of stat laboratory tests usually are tailored to measuring *levels of agents taken for therapeutic reasons* (e.g., lithium, theophylline, digoxin). Generally, tests for stimulants such as cocaine or amphetamines, hallucinogens, or narcotics are of no benefit in the management of an acute intoxication (Osterloh, 1990).

5. ***Other laboratory tests:*** Other tests that may be helpful in the diagnosis and management of alcoholism or substance abuse include:

a.   *Enzyme levels.* Mildly elevated liver enzymes are common in chronic drinkers, and markedly elevated in patients with acute alcoholic hepatitis. Classically, aspartate aminotransferase (AST) levels are higher than alanine aminotransferase (ALT). γ-Glutamyltransferase (GGT) elevation is an indicator of chronic alcohol abuse. Creatine phosphokinase (CPK) is important if rhabdomyolysis is considered.

b.   *Red blood cell indices* frequently show increased mean corpuscular volume (MCV), which is a direct effect of alcohol and also may be the result of a decreased folate intake in the malnourished alcohol-dependent patient.

c.   *Platelets:* Reversible thrombocytopenia is common in chronic alcoholism. Platelet counts <50,000 are not unusual, and recover to low normal levels (100,000 to 150,000) within 7 days in most cases.

d.   *Amylase and lipase* levels, although not perfectly correlated with severity of disease, are useful in the evaluation of pancreatitis.

e.   *Prothrombin time* may be helpful, because results are promptly available and give a rough measure of liver function.

6. ***X-ray studies:*** Radiographs that may be helpful in evaluating patients with alcohol or drug disorders include the following:

a.   *Cervical spine films* are helpful in trauma victims, patients who are found unconscious, or in patients with suspected fractures of cervical vertebrae. They should be obtained before manipulating the patient's neck, to avoid damage to the spinal cord.

b.   A *head CT* is helpful in finding intracranial bleeding, abscesses, fractures, or tumors. Contrast studies are useful when "isodense" areas, such as those caused by recent ischemia or inflammatory process, are suspected.

c.   *Chest x-ray films* are used in the diagnosis of any respiratory symptoms or when an infectious process is suspected.

7. *Electrocardiographs:* An ECG should be obtained if the patient is in shock, of advanced age, or if ischemia or drug overdose is considered to be a component of the problem.

III. Initial Management of the Inebriated Patient

A. Overview of the General Approach

The ED physician must have a systematic approach to the impaired patient. This systematic approach must always incorporate a very high index of suspicion (remember Murphy's law), must consider and manage the most immediate threats to life (first things first), but also must allow flexibility in the application of specific therapeutic interventions and diagnostic tests (apply common sense to algorithms). The algorithms in this chapter have been devised to help the physician consider and sort through the alternative interventions applicable to a variety of patient problems. They are often conservative, oriented toward ruling out worst case problems, and are intended to help the physician avoid the pitfalls of assuming that inebriation is the patient's only problem. The algorithms are intended to be guidelines, and are not substitutes for good clinical judgment applied to the individual case.

1. *Rapidly assess basic ABCs (airway, breathing, circulation) first:*

   An obstructed airway or a pulseless and/or nonbreathing patient requires immediate application of basic life support techniques. The management of cardiopulmonary arrest is outside the scope of this discussion. An arrest often can be avoided by careful attention to basics.

2. *Trauma:* Consider trauma as a potential part of the problem until it is ruled out. Caveats include the following:

   a. Stabilize the cervical spine until fracture or dislocation can be definitively ruled out.

   b. Ensure adequate ventilation by repeat examinations, pulse oximetry, repeat arterial blood gas levels (ABGs), and obtain an early chest x-ray film.

   c. Consider intracranial hemorrhage in the obtunded patient, and perform serial neurologic examinations and emergent head CT if focal neurologic findings develop or mental status continues to deteriorate.

   d. Look for and manage hypovolemic states or other causes of shock by performing a volume challenge and frequent monitoring of vital signs.

3. *Consider and treat reversible causes of coma:* After management of basic ABCs, establish IV access and give the following medications.

   a. Naloxone 2 mg IV push.

   b. Thiamine 100 mg IV push.

   c. Glucose 25 gm IV push.

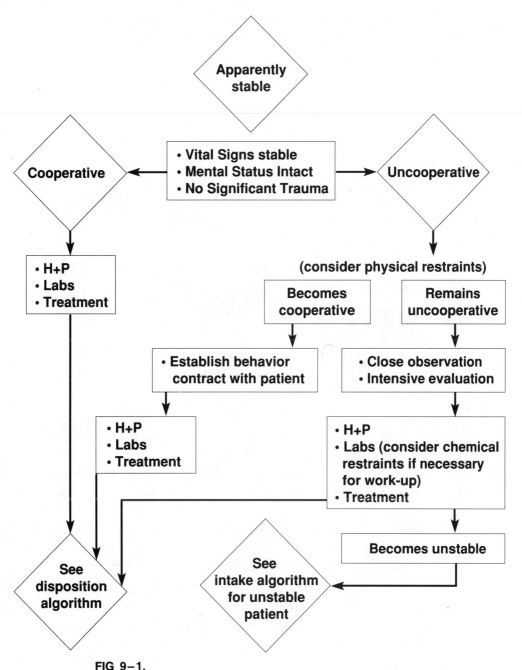

FIG 9–1.
Algorithm demonstrates management in inebriated patients who have stable vital signs, intact mental status, and no significant trauma.

4. ***Consider life-threatening medical emergencies,*** especially:
   a. Cardiorespiratory insufficiency.
   b. Multiple drug ingestions.
   c. CNS infection or bleeding.
   d. Cardiac arrhythmias.
   e. GI bleeding.
   f. Sepsis.

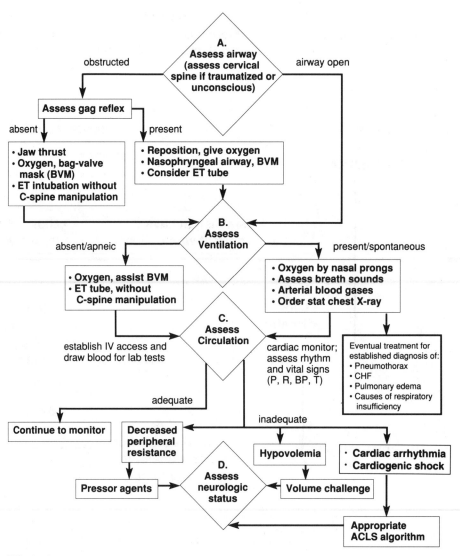

FIG 9–2.
The patient who enters the emergency department in unstable condition should be managed by assessing airway, ventilation, circulation, and neurologic status. Critical management strategies are listed for each of these areas of clinical care.

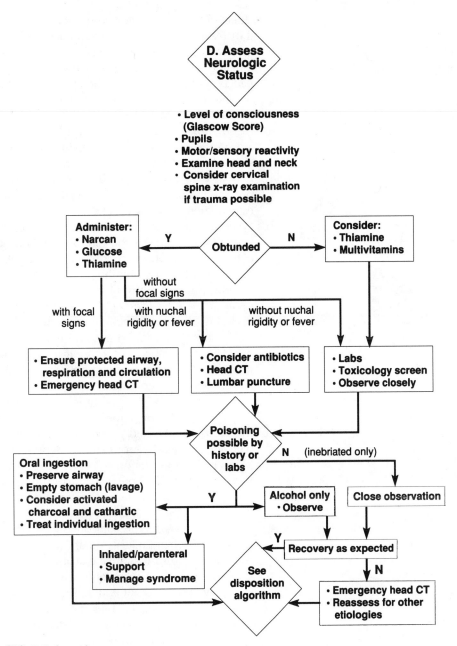

FIG 9-2 (cont.).

    g. Metabolic encephalopathies.

    h. Myocardial infarction.

B. Fundamentals of Initial Survey

Regardless of why the patient was brought to the ED, the general approach to the "apparently inebriated" should include rapid assessment of vital functions, using the techniques common to the evaluation of all medical or trauma emergencies. The initial assessment should be done in all patients, and can be accomplished in a few minutes in a patient with no major problems. The objective is to discover the potentially unstable patient and to manage life-threatening problems, as shown in Figures 9–1 and 9–2. The initial assessment includes:

1. ***Airway and cervical spine:***
   a. *Obstruction:* Ensure that there are no major obstructions and that a gag reflex is present. If the upper airway is obstructed, use basic life-support techniques, such as jaw thrust and chin lift, until definitive airway management with an endotracheal tube can be provided. A nasopharyngeal airway often is helpful in the intoxicated patient with a gag reflex.
   b. *Vomiting:* Be alert that vomiting is likely in intoxicated patients, and is even more common in those with head injury and concomitant intoxication. In nontraumatized patients, prevent aspiration by placing them on their sides in a slightly reversed Trendelenburg position. Always have ready access to suction.
   c. *Cervical spine injuries:* Cervical spine injuries should be suspected in all patients with a history of falls, assault, or motor vehicle crashes. Suspicion of trauma or signs of craniofacial injury mandate stabilization of the cervical spine with a hard collar and immobilization of the patient on a spine board. The cervical spine should be protected until fracture is ruled out by appropriate x-ray films or until the patient is capable of providing an unequivocally normal examination.
   d. *Intubation:* Inebriated patients with compromised gag reflexes or with serious head injuries should be intubated as soon as possible to prevent aspiration or obstruction. When cervical spine injuries cannot be ruled out, nasotracheal intubation or careful oral intubation while maintaining in-line traction may be necessary before complete radiographic evaluation.
   e. *Combative patient:* The combative inebriated patient suspected of having major head injury, multiple trauma, or multiple drug overdose may require definitive management of the airway by rapid-sequence induction techniques using neuromuscular blocking agents (with or without additional short-acting hypnotic agents), followed by endotracheal intubation. If unfamiliar with these techniques, physicians should get assistance *before* complications of vomiting and aspiration occur.

2. ***Breathing:***
   a. *Assess quality and rate:* Ensure an adequate respiratory rate and chest excursion. Reassess frequently.
   b. *Assess for trauma:* Examine the thorax quickly for signs of blunt or penetrating injury and ensure that breath sounds are clear and equal bilaterally.

    c. *Hypoxemia:* Acute hypoxic states should be considered in the confused or combative inebriate who has been traumatized or appears systematically ill. If hypoxia is suspected, give supplemental oxygen. Note irregular respiratory patterns such as apneustic breathing or Kussmaul respirations; these can be signs of overdose, head injury, CVA, or other severe illness.

    d. *Odor:* Assess breath odor for the presence of alcohol or acetone.

    e. *Opioid overdose:* Because the potency of street drugs is unpredictable, inadvertent narcotic overdose can produce respiratory depression. The effects of narcotics can be reversed by naloxone (Narcan), a narcotic antagonist. However, differences in potency and duration of action of narcotic drugs may require that repeated doses of naloxone be administered.

    f. *Pneumothorax:* Since intravenous drug abusers have discovered the ease with which the subclavian and internal jugular veins can be accessed, tension pneumothorax should be considered in patients with apparent respiratory distress. Spontaneous pneumothorax also has been reported in crack smokers. Look for signs of unequal breath sounds, hypertympany and asymmetric chest wall motion, tracheal deviation, and jugular venous distention in the presence of hypotension and tachycardia.

    g. *Respiratory depression in the young:* Occasionally, acute respiratory depression is seen in young drinkers who lack significant tolerance to CNS depressants but have consumed large quantities of alcohol alone or in combination with sedative-hypnotic agents. Even though their blood alcohol levels are not found to be in the "lethal" range, intubation and assisted ventilation may be necessary for several hours in a monitored intensive care unit.

    h. *Nondrug diagnosis:* Consider other medical causes of respiratory insufficiency, such as congestive heart failure, noncardiac pulmonary edema, pulmonary embolism, pneumonia, large pleural effusion, chronic obstructive pulmonary disease (COPD), or allergic or reactive airways disease.

3. **Circulation:**

    a. *Shock:* Assess for signs of shock by evaluating pulse rate and character. Causes of shock (including hypovolemic, cardiogenic, septic, and neurogenic shock) should be considered and managed. Cool, mottled skin should be considered a sign of inadequate perfusion, even in the face of "normal" blood pressure readings.

    b. *Monitoring:* Formal vital signs, including core temperature, should be obtained as soon as possible. Attach a cardiac monitor and consider pulse oximetry.

    c. *Hypotension:* In the absence of congestive heart failure, hypotension should be managed initially by rapid administration of 500 mL normal saline solution. If there is significant suspicion of severe hypovolemia (gastrointestinal bleeding or trauma), infuse 1 to 2 L normal saline solution, followed by frequent reassessment of vital signs.

4. ***Rapid neurologic evaluation:*** After assuring that the basic ABCs are either adequate or undergoing appropriate stabilization maneuvers, a focused neurologic examination should be performed. Inability to arouse an intoxicated individual to follow simple commands, even in the absence of focal findings, should promote a rapid evaluation for possible CNS trauma, sepsis, poisoning, or metabolic causes of diffuse encephalopathy. Key elements of this examination are:

   a. Mental status:
      (1) Speech.
      (2) Orientation.
      (3) Short-term memory.
   b. Pupils/eyes:
      (1) Size and reactivity.
      (2) Nystagmus and gaze.
   c. Gross motor and sensory evaluation.

The Glasgow coma score is helpful in quantifying the results of a rapid neurologic assessment, and may be done sequentially to follow a patient's progress in the ED. Scores less than 13 are suspect for very serious neurologic problems and generally should not be attributed to simple drunkenness or minor head injury. Most intoxicated persons are capable of following commands when roused.

Glasgow Coma Score

Eyes:	
Open spontaneously	4
Open on command	3
Open to pain only	2
Closed	1

Verbal:	
Oriented	5
Confused speech	4
Inappropriate words	3
Incomprehensible	2
None	1

Motor:	
Follows commands	6
Purposeful movement	5
Withdrawal to pain	4
Flexor response	3
Extensor response	2
Flaccid	1

Once the primary survey has been accomplished and serious illness and injury reasonably ruled out, the inebriate should be encouraged to interact with the examiner. Even moderately intoxicated patients often appear obtunded or somnolent if allowed to remain recumbent. However, most who are only inebriated will be surprisingly alert if aroused. A good practice is to require the impaired individual to sit upright at the edge of the gurney and answer simple questions.

C. Further Evaluation

1. *Stabilization of the patient:* Once the initial evaluation is completed, the clinician must stabilize the patient in the ED, establish pertinent diagnoses, begin treating emergent problems, and develop a disposition and follow-up plan. It is important to consider the following factors while the evaluation is in progress.

   a. Unsuspected trauma must always be considered in the unconscious or obtunded patient.

   b. Failure to respond in a manner consistent with the working diagnosis should lead to further investigation and a broadening of the differential diagnosis.

   c. Deterioration of the patient's condition in the ED should prompt the clinician to initiate procedures used in unstable patients.

2. *Potentially unstable or deteriorating patients:* The following common conditions, if they occur, should prompt an initial classification of *unstable* or, if the patient was previously considered stable, *change* the classification to unstable:

   a. Historical findings:

      (1) Chest pain or dyspnea.

      (2) GI bleeding.

      (3) Head injury (altercation or fall).

      (4) Major drug overdose.

      (5) Major premorbid illness.

      (6) Persistent neurologic deficit.

      (7) Possible major trauma (e.g., motor vehicle crash).

      (8) Polydrug ingestion.

      (9) Prolonged seizures.

      (10) Suicidal or self-destructive behavior.

      (11) Syncope.

   b. Physical findings:

      (1) Acute abdomen.

      (2) Agitated or obtunded.

      (3) Changing vital signs.

      (4) Compromised airway.

      (5) GI bleeding.

      (6) Respiratory distress.

      (7) Severe dehydration.

      (8) Shock (cool, mottled skin; tachycardia).

D. Caveats in Management

Serious problems are sometimes overlooked in the assessment of some inebriated patients.

1. *Motor vehicle crash victim:* Specific entities that might be overlooked and attributed to drunkenness alone include head injury, hypoxia, or hypovolemic shock.
2. *Belligerent patients:* Common problems that are missed include extremity fractures or functionally significant soft tissue injuries, such as flexor tendon and digital nerve transections in hand injuries.
3. *Patients with major medical problems:* In the face of intoxication, major medical problems, including multiple drug ingestions, poisoning, meningitis, ketoacidosis, and hypothermia or hyperthermia, may not be diagnosed.
4. *Patients seeking premature discharge:* Once a patient has come to the ED, the clinician is obligated to ensure that he or she is in satisfactory condition before discharge.
5. *Patients with seizures:* Patients with seizures require sufficient examination and observation in the ED to enable an appropriate disposition. The assumption that seizures are due to drug withdrawal leads to omission of necessary treatment in some patients.

E. **Approach to the Patient who has had a Seizure**

The substance abuse patient who has a history of seizures presents a special situation. The ED physician must differentiate between several possibilities and make the appropriate diagnosis and disposition. Not all seizures that develop in alcohol-dependent patients are related to alcohol withdrawal. Seizures may be due to infection, trauma, or the direct effect of other drugs of abuse, particularly stimulants such as cocaine. Patients who abuse alcohol often abuse other substances.

1. *Previous seizure history, prior workup:* Patients who have a history of seizures may be manifesting poor control of their underlying disorder, a subtherapeutic blood level of anticonvulsant medications, drug withdrawal, or complications of head injury. A high index of suspicion for trauma must be maintained, blood levels obtained, and seizures controlled. If the patient is stable in the ED and there is no evidence of trauma, appropriate doses of intravenous anticonvulsants may be given. Further care should parallel that given to other patients with alcohol or drug disorders.
2. *Previous seizure history, never evaluated:* These patients require a more complete ED evaluation than those whose previous seizures have been evaluated. Neurologic evaluation and a head CT should be done to rule out intracranial disease as the cause of the seizures. Once stabilized, and in the absence of compelling intracranial disease, the disposition of these patients is equivalent to that of other patients with drug or alcohol disorders.
3. *No previous seizure history:* Patients with a first seizure must be evaluated in an effort to determine a cause. Evaluation is similar to that described above. If the patient's condition stabilizes and no serious disease is found, treatment is the same as in other patients with alcohol or drug disorders.

4. ***Status epilepticus, complicated seizures, or medical-neurologic complications:*** These patients must be stabilized as much as possible in the ED and admitted to the appropriate level of care in the hospital. Surgical intervention may be in order for subdural or epidural bleeding, tumors, skull fractures, or other serious problems. Complicated seizures or status epilepticus must be treated with intensive medical management, perhaps in an intensive care setting.

IV. **Management of Behavioral Problems in the Emergency Department** Patients under the influence of alcohol or other drugs present special problems when their behavior is disruptive or threatens to compromise their care. The physician must find a solution that optimally balances patients' civil liberties and their expectation of good medical care.

A. **Patient Rights vs. Physician Responsibilities**

1. ***Implied consent:*** When patients come to an ED, there is an expectation and/or implied consent that appropriate medical care will be rendered.

2. ***Physician liability:*** Physicians are expected to establish appropriate and expeditious diagnosis and treatment plans. They are legally liable for failure to properly diagnose a primary alcohol and drug disorder and to provide appropriate care.

3. ***Informed consent:*** Patients under the influence of mind-altering substances cannot give informed consent (or informed refusal) for care. If family members are not present, the physician must use his or her own judgment.

4. ***Incriminating laboratory tests:*** Laboratory test results, such as blood alcohol levels or urinary cocaine screens, have both medical and potential legal significance. ED physicians must act in a medically appropriate fashion and order tests if their results might influence the medical care of the patient. While results from hospital laboratories are confidential, they are available to a court by subpoena. However, results usually are not admissible in criminal trials, because a urine or blood sample obtained by medical personnel in the ED does not usually follow the "chain of custody" required by the courts. In addition, laboratories must use legally acceptable test methods. Most medical laboratories perform a single test and do not use confirmatory testing procedures routinely used in forensic laboratories. Sometimes the police request a blood alcohol level in a patient. Patients can refuse this; however, legal penalties such as forfeiture of a driver's license may result. If the patient gives consent, the police usually ask the ED personnel to draw the sample, using provodine prep pads rather than alcohol prep pads to avoid introducing sources of error into the test.

5. ***Signing out against medical advice:*** It is dangerous and ill-advised to discharge inebriated and/or potentially unstable patients

from the ED, despite their demand to sign out against medical advice. The ED may want to contact a local police department for assistance.

B. Management Problems with Inebriated Patients

1. ***Delay of diagnosis is dangerous:*** There may be no time to delay diagnosis and treatment in an inebriated patient. A serious condition may worsen while a patient, assumed to be intoxicated, is allowed to "sober up."

2. ***Use of restraints:*** Physical restraints may be required to prevent the inebriated patient from injuring self or others. Chemical restraints may be indicated for sedation of an agitated patient who must lie still for a test, such as an emergent head CT.

3. ***Compromising the care of other patients:*** Inebriated patients in the ED can compromise the care of other patients by injuring or frightening those patients. The additional time spent with the unruly patient also takes staff and physician time and care from patients who may be equally sick but who do not exhibit behavioral symptoms.

4. ***Safety of ED staff:*** Inebriated patients who exhibit violent or abusive behavior also pose a threat to the safety of the ED staff. The early presence of security personnel can be helpful in preventing injury to the patient and others.

C. Techniques for Dealing with Inebriated Patients

1. ***Simple methods:*** There is a range of possible methods for handling an unruly inebriated patient. It may be possible to reason with an inebriated patient, especially if his or her ego is not at stake. Sometimes a patient who appears lethargic will wake up and cooperate with providers. If the patient's medical condition is stable, "quiet time" for sobering up may be allowed.

2. ***Use of restraints:*** Physical or chemical restraints may be used when there is no contraindication (e.g., trauma) and their implementation will improve the prognosis. It may become necessary to medically paralyze and ventilate a patient to permit the appropriate testing or treatment.

3. ***Aggressiveness of treatment:*** It is sometimes difficult to decide how aggressive to be when treating an uncooperative patient. A rule of thumb is that when a patient's "life or limb" is at risk, do what is necessary to provide treatment, even if the patient objects. It is more desirable to successfully treat a patient against his or her wishes than to fail to provide treatment and allow serious complications to result.

4. ***Specific methods:*** The following method for handling the disruptive patient in the ED may be helpful:

   a. Establish the therapeutic milieu with eye contact with the patient.

   b. Define the ED rules of conduct quickly, assertively, fairly, empathetically, and convincingly.

   c. If unable to proceed, or breech of contract occurs, and restraints are necessary, *go in force with a sufficient number of staff* to impress the patient; use "full leather" restraints, and secure all four extremities.

d. *Institute restraint precautions* by having staff present to clear the patient's airway in case of vomiting. *Never leave a restrained patient unattended.*

e. *Reduce the number of people* around the patient by dismissing as many staff and family members as possible, allowing the patient to save face.

f. *Try again* to obtain cooperation by offering the patient return of dignity and control in exchange for cooperation (e.g., "We will remove the restraints from your wrists if you stop spitting at the nurses.")

5. **Family members:** Family members may be helpful in dealing with the difficult inebriate. Frequently they are responsible for the patient being in the ED, and are anxious for successful treatment. A family member may obtain the patient's cooperation when others fail. Occasionally family members may obstruct medical efforts, especially when they are intoxicated themselves, and must be escorted out of the ED.

6. **Use of chemical restraints:** Medication for the treatment of agitation (e.g., neuroleptics and sedatives) may be helpful when they do not mask significant clinical signs. *Do not sedate the patient with suspected head injury unless a CT scan is to be obtained.* Chemical restraints are particularly useful for obtaining the compliance necessary for an urgent evaluation, to combat the effects of stimulant drugs, and to aid with severe acting out.

V. **Pharmacotherapy for Initial Treatment of the Medical Complications of Alcohol and Drug Disorders**

The ED provides treatment for a wide variety of conditions, many of which are present in patients with alcohol and drug problems. This section deals with only a few of these.

A. **Severely Intoxicated Patients**

Severely intoxicated patients may be malnourished and are susceptible to conditions associated with malnutrition. Wernicke encephalopathy syndrome may be prevented by administering thiamine. Multivitamins, additional folate, and magnesium help replenish depleted stores.

B. **Seizures**

Seizures can be induced by the toxic effects of acute ingestion or drug withdrawal. The primary drugs for treatment are benzodiazepines (diazepam and lorazepam). Respiratory depression is uncommon; however, bag, mask, and intubation equipment should be available.

C. **Status Epilepticus**

The patient with status epilepticus should be given intravenous benzodiazepines (as above). If this fails to control the seizures, an intravenous dose of phenytoin 15 mg/kg should be given *slowly*, over about 30 minues (rate ≤50 mg/kg). If the seizures continue, intravenous phenobarbital may be given at a dose of 15 mg/kg. The drug should be given *slowly*, at a rate <100 mg/kg, because of the combined respiratory depressant effects of phenobarbital and benzodiazepines. An alternative use of phenobarbital is to administer 250 to 300 mg IV, over about 10 minutes, and observe the patient's response. This dose may be repeated until the 15 mg/kg loading dose is reached.

D. Coma or Obtundation

The comatose patient may be suffering from the effects of drugs and immediately should be given 2 mg naloxone by IV push. A dose of 0.04 to 0.2 mg may be repeated every 3 minutes until the patient responds. If a total dose of 10 mg is reached without adequate response, other causes must be aggressively sought. Glucose 25 gm IV push should be administered after the first dose of naloxone, because hypoglycemia may be the cause; delay in treatment can increase permanent neuronal damage. Thiamine is useful in comatose patients, to prevent Wernieke's encephalopathy and/or Korsikoff syndrome.

E. Severe Agitation

Substance-abusing patients often are agitated, either from drug toxicity after acute ingestion or drug withdrawal. Once trauma and metabolic derangement have been ruled out, sedative medications may be helpful in the management of the patient. Phenobarbital, diazepam, and haloperidol are the drugs of choice. The following medications provide a summary of the treatment methods described:

Severe chronic alcohol use:
>   Thiamine 100 mg IM or IV.
>   Multivitamins 1 amp IV.
>   Magnesium sulfate 2 gm IM or IV.
>   Folate 1 mg IV or PO.

Seizures:
>   Lorazepam 2 to 4 mg IV push.
>   Diazepam 5 to 10 mg IV push.

Status epilepticus, loading (based on ideal body weight):
>   Phenytoin 12 to 15 mg/kg at a rate of ≤50 mg/min.
>   Phenobarbital 15 mg/kg at a rate of ≤100 mg/min; may repeat to a total of 400 mg

Coma or obtubation:
>   Naloxone 2 mg IV; may repeat doses of 0.04 to 0.2 mg every 3 minutes.
>   Glucose 50 gm IV.
>   Thiamine 100 mg IV.

Withdrawal:
>   Clonidine 0.1 to 0.2 mg PO tid.
>   Phenobarbital 60 mg PO tid.
>   Valium 10 to 20 mg PO every 2 hours for 3 doses.

Severe agitation:

Phenobarbital 120 to 240 mg IM.

Diazepam 5 to 10 mg IV.

Haloperidol 2 to 5 mg IV.

VI. Emergency Department Disposition

A. Overview

1. *Disposition algorithm:* Appropriate dispositions of patients with alcohol and drug disorders includes admission to an acute care hospital, discharge to a nonhospital setting that can provide competent care for the patient, or discharge to home under the supervision of a drug-free support person.

2. *Consultation:* The ED physician may proceed to disposition alone or consult with other physicians. Valuable input is often obtained from the patient's primary physician, who may be aware of information useful to the history and treatment plan. Consultation with other specialists, such as a surgeon or a neurologist, may be indicated before making a disposition plan. These physicians may want to evaluate the patient in the ED. If a dual diagnosis of alcohol or drug disorder and psychiatric illness is made, consultation with a psychiatrist may be important.

3. *Detoxification:* Many patients require a detoxification regimen to recover from the symptoms of withdrawal as well as to prevent seizures and delirium tremens. Protocols for detoxification are discussed in Chapter 3. Patient success in obtaining sobriety may depend on the treatment of intense withdrawal symptoms and drug craving in the first few days and weeks of sobriety.

B. Hospital Admission

1. *Medical indications:* Admission to the hospital may be necessary for several reasons. It may be required for medical reasons to treat acute medical, surgical, or psychiatric diagnoses or for patients at high risk of serious withdrawal complications.

2. *Social issues:* Admission may be necessary for patients with alcohol and drug disorders who are too impaired to function independently and may have no family or friends willing to care for them. Their resources may be limited, and their only alternative hospital admission.

3. *Combined medical and social issues:* Some patients addicted to alcohol may have a combination of problems that individually could be managed on an outpatient basis but taken in sum require admission for treatment and observation.

C. Non-Hospital Community Setting

1. *Community programs:* Frequently referred to as "social detox settings," these programs have received increasing support as important components of the alcohol and drug treatment system. They offer advantages over acute care hospital settings by reducing cost and improving staffing with personnel with expertise in the treatment of alcohol and drug disorders.

2. *Utilization:* Community programs may be used when patients require close observation by caretakers more familiar with withdrawal than family members. Medical staff coverage and physician follow-up at these sites is essential.

D. Discharge to Home

1. *Street discharge: Patients should not be discharged to the streets while under the influence of drugs.* When patients do not have homes or drug-free support persons to supervise their "drying out," alternate ED disposition must be sought.

2. *Support person:* Once sober, patients are able to go home directly from the ED. A drug-free support person must give needed medications, report changes to the managing physician, ensure that the patient attends follow-up visits, and encourage the patient to seek treatment for substance abuse. It may be prudent to get assurance of compliance in writing from any support people before discharging a patient home from the ED.

E. Alcohol and Drug Treatment Program

1. *Referral methods:* The ED physician may succeed in referring a patient directly to an alcohol and drug treatment program. The ED personnel should try to arrange the appointment and have the patient talk to a counselor at the treatment program before they leave the ED. Simply giving the patient a phone number with instructions to call when they are home is less helpful.

2. *Community AA groups:* Asking a member of the Alcoholics Anonymous (AA) community to come to the ED and talk to the patient may be helpful. The ED may want to fill in and post a treatment resource sheet shown in Chapter 4 to ensure ready access to the AA community.

BIBLIOGRAPHY

Aaron CK: Sympathomimetics. *Emerg Med Clin North Am* 1990; 8:513–526.

Advanced trauma life support course for physicians. American College of Surgeons, 1989.

Chang G, Astrachan VM: The emergency department's surveillance of alcohol intoxication after motor vehicle accidents. *JAMA* 1988; 260:2533–2536.

Chiang WK, Goldfrank LR: Substance withdrawal. *Emerg Med Clin North Am* 1990; 8:613–631.

Ellenhorn MJ, Barceloux DG: General approach to the poisoned patient, in Ellenhorn M, (ed): *Medical Toxicology: Diagnosis and Treatment of Human Poisoning.* New York, Elsevier Science, 1988.

Epstein FB, Eilers MA: Poisoning. *Emerg Med* 1988; 17:321–361.

Ewing JA: Detecting alcoholism: The CAGE questionnaire. *JAMA* 1984; 252:1905–1907.

Flomenbaum NE, Goldfrank LR, Kulberg AG, et al: General management of the poisoned or overdosed patient, in Goldfrank L (ed): *Goldfrank's Toxicologic Emergencies,* ed 3. East Norwalk, Conn, Appleton-Century-Crofts, 1986, pp 5–27.

Ford M, Hoffman RS, Goldfrank LR: Opioids and designer drugs. *Emerg Med Clin North Am* 1990; 8:495–511.

Hoffman RS, Goldfrank LR: The impact of drug abuse and addiction on society. *Emerg Med Clin North Am* 1990; 8:467–480.

Kamerow DB, Pincus HA, MacDonald DI: Alcohol abuse, other drug abuse, and mental health disorders in medical practice: Prevalence costs, recognition, and treatment. *JAMA* 1986; 255:2054–2057.

Kelen GD, Fleetwood D: HIV infection and intravenous drug users: Implications for emergency service. *Emerg Med Clin North Am* 1990; 8:653–664.

Levy M, Koren G: Obstetric and neonatal effects of drugs of abuse. *Emerg Med Clin North Am* 1990; 8:633–652.

Lieber CS: Biochemical and molecular basis of alcohol-induced injury to liver and other tissues. *N Engl J Med* 1988; 319:1639–1650.

Lowenstein SR, Weissberg MP, Terry D: Alcohol intoxication, injuries, and dangerous behaviors—and the revolving emergency department door. *J Trauma* 1990; 30:1252–1258.

Moore RD, Bone LR, Geller G, et al: Prevalence, detection, in treatment of alcoholism and hospitalized patients. *JAMA* 1989; 261:403–407.

Mueller PD, Benowitz NL, Olson KR: Cocaine. *Emerg Med Clin North Am* 1990; 8:665–681.

Osterhol JD: Utility and reliability of emergency toxicologic testing. *Emerg Med Clin North Am* 1990; 8:693–723.

Rall TW: Hypnotics and sedatives: Ethanol, in Gillman AG, Rall TW, Nies AS, et al (eds): *Goodman and Gilman's The Pharmacological Basis of Therapeutics,* ed 8. New York, Pergamon Press, 1990, pp 345–382.

Roberts R, Slovis CM: Endocarditises in intravenous drug abusers. *Emerg Med Clin North Am* 1990; 8:665–681.

Rund DA, Summers WK, Levin M: Alcohol use in psychiatric illness in emergency patients. *JAMA* 1981; 245:1240–1241.

Schauben JL: Adulterants and substitutes. *Emerg Med Clin North Am* 1990; 8:595–611.

Selden B, Clark R, Curry SC: Marijuana. *Emerg Med Clin North Am* 1990; 8:527–539.

Shepherd SM, Druckenbrod GG, Haywood GG: Other infectious complications in intravenous drug users: The compromised host. *Emerg Med Clin North Am* 1990; 8:683–692.

Soderstom CA, Cowley RA: The national alcohol and trauma center survey. *Arch Surg* 1987; 122:1067–1071.

Waller JA: Management issues for trauma patients with alcohol. *J Trauma* 1990; 30:1548–1553.

Weisman R, Howland M: The toxicology laboratory, in Goldfrank L (ed): *Goldfrank's Toxicologic Emergencies,* ed 3. East Norwalk, Conn, Appleton-Century-Crofts, 1986, pp 28–37.

PART FOUR

Clinical Approach in Specific Populations

CHAPTER 10

Care of Family Members and Other Affected Persons

Macaran A. Baird, M.D.

Everyone is affected by the behavioral and social effects of alcoholism and drug addiction. Twenty-eight percent of the general population have a close family member who is alcohol or drug dependent. Others are affected by neighbors, friends, colleagues, or patients who have primary addictive disorders. There are also accident and trauma victims. It is a rare person who has not been affected. Many secondarily affected individuals come to see physicians with medical and emotional problems associated with someone else's use. "Affected family members" and "affected persons" are the primary terms used in this chapter. This chapter focuses on constructive ways to discover affected family members, understand their dilemma, and assist them in establishing a realistic recovery effort.

I. Overview
A. Relationship of Family History to Current Patient Problem

How does growing up in a home influenced by drug or alcohol abuse affect people? Much has been learned about this over the past decade. Dr. Peter Steinglass has led this research effort by investigating the influence of alcohol on observed family interactions; other researchers have found similar, supportive evidence. Among the highlights of this research are the following points:

1. ***Impact:*** The impact of alcoholism on families is variable. Some families are devastated; some move along with few external signs of distress but pay a significant price for working hard to appear normal. In other families the observable consequences are minimal. Most alcoholic families are apparently successful.

2. ***Problem-solving ability of affected families:*** To maintain short-term stability, these families restrict behavior and become less creative problem solvers. Maintaining the appearance of normalcy becomes a dominating priority. Long-term problem solving is difficult to measure, because the families and the individuals may function within societal norms yet underexpress their own potential. Individual autonomy and creativity can be sacrificed to present a normal appearance to the community.

3. ***Long-term effects:*** In some families active alcohol use is associated with increased short-term spontaneity and creativity but with long-term inability to remain adaptive to new challenges, such as childhood growth and development, job changes, and economic stress.

4. ***Rituals:*** Family rituals (e.g., mealtimes, holidays, celebrations) play a strong role in shaping alcohol use in the next generation. In some families more "susceptible" to the transmission of alcohol disorders, family events become a powerful training process in which normal family activities are distorted with destructive behaviors influenced by the drug.

5. ***Genetics:*** A small percentage of families with alcohol and drug disorders have a strong genetic predisposition to alcohol and drug abuse. In these families severe alcohol and drug problems arise in adolescence or early adulthood. Early death from medical problems and violence is common.

6. ***Chronic illness paradigm:*** Alcohol- and drug-dependent families have much in common with families who experience other chronic illness (e.g., renal failure, cancer, schizophrenia, Alzheimer's disease). The unrelenting course of the alcohol or drug disorder and the intuitive but unsuccessful attempts to cope parallel the struggle of many families who struggle with other chronic illnesses. Social stigma, economic penalties, and unrealistic guilt and shame are shared themes across chronic conditions.

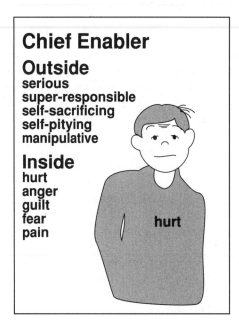

Chief Enabler

Outside
serious
super-responsible
self-sacrificing
self-pitying
manipulative

Inside
hurt
anger
guilt
fear
pain

hurt

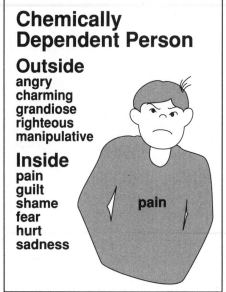

Chemically Dependent Person

Outside
angry
charming
grandiose
righteous
manipulative

Inside
pain
guilt
shame
fear
hurt
sadness

pain

FIG 10–1.
Primary behavioral characteristics in stereotypical roles noted in adult children of alcoholics. Clinical characteristics are categorized as external behaviors and internal feelings.

Hero

Outside
super-responsible
successful achiever
all-together
works hard for approval

Inside
inadequacy
loneliness
hurt
confusion
anger

inadequate

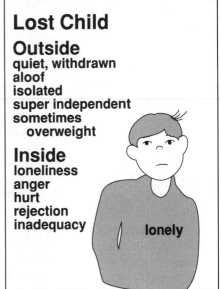

Lost Child

Outside
quiet, withdrawn
aloof
isolated
super independent
sometimes
  overweight

Inside
loneliness
anger
hurt
rejection
inadequacy

lonely

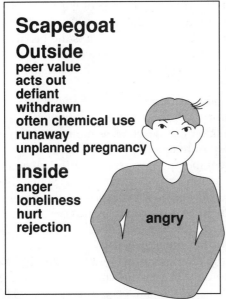

Scapegoat

Outside
peer value
acts out
defiant
withdrawn
often chemical use
runaway
unplanned pregnancy

Inside
anger
loneliness
hurt
rejection

angry

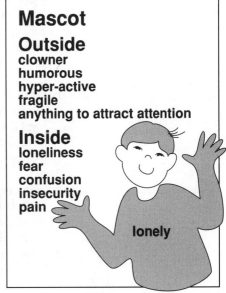

Mascot

Outside
clowner
humorous
hyper-active
fragile
anything to attract attention

Inside
loneliness
fear
confusion
insecurity
pain

lonely

FIG 10-1 (cont.).

B. Adult Children of Alcoholics Stereotyped Roles:
1. **Stress of illness:** Families with alcohol and drug disorders, as well as families with other chronic conditions, experience an ongoing high level of tension and stress. Children and other family members develop behavioral patterns to protect themselves from the continuous stress.

2. *Behavioral patterns:* There is little evidence that children and family members evolve into precise patterns of behavior. While individual family members may develop predominant patterns, they frequently use a wide range of coping behaviors.

3. *Importance of stereotypic roles:* While the stereotypic roles described by Wegscheider and others have been useful in identifying a common problem, these roles have limited diagnostic significance. Most patients who see a physician because of clinical problems secondary to growing up in a dysfunctional family do not fit any single stereotypic role. However, clinicians should be familiar with these roles, because many of their patients will use these roles to describe their family experience.

4. *Stereotypic roles:* These controversial but popularized behavioral roles include the chemically dependent person, the chief enabler, the scape goat, the mascot, the hero, and the lost child. The characteristics of each, as proposed by Wegscheider, are presented in Figure 10–1.

5. *Hazards of stereotyping:* It is important that clinicians recognize the negative implications of applying stereotypical roles to both children and adults, because they may view themselves as an embodiment of these roles for the rest of their lives. While many of the characteristics listed are useful to consider for therapy and may empower patients to engage in treatment, it is the behaviors that are important, rather than the cartoon-like roles described. We encourage clinicians to *refer to specific characteristics or behaviors* and avoid the use of these terms.

C. **Issues of Codependence**

1. *Definition:* Codependence is an emotional, psychologic, and behavioral condition that develops as the result of an individual's prolonged exposure to and practice of a set of oppressive rules—rules that prevent the open expression of feeling and direct discussion of personal and interpersonal problems (Subby, 1984). The term codependence has been used primarily in the chemical dependence treatment community, and originally was developed to explain some of the distinctive characteristics seen in persons closely involved with chemically dependent patients.

2. *Nurturing:* Although women often fulfill this codependent role, it has less to do with gender than with learned roles for survival in a stressed family. Codependence is associated with a person whose nurturing efforts have become distorted to the point that they deny their own basic needs.

3. *Unverifiable diagnosis:* Codependency is not a verifiable mental health diagnosis but a shared label for many family members of individuals with alcohol or drug disorders and other serious chronic illnesses. All serious chronic illnesses can lead to similar role distortions in family members.

4. **Hidden illness:** Negative social images associated with the primary illness in conjunction with the skilled manipulations of the primary addicted person work to keep the complex web of problems hidden from outsiders.

5. **Physician as codependent:** The physician also may become caught up in the same role distortions and become overly helpful, secretive about the primary problem, and self-destructive. It has long been suggested that this is a common problem, because such a high proportion of those in the helping professions come from families with alcohol problems. However, recent studies suggest that the percentage of medical students who come from families with alcohol disorders approximates the general population (28%).

II. Orientation to Physician-Patient-Family Triangle

A. Physician-Patient Interaction

1. **Complexity:** The interaction between a physician and patient is complex. Encounters can involve patient and physician health beliefs, the medical problems in question, and the presence of a third party. This third party usually is a key person in the patient's life, often a spouse, child, or other close family member. The person may or may not be physically present at the visit, but his or her values regarding the medical problem and possible treatments may be a powerful and influential factor in the patient's perceptions of the treatment encounter. This concept is visually represented as a triangle (Fig 10–2).

a. Case examples:

> Joe is a 47-year-old construction worker who has been treated for hypertension over the previous 6 months with no amelioration of symptoms. He recently began experiencing upper gastrointestinal distress. Joe drinks three or four beers a day, and occasionally binge drinks on weekends. When his physician has asked him about his alcohol use, Joe said he was just a social drinker. His wife has become increasingly frustrated with his drinking. She told him that she wanted to come along to find out what the physician could do for his hypertension and gastrointestinal pain. She also wants to find out if they are related to his drinking.
>
> Amanda is a 31-year-old computer programmer who has been married for 7 years to an attorney, and has two young boys, ages 5 and 3 years. Her husband grew up in a family with a father who was a heavy drinker and a mother who used pain medication and tranquilizers on a regular basis. He is opposed to drinking and to the use of any pain medications. Amanda has seen her physician on two previous occasions, because of recurrent migraine headaches. He prescribed butalbital (Fiorinal). Her husband was furious and threw the pills out. Her husband had told her before she came to the appointment that he did not want her to take any pain medication; by the time she entered the physician's office, she was very anxious.

2. **Successful treatment:** The patient-physician interaction is surrounded by values, medical problems, and family issues. While physi-

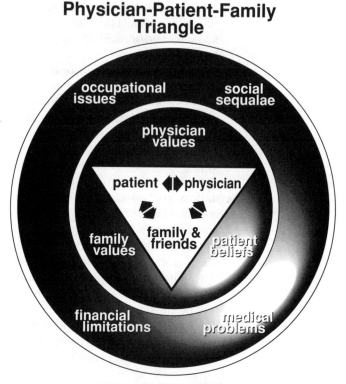

Physician-Patient-Family Triangle

occupational issues

social sequalae

physician values

patient ◀▮▶ physician

family & friends

family values

patient beliefs

financial limitations

medical problems

FIG 10–2.
Encounters between patient and physician involve health beliefs, medical problems, social sequelae, and family values. Diagram summarizes the complexity of the physician-patient-family triangle.

cians frequently focus on the medical problems and ignore individual and family beliefs, they are always present. The success of the treatment of chronic illnesses, such as alcohol disorders, often is determined by the provider's ability to recognize and work with these factors.

B. Victims:

When the patient is an affected family member of an alcohol-dependent person, an ongoing pattern of interactions may occur, resulting in three "victims": the alcoholic, the affected family member, and the physician or other health professional.

1. ***Who is the victim?*** While the family member usually is identified as the victim, the alcohol- or drug-dependent patient is as much a victim as the family member. The chemically dependent person did not choose to become alcohol or drug dependent any more than the family member consciously chose to become a victim of this devastating chronic illness.

2. ***Professional as victim:*** The physician or other health care pro-

vider becomes a victim by assuming the role of an overfunctioning family member and trying to do too much for the identified patient. Victimization can occur in a number of ways:

a. Becoming angry at either the primary chemically dependent person or affected family member.

b. Feeling unprofessional and/or incompetent by not being able to create rapidly successful outcomes for these patients or their affected family members.

c. Seeing the patient as a reflection of his or her own family member with active alcoholism or as a reminder of failed attempts to help their own family member.

d. Feeling a threat that the physician's secret alcohol or drug disorder will be discovered.

e. Trying so hard to help that the physician undermines the autonomy of the patient and fails to help.

f. Neglecting important physician self-care issues (e.g., getting home for supper, taking time off, paying bills). In other words, the physician becomes dysfunctional, like an overfunctioning family member does toward the alcohol- or drug-dependent patient.

C. **Reducing the Casualty Rate Among Victims**

1. *Reducing victimization:* Health care providers can reduce their risk of becoming victims by remaining respectful and by not becoming angry at the patient. They also need to have realistic treatment goals. Key elements in a physician's ability to be effective include taking a long-term perspective with the chronic illness and developing an optimistic and hopeful attitude toward the patient and the affected family member. By following these suggestions, *the physician has just reduced the "casualty rate" by one third.*

2. *Further reducing victimization:* If a physician patiently helps the affected family member to discover a way to avoid further despair and victimization to this disease, *the physician has reduced the casualty rate by two thirds.*

3. *Alcohol- or drug-dependent patient as casualty:* In a few instances the physician can assist the affected family member in a manner that leads to a healthy recovery for both the family member and identified alcohol- or drug-dependent person. *This is not common; although it is a rewarding clinical experience, this cannot be the expectation for all encounters.*

4. *Reduction in casualty rate:* A baseball analogy may help us to keep this complex process in perspective. Remember, even All-Star baseball players strike out frequently, get on base just over one third of the time, and rarely hit home runs. A completely successful interaction with an affected family member that leads to a 100% reduction in the casualty rate is equivalent to hitting a home run. Don't expect it often.

5. *Stick to the basics:* Be honest, respectful, and work with a team, if

possible. The "home runs" will occur at a reasonable but low rate if we do not become too anxious about either striking out or hitting home runs. Expectations about always hitting home runs only sounds good from the press box. In life, unrealistic fantasies lead to despair and anger, wasting energy that is needed for more modest goals.

III. Treatment Options to Assist Affected Family Members

A. Treatment Option 1: Wait for Patient to Discuss

1. *Most common option:* Ignoring family members until they become involved spontaneously is the most common current pattern of care (not recommended).
2. *Family member fears:* Often the affected family member is too afraid or intimidated to assertively ask for help in coping with another family member's problem drinking or drug use.

B. Treatment Option 2: Education on Disease Concept

1. *Share information* about the disease concept of alcoholism with family members when it arises as an issue during routine questioning about family illnesses or the use of genograms.
2. *The genogram* may provide an effective entry into many family illness and problems, including chemical dependency. (See IV, A: Case-finding, for a discussion of the use of genograms).

C. Treatment Option 3: Discussion of Feelings

Beyond the sharing of information, the physician can lead the discussion to feelings related to living with an alcohol- or drug-dependent person.

1. *Time and training:* This option requires more time and training, because the physician's own potentially powerful feelings about the issue must be addressed before he or she can lead this interaction in a balanced manner. This self-development may require a simple educational effort or more formal family therapy or psychotherapy.
2. *Initial time commitment:* Patient- and family-centered discussions about uncomfortable affective issues take more time in the initial treatment phase, but often save time later.
3. *Referral:* After the initial discussion the patient may agree to referral to a mental health professional with specific skills in alcohol- or drug-related family conflict.
4. *Self-help groups:* Close working relationships with self-help groups is important both as a potential resource for the patient and as a resource for the physician to discuss dilemmas as they arise (see Chapter 4 for a discussion of 12-Step self-help groups).

D. Treatment Option 4: Brief Advice Interventions

With some advanced training the practitioner may choose to provide short-term goal-oriented counseling, including brief interventions, to move a patient and/or family into a structured alcohol or drug recovery program.

1. *Brief interventions:* While brief interventions are a skill that can be learned and easily incorporated into routine patient care, this activity requires specific training and effort. See Chapter 2 for a more in-depth discussion of brief advice interventions.

2. ***Skills:*** Specific skills often are needed to engage reluctant family members in the conversation about a topic that is often "taboo" for the affected family. Some of these skills include the following:

   a. Make an initial assessment of the degree of impairment in the family.

   b. Support an individual family member (often the identified alcoholic or drug dependent person) while avoiding long-term coalitions that would undermine the process of change.

   c. Create a "team" with which to work in the community to avoid personal or emotional injury. Meet with local mental health workers, chemical dependency counselors, staff of nearby alcohol and drug treatment centers, and law enforcement personnel.

3. Ultimately, some patients and families will not accept help for alcohol or drug problems at the time it is offered. However, a respectful and honest attempt is never in vain. Someday, someone may remember the practitioner's earlier effort and be ready to hear the next one, or the next. We are like a chain. We may be the first link in a long chain of events and never know of the changes that are manifested years later. We may be the last link before recovery is attempted and actually be privileged to see the healing but painful changes. Affected family members deserve our best and most respectful effort no matter which link in the chain we become.

E. **Treatment Option 5: Standard Family Therapy**

   A few family physicians may become fully trained family therapists with special focus on alcoholism and other addictions or become certified addictionists. In either case, a 1- or 2-year fellowship is the usual method of gaining the extended training that leads to certification. The techniques used are beyond the scope of this chapter; a number of excellent resources are listed in Appendix B.

IV. **Case Finding**

A. **Method 1: Genograms**

   As part of a routine history, providers commonly inquire about illnesses experienced by other family members. A quick and convenient method of taking this family medical history is through a genogram, which includes illnesses and other major life events for important members of the family. Defining a family is difficult, but in general should be defined in the patient's terms. For example, cousins and uncles may play a more central role in a patient's life than siblings or parents. Friends or same-sex partners also may be critical to understanding a family unit. Genograms can facilitate the establishment of a sharing patient-physician interaction. The patient has the opportunity to offer viewpoints and share information in a collaborative manner with the physician. Figure 10–3 illustrates a common genogram in a family with a member who has an alcohol disorder.

   1. ***Family map:*** In addition to the information provided in Figure 10–3, brief notes about medical illnesses, dates of deaths, weddings, divorces, and such, may simply be written beside each person's sym-

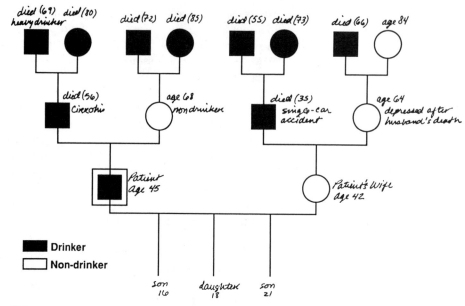

FIG 10–3.
This family genogram represents a patient with a strong family history of alcohol dependence. A similar pattern in the spouse's family would suggest that the children are at significant risk for alcohol dependence.

Patient: Construction worker. Hobbies include softball and hunting. Drinks daily; has binged once a week for years. Arrested once for DWI. Tried to cut down in last year, but couldn't.

Wife: History of depression. Employed half-time as secretary.

Son (21 years old): College student. Some binge drinking.

Daughter (18 years): Depressed. Eating disorder; quite thin; worried constantly about weight. Irregular menses.

Son (16 years): Does not appear to be using substance. Reported as somewhat withdrawn.

bolic circle or square on the genogram. With this "family map" the physician and patient together will discover patterns of problems experienced by the patient and the patient's family. A typical genogram can be constructed in 2 to 5 minutes without going into intricate detail.

2. ***How to introduce the subject:*** If the patient spontaneously mentions alcohol or drug abuse and/or dependency, the task for the physician interviewer is simplified. Occasionally the primary patient will not discuss another family member's drug or alcohol problems even if asked. Therefore it is often useful to use indirect inquiries about potentially related illnesses, such as liver disease, acid peptic disease, hypertension, and any unmanageable medical problems that ordinarily are successfully treated unless complicated by poor compliance and drug or alcohol abuse.

B. Method 2: Screening Questions

Specific screening questions can be useful if they are indirect and allow patients to discover for themselves if someone in their family has an alcohol or drug disorder. Many patients frequently choose not to think about a family member's use, and may need time to process specific questions.

1. **_CAGE:_** It may be useful to modify the CAGE questions (see Chapter 2) to seek data about family members' use of drugs and/or alcohol:
   a. Have you ever recommended that a family member _Cut_ down?
   b. Have you ever felt _Angry_ about a family member's use?
   c. Have you ever felt _Guilty_ about a family member's use?
   d. Does (did) anyone in your family have _Eye_ openers?
2. Other questions that may be helpful as part of the physician interview include:
   a. Has anyone in your family ever consumed more alcohol than _you_ thought was good for them?
   b. Does anyone in your family get _drunk_ at family gatherings?
   c. Does anyone in your family use _pot_ or drugs?
   d. Does anyone in your family use _tranquilizers_ or sleeping pills?
   e. Has anyone in your family ever seen a _psychiatrist?_ If yes, what for?
   f. Has anyone in your family ever been in the _hospital_ for a mental problem?
   g. Has anyone in your family ever been _arrested_ for drunk driving?
   h. Has anyone in your family ever gone to an _AA_ or _Alanon_ meeting?
   i. Has anyone in your family ever been in _treatment_ for an alcohol or drug problem?
3. Question _a_ of the CAGE modified for family members is subjective, and abstainers may respond that any alcohol use is inappropriate. However, the editors and contributors have found this to be a useful screening question. This is an excellent initial question to define the level of drinking and associated problems, often difficult to elicit with a direct approach such as "Is anyone in your family an alcoholic?"
4. Questions _b_ through _d_ attempt to establish use without trying to establish abuse or dependence.
5. As demonstrated in the second list of questions, inquiring about psychiatric care or hospitalizations is useful in screening, because alcohol and drug abusers often indicate that they have had mental health problems rather than drug or alcohol problems. Many recovering patients first entered treatment through the mental health care system rather than through alcohol and drug treatment programs. In addition, genetic studies clearly indicate that persons with a family history of affective disorders and/or antisocial personality (ASP) are at higher risk for alcoholism.
6. While an arrest for drunk driving is not an explicit sign of alcoholism, it is a clear indicator of risk, and is something patients usually will discuss.
7. The final questions are direct indicators of a problem that family members will usually reveal without much resistance.

C. **Method 3: Identification through Medical Complaints**
The practitioner may want to limit taking a family history of alcohol or drug dependence to those patients with problems frequently seen in affected family members. Common presenting problems include:
1. *Sleep disorders:* While there is no characteristic pattern, there usually are additional symptoms of anxiety and stress. A thorough alcohol and drug history in patients with sleep disorders is imperative. There is no place for the use of sedatives and hypnotics in the absence of a careful personal and family history of alcohol and mental health problems.
2. *GI complaints:* Gastrointestinal complaints range from chronic undifferentiated epigastric pain to classic symptoms of irritable bowel syndrome. These symptoms characteristically recur, and the symptoms frequently are exacerbated around the time of important family events such as holidays and family celebrations.
3. *Musculoskeletal complaints:* Fibromyositis, chronic muscle aches, and chronic back and leg pain may mask a family problem. Physical abuse also may be presented as chronic pain.
4. *Headaches:* A wide range of headache syndromes are seen in affected family members. Children often develop vascular headaches. Adults frequently have tension and muscle contraction headaches. Migraine headaches can be exacerbated by active problematic use of the addicted family member.
5. *Affective disorders:* Sadness, hopelessness, and other symptoms of an affective disorder are common. Depression may be severe, and pharmacotherapy may be required as a component of a comprehensive treatment plan. Risk of suicide also should be carefully assessed. If tricyclic antidepressants are used, the total number provided in each prescription should be limited to minimize the chance of a serious overdose.
6. *Undifferentiated syndromes:* The most common clinical problems seen are those referred to as undifferentiated problems. Patients may present with chronic fatigue and weakness; other complaints include lethargy, asthenia, dizziness, and anorexia.
V. **Treatment Issues: What to Do and Where to Refer**
   A. **General Concepts**
   1. *Respectful, noncoersive discussions:* Not all patients from alcohol- or drug-dependent families need referral or assistance. However, most are happy to have respectful and noncoercive discussions about these issues.
   2. *Self-help groups:* These groups often are helpful but quite variable in process and atmosphere. Referral should be accompanied by qualifying statements about variability in mood, anger, acceptance of newcomers, loyalty to popular movements (e.g., Adult Children of Alcoholics, ACOA), and support from local primary treatment centers. (See Chapter 4 for a discussion of standard 12-Step programs).

3. ***Spouse abuse:*** When the abusive spouse is impaired with an alcohol or drug disorder, denial by the abused patient may parallel denial by the abusing spouse. Accepting help and creating changes may come slowly (6 to 18 months).

4. ***Remain optimistic:*** It is not helpful to become angry with affected family members for not taking action against a loved one who continues to use or abuse drugs or alcohol. It is helpful to remain optimistic that change is always possible and to continue to recommend concrete steps toward getting help.

B. **Specific Steps that Lead to Intervention and Family Support**

1. ***Open discussion:*** Discuss the issues of alcohol and drug disorders openly and optimistically whenever possible with affected family members.

2. ***Primary disease model:*** Discuss alcohol and drug disorders from the perspective of the disease model. Reflect how all family members are involved just by living in the family.

3. ***Responsibility for self-care:*** Reinforce that affected family members are responsible only for their own well-being. Attending to their own needs for recovery and personal development is the most reliable way for the family member to "help" the addicted person. Often self-care is the only path to initiating changes in the other person and in the family unit.

4. ***Enlarging the circle of support:*** Once the affected family member is identified, the physician can help most by enlarging the circle of support for this person. Any group involvement that reinforces the inherent, but often damaged, self-esteem of the presenting family member is useful.

C. **What to Do When the Patient Does Not Respond to Simple Suggestions**

1. ***Build self-esteem:*** Certain questions may lead to self-esteem building: "Where can you go, or what do you do in small ways, that reminds you that you are a fine person?" or "Who can you talk to and not be criticized or treated like a failing child?"

2. ***Find a support system:*** Often these questions evoke slow and painful responses that there is no support system in place for this person at the moment. Perhaps this is the first time the "self-care" theme has been discussed. It may take weeks or months of supportive conversations with the physician to assist the patient to assume more responsibility for his or her own recovery.

3. ***Never too late to learn:*** It is never too early or too late to learn about the disease of alcoholism and other drug abuse or dependency and its potential effects on other family members. Sometimes the family member will want to discuss this topic long after the alcoholic's death or before there is a serious problem. It is important for the primary care physician to be comfortable with this topic and to respect the potential variability in impact on family members.

D. Protocol to Involve the Affected Family Member While Treating the Identified Patient With an Alcohol or Drug Disorder

The purpose of this protocol (Baird, 1985) is to encourage physicians to use a patient's social network, usually the family, in the initial diagnosis and management of suspected alcoholism or other substance abuse. After the physician suspects a problem with alcohol or other drugs in an identified patient, the following steps may be taken to engage the family in more fruitful discussion about the impact of drug and/or alcohol use.

1. *Genogram:* Take a family history (genogram) from the patient.

2. *Permission for family conference:* Once the provider has diagnosed the alcohol or drug disorder, ask the patient's permission to discuss this again with the patient and a family member together. The purpose is to "understand better whether your alcohol or drug use has any significant impact on family relationships or other major factors that might best be understood by other family members. This would help me better understand this problem."

3. *Schedule family conference:* Once the patient agrees to "prove you wrong," assemble the family for 15 to 30 minutes at the next convenient time, probably at the end of the day or at any time when heavy patient load is not a problem.

4. *Family interview:* Conduct a family interview. This type of interview may occur several times before a family can come to grips with an alcohol and/or drug problem in a family member.

   a. First discuss objective medical problems.

   b. Then ask what family members think may contribute to the identified medical problems or conflicts that led to seeking medical assistance in the first place. If no one mentions alcohol or drug use, the physician will have to decide whether to breech the code of silence and ask questions about the forbidden topic or schedule a follow-up visit.

   c. Once the drug or alcohol problem in discussed, the physician may ask, "What is it like to be in this family?" Be sure each family member is allowed to answer this question. Avoid detailed discussions of amount or frequency of drug or alcohol use unless spontaneously volunteered by family members. Early statements about consumption are often inaccurate.

   d. Focus on the observable consequences of the drug or alcohol use as seen by family members.

   e. Work toward some level of agreement between the physician and the family about the severity of the chemical problem. The CAGE questions and an objective list of negative consequences are objective measures of the degree of severity.

   f. Individual efforts at sudden abstinence or "cutting down" as the primary and sole treatment option often are volunteered by the patient and generally are ineffective.

   g. Do offer consultation from a drug or alcohol treatment counselor for verification of a suspected diagnosis. An alternative may be a discussion with an Alcoholics Anonymous (AA) or Narcotics Anonymous (NA) member.

h. Offer reading materials from a self-help group such as AA or NA to the patient with the alcohol or drug disorder. In addition, *offer materials from Alanon or Adult Children of Alcoholics to the family members.*

i. Arrange for direct referral to an inpatient or outpatient treatment center. This may not happen quickly, and could involve several sessions with the family over many weeks in order to arrive at the conclusion that an assessment is necessary. However, if there an is obvious need for such treatment, and if there is relative agreement in the midst of their ambivalence, help the patient and family to contact the treatment resource immediately. Sometimes this can be accomplished with a direct phone call from the physician's office. If the patient is unwilling but the family members are interested in help, they can be referred to a treatment program that has a family program.

j. Document this discussion in the patient's chart as evidence of one step in the negotiation and confrontation process.

5. Sometimes it takes many months for the identified patient and family members to understand the problem well enough to seek appropriate assistance. In the meantime, it is extremely helpful for the physician to remain supportive but firm in the professional role of assisting the family and maintaining a recommendation for appropriate treatment and/or management.

BIBLIOGRAPHY

Anderson SC, Henderson DS: Family therapy in the treatment of alcoholism. *Soc Work Health Care* 1983; 8:79–94.

Baird MA: Protocols. Chemical dependency: A protocol for involving the family. *Fam Syst Med* 1985; 3:216–220.

Black C: *It Will Never Happen to Me.* Denver, Medical Administration Co, 1982.

Cermak TL: *Diagnosing and Treating Co-dependence: A Guide for Professionals Who Work With Chemical Dependents, Their Spouses and Children.* Minneapolis, Johnson Institute Books Professional Series, 1986.

Cloninger CR, Bohman M, Sigvardsson S: Inheritance of alcohol abuse: Cross fostering analysis of adopted men. *Arch Gen Psychiatry* 1981; 38:861.

Cotton NS: The familial incidence of alcoholism: A review. *J Stud Alcohol* 1979; 40:89–116.

Dulfano C: Family therapy of alcoholism, in Zimberg S, Wallace J, Bloom S (eds): *Practical Approaches to Alcoholism Psychotherapy.* New York, 1978, pp 119–136.

Goodwin DW: Alcoholism and heredity: A review and hypothesis. *Arch Gen Psychiatry* 1979; 36:57.

Griner EG, Griner PF: *Alcoholism and the Family: A Guide for the Primary Care Physician.* New York, Springer-Verlag, 1987, pp 159–166.

Lanier DC: Familial alcoholism. *J Fam Prac* 1984; 18:417–422.

Shulamith LA, Strausner A, et al.: Effects of alcoholism on the family system. *Health Social Work,* 1979; 4:111–127.

Steinglass P: A life history model of the alcoholic family. *Fam Process* 1980; 19:211–226.

Steinglass P, Bennett LA, Wolin SJ, et al: *The Alcoholic Family.* New York, Basic Books, 1987.

Subby R: Inside the chemically dependent marriage: Denial and manipulation, in *Codependency: An Emerging Issue,* Hollywood, Fla, Health Communications, 1984.

Vernon J: *I'll Quit Tomorrow.* New York, Harper & Row, 1973.

Wegscheider S: *Another Chance: Hope and Health for the Alcoholic Family.* Palo Alto, Calif, Science and Behavior Books, 1981.

Wolin SJ, Bennett LA, Noonan DL, et al: Disrupted family rituals: A factor in the intergenerational transmission of alcoholism. *J Stud Alcohol* 1980; 41:199–214.

Wolin SJ, Bennett LA, Noonan DL: Family rituals and the recurrence of alcoholism over generations. *Am J Psychiatry* 1979; 16:589–593.

Woodside M: Children of alcoholic parents: Inherited and psychosocial influences. *J Psychiatric Treat Eval* 1983; 5:531–537.

CHAPTER 11

Care of Women and Children in the Perinatal Period

Hope Ewing, M.D.

Psychoactive substance use is associated with significant health effects to mothers, infants, and their families. Pregnancy brings women with drug- and alcohol-related problems into contact with the health care system and offers opportunity for early identification, education, and intervention. As a result of the need for prenatal care, fetal exposure to psychoactive substances, maternal substance dependence, and progressive family dysfunction can be prevented or ameliorated. This chapter presents an overview of the care of women and children who use or are exposed to mood-altering drugs in the perinatal period.

I. Overview

Tobacco use remains the most common drug used by pregnant women. Excluding alcohol-related effects, nicotine use in pregnancy causes more health problems to women and children than all other psychoactive drugs combined. Fetal alcohol syndrome is one of the few preventable types of birth defects. In addition, there is increasing evidence that cocaine and amphetamines have fewer adverse effects on pregnancy and newborns than previously feared.

A. Prevalence

1. ***Tobacco and alcohol:*** Twenty-five percent to 35% of women smoke cigarettes during pregnancy. Among women who are alcohol or drug dependent, almost half smoke more than one pack per day. Studies from several communities indicate that at least 5% of pregnant woman take two or more drinks daily, and 6% to 8% can be classified as "problem drinkers" (Sokol et al., 1981).

2. ***Drugs:*** In several research populations (primarily inner-city minority samples), 4% to 20% of pregnant women were found to use cocaine (Ostrea, 1990), and 14% to 32% used marijuana at least once during their pregnancy. These statistics are from studies using urine and meconium drug testing. Prevalence rates in community-based primary care samples are unknown, but unpublished data from ongoing projects suggest lower rates of use than those reported from inner-

city hospitals (Kokotailo, unpublished data). Six percent of women of childbearing age in the general population reported marijuana use in the past week. Five percent of pregnant women admit taking a narcotic at least once during pregnancy, and an estimated 300,000 children per year are exposed to heroin or methadone in the perinatal period (Zagon et al., 1982).

B. Patterns of Nicotine, Alcohol, and Other Drug Use

1. *Tobacco:* While the prevalence of tobacco use in women has gradually declined, use in pregnant women has fallen more slowly, and appears to be stable in minority populations and adolescents.

2. *Alcohol use:* The total number of women who use alcohol during pregnancy has decreased. The prevalence of heavy binge drinking or daily use is believed to be stable at 5% to 8%.

3. *Illicit drugs:* Women who use addictive drugs tend to use multiple substances. In a national membership survey of Alcoholics Anonymous (AA), 64% of alcohol-dependent women under 31 years of age reported addiction to at least one other prescription or illicit drug. Pregnant women often decrease use of one drug and increase use of another that is perceived as less problematic (e.g., cocaine to alcohol or marijuana).

C. Response of Health Care System

1. *Treatment barriers:* Feelings of anger, hopelessness, and helplessness on the part of professionals create special barriers to the delivery of health care. The education of health care providers, community leaders, and members of the legal system about the disease concept and the nature of recovery helps to restore therapeutic attitudes. The complex needs of this population make coordination between clinical and social services essential (e.g., medical, nursing, social services, drug and alcohol programs, smoking cessation clinics, and the courts).

2. *Ethical issues:* Policies on confidentiality, consent, and reporting need to be defined in each setting to assure clarity and enhance teamwork. Inasmuch as any medical record can be subpoenaed by the courts, health care professionals must be careful with the information that is obtained and recorded. Unless there is a medical emergency, women should always be asked to consent to drug testing for themselves or their newborns. Also, when taking a history clinicians should carefully record major use patterns and symptoms and be cautious about labeling a patient as an alcoholic or an addict. The use of illicit drugs by pregnant women is such a value-laden issue in our society that we may need to protect our patients from inappropriate legal penalties.

3. *Education of community leaders and courts:* Educating community leaders, the courts, and district attorneys at the community level about the use of treatment models rather than punitive ap-

proaches to the problem can be important. While we need to use procedures to help pregnant woman become abstinent, imprisonment is not an effective method. Asking community leaders and the courts to work with physicians and the treatment system to create more treatment opportunities and resources for women and their families is the only method that will break the current cycle of drugs and the breakdown of many urban communities. The management of illicit drug use in pregnancy is primarily a family and social, rather than a medical, problem.

II. Reproductive Health Effects of Maternal Use of Cigarettes, Alcohol, and Other Drugs

Table 11–1 presents an overview of adverse health effects associated with psychoactive drugs. The rest of this section describes each of these findings in more detail.

A. Limitation of Current Research

1. *Health effects:* Since most women at risk for drug-related adverse health effects use multiple psychoactive substances, it is difficult to separate the individual effects of tobacco, alcohol, and illicit drugs. In addition, sociocultural effects—higher rates of sexually transmitted diseases, poor nutritional habits, and a variety of other life-style differences in this population—may produce health problems. The stress produced in many communities by the sale of drugs and associated violence also has important ramifications.

2. *Determining level of use:* Self-report alone underestimates current level of substance use by one fourth or more when compared with urine testing plus interviewing (Frank, 1988). Specimen collection is complicated by legal, ethical, and practical considerations. Meconium testing can detect use of cocaine, marijuana, and opioids during the last weeks of pregnancy (Ostrea, 1990). However, one of the best methods to identify women at risk is to ask about previous use or about alcohol or drug treatment, and in particular, *use in the 6 months before they became pregnant.* Women are more likely to reveal use in the past when they were not pregnant. This information can be used to develop a counseling plan to minimize use during pregnancy.

3. *Generalizing results:* Patterns and effects of drug and alcohol use are influenced by cultural variations. Data from one subculture or class of drugs may not predict effects in other groups (e.g., rural vs. urban, poor vs. affluent, teens vs. mature gravidas, heroin vs. marijuana). The patterns of use have changed as cocaine has replaced much of the opioids used by pregnant women and reduced the number of newborn infants with abstinence syndrome.

B. Nicotine

1. *Pharmacology:* Nicotine-induced catecholamine release produces uterine vasoconstriction and decreased uterine blood flow. Fetal car-

TABLE 11–1.
Overview of Reported Drug Effects

	Fertility	Pregnancy	Fetal Effects	Newborn	Infant	Toddler
Alcohol	Males: Decreased testicular testosterone synthesis; sperm abnormalities Females: Anovulation	Spontaneous abortion with 2 drinks twice/wk (Kline et al., 1980) Preterm labor, placental abruption; precipitous labor with heavy alcohol use	Fetal alcohol syndrome Fetal alcohol effects	Newborn withdrawal syndrome (questionable) Irritability, sleep and feeding disturbances	Fetal alcohol syndrome Fetal alcohol effects	
Benzodiazepines	No physiologic impairment	No physiologic impairment	Diazepam accumulates in fetal circulation	Levels of benzodiazepines 1–3 times maternal levels Sedation, feeding problems, parental bonding problems	Long-term adverse consequences have not been demonstrated	
Stimulants: Cocaine, methamphetamines	No physiologic impairment	Increased rates of miscarriage, placental hemorrhage, preterm labor and delivery. *higher cesarean section rates	Intrauterine growth retardation Microcephaly Proposed *congenital malformations: Prune belly syndrome Missing digits Kidney malformations	Stimulant neonatal syndromes (see p 229)	Abnormalities on Brazelton scores Increased motor tone and visual processing >9 mo "W" position, with arms flexed on either side of head	Poor impulse control Attachment problems Decreased spontaneous play

	Fertility effects	Pregnancy/labor effects	Fetal effects	Neonatal effects	Long-term effects
Marijuana	*Decreased male and female fertility	*Precipitous delivery	Prematurity	No effects	Low-frequency high-amplitude tremors Poor visual response
Cigarettes (nicotine)	May decrease	*Increased 1st trimester bleeding Premature rupture of membranes Placental separation and bleeding Preterm delivery	Intrauterine growth retardation Prematurity	*Increased sudden infant death syndrome (controversial) Suppressant lactation	Respiratory tract and middle ear infections
Opioids	Decreased with heroin Frequent absence of menses (restored with methadone)	Miscarriage Preterm labor *Infections *Toxemia *Premature rupture of membranes *Breech presentation Stillbirth *Cord prolapse	Low birth weight *Decreased head circumference Prematurity No known association with congenital abnormalities	Neonatal abstinence syndrome (rare with methadone dose <20; clinically significant in >66% at higher doses mg/day) Higher doses (50%–60% require medication) Hyperbilirubinemia and hyaline membrane disease may be decreased	Minor neurologic abnormalities Low development scores through 36 wk

*Many of the effects listed are controversial and not well accepted in the scientific community.

boxyhemoglobin levels are 15% to 20% higher than maternal levels. Intravillous placental blood flow decreases acutely with maternal smoking.

2. ***Pregnancy and breast-feeding:*** There is an increased risk of first-trimester bleeding, spontaneous abortion, premature rupture of membranes, and placental abruption (Murphy and Mulcahy, 1978; Department of Health and Human Services, 1980). Decreased milk supply is associated with tobacco use during lactation.

3. ***Fetus, infant, toddler:*** Congenital anomalies are not associated with maternal tobacco use. Reversible intrauterine growth retardation can be seen on ultrasound beginning at 21 weeks gestation. Decreased fetal movement and heart rate beat-to-beat variability are commonly reported. Sudden infant death syndrome (SIDS) is higher in families with heavy smokers. Respiratory tract and middle ear infections are significantly increased with passive cigarette smoke exposure. Babies of mothers who continue to smoke have delayed cognitive development at least to the third year of life (Bolton, 1987; Goodman et al., 1984; Sexton et al., 1990).

C. Alcohol

1. ***Pharmacology:*** Alcohol is metabolized in pregnant women at a rate of approximately one drink every 60 to 90 minutes. Fetal blood alcohol is eliminated mostly by reverse diffusion across the placenta. In the second to third hour after maternal drinking, fetal blood alcohol concentrations exceed maternal levels (Pratt, 1980).

2. ***Adverse effects of alcohol in pregnancy:*** Spontaneous abortion, preterm labor, and placental abruption may be slightly increased with consumption of more than three drinks two or more times a week (AMA, 1983; Marbury et al., 1983).

3. ***Breast-feeding:*** Alcohol levels in breast milk are similar to maternal blood levels. Maternal levels must be very high (300 mg/dL) to produce a sedative effect in the infant. Studies in breast-fed infants of heavy drinking mothers showed equivalent mental development but decreased psychomotor development, compared with controls, at 1 year of age (Little, 1989).

4. ***Fetal Alcohol Syndrome:*** The incidence of fetal alcohol syndrome (FAS) in the general population is 1.5 per 1,000 live births. Seven percent to 10% of women who are daily heavy drinkers will give birth to a child with the clinical characteristics of FAS. FAS appears to be limited to the offspring of women who are daily heavy drinkers in the first trimester. Dizygotic twins have been born to alcoholic mothers, with only one twin affected (Cristoffel et al., 1975). The clinical characteristics of FAS are listed below and are illustrated in Figure 11–1.

   One abnormality from each of three categories:

   a. Prenatal and/or postnatal growth retardation.

   b. CNS involvement (neurologic, intellectual, or developmental).

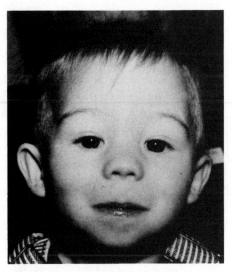

FIG 11–1.
Clinical characteristics of fetal alcohol syndrome.

   c. *Two* of three characteristic facial features:
     (1) Microcephaly,
     (2) Microphthalmia,
     (3) Midfacial abnormalities (philtrum, nasal bridge, maxillary area, thin upper lip)

5. ***Fetal alcohol effects and intrauterine growth retardation:***
Fetal alcohol effects (FAE) or alcohol-related birth defects (ARBD) are partial expressions of FAS, and occur in an additional 3 to 5 per 1,000 live births. Low birth weight due to both prematurity and intrauterine growth retardation (IUGR) is perhaps the most prominent effect of in utero alcohol exposure. These effects have been observed in daily drinkers who consume as little as two drinks per day (Little, 1977; Mills and Graubard, 1987). While these partial effects are difficult to define and separate from other factors, there is widespread agreement that alcohol can cause them.
   a. Fetal alcohol effects are defined as one or two but not all three of the FAS criteria.
   b. Associated features include cardiac abnormalities; neonatal irritability and hypotonia; hyperactivity; hemangiomas; genitourinary, skeletal, muscular, and ocular abnormalities; dental malalignment, malocclusion; eustachian tube dysfunction; increased body fat in adolescent girls.

6. ***Intrapartum abnormalities:*** Amnionitis, preeclampsia, bleeding, precipitous delivery, and meconium staining are increased in mothers with histories of "risk level" drinking (Abel, 1982). Of infants born to mothers consuming less than two drinks per day, 27.9% had

fetal heart rate abnormalities, usually bradycardia or variable decelerations, compared with 16.9% of controls (Streissguth et al., 1982).

7. ***Infants and children:*** Measurable mental and psychomotor developmental delays have been recorded in non-FAS infants with maternal intake of more than two drinks per day (Streissguth et al., 1980). Although the offspring of alcoholic mothers may have normal intelligence and few features of FAE, attention deficits, learning disabilities, and behavioral problems may be increased (Shaywitz, 1980). This whole area of long-term alcohol effects on childhood behavior and learning remains controversial because long-term studies are difficult to conduct and often lack adequate controls.

C. **Cocaine and Methamphetamine**

There is little convincing data to document the potential teratogenic and maternal effects of stimulants. Nearly all studies that have examined the effects of stimulants on the fetus and on pregnant women have been conducted in small, uncontrolled, inner-city samples. Results of the studies presented in this section must be interpreted cautiously.

1. ***Pharmacology:*** Cocaine increases circulating catecholamines that produce maternal tachycardia, vasoconstriction, hypertension, and uterine contractions. Levels of plasma and liver cholinesterases, which are responsible for the metabolic breakdown of cocaine, are decreased in pregnancy. This leads to an increased cocaine half-life. Fetal metabolism produces an active metabolite (norcocaine) that further prolongs the stimulant effects of cocaine. Despite pharmacologic differences, the effects of both cocaine and methamphetamines on pregnancy and the newborn are similar (Oro and Dixon, 1987).

2. ***Fertility:*** There is no known physiologic impairment of fertility from use of cocaine or methamphetamines. "Sex for drugs" practices in the cocaine subculture may increase pregnancy rates.

3. ***Pregnancy:*** Decreased appetite leading to poor nutrition often accompanies regular cocaine use. Placental abruption and preterm labor with premature delivery are slightly increased in pregnant women who use cocaine and amphetamines. Women may freebase cocaine to induce uterine contractions and labor. Prenatal cocaine use has been associated with rupture of an intracranial aneurysm and postpartum intracerebral hemorrhage (Bingol et al., 1987).

4. ***Breast-feeding:*** Case reports suggest that newborns exposed to cocaine through breast milk can develop tachycardia, tachypnea, hypertension, irritability, and tremulousness from maternal use of intranasal cocaine (Chasnoff et al., 1987).

5. ***Fetal effects:*** IUGR may occur, with use in the second and third trimesters causing the most damage. While a number of abnormalities have been suggested by small uncontrolled studies, the teratogenic effects of cocaine remain controversial. Fetal effects reported include prune belly syndrome, missing digits, limb reduction defects, intestinal atresia, genitourinary tract anomalies, and cerebral infarc-

tion (Chasnoff et al., 1988; Dixon, and Bejar, 1988; Cherukuri et al., 1988). The only fetal effects for which there is widespread agreement are growth retardation and microcephaly.

6. ***Newborn:*** Adverse effects include stimulant neonatal syndrome (see section V), increased heart rate and blood pressure on day 1 of life, and a possible predisposition to necrotizing enterocolitis.

7. ***Infant and toddler:*** Infants may exhibit the "W" position, with arms flexed on either side of the head. There may be increased motor tone and impaired visual processing through 9 months (Lewis et al., 1989). Several small studies on users of multiple drugs, including stimulants, suggest poor impulse control, attachment problems, difficulty with transitions, and decreased quality of spontaneous play (Rodning et al., 1989).

D. Marijuana

1. ***Pharmacology:*** Tetrahydrocannabinol (THC) in street marijuana increased from less than 1% to 4% between 1975 and 1984. This effect has increased the amount of cannabinoids in the fetal circulation. Maternal blood concentration of THC is two and one-half to six times higher than fetal blood concentration (Gold, 1989).

2. ***Fertility:*** Decreased sperm count has been noted in men after long-term exposure to marijuana. Women who smoke marijuana more than three times a week have shorter menstrual cycles, shorter luteal phases, and a 30% reduction in lutenizing hormone concentrations.

3. ***Pregnancy and breast-feeding:*** A slight dose-dependent decrease in the duration of gestation has been suggested. Cannabinoids concentrate in breast milk at eight times maternal plasma levels. There have been no adverse effects reported, but there is inadequate long-term follow-up.

4. ***Fetus, newborn, infant:*** Most studies show no increase in fetal anomalies or birth defects (O'Connell and Fried, 1984; Zuckerman et al., 1989). Multiple studies have produced conflicting data regarding the effect of marijuana on birth weight. Studies that have examined the long effects of marijuana are contradictory.

E. Opioids (heroin, methadone, oxycodone, codeine, propxyphene)

1. ***Fertility:*** Decreased pregnancy rates, decreased desire and performance, and frequent amenorrhea are reported (Stoffer, 1986). Fertility is restored with methadone.

2. ***Pregnancy and breast-feeding:*** Miscarriage, preterm labor, infections (heroin only), toxemia, premature rupture of membranes, breech presentation, stillbirth, and cord prolapse are more common in women who use opioids. Heroin passes into breast milk, but no milk/plasma ratio studies have been reported. In addition, while there are case reports of infants addicted to heroin in breast milk, there have been no controlled studies to document this clinical finding. It is unlikely that sufficient methadone is excreted into breast milk to affect the newborn.

3. ***Fetal and newborn issues:*** While there is no evidence linking opioids with congenital anomalies, heroin and methadone are associated with low birth weight and prematurity (Kandall, 1977). Significant neonatal abstinence syndromes have been reported with maternal addiction to heroin, methadone, codeine, and pentazocine. Withdrawal is rare with maternal methadone doses <20 mg/day. Acute symptoms may last for 6 days to 8 weeks. Hyperbilirubinemia and hyaline membrane disease may be *decreased* in newborns chronically exposed to opioids.

III. Case Finding for Mothers and Infants at Risk

The primary purposes of case finding for perinatal alcohol and drug use are to (1) prevent complications of pregnancy; (2) treat the primary maternal addictive disorder; (3) prevent, or at least reduce, fetal exposure to these drugs; and (4) identify families at risk for problematic parent-child relationship issues. There are a number of factors to consider when establishing a case finding system in clinical settings. Some of these factors include specific clinical issues, such as which screening tests are effective, as well as practice and community issues, such as literacy rates, prevalence, cost, legal codes, and acceptability of the case finding system to staff and patients.

A. Self-Report Screening Questions

Two sets of questions that clinicians can use as part of the routine history are the *4 Ps* questionnaire developed by Ewing (1991) and the *T-ACE,* which is a modified version of CAGE (Sokol et al., 1989). Examples of self-administered screening questionnaires are the *Kaiser Permante Prenatal Questionnaire* (Appendix C–6) and the *Perinatal Health Screening Instrument* (Appendix C–7).

1. ***Ewing's 4 Ps screening tool:*** These questions are weighted toward family ramifications of prenatal substance use. "Problem" is defined as continued use despite adverse consequences. *One or more positive answers* indicates a positive screening interview. A more in-depth diagnostic interview is recommended for patients who screen positive. The major advantages of these questions are that (1) they include questions about both alcohol and drugs, (2) there is an orientation toward family issues, and (3) the questionnaire is brief.

   a. Ewing 4 Ps screening questionnaire:
      (1) *Parent* with a drug or alcohol problem   ❑ Yes   ❑ No
      (2) *Partner* with a drug or alcohol problem   ❑ Yes   ❑ No
      (3) *Past* problem with drugs or alcohol   ❑ Yes   ❑ No
      (4) *Pregnancy* use of drugs, alcohol, or cigarettes   ❑ Yes   ❑ No

2. ***T-ACE:*** The T-ACE is based on the CAGE questions. A question on tolerance was substituted for the question "Do you ever feel guilty about your drinking?" Many women who consume even one alcoholic drink may feel guilty. The test has been found to have similar psychometric properties to the CAGE in perinatal settings (Sokol et al., 1989). A response of *three or more drinks to feel high* is consid-

ered a positive score on question (1). Persons who have two or more positive responses to these four questions are considered at risk for problematic alcohol use.

   a. T-ACE questions:

      (1) How many drinks does it *t*ake to make you feel high?   _____

      (2) Have people *a*nnoyed you by criticizing your drinking?   Yes No

      (3) Have you felt you ought to *c*ut down on your drinking?   Yes No

      (4) Have you ever had an *e*ye opener first thing in the morning to steady your nerves?   Yes No

B. Laboratory Screening

Screening with biologic materials such as blood, urine, or meconium determines use, not addictive disease. In contrast to most laboratory studies used in the care of patients, drug screens are complicated by legal and ethical issues, including confidentiality, consent, and the clinical and potential legal uses of the results.

   1. *Urine testing:* Testing for drugs at the time of the first prenatal visit is being used in a number of clinical settings as a screening procedure. While there are ethical and legal issues that require careful deliberation, urine testing will detect a larger number of users than can be detected by self-report. As discussed in Chapter 6, metabolites of many drugs remain in maternal urine for 3 to 7 days. Urine collection in newborns is problematic and is being replaced by meconium testing.

   2. *Meconium testing:* While not widely available, testing for drugs in meconium is expected to become the standard method for drug testing in the newborn (Ostrea, 1989). Chapter 6 provides a review of this test and information about where to send samples.

   3. *Breathalizer testing:* This is a simple and cost-effective test for alcohol and carbon monoxide in smokers.

C. Diagnosis of Maternal Dependence

   1. *Use of screening information:* Prenatal patients who screen positive for possible drug or alcohol abuse should be interviewed. The interview should include a diagnostic assessment, a preventive counseling session, and if appropriate, referral to a local recovery support service.

   2. *Diagnostic questions of use in prenatal patients:* The following are examples of diagnostic questions examining control problems, compulsion, and continued use despite adverse consequences in the childbearing population.

      a. Do you ever spend more of your money than you planned on drugs or alcohol?

      b. Does anyone in your family ever complain about your drinking or using?

c. Has your partner ever been violent with you when you were using drugs or alcohol?

d. Have you ever left your children longer than you intended or with someone you didn't quite trust when you were using alcohol or drugs?

e. Do you have any children placed out of your custody?

3. American Psychiatric Association DSM criteria should be used for formal diagnosis of use, abuse, and dependence.

IV. Management of Pregnant Women at Risk

A. Identification of Potential Alcohol- and Drug-Related Health Effects in Pregnancy

A number of clinical methods may be used to detect the adverse effects of alcohol and other psychoactive drugs in the perinatal period.

1. *Cardiovascular effects:* Patients with cardiac problems may present with labile hypertension, arrhythmias, or unexplained tachycardia. These effects are associated with stimulant use or sedative withdrawal. Auscultation of the heart to assess for cardiac murmurs (subacute bacterial endocarditis, SBE), arrhythmias, and heart rate during each prenatal visit may detect these problems before significant morbidity develops. Examining patients' arms for needle tracks also may provide clues.

2. *Infectious diseases:* Infections are more common in alcohol- or drug-dependent persons. Potential infections include tuberculosis, tetanus, hepatitis, syphilis, human immunodeficiency virus (HIV) infection, gonorrhea, *Chlamydia,* herpes, condylomas, mycoses, skin abscesses, dental abscesses, pneumonia, and endocarditis. Routine care should include HIV testing, preferably in the first trimester; VDRL, cultures for gonorrhea and *Chlamydia;* PPD (purified protein derivative of tuberculin) and hemoglobin S antigen (HbSAg).

3. *Trauma:* Women are sometimes exposed to physical abuse by their partners, a family member, or acquaintances. These violent acts often start or increase during pregnancy. Patients should be examined for bruises and asked about trauma or recent emergency department visits.

4. *Intrauterine fetal effects:* Fetal and intrauterine abnormalities are more common in this group, and routine ultrasonography at 16 to 20 weeks has been recommended (Evans, 1991). Because amenorrhea is common, this examination also will assist in determining the expected date of confinement.

B. Practical Clinical Issues in Intrapartum and Postpartum Periods

1. *Clinical effects:* Cocaine use in the preceding 12 to 24 hours may be associated with maternal and fetal tachycardia. Contrary to popular belief, duration of labor is not shortened with intrapartum cocaine use (Dombrowski, 1991). While fetal heart rate abnormalities have been observed, their clinical significance is unknown (Evans, 1991). The major clinical issue associated with these tracing abnormalities is

the potential for an inappropriate medical intervention, such as a cesarean section or instrument-assisted delivery.

2. *Analgesia:* Withdrawal may be precipitated in persons who are opioid dependent. Avoid the use of opioids with partial agonist-antagonists properties (e.g., buprenorphine or pentazocine) in pregnant women. Patients receiving methadone should maintain their normal schedule. Additional opioids may be necessary.

3. *Postpartum clinical issues:* Warn patients about contraindications to stimulant and sedative use in breast-feeding. Support breast-feeding in stable methadone-maintained mothers who are not using other drugs and alcohol. Advise mothers about dangers of ambient smoke containing nicotine or other drugs.

C. **Intervention and Treatment of the Primary Disorder**

1. *Goals:* The primary goal of intervention and treatment is total abstinence from all addictive psychoactive drugs. A related goal is acceptance by the patient that she is unable to control use by herself. *Safe levels* for drug and alcohol use in pregnancy have not been determined. A single episode of use of drugs or alcohol may harm the fetus or compromise the pregnancy. Although decreased use reduces risk to the fetus and the mother, clinicians should not recommend decreased use, because safe limits have not been established. In addition, women who are dependent and exhibit loss of control when they use may not be able to stop with one drink.

2. *Presenting the diagnosis and working with denial:* Most patients are cooperative and appreciative, despite an overlay of denial. A therapeutic position of acceptance, a positive caring outlook, and hope for recovery are most effective. Specific points clinicians may want to consider include the following:

   a. Address the issue of control directly.
   b. Avoid lecturing the patient.
   c. Stress the goal of abstinence from all psychoactive substances.
   d. Since many patients with alcohol and drug disorders started using substances in their formative adolescent years, they may have missed some of the normal developmental stages. Allow denial and adolescent behavior to emerge during the interview.

3. *Patient reaction:* It is important to listen to the patient's perspective, support the "feelings behind the words," and work with their denial to help them obtain the needed treatment.

   a. Common responses of women in denial:
      (1) I use, but it's not a problem.
      (2) I had a problem in the past, but I stopped using/drinking as soon as I found out I was pregnant.
      (3) I have a problem, but I have to solve it on my own.
      (4) I have a problem, but I just don't care (whether I or the baby lives or dies).

     (5) I have a problem, but I can't accept help because (e.g., my boyfriend won't let me, no transportation, no child care)

     (6) It would be a problem, but (e.g., my parents, my boyfriend) always takes care of everything.

     (7) I wish I could tell you about my problem, but I'm afraid what it will mean to me and my children.

4. ***Brief intervention/preventive counseling:*** While reviewing the effects of substances on pregnancy and the fetus, consider the patient's feelings of shame, guilt, and fear. Discuss how the health care system relates to toxicology testing, protective services, or criminal justice reporting, confidentiality, and consent. Mirror to the patient the reality of her situation as you have heard it. Clinicians may want to use the following statements when conducting a brief intervention.

   a. We care about you and your baby and believe in your ability to change.

   b. This is a disease that is not your fault.

   c. It is a chronic relapsing illness.

   d. In many cases alcohol and drug problems are passed down through the family.

   e. Recovery starts with the first step of admitting you have a problem.

   f. Admit that you may not be able to do it on your own.

   g. Treatment works with most patients who participate in a chemical dependency treatment program and helps them remain abstinent.

5. ***Referral:*** If it is difficult to conduct a diagnostic assessment within the practical restraints of a busy practice, women who are identified as at risk can be referred for an assessment. One way to make the referral is to tell the patient you would like a second opinion. General guidelines for referral are listed below.

   a. Do not wait for a firm diagnosis.

   b. Refer to community programs, even if it seems none are geared for a pregnant woman with small children. Referrals generate resources. Motivated women may find recovery with scant resources.

   c. Consider involving other family members in the referral.

   d. Patients requesting help immediately can be given the handout called "First steps," which outlines how to begin abstinence and use local support over the next 24 hours.

First Steps for Yourself and Your Baby When You Want to Stop Using Drugs and Alcohol

Step 1: Get all drugs and alcohol out of your house.

Step 2: Get all drug paraphernalia out of your house.

Step 3: Tell the people you live with you cannot have any drugs, alcohol, or paraphernalia around.

Step 4:   Tell roommates, family, and father of the baby to stay away unless they are clean and sober.

Step 5:   If you can't clean up where you live, find a safe place to live.

Step 6:   Stay away from people, places, and things that make you think of drinking and/or using.

Step 7:   Plan other activities for the time of day when you used to use.

Step 8:   Get and use the phone number of someone who understands.

Step 9:   Use your local recovery resources (AA, NA, CA, and programs).

D. Pharmacologic Treatment of Addiction in Pregnancy

Pharmacologic treatment is not essential for cocaine, amphetamine, nicotine, PCP, hallucinogen, or inhalant withdrawal. While withdrawal from these drugs may be uncomfortable, there are few serious health problems. However, withdrawal from opiates can be life-threatening to the fetus, and sedative withdrawal (e.g., alcohol, benzodiazepines) may be fatal to both the fetus and the mother in the rare event of maternal seizures or vascular collapse.

1. ***Methadone maintenance for opioid dependence*** (also see Chapter 3): One daily dose usually blocks the effects of withdrawal. Methadone clearance increases as pregnancy progresses, because of decreased plasma protein binding and the more rapid metabolism associated with increasing progestin levels.

2. ***Fetal effects:*** Maternal opiate withdrawal can cause fetal death (Hoegerman and Schnoll, 1991). Significant opiate use is associated with increased pregnancy loss and decreased fetal growth, which are partially reversed with methadone maintenance. Therefore methadone maintenance usually is recommended for established opioid-dependent patients who become pregnant.

   a. *Legal issues:* Methadone may be legally prescribed only for maintenance or outpatient detoxification by licensed clinics, and many communities lack such clinics. Any licensed physician with a DEA number, can prescribe methadone for a patient who is in a hospital setting for up to 3 days (Code of Federal Regulations, 1990).

   b. *High vs. low dosage:* Divergence occurs between programs using mostly high methadone doses (50 to 80 mg) in pregnancy and those using low doses (20 to 30 mg). With high doses mothers are less likely to use heroin, but with low doses they are less likely to produce newborn withdrawal syndrome.

   c. *Increased dosing requirements:* Maternal methadone needs may increase as pregnancy progresses (see 1, above). Split doses (two thirds given in the morning and one third given in the afternoon as a take-home dose) may be helpful in preventing early morning withdrawal symptoms. Blind dosing may facilitate successful dose reduction.

d. *Conflict with 12-Step programs:* There are philosophic differences between methadone treatment programs and the standard sobriety-based 12-Step approach. Women receiving methadone may be denied full access to other recovery resources, such as drug-free residential recovery programs and full participation in Narcotics Anonymous.

3. ***Sedative withdrawal:*** Phenobarbital is the drug of choice for withdrawal. Treatment protocols are given in Chapter 3. Inpatient medical withdrawal by a physician with expertise in detoxification in women may be indicated for women with a history of withdrawal seizures or delirium tremens. While treatment parallels that in women who are not pregnant, a baseline fetal ultrasound and monitoring of fetal activity and heart rate are necessary.

4. ***Safety of other pharmacologic agents used to treat primary addictive disorder:***

    a. *Clonidine,* used for treatment of withdrawal from many substances, lowers the blood pressure. Use in pregnancy is experimental.

    b. *Disulfiram (Antabuse)* is teratogenic and contraindicated in pregnancy and lactation.

    c. *Use of tricyclics* to decrease craving for cocaine is experimental in pregnancy.

V. Pharmacologic Treatment of Newborn Syndrome

The recent epidemic of cocaine use by pregnant women complicates the management of newborn abstinence syndrome because stimulants, opioids, and sedatives often are used in combination. If cocaine is the primary drug of choice, newborns do not usually require medication, and may be discharged after 4 days if symptoms do not develop.

A. Opioid Abstinence Syndrome

Neonatal opiate withdrawal may be life-threatening as a result of diarrhea, dehydration, and seizures.

1. ***Clinical diagnosis:*** Opioid abstinence syndrome consists of yawning, fist sucking, irritability, poor feeding, poor weight gain, tremulousness, and seizures. Opiate abstinence syndrome usually is scored on the Finnegan scale (Table 11–2). The abstinence score lists 21 symptoms most commonly found in the passively opioid addicted newborn. The symptoms are assessed within 2 hours of birth, and then every 4 hours for 96 hours unless the score exceeds 8. If the score exceeds 8, the assessment is repeated at 2-hour intervals, and if the average score for the three consecutive assessments is ≥8, pharmacotherapy usually is initiated.

    a. *Heroin abstinence syndrome* begins within the first 4 days of life. The acute phase of the syndrome may last as long as 1 week. A

TABLE 11-2.

Neonatal Abstinence Scoring System*

Central nervous system disturbances	
Excessive high-pitched (or other) cry	2
Continuous high-pitched (or other) cry	
Sleeps <1 hour after feeding	3
Sleeps <2 hours after feeding	2
Sleeps <3 hours after feeding	1
Hyperactive Moro reflex	2
Markedly hyperactive Moro reflex	3
Mild tremors disturbed	1
Moderate to severe tremors disturbed	2
Mild tremors undisturbed	3
Moderate to severe tremors undisturbed	4
Increased muscle tone	2
Excoriation (specific areas)	1
Myoclonic jerk	3
Generalized convulsions	5
Metabolic vasomotor respiratory disturbances	
Sweating	1
Fever (temp <38° C, <101° F)	1
Fever (temp >38° C, >101° F)	2
Frequent yawning (>3-4 times/interval)	1
Mottling	1
Nasal stuffiness	1
Sneezing (>3-4 times/interval)	1
Nasal flaring	2
Respiratory rate >60/min	1
Respiratory rate >60/min with retractions	2
Gastrointestinal disturbances	
Excessive sucking	1
Poor feeding	2
Regurgitation	
Projectile vomiting	3
Loose stools	2
Watery stools	3

*From Finnegan LP: Neonatal abstinence syndrome, in Nelson RM (ed): *Current Therapy in Neonatal-Perinatal Medicine*, vol 11. Philadelphia, BC Decker, 1990. Used by permission.

protracted abstinence syndrome may develop with persistent symptoms for up to 6 weeks.

  b. If the mother's dose of *methadone* was >30 mg/day, 50% to 60% of newborns will have symptoms requiring treatment. Methadone withdrawal may require 1 to 6 weeks, and some signs or symptoms may last several months.

2. ***Pharmacologic treatment:*** Before therapy is begun, a thorough workup should be conducted, including serum glucose, calcium, and magnesium levels, cultures of urine and blood, and toxicology screen. Pharmacotherapy is not indicated unless the Finnegan score is more than 7 for three consecutive assessments or is more than 12 on two assessments. The primary drugs of choice are paregoric or phenobarbital. The dosing schedule is based on the Finnegan scoring system. Since a number of clinical problems are encountered when treating newborn opioid abstinence syndrome, infants should be treated in an intensive care unit under the supervision of a neonatologist or physician with expertise in this area.

3. ***Paregoric:*** The following are general guidelines for the use of these medications. The clinician should consult Finnegan (1990) for a more complete description of use of paregoric and phenobarbital.

   a. For initial treatment with a Finnegan score of more than 8, paregoric should be given every 4 hours. The recommended dose is 0.8 mL/kg/day for a Finnegan score of 8 to 10, 1.2 mL/kg/day for a score of 11 to 13, and 1.6 for a score of more than 13.

   b. The dose should be increased 0.4 mL/kg/day every 4 hours until symptoms are controlled and the score falls below 8.

   c. Once symptoms have been controlled, maintain the dose for 72 hours. The clinician may need to recalculate the dose if the newborn loses weight.

   d. After stabilization is achieved, reduce the daily dose by 10% for every 24-hour period.

   e. When the dose reaches 0.5 mL/kg, paregoric may be discontinued.

4. ***Phenobarbital:***

   a. An initial loading dose of 20 mg/kg is recommended for three consecutive Finnegan scores of more than 8. The initial serum level drawn 12 hours after the first dose should range from 18 to 22 μg/mL.

   b. Twelve hours after the loading dose, additional phenobarbital is given using the Finnegan score. For a score of 8 to 10, phenobarbital 6 mg/kg every 8 hours should be administered; for a score of 11 to 13, phenobarbital 8 mg/kg; and for a score of more than 13, 10 mg/kg every 8 hours. It may be necessary to push phenobarbital to a serum level of 70 μg/mL to achieve controlled withdrawal symptoms.

   c. Once the infant's condition has stabilized, phenobarbital should be reduced by 10% per day.

5. ***Evaluation of CNS depression during pharmacotherapy is critical.*** Newborns receiving drugs for the treatment of abstinence syndromes may develop precipitous changes. The following clinical changes should be assessed regularly and may indicate a life-threatening event.

   a. Altered state of arousal.

    b. Diminished response to painful stimuli.

    c. Central or circumoral cyanosis or persistent mottling.

    d. Altered respirations (irregular breathing, apneic episodes, rate of more than 20).

    e. Cardiac problems (irregular rate, poor peripheral perfusion, rate of more than 100).

    f. Hypothermia.

    g. Diminished or absent reflexes (Moro, sucking, swallowing, tonic neck, grasp).

B. Stimulant Withdrawal Syndrome

1. ***Clinical recognition:*** Neonatal stimulant syndrome is seen in newborns exposed in utero to chronic high doses of cocaine or amphetamines. The effects of cocaine and methamphetamine are similar. The prevalence of this syndrome has been reported to vary from 0% to 80% in exposed newborns. A 1991 telephone survey of six neonatal intensive care units in Wisconsin suggested that the prevalence is very low, with most centers reporting fewer than two known cases per year, none of which have required the use of pharmacotherapy (Fleming, unpublished data). It is unclear whether the syndrome represents withdrawal, acute toxicity, or other effects (Oro and Dixon, 1987). Effects begin at 1½ days, and peak at 2½ days after birth. The clinical picture is extremely variable, and may be incorrectly attributed to a difficult labor or some unknown self-limited process. The major signs, symptoms, and frequency of occurrence are as follows:

    a. Tremor 70%

    b. Poor feeding 58%

    c. Hypertonia 52%

    d. Vomiting 51%

    e. Sneezing 45%

    f. Tachypnea 19%

    g. Loose stools 16%

    h. Hyperreflexia 15%

    i. Yawning 12.9%

2. ***Treatment:*** Management usually is limited to nonpharmacologic methods:

    a. Swaddling or positioning the infant to bring hands together.

    b. Using pacifiers.

    c. Avoiding sudden noises and eye contact and judiciously reintroducing eye contact.

    d. Avoiding walkers and jumpers that encourage arching of back.

    e. Minimizing abrupt transitions.

    f. Educating parents.

    g. Giving benzodiazepines or barbiturates for severe agitation.

BIBLIOGRAPHY

Abel EL: Consumption of alcohol during pregnancy: A review of effects on growth and development of offspring. *Human Biol* 1982; 54:421.

American Medical Association Council on Scientific Affairs: Fetal effects of maternal alcohol use. *JAMA* 1983; 249:2517.

Bingol N, Fuchs M, Diaz V, et al: Teratogenicity of cocaine in humans. *J Pediatr* 1987; 110:93.

Bolton PJ: Drugs of abuse, in Hawkins DF (ed): *Drugs and Pregnancy.* New York, Churchill Livingstone, 1987.

Chasnoff IJ, Chisum GM, Kaplan WE: Maternal cocaine use and genitourinary tract malformations. *Teratology* 1988; 37:201.

Chasnoff IJ, Lewis DE, Squires L: Cocaine intoxication in a breast-fed infant. *Pediatrics* 1987; 80:836–838.

Cherukuri R, Minkoff H. Feldman J, et al: A cohort study of alkaloid cocaine ("crack') in pregnancy. *Obstet Gynecol* 1988; 72:147.

Code of Federal Regulations: Administering or dispersing of narcotic drugs. Office of the Federal Register, Washington, DC, US Government Printing Office, Title XXI, Section 1306.07, subpart b, p 72, April 1990.

Cristoffel KK, Salafsky I: Fetal alcohol syndrome in dizygotic twins. *J Pediatr* 1975; 87:963.

Department of Health and Human Services: Health Consequences of Smoking for Women: A report of the Surgeon General. Bethesda, Md, 1980, 0–326–003.

Dixon SD, Bejar R: Brain lesions in cocaine and methamphetamine exposed neonates (abst). *Pediatr Res* 1988; 23:405.

Downing GJ, et al: Characteristics of perinatal cocaine-exposed infants with necrotizing enterocolitis. *Am J Dis Child* 1991; 145:26.

Evans A, Gillogley K: Drug use in pregnancy: Obstetrical perspectives. *Clin Perinatol* 1991; 18:23.

Ewing H: Management of the pregnant alcoholic/addict. Presented at American Society on Addiction Medicine, Medical Scientific Conference, Boston, April 20, 1991.

Finnegan LP: Neonatal abstinence syndrome, in Nelson RM (ed): *Current Therapy in Neonatal-Perinatal Medicine,* vol 11. Philadelphia, BC Decker, 1990.

Frank DA, Zuckerman BS, Amaro H, et al: Cocaine use in pregnancy: Prevalence and correlates. *Pediatrics* 1988; 82:888–895.

Gold MS: *Marijuana.* New York, Plenum Press, 1989.

Goodman JDS, Visser FGA, Dawes GS: Effects of maternal cigarette smoking on fetal trunk movements, fetal breathing movements, and the fetal heart rate. Br J Obstet Gynecol 1984; 91:657.

Hoegerman G, Schnoll S: Narcotic use in pregnancy. *Clin Perinatal* 1991; 18:51.

Kandall SR, Albin S, Gartner LM, et al: The narcotic-dependent mother: Fetal and neonatal consequences. *Early Hum Dev* 1977; 12:159–169.

Kline J, Shrout P, Stein Z, et al: Drinking during pregnancy and spontaneous abortion. *Lancet* 1980; 2:176–180.

Lewis K, Bennett B, Schmeder N: The care of infants menaced by cocaine. *Maternal Child Nurs* 1989; 14:324.

Little RE, Anderson KW, Ervin CK, et al: Maternal alcohol use during breast-feeding and infant mental and motor development at one year. *N Engl J Med* 1989; 321.

Little RE: Moderate alcohol use during pregnancy and decreased infant birth weight. *Am J Public Health* 1983; 67:1161.

Little RE: Moderate alcohol use during pregnancy and decreased infant birth weight. *Am J Publ Health* 1977; 67:1154–1156.

Marbury M-C, Linn J, Monson R, et al: The association of alcohol consumption with outcome of pregnancy. *Am J Publ Health* 1983; 73:1165.

Mendelson JH, Mello NK, Ellingboe J, et al: Marihuana smoking supresses leuteinizing hormone in women. *J Pharmacol Exp Ther* 1986; 237:862.

Mills JL, Graubard BI: Is moderate drinking during pregnancy associated with an increased risk of malformations? *Pediatrics* 1987; 80:309.

Murphy J, Mulcahy R: Cigarette smoking and spontaneous abortion. *Br Med J* 1978; 1:988.

O'Connell CM, Fried PA: An investigation of prenatal cannabis exposure and minor physical anomalies in a low resk population. *Neurobehav Toxicol Teratol* 1984; 6:345.

Oro AS, Dixon SD: Perinatal cocaine and methamphetamine exposure: Maternal and neonatal correlates. *J Pediatr* 1987; 111:571–578.

Ostrea EM, Parks P, Brady M: The detection of heroin, cocaine, and cannabinoid metabolites in meconium of infants of drug dependent mothers. *Ann NY Acad Sci* 1989; 562: 373–374.

Pratt OE: The fetal alcohol syndrome: Transport of nutrients and transfer of alcohol and acetaldehyde from mother to fetus, in Sandler M (ed): *Psychopharmocology of Alcohol.* New York, Raven Press, 1980.

Ramer C, Lodge A: Clinical and developmental characteristics of infants of mothers on methadone maintenance. *Addict Dis* 1975; 2:227.

Rodning C, Beckwith L, Howard J: Characteristics of attachment organization and play organization in prenatally drug-exposed toddlers. *Dev Psychopathol* 1989; 1:227.

Sexton MJ, Fox NL, Herbel JR: Prenatal exposure to tobacco: Effects on cognitive functioning at age three. *Int J Epidemiol* 1990; 19:72–77.

Shaywitz SE, Cohen DJ, Shaywitz BA: Behavior and learning difficulties in children of normal intelligence born to alcoholic mothers. *J Pediatr* 1980; 96:978.

Sokol RJ, Martier SS, Ager JW: The T-ACE questions: Practical prenatal detection of risk-drinking. *Am J Obstet Gynecol* 1989; 160:863–870.

Sokol RJ, Miller SI, Debanne S, et al: The Cleveland NIAAA prospective alcohol-in-pregnancy study. *Neurobehav Toxicol Teratol* 1981; 3:203.

Stoffer SS: A gynecologic study of drug addicts. *Am J Obstet Gynecol* 1986; 101:779.

Streissguth AP, Barr HM, Martin D: Offspring effects and pregnancy complications related to self-reported maternal alcohol use. *Dev Pharmacol Ther* 1982; 65:21.

Streissguth AP, Barr HM, Martin DC, et al: Effects of maternal alcohol, nicotine, and caffeine use during pregnancy on infant mental and motor development at eight months. *Alcohol Clin Exp Res* 1980; 4:152.

Woods JR, Plessinger MA, Clark KE: Effect of cocaine on uterine blood blow and fetal oxygenation. *JAMA* 1987; 257:957–961.

Zagon IS, McLaughlin PJ, Weaver DJ, et al: Opiates, endorphins and the developing organism: A comprehensive bibliography. *Neuro Behav Rev* 1982; 6:439.

Zuckerman B, Frank D, Hingson R, et al: Effects of maternal marijuana and cocaine use on fetal growth. *N Engl J Med* 1989; 320:762.

CHAPTER 12

Adolescent Substance Abuse

Stephen Flynn, M.D.

Adolescence is a time of rapid change and experimentation. Nicotine, alcohol, and drug use as well as eating disorders frequently begin during this period. While some adolescents develop serious problems related to substance use, most progress through this period of increased experimentation and develop healthy patterns of limited use. The one major exception is the use of tobacco products, which often continues in the form of physical dependence and addiction to nicotine. While communicating with and treating adolescents is often difficult, it also provides the clinician with a unique opportunity to ask about alcohol and drug use. This chapter reviews the recognition and treatment of nicotine, alcohol, and drug use and abuse in adolescents.

I. Introduction
A. How Common are Alcohol and Drug Problems?
1. **Prevalence:** The best estimate of the frequency of tobacco, alcohol, and drug use is derived from an annual survey conducted by the National Institute of Drug Abuse (NIDA) of more than 17,000 seniors in 133 public and private high schools in the United States. The findings of this survey are displayed in Figure 12–1. Nine of 10 high school seniors report some lifetime experience with alcohol. Two thirds of the seniors have tried smoking, and about half have experimented with illicit drugs.
   a. These figures may underestimate the true prevalence of use, because they are based on responses from high school seniors and do not include students who have dropped out of school.
   b. Similar results were noted for the 18- to 25-year-old cohort in the 1990 National Household Survey on Drug Abuse. This survey sampled 8,814 households, representing 98% of the population in the contiguous United States.
2. **Risk of drug use:** A small but significant group of adolescents will become regular users and develop problems with chemical abuse. Even occasional users or nonusers are at risk of serious injury from alcohol or drug-related automobile accidents.
3. **Downward trend:** Despite the slight downward trend in use in

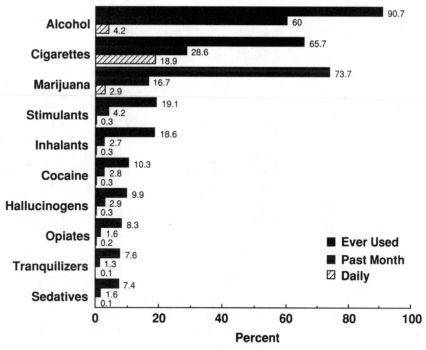

FIG 12–1.
Best estimate of tobacco, alcohol, and drug use in high school seniors. The survey was conducted in 1990 in 17,000 students in 133 public and private schools in the United States. (From *NIDA Capsules,* 1990.)

some adolescent populations over the past few years, the use of drugs, especially alcohol, tobacco, and marijuana, remains widespread and poses a major health hazard for the adolescent population.

4. ***Gateway drug exposure:*** First exposure to the "gateway drugs" of cigarettes, alcohol, and marijuana usually is in grades 4 through 8; thus education and screening must begin with elementary school age children.

B. Definitions

In contrast to adults, physical dependence, with the development of withdrawal and tolerance, is uncommon in adolescents. As a result, it is more difficult to diagnose an alcohol or drug disorder in an adolescent. Clinicians should use the labels "alcoholic" or "drug addict" sparingly in this population; the terms "abuse" or "problematic use" are more appropriate and better describe the clinical issues.

1. ***Adolescent substance abuse:*** Problematic alcohol and drug use in adolescents probably is best defined as the *recurrent, compulsive use* of any chemical substance that is *causing negative consequences* in some area of the adolescent's life, including:

   a. Health.

   b. Family or social relationships.

    c. School or work performance.

    d. Legal or financial problems.

    e. Personal development.

Adolescent substance abuse also includes any chemical use that places the adolescent *at risk of physical injury* (e.g., driving under the influence of alcohol or drugs).

2. **Dependence:** The use of the term "chemical dependency" in adolescents is confusing because physical dependence is uncommon. "Substance abuse" is more descriptive, and includes a greater number of youth who are in trouble and could use help.

3. **Abuse definitions:** For clinical purposes, several working definitions of nicotine, alcohol, and drug abuse in adolescents can be used:

    a. *Cigarette smoking* is never healthy, and constitutes nicotine abuse at any level of use.

    b. *Alcohol* use is illegal for teenagers. Any use of alcohol can be considered misuse and must be viewed with caution. The use of alcohol can be considered abuse if it disrupts or has any negative impact on the adolescent's life or if it places the adolescent at risk of serious injury.

    c. Any use of *illicit drugs* may be considered misuse. Continuing use of illicit drugs poses significant health, social, and legal risks to the adolescent and constitutes abuse. While the primary illicit drugs used are street drugs, such as marijuana, cocaine, amphetamines, PCP, and LSD, use of sedatives obtained surreptitiously from family member's prescription bottles, over-the-counter (OTC) amphetamine-like agents, and inhalants are of increasing concern.

C. Stages of Adolescent Substance Abuse

Adolescent substance *abuse* generally progresses from experimentation with gateway drugs (tobacco, beer, wine, wine coolers, marijuana) to more frequent use of a wider variety of substances, with increasing negative consequences. This progression can be divided into *four stages*. Although these stages are not always applicable, they may be helpful in understanding adolescent substance abuse and deciding when and what type of treatment is necessary.

1. **Stage 1: Experimentation (misuse):**

    a. The adolescent often has his or her first experience in elementary or junior high school, and may experience a first hangover at this time.

    b. The use is infrequent and usually involves cigarettes, beer, wine coolers, or marijuana, but may include inhalants, OTC drugs, or cocaine, depending on availability and setting.

    c. The adolescent is learning to handle the mood-altering effects of psychoactive substances. Adolescents usually have a low tolerance to these substances.

    d. Parental modeling is an important influence. Parents who use alcohol or drugs on a regular basis send a clear message to their adolescent children regarding normal standards of use.

  e. Peer pressure is the single most powerful predictor of use.

  f. Consequences are generally few, but may involve serious physical injury while intoxicated.

2. ***Stage 2: Seeking the mood swing (early abuse):***

  a. The adolescent begins using regularly, but often only on weekends.

  b. Tolerance increases, and the teenager begins to experiment with other drugs, including liquor, stimulants, hallucinogens, and cocaine.

  c. They rationalize use, including relief of negative feelings, to impress friends, and to get ready for social occasions.

  d. Consequences may include:

    (1) School problems.

    (2) Truancy.

    (3) Loss of nonusing friends.

    (4) Sneaking out.

    (5) Hangovers.

    (6) Mood swings.

3. ***Stage 3: Preoccupation with the mood swing (abuse):***

  a. The adolescent is preoccupied with alcohol or drugs and uses during the week as well as on weekends.

  b. Activities revolve around the chemical use, and almost all friends are users.

  c. Tolerance continues to increase, and the adolescent maintains a supply of drugs and paraphernalia.

  d. The adolescent becomes more withdrawn from the family and begins using drugs alone.

  e. Consequences continue to increase, and may include stealing, fighting, injuries, blackouts, depression, overdoses, physical hygiene deterioration, and legal problems.

4. ***Stage 4: Compulsion and burnout (addiction):***

  a. The adolescent uses alcohol or drugs compulsively, usually daily.

  b. The adolescent uses the chemical to feel normal, and continues to use despite increasing negative consequences, including criminal activity, dealing, withdrawal symptoms, paranoia and self-hate, suicide attempts, and severe emotional and spiritual pain.

  c. Multiple drugs commonly are used, and the adolescent may remain high for several days.

D. Risk Factors

Several factors are associated with an increased likelihood of adolescent substance abuse. The following risk factors are warning signals that should raise the provider's index of suspicion for substance abuse:

1. Family history of addiction, including drugs or alcohol, gambling, eating disorders.

2. Family attitudes favorable to smoking and drinking.
3. Friends who smoke, drink, or use drugs.
4. Antisocial or criminal behavior.
5. History of conduct or affective disorder.
6. Involvement in drug trafficking.
7. Chronic family stress.
8. Excessive parental discipline or permissiveness.
9. Physical or sexual abuse.
10. Low self-esteem.
11. Transfer to new school or other form of social isolation.
12. Poor academic performance or lack of interest.

II. Diagnosis of Substance Abuse in Adolescents
A. General Comments
1. *Frequency of physician visits:* Teenagers generally are healthy and visit the doctor infrequently. Physicians need to take advantage of these limited contacts to identify nicotine, alcohol, and drug use.
2. *Screening opportunities include:*
   a. Health maintenance visits, such as school, camp, or sports physical examinations.
   b. Suggestive symptoms, such as fatigue, chronic cough, headache, palpitations, or indigestion.
   c. Acute care visits for trauma.
   d. Behavioral changes at home or school.
   e. Any hospital or office encounter.
3. *Time without parents:* It is important to have some time alone with the adolescent, starting at around age 11 years. Demonstrating a *sincere respectful attitude* is essential to establish trust with a teenager.
4. *Confidentiality:* While physicians are often viewed with respect, discussing issues of confidentiality may facilitate the development of trust. Clinicians need to be honest and not promise total confidentiality unless they can adhere to the decision no matter what the adolescent reveals.
5. *Gaining trust:* There is no short-cut to making the diagnosis. It takes time to gain the adolescent's trust and gather sufficient information about chemical use and the associated consequences.

B. How to Conduct the Interview
Questions about chemical use can be asked as part of the social history during the routine history and physical examination process. One useful method is to start with general questions about psychosocial function, then proceed to indirect and direct questions about chemical use.
1. *Step 1:* Inquire about psychosocial function and potential consequences of alcohol and drug use.
   a. *School:*
      (1) How are your grades this year (compared with last year)?
      (2) Are you having any trouble with your teachers?
      (3) Have you been absent frequently, or suspended?

    b. *Friends:*
      (1) Do you have any close friends?
      (2) Are they your age?
      (3) What do your parents think about your friends?
      (4) Have you changed friends in the past year?
    c. *Recreation/work:*
      (1) Are you involved in sports or other extracurricular activities?
      (2) Do you have an after school job?
      (3) Have you dropped any activities in the past year?
      (4) What do you do at night and on weekends with your friends?
    d. *Family relationships:*
      (1) Who do you go to for support in your family?
      (2) Who sets limits in your family?
      (3) Are there family rules about curfew, driving, etc?
      (4) What does your family like to do together?
    e. *Legal:*
      (1) Have you ever been in trouble with the police?
2. ***Step 2:*** Ask questions that provide *indirect* information about possible chemical use; ask questions that permit positive responses.
    a. What do you do to have fun? Parties? Clubs?
    b. How many kids at your school smoke (drink, use marijuana)?
    c. How many of your friends smoke?
    d. How many of your friends are into drinking or doing drugs?
    e. How much drinking or drugs do you see at parties or dances?
    f. What brand of cigarettes (beer) is popular with kids you know?
    g. Have you ever ridden in a car when the driver had been drinking or using drugs?
    h. Do any of your family members smoke, drink, or use drugs?
3. ***Step 3:*** Once trust has been established, *direct questions* often are answered with surprising candor and honesty. Ask about individual chemical use, progressing from cigarettes to alcohol, marijuana, cocaine, and other street drugs. Ask specifically about each drug of concern. Be nonjudgmental.
    a. It may help to ask about past behavior first, and to phrase questions such that positive answers are expected; for example:
      (1) Tell me about the first time you tried a cigarette (beer, marijuana).
      (2) Many kids your age have tried drinking at some time. Have you?
      (3) Not even once?
    b. Then ask about current use. You may purposely overestimate use to allow the adolescent to admit use at a seemingly more acceptable level.
      (1) How often are you drinking these days? Three times a week?
      (2) How much do you drink at a time? A case?
      (3) When was the last time you drank?

        (4) Do you smoke now? A pack a day?

        (5) Do your friends or family think you drink or use drugs too much?

C. Self-Administered Written Screening Instruments

Another method of screening in the office setting is the use of a self-administered written questionnaire. Adolescents often will divulge more in this manner than in a direct interview. The questionnaire could be completed while the patient is waiting to be seen.

    1. ***Recommended screening test for adolescent self-report:*** An example of a simple screening questionnaire for adolescent substance abuse is displayed in Figure 12–2. This instrument was developed for the Society of Teachers of Family Medicine, Physician Intervention Kit. While this test has face validity and allows clinicians to obtain screening information, it is not diagnostic. A study to determine the psychometric properties of this instrument in a primary care setting has not been completed.

    2. ***Recommended screening test for parental report on adolescent child:*** *Parents* can be screened for concerns about possible substance abuse in their children using questions such as those listed in Figure 12–3.

How a Teenager Can Tell if Substance Abuse is a Problem*

YES	NO		
❏	❏	1.	Do you lose time from school because of drugs or alcohol?
❏	❏	2.	Do you use drugs or alcohol to lose shyness and build up self-confidence?
❏	❏	3.	Are drugs or alcohol use affecting your reputation?
❏	❏	4.	Do you use drugs or alcohol to escape from study or home worries?
❏	❏	5.	Does it bother you if somebody says you "use" too much?
❏	❏	6.	Do you have to use a drug or alcohol to go out on a date?
❏	❏	7.	Do you ever get into money trouble buying drugs or alcohol?
❏	❏	8.	Have you lost friends since you've started using drugs or alcohol?
❏	❏	9.	Do you hang out now with a crowd where stuff is easy to get?
❏	❏	10.	Do your friends use less than you do?
❏	❏	11.	Do you drink until the bottle is empty (or use excessively)?
❏	❏	12.	Have you ever had a loss of memory from drinking or taking drugs?
❏	❏	13.	Has drunk driving ever put you into a hospital or jail (you or any others)?
❏	❏	14.	Do you get annoyed with classes or lectures on drugs or alcohol abuse?

A "yes" answer to one question is a warning. A "yes" to as few as three questions means that chemical abuse has almost certainly become, or is becoming, a serious problem.

*From STFM Substance Abuse Intervention Kit. Used by permission.

FIG 12–2.
Screening test for adolescent substance abuse.

3. ***Screening instruments used for adults:*** Several excellent screening instruments used for adults, including the CAGE and Michigan Alcoholism Screening Test (MAST) questionnaires, have not been validated for use with adolescents. Many items are not pertinent to adolescent substance abuse behavior. They have not gained acceptance as clinically useful tools in the adolescent population.

4. ***Other adolescent screening instruments:*** Several more extensive written questionnaires have been or are currently being developed. These instruments have been designed and used for research studies in the general population or for clinical use in treatment centers. They have not been validated in primary care settings. At this time, there is no widely accepted and validated written screening instrument for adolescent substance abuse in a primary care setting. Despite these limitations, several written instruments may have some utility for the primary care physician.

Test for Adolescent Substance Abuse Using Parent Report

To help you determine if there is a teenager in your home who might have an alcohol or drug problem, the following test was developed by the staff of St. Mary's Hospital Drug Unit and the Minneapolis Public Schools.

YES	NO		
☐	☐	1.	Has your teenager's type of friends changed?
☐	☐	2.	How much do you know about these friends?
☐	☐	3.	Does your teenager spend a lot of time alone?
☐	☐	4.	When you ask where he or she has been, do you get a vague answer?
☐	☐	5.	Are drugs missing from the medicine chest?
☐	☐	6.	What about the liquor cabinet?
☐	☐	7.	Have you noticed an erratic behavior pattern in your teenager?
☐	☐	8.	Does he or she have an extremely negative attitude and lower motivation to do things?
☐	☐	9.	Have you received reports from school of frequent truancy?
☐	☐	10.	Are grades dropping?
☐	☐	11.	Have there been frequent flulike symptoms such as red eyes, coughing, fatigue?
☐	☐	12.	Does your teenager have extra money you cannot account for?
☐	☐	13.	Is he or she buying more records, clothes, or other items than usual?
☐	☐	14.	Are other kids coming to your home but not staying long? (They could be buying their drugs from your child, the dealer).

A positive response to these questions may indicate an alcohol or drug problem. Clinicians and parents may want to discuss their concerns with alcohol and drug counselor or a physician with expertise in adolescent substance abuse.

FIG 12–3.
Screening test for parental report on adolescent child.

a. ***Adolescent Alcohol Involvement Scale*** (AAIS): This scale includes 14 items, related to alcohol only. The instrument is included in appendix C–1.

   (1) *Advantages:* This instrument was developed in 1979, and has considerable use and validation. Scoring permits some categorization into levels of alcohol use. It has been published, and is available at no cost.

   (2) *Disadvantages:* Applies to alcohol use only.

   (3) *Reference:* Mayer J, Filstead WJ: The adolescent alcohol involvement scale: An instrument for measuring adolescents' use and misuse of alcohol. *J Stud Alcohol* 1979; 40:291–300.

b. ***Drinking and You*** (Adolescent Drinking Inventory): This is a 24-item instrument for alcohol only.

   (1) *Advantages:* Well-designed; assesses loss of control as well as social, psychological, and physical indicators of abuse. Can be completed in 10 minutes.

   (2) *Disadvantages:* Alcohol use only. Newly developed and has limited use in primary care settings. Proprietary; questionnaires available commercially for a fee.

   (3) *Reference:* Psychological Assessment Resources, Inc., PO Box 998, Odessa, FL 33556; (813) 968-3003.

c. ***Personal Experience Screen Questionnaire*** (PESQ): Contains 38 items related to alcohol and other drugs.

   (1) *Advantages:* This is an offshoot of a more extensive and validated assessment instrument, the Personal Experience Inventory (PEI).

   (2) *Disadvantages:* This instrument consists of items culled from the more comprehensive and validated PEI. It is newly developed and has had limited use in a primary care setting. Proprietary; questionnaires available commercially for a fee.

   (3) *Reference:* Adolescent Assessment Project, Publishing Division, 907 W. Arlington, St. Paul, MN 55117; (612) 647-4625.

d. ***Problem Oriented Screening Inventory for Teenagers*** (POSIT): This comprehensive alcohol and drug inventory consists of 139 items and addresses 10 problem areas.

   (1) *Advantages:* This is an excellent instrument for use in inpatient settings, educational settings such as high schools and colleges, or as part of a comprehensive assessment. This screening tool was authored by a panel of national experts as part of the Adolescent Assessment and Referral System project, sponsored by the National Institute on Drug Abuse (NIDA).

   (2) *Disadvantages:* Designed primarily for adolescents suspected of being users, not as a general screening instrument for the general population of adolescents seen by clinicians. It is too long for general office screening, and has limited use in pri-

mary care setting. Studies are currently under way to determine the psychometric properties of POSIT.

(3) *Reference:* National Clearinghouse for Alcohol and Drug Information, PO Box 2345, Rockville, MD 20852; (301) 468-2600.

D. **Follow-up Questions**

1. *Diagnostic questions:* If the interview or written questionnaire indicates possible substance abuse, follow-up questions should examine consequences of alcohol and drug use in more detail.

    a. Physical: Hangovers, blackouts, injuries, automobile accidents, poor hygiene, depression, suicide attempts.

    b. Family/social: Family problems, fighting, isolation, change or loss of friends, running away, marked change in behavior, previous treatment for substance abuse.

    c. School/work: Poor grades, truancy, suspensions, absenteeism, loss of job, discontinuation of sports/extracurricular activities.

    d. Legal/financial: DUI or other arrests, stealing, money spent on drugs, drug trafficking.

E. **Physical Examination and Laboratory Tests**

1. *Physical findings:* Important findings that may signify an alcohol or drug problem include:

    a. Lack of eye contact.

    b. Weight loss.

    c. Nasal congestion.

    d. Singed eyebrows (from crack pipes).

    e. Scars from burns or self-mutilation.

    f. Poor hygiene.

    g. Chronic cough.

    h. Conjunctivitis.

    i. Needle tracks.

2. *Routine laboratory tests often are nondiagnostic:* Cholesterol and liver function tests may be useful to detect the health effects of anabolic steroids. Urine drug screens may be helpful diagnostic tests in an acute care setting in adolescents with serious medical problems. They also can be used to confront adolescents who deny use.

F. **Suspected Substance Abuse Problem**

1. *Urine drug screen:* If a substance abuse problem is suspected at the conclusion of the visit, the physician may want to seek the adolescent's consent to question his or her parents and others and to perform a urine drug screen (see Chapter 6 on urine drug testing).

2. *Family member interview:* The purpose of the parental interview is to gain more information about the adolescent's behavior and to assess the denial, dysfunction, and level of support in the family system. Information about chemical use in other family members is important.

3. ***Referral to a treatment program:*** If the history, physical examination, laboratory tests, and family interview indicate a probable or definite substance abuse problem, the primary care physician should refer the patient and family to a chemical dependency specialist for further assessment.

4. ***Confidentiality and safety issues:*** If the adolescent refuses parental contact or formal assessment by a treatment specialist, the physician must make a decision as to whether to breach confidentiality and pursue the investigation as above or to arrange a follow-up visit with the adolescent. The decision is based on the severity of the problem and immediate danger to the adolescent or others.

III. Treatment and Referral
A. Nicotine use

1. ***Dependence factors:*** Factors that contribute to nicotine dependence in adolescents include social pressures, the absence of major physical consequences, and the use of nicotine to control weight, especially in young women.

2. ***Brief interventions with tobacco addiction:*** While it is very difficult to motivate habituated adolescent smokers to quit, brief interventions can be effective. Intervention with habituated adolescent smokers is similar to adult smoking cessation. There are four stages in the office intervention:

   a. *Step 1: Ask.*

      (1) Start asking about smoking in elementary school children.

   b. *Step 2: Challenge and motivate.*

      (1) Give a clear recommendation to quit smoking and challenge the adolescent to do so, especially at times of acute illness aggravated by smoking.

      (2) Assess motivation to quit with questions such as the following:

      > Have you thought about quitting smoking?
      > What would make you want to quit smoking?
      > Are you willing to quit smoking now?

      (3) Stress the immediate negative social consequences of smoking (e.g., bad breath; odors and stains on fingers, teeth, and clothing), which may seem more important to the adolescent than the long-term health effects.

      (4) Some adolescents may respond to the idea of improved athletic performance after cessation of smoking.

      (5) If the adolescent is unwilling to quit at that time, remain supportive and tell the adolescent you will be available to help if he or she does decide to quit.

      (6) Take the opportunity to ask again at future visits.

   c. *Step 3: Set a quit date.*

      (1) If the adolescent agrees to quit, set a specific quit date. This is the date in the near future when the adolescent would quit smoking entirely.

(2) A date with special significance to the individual is best.

(3) Preparation includes identifying reasons for quitting, recognizing cues for smoking, planning alternative activities, and rallying support from family and friends by announcing the quit date.

(4) An office visit on or around the time of the quit date is important.

(5) Role playing and practicing answers to use in specific smoking situations may be helpful to the adolescent.

(6) A written contract with the patient is useful.

d. *Step 4: Reinforce.*

(1) Smoking cessation efforts must be reinforced in subsequent visits or phone calls.

(2) It is helpful to plan a visit a few weeks after the quit date to praise the adolescent's progress and explore any problems that have arisen.

(3) Smoking cessation efforts commonly end in relapse, but should be viewed positively as practice for future success. Quitting is a process, not a single event.

(4) In resistant or recurrent cases, referral to a multicomponent community smoking cessation program is indicated. These are often sponsored by local hospitals or chapters of the American Cancer Society and the American Lung Association.

B. Treatment Options for Alcohol and Drug Abuse

The appropriate treatment of alcohol and drug abuse depends on a number of factors, including the stage of chemical use, the amount of denial in the patient and family, the degree of disruption in the adolescent's life, coexisting psychiatric or medical illness, family support, financial resources, and the availability of treatment facilities in the community. Adolescents with substance abuse problems often are protected by a large network of enablers, including parents, friends, relatives, teachers, coaches, and clergy, among others. Treatment begins with the dismantling of this enabling system and requires teamwork and cooperation with other professionals, including school and court officials as well as chemical dependency treatment specialists. It takes a system to beat a system. The physician can play a valuable role in this process. A variety of treatment options with suggested criteria for use are listed below in order of increasing intensity. Each level includes the components of preceding levels and adds further steps in the treatment process.

1. *Physician Management:*

a. *Treatment components:* These include careful monitoring, regular office visits, referral to drug information classes (at school and the local treatment center), and urine drug testing as necessary. A supportive and drug-free household and safe social environment are essential. Parents may need advice and help with parenting skills for dealing with adolescents. Parents can be referred to Families Anomymous or Toughlove for support. The school system can be invaluable for educating the adolescent about drug abuse and for monitoring his or her behavior in school.

b. *Indications:* May be appropriate for experimentation and misuse stages with the adolescent who admits a problem and is motivated;

c. *Goal of treatment:* No-use contract.

2. ***Low-intensity outpatient treatment*** (4 to 6 weeks):

a. *Treatment components:* Counseling sessions occur once or twice a week with a therapist. Other aspects are an educational program, group therapy, and self-help groups. While not a specific component, the local schools usually provide additional counseling support and facilitate the creation of a drug-free environment.

b. *Indications:* Low-intensity treatment is appropriate for an adolescent who is misusing or abusing chemicals but is physically and psychologically stable. Family support and a nonchemical social environment are necessary to provide stability. Adolescents who participate in low-intensity programs need peer support to remain abstinent.

3. ***Intensive outpatient treatment:***

a. *Treatment components:* The treatment program consists of four to five sessions per week for 12 to 16 weeks. The time utilized can be 3 to 4 hours after school, in the early evening, or an all-day structured experience. Specific components are structured individual and group therapies and multidimensional treatment (e.g., social, educational, vocational, and recreational). A structured family involvement and aftercare therapy program for 12 to 24 months also are essential components.

b. *Indications:* Useful for more intermediate stages of substance abuse and for those adolescents who acknowledge that chemical use is a problem. There should be no history of a major psychiatric disorder. As in other methods, family support and a drug-free environment are necessary for a successful outpatient program.

4. ***Inpatient treatment:***

a. *Treatment components:* Include all activities described in the high-intensity outpatient program, with the addition of a medically supervised inpatient setting with the availability of a physician and skilled nursing care. Many programs provide tutoring to prevent students from falling behind in their academic studies.

b. *Indications:* Inpatient treatment is appropriate for adolescents in denial or those who have failed less intense modes of treatment. Other indications for inpatient treatment are coexisting major psychiatric disorders, nonsupportive families, or unstable social environments. Adolescents who live in situations of physical or sexual abuse and parental chemical dependency are best treated in a hospitalized setting.

    c. *Cost:* Expensive ($10,000–$25,000), and may not be covered completely by insurance.

5. ***Extended-Care or Transitional Living Program:***

    a. *Treatment components:* A wide range of services and treatments are available in these settings. Most have counselors, group therapy, and educational programs. Work study programs, academic classes, and vocational training are important components. Peer support groups and peer counseling are also used.

    b. *Indications:* Extended care may follow inpatient treatment for adolescents who need a long-term supervised treatment setting. It is often used for adolescents who need a structured living environment with low-intensity but long-term supervision. It is appropriate in cases of nonsupportive or unstable family situations with sexual or physical abuse and for those adolescents who are severely impaired by lack of social, academic, and vocational skills.

C. **Establishing a Treatment Referral System**

1. ***Relationship with a local treatment program:*** It is critical for the physician to have a good working relationship with a chemical dependency specialist and/or treatment center. Initial recommendations can be obtained from the local medical society, Alcoholics Anonymous, community alcoholism service agencies, and the National Clearinghouse for Alcohol and Drug Information.

2. ***How to evaluate a treatment program:***

    a. The program should have a treatment philosophy that recovery involves permanent abstinence from alcohol and drugs.

    b. The center should use a multidisciplinary approach, with attention to specific adolescent behavioral and developmental issues.

    c. The staff includes medical professionals actively involved in treatment.

    d. Treatment components include the use of self-help groups such as AA, NA, and CA.

    e. There is a credible family treatment program of at least 4 to 6 weeks in duration.

    f. The ratio of counselors to adolescent patients in active treatment (this may include aftercare) is less than 20:1.

    g. They are committed to an aggressive aftercare program and place adequate resources in follow-up for 12 to 24 months.

    h. There is a willingness to communicate and work with physicians and other health care professionals.

D. **Initiating Treatment and Referral**

Placement in appropriate treatment depends on a thorough evaluation and accurate diagnosis.

1. ***Early problems:*** In cases of experimentation or misuse in a stable social situation, the physician can make the diagnosis and initiate treatment as described in treatment options 1 and 2.

2. ***Referral for assessment:*** More often, because of a more advanced stage of use, individual and family dysfunction, or a failure to comply with management, referral to a chemical dependency specialist is necessary for further assessment and treatment. Referrals should be handled in a nonjudgmental and supportive manner, just as referral to any other specialist. The assessment may be conducted during a 3- to 5-day inpatient admission.

3. ***Resistant patient:*** If the adolescent is resistant but the parents are interested, the family can be referred to a self-help group, such as Alanon or Families Anonymous. The parents also can be advised to contact a treatment specialist or center about various methods (including a formal intervention) to motivate the adolescent to enter treatment.

4. ***Motivated patient who refuses to tell family:*** If the adolescent is motivated but *refuses to tell the family* or the family is nonsupportive, the physician may monitor the adolescent, refer to a self-help group such as AA, NA, or CA, and continue to work with the adolescent and the family, if possible, to seek further treatment.

5. ***Patient and family resistance:*** If both the adolescent and parents deny a problem and refuse referral, the physician should maintain a respectful and supportive relationship and continue to express concern about the substance abuse problem. Patients and families often return for treatment later as further negative consequences develop.

E. Monitoring Recovery

1. ***Physician participation in the aftercare program:*** The physician should communicate with the treatment specialist and/or center about his or her role in monitoring the recovery process. At minimum, the physician needs to maintain an ongoing and supportive relationship with the adolescent and family, encourage compliance with the treatment program (including attendance at aftercare programs and self-help meetings), and avoid prescribing mood-altering drugs.

2. ***Relapse prevention:*** Monitoring adolescents for signs of relapse is a critical role of the primary care physician. Adolescents tend to relapse at least once, because of their sense of invulnerability and need to test the system. Relapse should be anticipated, along with the need for further treatment.

IV. Legal and Ethical Issues

A. Consent for Health Care

1. ***Age issues:*** All individuals 18 years and older are considered adults and are able to consent to their own medical care if they are mentally competent. Adolescents younger than age 18 years are consid-

ered minors and usually require parental approval for medical care, except as discussed below.

2. ***Emergency care:*** In an emergency, care can be provided without parental approval if a delay would cause significant pain or compromise the child's well-being.

3. ***Adolescent consent:*** Two categories of adolescents can provide consent to care: the mature minor and the emancipated minor.

   a. The *mature* minor is judged to possess the adult cognition and judgment necessary for making health care decisions. This definition is subjective, but generally is applicable to the following situations.

      (1) Treatment was undertaken clearly for the benefit of the minor.

      (2) The minor was near majority (age 15 to 17 years).

      (3) The medical procedure was not "major."

   b. The *emancipated* minor is one who has joined the armed services, is married, or is otherwise living apart and financially independent of his or her parents.

4. ***Medical indications for adolescent consent:*** The law recognizes minors' rights to consent to treatment for certain specific medical conditions without parental approval. All states permit minors to secure medical care for sexually transmitted diseases without parental knowledge or consent.

5. ***Adolescent consent for treatment of alcohol and drug disorders:*** More than half of the states have statutes that permit minors to get treatment for substance abuse without parental consent. Even in states without such laws, it is extremely unlikely that the physician would be held liable for providing nonnegligent care to a minor for substance abuse if the adolescent refused to tell his or her parents.

B. Confidentiality

1. ***Legal issues:*** The physician is required by law to report certain specific conditions, such as sexually transmitted diseases and suspected child abuse. The physician also may breach confidentiality in cases where the patient's behavior may harm him or her or another (e.g., the suicidal patient).

2. ***Legal guidelines:*** It is often helpful to inform the adolescent that confidential information may be shared with the parents only if the adolescent requests parental involvement, the adolescent provides consent to inform the parents, or the physician feels that the adolescent is at risk for serious harm.

3. ***Breaching confidentiality:*** If the adolescent refuses to tell his or her parents about a substance abuse problem, the physician must decide whether to treat without parental consent or to breach confidentiality. The physician should inform the adolescent if and when it is necessary to breach confidentiality.

C. Treatment Without the Adolescent's Consent

Occasionally an adolescent will be brought in by the parents or referred by school or legal authorities for drug screening or treatment without the adolescent's consent.

1. ***Honest straightforward approach:*** The physician should be frank and honest with the adolescent and the family about the purpose of the visit. If the adolescent continues to object to evaluation and treatment, the physician may wish to refer the family to a colleague or a chemical dependency treatment center.

2. ***Forced treatment:*** While imposition of treatment would disrupt the ongoing relationship of trust, the physician may need to recommend enforced treatment. There are no cases reported in which a physician has been held liable for care imposed on an adolescent with the parents' consent.

BIBLIOGRAPHY

Ash KH, Schiks MA, Schwartz RH: Helping the teenage drug user. *Patient Care* 1989; 15:58–85.

Johnson L, O'Malley P, Bachman JG: Drug use, drinking, and smoking: National survey results from high school, college, and young adult population. Bethesda, Md, Department of Health and Human Services, 1989.

Mayer J, Filstead W: The Adolescent Alcohol Involvement Scale: An instrument for measuring adolescents' use and misuse of alcohol. *J Stud Alcohol* 1979; 40:291–300.

Rogers PD: Chemical dependency. *Pediatr Clin North Am* 1987; 34:275–544.

Schaefer D: *Choices and Consequences: What To Do When a Teenager Uses Alcohol/Drugs.* Minneapolis, Johnson Institute Books, 1987.

Schonberg SK (ed): *Substance Abuse: A Guide for Health Professionals.* Elk Grove Village, Ill, American Academy of Pediatrics/Pacific Institute for Research and Evaluation, 1988.

STFM Substance Abuse Working Group: Physician intervention kit for substance abuse. Contact Michael Fleming, MD, University of Wisconsin, Department of Family Medicine.

CHAPTER 13

Drugs in Sports

Patricia K. Kokotailo, M.D., M.P.H.

Gregory L. Landry, M.D.

Physicians and other health care providers deal with many children, adolescents, and adults who are involved in recreational and competitive sports. Although physicians should be aware of the possibility of alcohol and other drug problems in all patients, alcohol and other drug use in athletes can present unique concerns and problems. The use of performance-enhancing drugs such as anabolic steroids is an issue for athletes at many levels. This chapter focuses on drug use most problematic and unique to athletes and reviews types of drugs related to sports, their desirable and undesirable effects, and ethical issues concerning the use of drugs by athletes. The physician's role in drug use by athletes also is discussed.

I. **Types of Drugs Related to Sports**
   A. **Performance-Enhancing or Ergogenic Drugs**
      These are drugs used to potentially improve athletic performance. Anabolic steroids are probably the most publicized performance-enhancing drugs, but others include amphetamines, caffeine, beta blocking agents, alcohol, cocaine, marijuana, human growth hormone, and erythropoietin. The intent of use may be unclear between performance-enhancing and social use with drugs such as amphetamines, which may be used to obtain a high or build confidence as well as increase endurance.
   B. **Personal or Social Use of Mood-Altering Drugs**
      These drugs include alcohol, tobacco, caffeine, marijuana, cocaine, phencyclidine (PCP), amphetamines, and hallucinogens. The use of these drugs probably is similar in the athlete vs. nonathlete populations, but there are few studies comparing the two groups.
   C. **Restorative Drug Use**
      These drugs, most of which are not controversial, are used to treat injuries or illness. Medications such as nonsteroidal anti-inflammatory drugs, oral and/or injectable corticosteroids, dimethylsulfoxide (DMSO), and short- and long-acting local anesthetics, however, can be controversial because of potential overuse or abuse of these medications.

II. Ethics of Drugs in Sports

A. Introduction

1. *Use of performance-enhancing drugs.* Many of the ethical issues of drugs used by athletes revolve around performance-enhancing drugs. Reports of drug use, most likely herbs and mushrooms, date back to the ancient Greek Olympiads. Coca leaf extracts were widely available to athletes in the early 19th century, and drugs, most likely stimulants, are reported to have been used by athletes in the modern Olympics in the 1950s. Anabolic steroids appear to have been widely used by male and female athletes from the 1960s to the present.

2. *Newer methods to enhance performance:* Techniques such as use of growth hormone, erythropoietin use, and blood doping or packing (blood transfusions using another's or one's own blood before an endurance event to produce erythrocythemia) are considered performance-enhancing drugs.

3. *Definition of Doping:* The term "doping" often is used in reference to performance-enhancing drugs and techniques. The International Olympic Committee (IOC) defines doping as "the administration of or use by a competing athlete of any substance foreign to the body or any physiologic substance taken in abnormal quantity or taken by an abnormal route of entry into the body with the sole intention of increasing in an artificial and unfair manner his or her performance in competition. When necessity demands medical treatment with any substance which, because of its nature, dosage, or application, is able to boost the athlete's performance in competition in an artificial and unfair manner, this too is regarded as doping." The term "blood doping," however, usually refers to the specific methods of blood transfusion to produce erythrocythemia.

4. *Position of sports officials:* Sports officials and governing bodies currently express unequivocal disapproval of doping or use of performance-enhancing drugs, and formally ban them. Yet punishment and restrictions have been inconsistent when violations have been found. Even with definitions as above, confusion about the definition of performance-enhancing drugs exists, as well as confusion about the moral grounds for prohibiting such drug use in athletic competition.

5. *Position on use of illicit drugs:* Social or personal use of illicit drugs used for recreational purposes is banned by some regulatory commissions (e.g., National Collegiate Athletic Association, NCAA).

B. Ethical Issues Vary With Type of Drug Used

1. *Performance:* It is generally agreed that the common goal of sports is to identify and reward certain forms of human excellence. The use of athletic ability, skilled coaching, individual training, teamwork, and strategic ability all are regarded as legitimate means of attaining excellence.

2. ***Cheating:*** Sabotaging competitors, using banned equipment, and seeking unfair advantage are viewed as illegitimate means of attaining excellence. The use of banned performance-enhancing agents, such as drugs, hormones, and/or blood doping, are seen as theoretically giving an unfair advantage to an athlete. Use of a banned substance is considered a form of cheating.

3. ***Health risks:*** Use of performance-enhancing drugs may pose short-term and long-term health risks to an athlete. Although there is debate on the role of regulatory bodies in minimizing health risks associated with competitive sports, most people feel that the health risks of drug use justify official intervention.

4. ***Social or personal use drugs:*** Drugs such as cocaine and opiates are banned because some regulatory bodies expect athletes to be "model" citizens. Inconsistencies exist when professional sports figures promote drugs such as alcohol and tobacco. The sports figures who are used by the alcohol industry to advertise alcohol may have a profound influence on alcohol use by young persons.

C. **Banned Drugs**

1. ***Guidelines on drug use:*** Rulings as to which drugs are banned as well as testing procedures and how violations of bans are dealt with vary by regulatory body. The IOC, the NCAA, and individual universities have slightly different lists of specific drugs that are banned or subject to certain restrictions. Club and high school athletic departments usually cannot afford formal testing procedures but often have written policies about use of alcohol and other drugs.

2. ***Banned drugs (by IOC and NCAA):***
   a. All types of blood doping.
   b. Stimulants.
   c. Anabolic steroids.
   d. Diuretics.
   e. Narcotics.
   f. Beta blockers (in rifle competition).
   g. Peptide hormones and analogues.

3. ***Restricted use:*** The following classes of substances generally are subject to certain restrictions:
   a. *Alcohol and marijuana* use is discouraged, but might not be sought in drug testing (IOC).
   b. *Local anesthetic and corticosteroid* use is not banned, but must be reported by the physician who prescribes them (NCAA and IOC).

4. ***Free information:*** Publications from regulatory bodies, such as *Drug Free,* the US Olympic Committee Drug Education Handbook, list not only banned drugs but also substances that are not banned. These publications give facts about many substances capable of being abused, in an attempt to provide education to athletes, athletic trainers, coaches, and parents.

D. Enforcement of Drug Bans by Testing

Testing for banned drugs has been a controversial area in sports. Although the impetus for doing analytical chemistry testing on body fluids to detect drug use began in the 1950s and 1960s with reports of widespread drug misuse in the athletic community, formal drug testing was not conducted at a major international athletic event until the 1972 Summer Olympics in Munich. Many testing issues are the same for athletes as for nonathletes (see Chapter 7). The following issues are more specifically related to drug testing in athletes.

1. *Expense:* It is expensive and time consuming to run a high-quality drug testing program for any athletic organization, yet it is the best way to enforce a banned drug list if performed frequently.

2. *Limitations of detection methods:* Many drugs or performance-enhancing agents used by athletes cannot be detected by routine urine drug metabolite screening for drugs of abuse. Anabolic steroid detection requires use of gas chromatography and mass spectrometry. There are no current reliable testing methods for blood doping, erythropoietin use, or growth hormone use by current urine testing methods.

3. *Accuracy:* Sensitivity and specificity of detection of metabolites vary with the laboratory used, so a user may not always screen positive following use. Because false positive results can be disastrous to the future career of the athlete, positive tests must always be confirmed by gas chromatography or mass spectrometry.

4. *Discontinuation of drugs before event:* Drugs such as anabolic steroids (see IIIC, below) may be stopped far enough in advance of an athletic event so as not to be detected by urine testing. Anabolic steroid testing is also very expensive and is not widely available.

5. *Invasion of privacy issues:* Legality of testing athletes has continued to be controversial, especially at the collegiate level. Invasion of privacy is a risk, especially with publication of names of those who test positive. Every effort must be made to ensure that proper informed consent is obtained before screening at any time.

6. *Clinical signs of use:* Since urine screening is not a "gold standard" for detecting drug use by athletes or nonathletes, efforts must be made to monitor athletes for clinical signs of drug use.

III. Effects of Drugs in Sports

A. Amphetamines

1. *Efficacy:*
   a. Amphetamines are potent stimulants as well as appetite suppressants, and probably enhance performance in selected events.
   b. Use of amphetamines currently is being replaced by cocaine use and abuse.

2. *Desirable effects:*
   a. Increase in energy level.
   b. Increase in concentration.

     c. Decrease in sense of fatigue.

     d. Self-perceived improvement in reaction time.

     e. Decrease in body fat (especially desired by athletes in sports where weight control is important, such as wrestling and gymnastics).

     f. Increasing self-confidence.

   3. ***Adverse effects:***

     a. Cardiac arrhythmias severe enough to cause death.

     b. Paranoia with possible toxic psychosis.

     c. Anxiety, distractibility, and agitation.

     d. Hyperthermia due to peripheral vasoconstriction.

     e. Post-use fatigue and depression.

     f. Dependency.

B. Caffeine

   1. ***Efficacy:***

     a. Caffeine has been demonstrated to enhance performance in endurance athletic events.

   2. ***Desired effects:***

     a. Enhanced fatty acid utilization during activity and increased glycogenolysis, thereby sparing muscle glycogen; increased skeletal muscle contractility by increased amount of intracellular calcium, resulting in increased endurance.

     b. The CNS effect of limiting the adenosine inhibition of the release of neurotransmitters by blocking receptors, resulting in stimulation and a decreased perception of fatigue.

   3. ***Adverse effects:***

     a. Cardiac arrhythmias and transient hypertension.

     b. Gastrointestinal upset.

     c. Diuretic effect may be bothersome in distance events.

     d. Withdrawal syndrome of headache, drowsiness, irritability, lethargy, and nervousness.

C. Anabolic Steroids

   1. ***Efficacy:***

     a. All anabolic steroids are both anabolic (tissue building) and androgenic (masculinizing). Most athletes use anabolic steroids for their anabolic effects. They may be taken by mouth, by injection, or by both methods.

     b. The numerous studies of anabolic steroids do not conclusively answer the question of efficacy. Problems and inconsistencies in studies include the following:

       (1) Many studies were not adequately blinded, and therefore placebo effects may greatly influence outcomes.

       (2) Anabolic steroids are psychoactive, and separating psychoactive effects from physiologic effects may be difficult.

       (3) Variations in anabolic steroid preparation and dosage, as well as concomitant training routines and diets influence study outcomes.

    c. The best scientific studies show that anabolic steroids *can* cause an increase in muscle mass and strength under the following conditions:

        (1) The individual has been involved in regular intensive strength training prior to taking anabolic steroids and continues this training while taking the anabolic steroids.

        (2) The individual's strength is measured by the single repetition–maximal weight technique testing the same movements and exercise the individual had used in regular weight training, rather than testing strength by other means such as dynamometers.

        (3) The individual maintains a proper diet with an adequate amount of protein.

2. *Desirable effects:*
   a. Increase in lean body mass.
   b. Increase in strength.
   c. Increase in aggressiveness.

3. *Adverse effects:*
   a. These side effects were observed in patients using anabolic steroids for medical conditions, but most have also been reported in athletes.

        (1) Gastrointestinal (liver):
            Hepatocellular damage
            Cholestasis
            Pelosis hepatitis
            Hepatoadenoma
            Hepatocarcinoma

        (2) Integument:
            Acne
            Striae
            Hirsutism
            Male-pattern baldness
            Edema

        (3) Reproductive:
            Males:
                Testicular atrophy
                Oligospermia or azoospermia
                Impotence
                Prostatic hypertrophy
                Prostatic carcinoma
                Gynecomastia
            Females:
                Amenorrhea
                Clitoromegaly
                Uterine atrophy
                Breast atrophy
                Teratogenicity

(4) Respiratory (larynx):
   Deepening of the voice
(5) Cardiovascular:
   Increase in cholesterol level
   Decrease in high-density lipoprotein (HDL) level
   Increased blood pressure
(6) Urinary:
   Wilm's tumor (case reports)
(7) Musculoskeletal:
   Early physes closure in children (shorter adult height)
   Increased rate of muscle strain
(8) Endocrine (other than reproductive):
   Decreased glucose tolerance
(9) Psychologic:
   Mood swings
   Aggressiveness
   Depression
   Psychosis
(10) Immunologic (infections):
   Decreased IgA levels
   (Hepatitis or HIV infection if needles are shared)

b. The incidence of side effects in athletes using anabolic steroids compared with individuals using medically indicated anabolic steroids is unknown. In general, most of the mild side effects are seen frequently, and the more severe and life-threatening effects rarely.

c. In males, all side effects appear reversible except baldness, liver tumors, and some cases of gynecomastia. In females, clitoral enlargement, virilization, and male-pattern baldness are permanent.

d. Although some psychologic effects of anabolic steroids, such as increased aggressiveness and euphoria, may be beneficial to an athlete during competition, aggressiveness and mood swings off the field may cause severe repercussions.

e. Psychotic symptoms have been associated with anabolic steroid use, and there have been anecdotal reports of suicides associated with use. Although abrupt withdrawal of anabolic steroids may cause significant clinical depression, the incidence of severe psychologic reactions is unknown.

f. Case reports support the addictive potential of anabolic steroids, with both physiologic and psychologic components seen to develop, as well as withdrawal, as evidenced by such symptoms as lethargy, abdominal muscle cramps, constipation, headache, and reactive depression.

D. Human Growth Hormone
   1. *Efficacy:*
   a. Growth hormone appears to affect the growth of nearly every organ and tissue in the body. There are no studies on its effect on athletic performance.

2. *Desirable effects:*
   a. Anabolic or tissue building, including speeding up repair of in-jured tissue.
   b. Stimulation of the mobilization of lipids from adipose tissue, in-creasing their oxidation as a source of energy.
   c. Stimulation of collagen synthesis.
   d. Use not detectable by current urine testing methods.
3. *Adverse effects:*
   a. Acromegaly, proximal muscle weakness, cardiomyopathy, viscero-megaly, osteoporosis, and sexual dysfunction.
   b. Development of diabetes.
   c. Diseases transmitted parenterally, such as hepatitis and acquired immune deficiency syndrome (AIDS).
E. **Erythropoietin and Blood Doping**
   1. *Efficacy:*
      a. The increase in oxygen-carrying capacity of these methods due to erythrocytosis may produce a 1% to 37% increase in endurance, based on research on blood doping.
      b. Blood doping may be used in conjunction with anabolic steroids to increase endurance.
   2. *Desirable effects:*
      a. Improve endurance.
      b. Use not detectable by current testing methods.
   3. *Adverse effects:*
      a. Increase in blood pressure and workload on the heart may cause heart failure and pulmonary edema.
      b. Those related to polycythemia and increased blood viscosity (e.g., cerebrovascular accidents, embolic phenomenae).
      c. Blood-borne infections such as AIDS and hepatitis, or transfusion reactions if transfused with someone else's blood.
IV. **Physician's Role in Drug Use by Athletes**
   A. **Overview**
      1. *Awareness:* To be able to fully participate in the medical and psy-chologic care of athletes, a physician must be aware of alcohol and other drug use by athletes. It is essential that the physician have knowledge of the availability and presumed benefits and risks of both ergogenic drugs and drugs used for social and personal reasons by athletes.
      2. *Athlete specific:* The medical provider also needs to be aware of proclivities for use of certain drugs by specific teams, such as use of amphetamines for weight loss by wrestlers or gymnasts or use of ana-bolic steroids by football players or weight lifters.
   B. **Identification and Case Finding**
      1. *Principles:* Screening for alcohol and other drug use by athletes should incorporate many of the same principles as screening among adolescent and young adult populations (see Chapter 12). Since there

may be considerable overlap between performance-enhancing drugs and drugs used for social and personal reasons, as well as misuse of restorative drugs, a medical provider needs to consider all of these types of drug misuse in an athlete.

2. *Specific clues:* Clues to drug misuse could include:
   a. *All drugs:*
      (1) Frequent injuries on and off the field.
      (2) Drop in athletic as well as school or job performance.
      (3) Change in personality.
      (4) Mood swings, aggression, or depression
   b. *Anabolic steroids:*
      (1) Large weight and muscle mass gain in a relatively short amount of time.
      (2) Virilizing changes and acne.
      (3) Unexplained peripheral edema (i.e., moon face).
      (4) Gynecomastia or sexual dysfunction in men.
      (5) Any liver dysfunction.
      (6) Stress fractures and significant muscular strains.
      (7) Abrupt onset of temporary hyperkinesia with rapid speech pattern.

3. *Screening questions:* Screening questions for anabolic steroids can be included when one is inquiring about alcohol or other drug use during a preparticipation examination or other appropriate medical encounter. Suggested opening questions include:
   a. "Do any of your friends use anabolic steroids?"
   b. "Have you ever been tempted to use anabolic steroids?"
   c. If there is a positive response to either question, then more direct questions are appropriate, such as, "Have you ever used them?"

C. Physician Role as Educator:
1. *Strategies:* A physician's role is seen to be that of an educator about the risks and consequences of drug use by athletes, including licit drugs such as nicotine and alcohol. Education alone probably does not deter use, and some educational tactics may actually increase use.
2. *Combination:* Drug education combined with drug testing may better deter the use of drugs by athletes.

D. Physician Involvement With Drug Testing Programs
1. *Random testing:* Random drug testing has been mandated by more and more athletic regulatory bodies and schools. Drug testing requires strict collection protocols, including witnessed voiding. Accurate testing and confirmation techniques are essential, and the physician should maintain a good working relationship with the toxicologist.
2. *Informed consent:* If a physician believes an athlete should have a urine drug screen based on clinical information, informed consent should be obtained and the same strict collection and testing procedures should be followed. It should also be realized that urine drug

screening needs to be used in conjunction with clinical assessment and counseling of athletes.

E. Referral

1. ***Network:*** It is necessary for a physician to develop a referral network for counseling and drug treatment. Counselors and therapists sensitive to adolescent and young adult developmental issues as well as the stresses of athletics should be identified in the physician's community.

2. ***Aftercare:*** Physicians should be involved in long-term follow-up and aftercare planning with the athlete. These plans should include the athletic trainer and the coach whenever possible.

F. Future Directions

1. ***Prevention research:*** Further research is necessary to develop better educational programs to prevent drug misuse among athletes and other young people.

2. ***Research on risk factors:*** Further research is needed to determine risk factors for drug use among athletes. The idea that athletes use drugs for the same reasons as other young people, apart from ergogenic use, is not well proved. Research regarding long-term effects of drugs such as growth hormone and anabolic steroids is difficult to perform, because it is unlikely all users would be willing to participate in a study. Longitudinal studies, however, are the best way to determine true incidence of side effects of drug use in athletes.

3. ***Financing of research:*** For drug testing to become a better deterrent to use, regulatory bodies must support and finance more research on testing methods and perform more frequent unannounced testing.

4. ***Societal expectations:*** Physicians and other responsible adults must give young athletes reasons not to use drugs by encouraging moral development. The value of sports should be kept in perspective in society, and young people should be taught that the use of drugs in sports is a form of cheating, as well as being potentially harmful to the athlete.

BIBLIOGRAPHY

ACSM Position Stand: Blood doping as an ergogenic aid. *Physician Sports Med* 1988; 16:131–134.

American Medical Association Council on Scientific Affairs: Drug abuse in athletes: Anabolic steroids and human growth hormone. *JAMA* 1988; 259:1703–1705.

American Medical Association Council on Scientific Affairs: Scientific issues in drug testing. *JAMA* 1987; 257:3110–3114.

Gall SL, Duda M, Giel D, et al: Who tests which athletes for what drugs? *Physician Sports Med* 1988; 16:155–161.

Haupt HA: Drugs in athletes. *Clin Sports Med* 1989; 8:561–582.

Landry GL, Primos WA: Anabolic steroid abuse. *Adv Pediatr* 1990; 37:185–205.

Ramotar JE: Cyclists deaths linked to erythropoietin? *Physicians Sports Med* 1990; 18:48–50.

Strauss RH (ed): *Drugs and Performance in Sports*. Philadelphia, WB Saunders, 1987.

Taylor WN: *Anabolic Steroids and the Athlete*. Jefferson, NC, McFarland and Co., 1982.

Voy R: *Drugs, Sport and Politics*. Champaign, Ill, Leisure Press, 1991.

Wadler G, Hainline B: *Drugs and the Athlete*. Philadelphia, FA Davis, 1989.

CHAPTER 14

Management of Addictive Disorders in Women

Patricia A. Lane, M.D.

Sandra Burge, Ph.D.

Antonnette Graham, Ph.D., M.S.W., R.N.

Addictive disorders traditionally have been viewed as "male diseases." It is only in the past decade that society and the medical community have begun to recognize the seriousness of problematic substance use in women. As a result of the male-limited perspective, most clinical research and treatment methods were designed for use in men. The limited clinical and research findings available indicate significant differences in susceptibility to the adverse effects of psychoactive drugs, gender differences in metabolism, and conflicting social and cultural norms. It is important to recognize that the clinical methods used for recognition and treatment are based primarily on treatment programs developed for men. The efficacy of many of these therapeutic methods currently is being testing in women. This chapter focuses on the unique problems of managing addictive disorders in women.

I. Problematic Nicotine, Alcohol, and Drug Use in Women
A. Epidemiology

1. *Prevalence of nicotine use:* Nearly 24% of American women smoke cigarettes. The fastest growing group of smokers in this country are women younger than 23 years. Everyday 2,000 young women start smoking. The percentage of women who smoke 25 or more cigarettes a day increased from 13% in 1965 to 23% in 1985 (Department of Health and Human Services, Feb 1990). Lung cancer has emerged as the number one cause of cancer deaths among women, surpassing breast cancer (Boring, 1991). Specific smoking cessation strategies are discussed in Chapter 5, and apply to both genders.

2. *Prevalence of alcohol use:* National surveys from 1971 to 1981 indicate that approximately 60% of women drink alcohol. It is estimated that six million American women have an alcohol disorder.

The percentage of women drinkers is related to age and ethnic group.

a. Younger women are more likely to drink and to be heavy drinkers than are older women. However, during adolescence and young adulthood the gender differences in alcohol and drug use decrease dramatically. Many clinicians believe that females and males in these two populations may be drinking in equal proportions.

b. Despite stable drinking patterns among the general population from 1965 to 1990, recent studies indicate an increase in younger women who are heavy drinkers (5 or more drinks a day) (US House of Representatives, 1990).

c. Several studies have explored whether drinking patterns and alcohol-related problems vary among women of different racial and ethnic groups. Although it has been commonly assumed that a larger proportion of African-American women drink heavily, researchers have disproved this assumption. They drink in equal proportions to white women, and report fewer alcohol-related personal and social problems than white women do. However, a greater proportion of African-American women experience alcohol-related health problems (Herd, 1989).

d. Data from self-report surveys suggest that Hispanic women are either infrequent drinkers or abstainers (Caetano, 1989), but this may be changing as they enter new social and work arenas. One study found that rates of abstention are greater among Hispanic women who have immigrated to the United States. Reports of moderate or heavy drinking are greater among younger, American-born Hispanic women (Gilbert, 1987).

3. ***Prevalence of drug use:*** Illicit drug use has increased among millions of women across all socioeconomic groups.

a. More than five million women of childbearing age (15 to 44 years) currently use an illicit drug, including one million who use cocaine and 3.8 million who use cannabis (National Institute of Drug Abuse [NIDA], 1990).

b. Women are more likely than men to report the medical use of psychotherapeutic drugs (NIDA, 1990).

c. Younger women are more likely to abuse sedatives, stimulants, and opioids then are men or older women (NIDA, 1990).

B. Physiologic Factors Affecting Development of Alcohol and Drug Disorders in Women

1. ***Physiologic characteristics and alcohol disorders:*** Research has shown that women appear to be more prone than men to the medical consequences of heavy drinking. Women become intoxicated after drinking smaller quantities of alcohol than are needed to produce intoxication in men. Three possible mechanisms have been suggested to explain this response.

a. *Absorption rates:* Women have lower total body water content than men of comparable size. When alcohol is consumed it diffuses into the body water inside and outside the cells in a uniform manner. Because women have a smaller quantity of body water, they achieve higher concentrations of alcohol in their blood than men after drinking equivalent amounts. Since women metabolize most substances 10% to 20% faster than men of equal size, the effect of using other drugs is similar to that of the effect of alcohol use.

b. *Diminished activity of alcohol dehydrogenase:* Frezza et al. (1990) reported that women have lower levels of alcohol dehydrogenase (the primary enzyme involved in the metabolism of alcohol) in their gastric mucosa than men do. As a result of this difference in enzyme levels, women absorb about 30% more alcohol into the blood stream.

c. *Hormonal absorption effects:* Gonadal hormone levels during the menstrual cycle may affect the rate of alcohol metabolism, increasing the vulnerability of women to the physiologic consequences of drinking. Research findings to date, however, have been variable (Marshall et al., 1983; Sutker et al., 1987).

2. ***Physiologic characteristics and drug disorders:*** Because of the increased fat-muscle ratio in women, detoxification may be delayed with drugs such as marijuana and long-acting benzodiazepines, which are deposited in fatty tissue.

C. **Telescoping of Symptoms**

1. ***Accelerated time course:*** The problematic use of alcohol has been documented to escalate into severe consequences at a faster rate for women than for men. This process has been referred to as "telescoping of symptoms." The telescoping of symptoms in female alcohol disorders may include an increase in severity and progression of hypertension, anemia, malnutrition, gastrointestinal hemorrhage, and liver damage.

2. ***Physical effects:*** Chronic alcohol disorders exact a greater physical toll on women than on men. Women who are alcohol dependent have death rates 50% to 100% higher than in men who are alcohol dependent. Further, a greater percentage of alcohol-dependent women die of suicide, alcohol-related accidents, circulatory disorders, and cirrhosis of the liver (Hill, 1983).

3. ***Progression of illicit drug use:*** Compared with men, rapid progression of an addictive disorder has not been documented for illicit drug use in women. However, many women who enter treatment are using more than one substance, including alcohol, and are experiencing depression or anxiety, complicating the establishment of causal links in the disease process.

D. **Social and Psychologic Characteristics**

1. ***Common characteristics across groups of women:*** Although women who use and abuse alcohol and other mood-altering drugs

are a heterogeneous group, there are some common characteristics across subpopulations. These characteristics may include the following (Wilsnack, 1987):

a. Young women (20s to early 30s).
b. Unemployed (particularly those looking for work).
c. Heavy-drinking or drug-using partner or spouse.
d. Low self-esteem.
e. Sexual dysfunction.
f. Reproductive health problems.

2. ***Marital status:*** Marital status affects problems with substance use, alcohol in particular, with the highest incidence of problematic use found among divorced or separated women. This finding is supported by the clinical observation that men tend to leave wives who have alcohol disorders, whereas women tend to stay with a spouse who has an alcohol problem.

3. ***Polydrug use:*** Women problem drinkers are also more likely to abuse prescription drugs such as tranquilizers, sedatives, and opioids.

4. ***Partner's use:*** Women with alcohol and drug disorders are more likely to have drinking spouses than are men with alcohol disorders. With regard to drug use, studies indicate that women's drug use often is initiated by male partners, and it is rare for drug-using women to have nonaddicted partners.

5. ***Stereotype of promiscuity:*** One stereotyped presumption about women who drink heavily is that this particular "social deviance" is indicative of other "deviant" behavior patterns, including sexual promiscuity. Alcoholism is associated with high rates of sexual, gynecologic, and reproductive problems in women. "Disorders of sexual desire" and dysfunctional sexuality are more frequent among women who are heavy drinkers than those who are not. Women who drink the most have the highest rates of sexual disinterest over their lifetimes and are most likely to report lack of orgasm (Klassen and Wilsnack, 1986).

6. ***Lack of support:*** Women seeking treatment have been found to feel more isolated, have fewer friends or relatives to provide emotional support, and experience more stressful relationships than women who do not have alcohol or drug disorders.

7. ***Vulnerability to assault:*** Heavy use of alcohol and drugs appears to make women more vulnerable to assault. Women are likely to experience sexual aggression from male drinkers. Studies indicate that between 29% and 54% of women alcoholics in treatment have been rape victims. Two studies indicate that alcoholic women are at high risk for wife-battering (Kantor and Straus, 1989; Miller et al., 1989). Severe violence, however, is more strongly associated with the husband's drug use and drinking.

8. ***Depressed feelings:*** General population surveys show that women with drinking problems are more likely than men with drinking

problems to be depressed and have symptoms of anxiety. The rates of attempted and completed suicide among women with alcohol disorders are higher than those in alcohol-dependent males in a general population.

9. *Life events:* One widely explored hypothesis is that women begin heavy drinking after a stressful life event, whereas men begin drinking as a social activity. Research has failed to consistently support this hypothesis, but scholars have found that women use alcohol and other drugs to help them cope with different problems in their lives. Reed (1987) noted that female alcoholics often seek help for other problems, viewing their drinking as a method of coping rather than an issue for treatment.

II. Recognition of Alcohol and Drug Disorders in Women

A. Barriers to Recognition

1. *Cultural beliefs:* Heavy use of alcohol and drugs has been considered a masculine behavior. Women with alcohol and drug problems are more likely to feel an even stronger stigma than men.

2. *Denial:* The strong stigma against substance abuse by women may cause both them and their families deep shame. Female substance abusers often may go unrecognized by professional caregivers because family members shield them from public detection more than they might male substance abusers.

3. *Diagnostic criteria:* A diagnosis of alcohol abuse and/or dependence is based on a history of acting out behaviors, legal problems, tolerance, and withdrawal symptoms. These criteria are most likely to fit men with alcohol and drug disorders. Women are rarely arrested for driving while under the influence; they more often are escorted home rather than taken to the station (Hennecke and Gitlow, 1985). They are also less likely to get into physical fights while using alcohol or other drugs. Women exhibit more passive alcohol and drug-related symptoms (e.g., depression), and more often enter the mental health treatment system than the alcohol and drug treatment system.

B. Recognition in the Office

1. *Practical issues:* Time constraints often preclude screening all patients for alcohol and drug disorders. There are, however, some signs and symptoms that provide the clinician with the opportunity to ask questions about alcohol and drugs, including prescribed and over-the-counter medications.

   a. Stressful events such as divorce, financial problems, employment issues.

   b. Depression, insomnia, suicidal ideation, self-mutilation.

   c. Anxiety, panic disorders, hyperventilation.

   d. Amenorrhea, premenstrual syndrome (PMS), dysmenorrhea, pelvic pain.

   e. Requests for tranquilizers, narcotics, or sedatives.

   f. Chronic pain syndromes, such as headache, abdominal pain, musculoskeletal pain.

g. Family problems, family illness, behavioral problems in children.

h. Spouse or significant other with alcohol or drug problem.

2. ***Role of family stress:*** Look for stressful events in the lives of female patients. Although the research indicating that life events precede alcohol and drug disorders is sketchy, women are more likely to date the onset of their problem drinking to a stressful event, such as divorce. Their reasons for entering treatment are more likely related to medical and family problems, whereas for men the reasons are more likely related to job or legal problems.

C. Screening Questions

1. ***Limitations of "consequence" questions:*** Screening tests to identify problem drinking or drug use include standard laboratory studies and verbal or written questionnaires. Since women, at least those most often seen in primary care settings, are less likely to have experienced social and legal consequences of prolonged drug and alcohol use, traditional screening questionnaires such as MAST have been less useful (Fleming and Barry, 1989). Use of the CAGE questionnaire or the CAGE Adapted for Drugs (CAGEAID; see Chapter 2) may be problematic with female patients, since many women experience guilt about use whether they have alcohol or drug-related problems.

2. The following questions can be used in screening women for potential alcohol and drug problems. Responses may indicate the need for further assessment to determine level of risk.

a. How many drinks does it take for you to feel high? (>3 = tolerance).

b. Have you felt you should cut down on your use of alcohol, medications, or drugs?

c. Has anyone close to you been affected by your use of alcohol, medications, or drugs?

d. Do you ever use more alcohol, medications, or drugs than you intended?

e. Do you ever use alcohol, medications, or drugs to relieve problems?

f. Do you think you have had a past problem with alcohol, medications, or drugs (patients with a current problem often are willing to admit to a past problem)?

3. *Whatever screening questions are chosen, clinicians need to be aware of the need to maintain a nonthreatening supportive approach.*

III. Treatment

A. Getting Patient into Treatment

Women represent approximately 25% of the clients in traditional chemical dependency treatment centers in the United States (NIAAA, 1990). Although it appears that they comprise a smaller proportion of the treatment population (25% vs. 75% for men), the proportion of all females to all males with alcohol dependence, in particular, is similar (30% female, 70% male). However, women with alcohol and drug problems may encounter some barriers to treatment not encountered by men. Some of the same barriers that make it difficult for clinicians and families to recognize alcohol and drug problems in women also present obstacles to women in seeking treatment. *The clinician's knowledge of the local treatment programs and available community resources can help patients to overcome some of these barriers.*

1. ***Social stigma:*** Seeking treatment represents a public admission of a highly stigmatized behavior.
2. ***Family denial:*** The family of a woman with an alcohol or drug disorder shares the stigma and wants to avoid public exposure. As part of the treatment process, the clinician has the opportunity to steer the family toward help for themselves. Educating the family about the disease process can be useful.
3. ***Ambivalence toward treatment:*** Even women who want help with an alcohol or drug problem often are reluctant to enter treatment if it takes them away from family responsibilities. They either need reassurance that their family responsibilities can be maintained by others while they are in treatment or they may need help to find community resources to assist them during treatment.
4. ***Child care:*** Women with young children may not have the support network or the financial resources to obtain child care if they need inpatient treatment.
5. ***Insurance:*** Since more women than men with alcohol and drug problems are divorced, their standard of living, employment opportunities, and insurance benefits may preclude treatment options. Knowledge of the treatment programs and insurance options can aid patients in decisions to seek treatment.

B. **Specific Treatment Issues for Women**

When searching for treatment resources for female patients with alcohol or drug disorders, programming that is sensitive to women's needs is essential to retain them in treatment and to minimize the chances for relapse. Although most community treatment programs cannot afford to directly offer all of the services many women in treatment need, they can assure their availability through formal and informal arrangements with other service providers. In essence, treatment can be conducted by a team that includes a primary care physician, vocational counselors, and legal consultants, as well as the chemical dependency treatment program staff. Recovery for women, as well as for men, needs to be envisioned as a long-term process. *Not all of the elements listed below are necessary during the short period the patient is in inpatient or outpatient treatment; however, most of these services will be needed to enhance long-term recovery.* Core services for women during and after treatment include:

1. ***Prescription drug assessment and treatment:*** Many women entering treatment have experienced problems with prescription drugs as well as with alcohol or illicit drugs.

2. ***Gynecologic services:*** Diagnosis and treatment of medical problems, including gynecologic services, are important components of care. These services may be provided by a primary physician working in conjunction with the treatment program.

3. ***Psychiatric assessment:*** Women are generally more willing than men to seek help for emotional problems, and many acknowledge that substance use is a problem for them. Many women need assessment and treatment for concurrent depression or anxiety to minimize the likelihood of relapse.

4. ***Violence counseling:*** Because of the high rate of physical abuse among women with alcohol and drug problems, counseling for women who have been battered and/or have been victims of incest has become an increasingly important component of alcohol and drug treatment programs. Ideally, this should begin while the patient is in treatment, but generally should continue past the acute phase of alcohol and drug treatment.

5. ***Social support:*** Because social supports of women with alcohol and drug-related problems are generally poor, treatment agencies for women should offer programs that bolster social support. Moyar (1987) recommends programs that encourage healthy relationships between women, to avoid overdependency on male partners who are frequently substance dependent and may increase the possibility of relapse (Tunving & Nilsson, 1985). Beginning to establish these ongoing support networks in treatment can assist in relapse prevention. Components of social support groups can include:
   a. Assertiveness training.
   b. Financial management.
   c. Stress and crisis management.
   d. Communication skills to develop a support system.
   e. Basic survival skills.

6. ***Child care services:*** Very few treatment programs in the United States have on-site child care, and many women entering treatment worry about being separated from their children and child care arrangements. Some are also concerned about the loss of child custody if they publicly acknowledge their alcohol or drug disorder. Knowledge of both the patient's family system and the community child care agencies can provide child care options to the patient.

7. ***Health promotion.*** Exercise and nutrition planning are included to increase the likelihood of healthy life-style changes during recovery.

8. ***Legal assistance:*** Both criminal and civil issues (e.g., child custody, landlord disputes, divorce or separation) may need resolution for the patient during or after acute alcohol and drug treatment.

9. ***Vocational assistance:*** Some women entering treatment need job readiness training, vocational skill training, and job-seeking support and coaching. These programs can be especially helpful in the recovery phase of treatment.

BIBLIOGRAPHY

Boring C, Squires T, Fong T: Cancer statistics, 1991. *CA* 1991; 41:19–36.

Brownell KD, Marlatt GA, Lichtenstein E, et al: Understanding and preventing relapse. *Am Psychol* 1986; 41:765–782.

Caetano R: Drinking patterns and alcohol problems in a national survey of US Hispanics, in Spieger D, Tate D, Aitkon S, et al (eds): *Alcohol Use Among US Ethnic Minorities.* Bethesda, Md, National Institute of Alcohol Abuse and Alcoholism, 1989, Research Monograph No. 18, DHHS Publ. No. (ADM)89–1435.

Dahlgren L, Willander A: Are special treatment facilities for female alcoholics needed? A controlled 2-year follow-up study from a specialized female unit (EWA) versus a mixed male/female treatment facility. *Alcohol Clin Exp Res* 1989; 13:499–504.

Smoking and Health: A National Status Report, ed 2. DHHS Publ No (CDC)87–8396. Rockville, MD, Department of Health and Human Services, 1990.

Fleming M, Barry K: A study examining the psychometric properties of the SMAST-13. *J Subst Abuse* 1989; 1:173–182.

Frezza M, DiPadova C, Pozzato G, et al: High blood alcohol levels in women: The role of decreased gastric alcohol dehydrogenase and first pass metabolism. *N Engl J Med* 1990; 322:95–99.

Gilbert J: Alcohol consumption patterns in immigrant and later generation Mexican American women. *Hispanic J Behav Sci* 1987; 9:209–213.

Harrison PA, Belille CA: Women in treatment: Beyond the stereotype. *J Stud Alcohol* 1987; 48:574–578.

Hennecke and Gitlow: Alcoholism in women: A growing problem. *Med Aspects Hum Sex* 1985; 19:150–155.

Herd D: Drinking by black and white women: Results from a national survey. *Social Probl* 1988; 35:493–505.

Herd D: The epidemiology of drinking patterns and alcohol-related social problems among U.S. blacks, in Spieger D, Tate D, Aitkon S, et al (eds). *Alcohol Use Among US Ethnic Minorities.* Bethesda, Md, National Institute of Alcohol Abuse and Alcoholism, 1989; Research Monograph No. 18, DHHS Publ. No. (ADM)89–1435.

Highlights from the 1989 National Drug and Alcoholism Treatment Unit Survey (NDATUS) Bethesda, Md, National Institute of Alcohol Abuse and Alcoholism 1990.

Hill S: Biological consequences of alcoholism and alcohol-related problems among women, in *Special Populations Issues.* Bethesda, Md, National Institute of Alcohol Abuse and Alcoholism, 1983, Alcohol and Health Monograph No. 4, DHHS Publ. No. (ADM)82–1193.

Kantor GK, Straus MA: Substance abuse as a precipitant of wife abuse victimizations. *Am J Drug Alcohol Abuse* 1989; 15:173–189.

Klassen AD, Wilsnack SC: Sexual experience and drinking among women in a U.S. national survey. *Arch Sex Beh* 1986; 15:363–392.

Marsh JC, Miller NA: Female clients in substance abuse treatment. *Int J Addict* 1985; 20:995–1019.

Marshall A, Kingstone D, Boss M, et al: Ethanol elimination in males and females: Relationship to menstrual cycle and body composition. *Hepatology* 1983; 3:701–706.

Miller BA, Downs WR, Gondoli DM: Spousal violence among alcoholic women as compared to a random household sample of women. *J Stud Alcohol* 1989; 50:533–540.

Moyar M: Female alcoholism and affiliation needs. *Women Ther* 1987; 6:313–321.

Ray BA, Braude MC: Women and drugs: A new era for research. Bethesda, Md, National Institute of Drug Abuse, NIDA Monograph 65, 1990.

Reed BG: Developing women-sensitive drug dependence treatment services: Why so difficult? *J Psychoact Drugs* 1987; 19:151–164.

Schilit R, Gomberg EL: Social support structures of women in treatment for alcoholism. *Health Social Work* 1987; summer, 187–195.

Sutker P, Goist K, King A: Acute alcohol intoxication in women: Relationship to dose and menstrual cycle phase. *Alcohol Clin Exp Res* 1987; 11:74–79.

Tunving K, Nilsson K: Young female drug addicts in treatment: A twelve year perspective. *J Drug Issues* 1985; 15:367–382.

Underhill BL: Issues relevant to aftercare programs for women. *Alcohol Health Res World* 1986; fall, 46–47.

US House of Representatives, Select Committee on Children, Youth, and Families: *Women, Addiction, and Perinatal Substance Abuse: Fact Sheet.* Washington, DC, 1990.

Werner EE: Resilient offspring of alcoholics: A longitudinal study from birth to age 18. *J Stud Alcohol* 1986; 47:34–40.

Wilsnack SC: Drinking and drinking problems in women: A US longitudinal survey and some implications for prevention, in Loberg T, Miller WR, Nathan PE, et al (eds): *Addictive Behaviors: Prevention and Early Intervention.* Amsterdam, Swets and Zeitlinger, 1987, pp 1–39.

Women and Alcohol Use: A Review of the Research Literature. Washington, DC, *Department of Health and Human Services,* Alcohol, Drug Abuse, and Mental Health Administration, 1988.

Zankowski GL: Responsive programming: Meeting the needs of chemically dependent women. *Alcohol Treat Q* 1987; 4:53–67.

CHAPTER 15

Substance Use in Older Adults

James Finch, M.D.

Kristen Lawton Barry, Ph.D.

The use of mood-altering drugs, such as alcohol and tranquilizers, by persons older than 65 years is an important medical concern with a wide range of consequences. Most of the people in this age group visit a clinician on a regular basis, furnishing these providers with a unique opportunity to recognize and intervene with substance abuse problems. Even though the prevalence of alcohol and drug use decreases with age, it remains a common problem, and prescription and over-the-counter (OTC) medication abuse actually may become more common. Brief physician advice and social support may be particularly effective in reducing nicotine, alcohol, and other drug problems in older patients.

I. Overview of Nicotine, Alcohol, and Drug Use in Older Adults
A. Magnitude of the Problem
1. ***Significance:*** Older adults are the fastest growing segment of our society. There are seven million smokers older than 65 years of age. Alcohol, nicotine, and prescription drug abuse comprise one of the most important health problems in patients over 65 years. OTC medication abuse is an additional problem in this age group. Although older adults represent 11% of the population, they take 25% of all prescribed medications, many of which have the potential for misuse or abuse (Carty and Everitt, 1989).
2. ***Underreporting:*** In the last decade researchers have acknowledged that alcohol and drug abuse among older adults is a substantial but underrecognized problem. There has been an increase in reported mortality from alcohol abuse in this age group in spite of the fact that many alcohol-related deaths are not reported. This underreporting is due, in part, to a failure to recognize how alcohol and other medications contribute to deteriorating health in older patients.

B. Specifics of Nicotine Abuse
1. ***Age differences:*** National surveys have found that the proportion of smokers who say they would like to stop smoking is lower for smokers over the age of 50 years (57%) than for smokers aged 18 to 29

years (68%) or 30 to 49 years (67%) (US Department of Health and Human Services, 1990).

2. *Motivation:* The older smoker may be less motivated to quit for the following reasons:
   a. The highly motivated may have quit at younger ages, leaving the "hard core" group still smoking.
   b. Some elderly may believe that they are no longer at risk for smoking-related diseases because they have already survived smoking for so many years.
   c. Some may believe that the damage caused by smoking is irreversible after so many years of smoking, so why quit. For similar reasons, physicians may be reluctant to encourage older smokers to quit.

3. *Benefits of quitting:* The Surgeon General's 1990 report (US Department of Health and Human Services, 1990) on smoking shows data indicating that the benefits of cessation extend to quitting at older ages.
   a. A healthy man aged 60 to 64 years who smokes one pack of cigarettes or more a day reduces his risk of dying during the next 15 years by 10% if he quits smoking.
   b. Age of menopause appears to be affected by smoking. Smoking women cease menstruating 1 to 2 years earlier than otherwise similar nonsmokers.
   c. Smokers who have already developed cancer may also benefit from smoking cessation. A few studies have indicated that smokers who stopped after a diagnosis of cancer was made, compared with those who continued to smoke, reduced their risk for a second primary cancer.

4. *Smoking cessation techniques:* Specific smoking cessation strategies (see Chapter 5) apply to both younger and older patients.

C. **Alcohol Use**

1. *Prevalence:* Conservative estimates of the prevalence of alcohol abuse and dependence after age 65 years range from 2% to 8% (higher in men than in women). Problematic use, however, may be significantly higher, since minimal use can exacerbate many medical problems seen in this age group.

2. *Categorization by age at onset:* Older patients with alcohol disorders have been divided into two major groups.
   a. *Early-onset disorders:* Often termed "survivors," this group comprises two thirds of the alcohol problems in older patients. Patients in this category are the easiest to identify in the office. Most have numerous medical problems, such as cirrhosis, dementia, psychiatric problems, and other alcohol-related medical conditions. Some of these survivors may be more difficult to recognize because occasional binge drinkers are difficult to recognize in the office at any age.

b. *Late-onset or reactive disorders:* One third of elderly patients with alcohol disorders are people who initiate problematic drinking later in life. Problematic alcohol use is believed to be secondary to the stresses or losses associated with the normal aging process. These patients show fewer of the classic physical consequences and life-style disruptions seen in younger patients with alcohol disorders (e.g., acute hepatitis, arrests). Women are more likely than men to start drinking in later life, and single older women are more likely to drink than married women. Alcohol use by older people who are isolated, such as those widowed, single, or living in disadvantaged circumstances, are of particular concern.

3. ***Prognosis:*** Although patients with early-onset disorder often are thought to have a worse prognosis, this has not been clearly borne out by follow-up studies. Prognosis is more clearly related to associated chronic physical problems, psychiatric comorbidity, social isolation, and family drinking practices that facilitate continuing abuse.

D. **Illicit, Prescription, and Over-the-Counter Drug Use**

1. ***Illicit drug abuse:*** Information on illicit drug abuse in older patients is limited. Clearly, many street addicts die of violence, trauma, overdose, or medical complication before reaching advanced age. For example, only about 5% of those receiving long-term methadone treatment are older than 45 years of age. Those who do survive generally adapt or alter their drug life-style as they age ("maturing out"). Changes include a decrease in criminal activities and street drug use as well switching their "drug of choice" to legal prescription drugs.

2. ***Prescription drugs:*** The majority of persons older than 65 years take regular prescription medication. Tranquilizers and anti-insomniacs are the two most commonly used psychotropic prescriptions.

a. Studies have estimated that between 11% and 25% of persons over 65 have used tranquilizers in the previous year. Tranquilizers are most often prescribed for women. These findings are worrisome in view of the limited usefulness of these medications on a long-term basis and the potential for problems with prolonged half-lives (e.g., half-life for diazepam is 20 hours in young adults, and 90 hours in 80-year-old persons). See Table 15–1 for the specific effects and dosages of benzodiazepines by age. See Table 15–2 for maximum recommended daily doses by age for antidepressants and neuroleptics. These sedative drugs also have cross-addiction potential with alcohol, and alcohol can potentiate the sedative effect of these drugs.

b. Chances for misuse are acute in this age group (many experts believe this is more common than true abuse or dependence). The potential reasons for this are many. Multiple prescriptions increase the chance for error. Additional reasons for misuse include cognitive or visual impairment, erratic compliance, self-

TABLE 15–1.

Benzodiazepines: Pharmacokinetic Characteristics in Older Adults

Generic Name	Geriatric Dose (mg)	Half-life in Young (hr)	Half-life in Elderly (hr)	Maximum Dose in Young (mg)	Maximum Dose in Elderly (mg)
Flurazepam HCl	15	40–100	40–150 (active metabolite)	—	—
Diazepam	2–5	24	75	60	20
Chlordiazepoxide HCl	5	10	18–30	100	40
Oxazepam	7.5–20	7–10	7–10	90	60
Temazepam	15	11	10	—	—
Lorazepam	0.5	12	12	6	3
Triazolam	0.125	2.6	3.3	—	—
Alprazolam	0.25	12.4	12	2	4

medication, and use of medications in combination with alcohol or OTC drugs.

3. ***OTC drugs:*** Since many OTC drugs have sedative effects (e.g., antihistamines such as Benadryl, sleep aids such as Sominex), their use may become problematic alone or in conjunction with alcohol or prescription sedatives. In addition, the anticholinergic side effects of antihistamines, which may impair memory and bring out a behavioral disorder in a patient with dementia.

E. **Physiological Factors in Alcohol and Drug Disorders**

1. ***Changes in physiologic responses with age:*** The physiologic responses to mood-altering chemicals differ with aging. Compared with younger people, older adults have increased sensitivity to alcohol, OTC medications, and other drugs. The elderly often have a *dysphoric reaction* to alcohol, whereas younger drinkers generally experience some euphoria.

TABLE 15–2.

Maximum Dose of Frequently Used Antidepressants and Neuroleptics in Older Adults*

Drug	Usual Maximum Dose Age 12–64 Yr (mg)	Usual Maximum Dose Age ≥65 Yr (mg)
Antidepressants		
Amitriptyline	200	150
Desipramine	200	150
Doxepin	200	150
Imipramine	200	150
Nortriptyline	150	75
Trazodone	400	200
Antipsychotics†		
Chlorpromazine	1,600	800
Haloperidol	100	50

*Note maximum doses are 25% to 100% less than in patients 12 to 64 years of age.
†Maximum daily dose of chlorpromazine and haloperidol in patients with organic mental disease is 400 mg and 15 mg, respectively.

a. There is an age-related decrease in lean body mass as opposed to total volume of fat. The resultant decrease in total body volume increases the total distribution of alcohol and other mood-altering chemicals in the body.

b. Liver enzymes that metabolize alcohol or certain other drugs (e.g., diazepam) are less efficient with age. Hepatic blood flow decreases with age.

c. Central nervous system sensitivity to alcohol increases with age.

d. Decreased cardiovascular and renal function, reducing clearance of some drugs. Reactions include headache, reduced cognitive abilities, and memory problems, even at low levels of use.

2. ***Increase in physiologic consequences with age:*** The following systems can be affected by alcohol and/or drug disorders with aging.

a. *Cardiovascular system:* Since older patients generally have more cardiovascular disease, patients who are problematic alcohol or drug users can be at higher risk for serious complications (e.g., angina pain may be dulled by alcohol or drug use and could lead to myocardial infarction). Cardiac output and efficiency decrease, because cardiac function is impaired by alcohol.

b. *Pulmonary system:* Problematic use of alcohol or other drugs can cause decreased respiratory drive, which can lead to increased frequency of mental confusion in patients who have chronic obstructive pulmonary disease.

c. ***Gastrointestinal system:*** Diarrhea secondary to the direct effect of alcohol on the small intestine is common in the elderly patient with an alcohol disorder. Peptic ulcer disease is more common in elderly drinkers, particularly in those who have long-term patterns of binge drinking. As a result of low grade gastrointestinal bleeding, which is often silent, patients may develop chronic iron-deficiency anemia.

d. ***Neuromuscular system:*** There can be an increase in alcohol-related disorders, such as myopathy, neuropathy, and cerebellar dysfunction. Alcohol lowers the seizure threshold and decreases coordination. This is associated with an increased rate of falls and subsequent fractures of the wrist, back, and hips.

e. ***Sexual function:*** Sexual dysfunction is a common complication of problematic use of alcohol and other drugs. This may result from hormonal dysfunction, CNS depression, peripheral neuropathy, and/or emotional consequences. Because of the increased sensitivity of older adults to alcohol and other drugs, these effects can occur with relatively low use.

3. ***Risk with even low to moderate use:*** Adverse health effects are not limited to patients identified as heavy drinkers or drug abusers. Older patients who have chronic medical conditions can have adverse consequences from even moderate consumption of alcohol, cigarettes, or other drugs.

F. Psychosocial Factors in Alcohol and Drug Disorders

1. *Transitions:* Late adulthood is a time of transitions. Some of these changes are physical; some are social, psychologic, and emotional. Coping responses can be positive or negative, and some changes can contribute to increased use of nicotine, alcohol, or other drugs. Retirement can be especially difficult for the person who has worked hard, been productive, and never found time for hobbies and leisure activities. A person with unrealistic expectations of retirement may become depressed and bored. Some patients may be unprepared for a decline in economic status. Mood-altering chemicals may be used to try to relieve boredom and ease depression.

2. *External losses:* External losses and the accompanying loneliness can cause overwhelming stress. The longer individuals live the more likely they are to experience the death of friends and spouse.

3. *Internal losses:* Hearing and vision changes normally accompany aging. Arthritis, osteoporosis, cognitive deficits, and memory losses can be aggravated by overmedication or alcohol use.

4. *Depression:* Depression can result in a tendency to stop trying to change the unfavorable conditions and an increase in the use of alcohol and/or prescription drugs. Depression can be assessed using screening instruments. The Geriatric Depression Scale (GDS)—Short Form (Fig 15–1) is one example of these instruments.

II. Making a Diagnosis

A. Missed Opportunities

1. **Why are alcohol and drug abuse in older adults underdiagnosed?** Behavior problems in older patients are frequently attributed to other causes. Alcohol and other drug use often is overlooked as contributing to psychiatric syndromes such as depression, anxiety, agitation, insomnia, or sexual dysfunction. Decreases in cognitive function due to alcohol or other drug use may be attributed to senile or multi-infarct dementia. In addition, manifestations may be subtle, such as falls or poor attention to activities of daily living.

2. *Normal aging:* Many conditions, including dementia, depressive symptoms, and symptoms of substance use, are attributed to the normal aging process. They are *not* symptoms of normal aging, but are symptoms of diseases that need to be sorted out to allow older patients to function optimally.

B. Is it a Substance Abuse Problem?

1. *The good news:* Despite some of the limitations to diagnosis in this age group, elderly persons do seek medical attention more frequently than younger individuals. As a result, health care providers have more opportunity for screening, diagnosis, and follow-up in elderly patients than in any other group of patients.

2. *Team approach to diagnosis:* Maintaining a working relationship with other health care providers (e.g., visiting nurse, "Meals-on-Wheels" programs, services for elderly) who are more likely to no-

---

GERIATRIC DEPRESSION SCALE—SHORT FORM

Choose the best answer for how you felt over the past week.

1. Are you basically satisfied with your life? ☑ Yes ☐ No
2. Have you dropped many of your activities and interests? ☐ Yes ☑ No
3. Do you feel that your life is empty? ☐ Yes ☑ No
4. Do you often get bored? ☑ Yes ☐ No
5. Are you in good spirits most of the time? ☑ Yes ☐ No
6. Are you afraid that something bad is going to happen to you? ☐ Yes ☑ No
7. Do you feel happy most of the time? ☑ Yes ☐ No
8. Do you often feel helpless? ☐ Yes ☑ No
9. Do you prefer to stay at home, rather than going out and doing something? ☐ Yes ☑ No
10. Do you feel you have more problems with memory than most? ☑ Yes ☐ No
11. Do you think it is wonderful to be alive now? ☑ Yes ☐ No
12. Do you feel pretty worthless the way you are now? ☐ Yes ☑ No
13. Do you feel full of energy? ☐ Yes ☑ No
14. Do you feel that your situation is hopeless? ☐ Yes ☑ No
15. Do you think that most people are better off than you are? ☑ Yes ☐ No

Scoring: 1 point for each answer; Cutoff: normal (0–5),
5 suggests depression.

1. No	4 Yes	7. No	10. Yes	13. No
2. Yes	5. No	8. Yes	11. No	14. Yes
3. Yes	6. Yes	9. Yes	12. Yes	15. Yes

FIG 15–1.
Geriatric Depression Scale—Short Form.

tice household or community problems can facilitate the recognition of substance abuse problems in older patients in your practice. This same network will be critical to intervening with these patients. The following problems can alert the clinician to a potential substance abuse problem. The italicized symptoms are particularly telling in patients older than 65 years.

a. Anxiety
b. Blackouts, dizziness
c. *Depression*
d. *Disorientation, confusion*
e. Extended grieving
f. Excessive mood swings
g. *Falls, bruises, burns*
h. Family problems
i. Financial problems
j. Headache
k. *Incontinence*

l. *Increased tolerance to alcohol or medications/drugs*
m. Legal difficulties
n. *Memory loss*
o. Nausea
p. New difficulties in decision making
q. Persistent coughing, wheezing (specific to nicotine use)
r. *Poor hygiene*
s. *Poor nutrition*
t. Seizures, idiopathic
u. Sleep problems
v. *Social isolation*
w. Suicidal ideation
x. Sweating/tremor
y. *Unusual response to medication*
   If an older patient exhibits any of these symptoms, questions about alcohol, tobacco, and other medications/drugs should be part of a differential diagnosis.

C. Case Finding

1. ***Guidelines for asking older patients questions about substance use:*** Patients with early-onset disorders ("survivors") usually have health problems that can open up the discussion of treatment. Those with late-onset ("reactive") disorders have their earlier successes in life to reflect on with pride, as well as self-esteem to maintain or regain.

   a. Place questions in a medical context (e.g., drinking as a possible cause of gastrointestinal distress, insomnia).
   b. Gentle persistence, mutual respect, and patience on the part of the physician is the most effective method for guiding a patient and/or their family through the consequences and an awareness of a problem. This approach can help older patients break through the "learned helplessness" they may be experiencing. Strong confrontation, as sometimes used with younger alcohol and drug users, is less effective in the elderly.
   c. Focus on problems not amounts. Due to metabolic changes in aging, amounts of medication and alcohol considered acceptable in younger patients can produce adverse reactions in older adults.
   d. Talk with the family or other care givers. People who see older patients in their home environments are most likely to notice functional changes before they come to the attention of medical personnel.
   e. Ask about all drug use (alcohol, nicotine, prescription and OTC drugs). Each type of drug and/or the interaction between drugs can produce negative symptoms in the elderly. Look for the social context of alcohol and/or other drug use and for the connections between misuse or abuse and psychosocial history.

2. ***Screening questions:*** The CHARM questionnaire (Fig 15–2) is a face valid instrument that provides a clinically useful format in which to consider alcohol and prescription medication use in older patients. The instrument was developed to ask questions about alcohol use, but has been applied to any medication or OTC drug for which the clinician has concerns. Each letter in the acronym represents a short series of questions that can be useful in initial assessment of a potential problem with alcohol or other medications or drugs. The acronym CHARM was chosen for this particular age group to enhance the clinician's awareness of the need to maintain a nonthreatening, supportive approach.

3. ***Family member interview:*** If no family member is present at this interview, ask the patient if a family member can be contacted by phone or can come in for an interview. Ask either the patient or family member, as needed, to bring all medications (OTC and prescription) to an office visit ("brown bag" technique). A family meeting may include the following.

   a. Begin with open-ended questions regarding any information the family member(s) may have about the patient's health or functioning (wait to see if they bring up alcohol or other medicines or drugs).

   b. If misuse or abuse is recognized by the family, focus *first* on the problems and dysfunction as a result of the use, and *second* on the amount or frequency.

4. ***Physical examination:*** A thorough physical examination is particularly important in older problematic alcohol or drug users. They are more likely to show evidence of the chronic stigmata of prolonged abuse (e.g., hepatomegaly, gynecomastia, palmar erythema). They are more likely to have chronic medical conditions (both drug- and non-drug-related) than both the general older population and younger abusers and are at greater risk for complications of withdrawal. However, findings on the physical examination still frequently are normal and should not be relied on to confirm or reject the diagnosis.

5. ***Mental status examination:*** Finlayson et al. (1988) found that 44% of older alcoholic patients have significant organic brain syndrome. Even though it is often not possible to differentiate the diagnosis of alcohol-related dementia vs. Alzheimer's or multi-infarct dementia, it is still important diagnostic and therapeutic information, and a brief formal mental status examination can be useful.

   a. Short Portable Mental Status Questionnaire (SPMSQ; Pfeiffer, 1975):

      (1) What is the date today?

      (2) What day of the week is it?

      (3) What is the name of this place?

      (4) What is your telephone number? (If person does not have a phone, "What is your street address?")

C   *Cut* down?

H   *How* do you use?

A   *Anyone* concerned?

R   *Relief* use?

M   *More* than intended?

C   "Have you ever *Cut* down or quit drinking?"

"When, in your life, would you say your drinking was the heaviest?

"Have you thought recently that you should cut down?"

H   "*How* do you use alcohol?"

"What are your rules about alcohol use?"

"Has your drinking changed in the last 3 months? Year?"

A   "Has *Anyone* ever seemed concerned about your drinking?"

"People have different feeling about drinking alcohol.

How do your friends and family view your drinking?"

"Have you ever had health problems that caused your doctor to ask you to alter your drinking habits?"

R   "Have you ever used alcohol to *Relieve* problems?" (Look for social or emotional discomfort such as loneliness or depression.)

 "When you drink alcohol, what's usually the reason?"

"Do you ever have a drink when you feel lonely or upset?"

"How is your sleep?" "What do you use to help you fall asleep?"

M   "Do you ever drink *More* than you intended?" What were the circumstances?"

"Most people have times when they drink more than they intended to.

What situations might cause you to drink more than you expected to?"

FIG 15-2.

CHARM questionnaire for use in screening for alcohol and prescription medication use in older patients. (From Sumnicht G: *Sailing White Horses: Adventures With Older Substance Abusers.* Madison, Wis, PICADA, 1991. Used by permission.)

(5) How old are you?

(6) When were you born?

(7) Who is the president of the United States now?

(8) Who was the president just before that?

(9) What was your mother's maiden name?

(10) Subtract 3 from 20 and keep subtracting 3 from each new number you get, all the way down.

Scoring: Allow one more error if the patient has only a grade school education; allow one less error if the patient has an education beyond high school:

0–2 errors, intact intelligence function; 3–4 errors, mild intelligence impairment; 5–7 errors, moderate intelligence impairment; 8–10 errors, severe intelligence impairment.

6. *Laboratory tests:* A number of routine laboratory tests frequently yield abnormal results in patients who abuse drugs. Alcohol is by far the drug most commonly associated with a pattern of irregularities. Older patients with alcohol problems are more likely to demonstrate these abnormalities than their younger counterparts are. The most common abnormalities noted are increased liver function tests (e.g., alanine and aspartate transaminases, ALT and AST), elevated mean corpuscular volume (MCV) (with or without anemia), increased uric acid, decreased albumin level.

CAUTION: Values for MCV tend to be higher in older patients, and albumin values tend to be lower. In addition, older patients may be taking medications that affect laboratory values (e.g., thiazide diuretics raise uric acid levels). Look for a pattern of abnormalities to support the diagnosis, rather than an isolated value. In addition, although laboratory abnormalities are common in older alcohol abusers, they are frequently not present and should not be relied on to confirm the diagnosis. In a study of alcohol-dependent inpatients over the age of 65 years, AST was increased in 60% and MCV in 42% (Hurt et al., 1988).

III. Treatment for Alcohol and Drug Disorders in Older Adults

A. Overview: Do Treatment Issues Differ by Age of Patient?

1. *Reluctance of patient:* Older patients often are reluctant to enter a hospital or residential treatment center because they are concerned about leaving their homes unprotected or about making arrangements for their stay. Some older patients may be reluctant to turn to "outsiders" for help.

2. *Detoxification:* More patients over the age of 65 years require hospital detoxification, because of the general condition of their health, age-related medical conditions (e.g., heart disease, chronic lung disease), and increased morbidity and mortality associated with detoxification. Generally the use of medications (e.g., benzodiazepines) in detoxification in older patients should be reserved until there is physical evidence of withdrawal. Prophylactic treatment before the

onset of symptoms, as is often done in younger patients, may be dangerous in older patients. Detoxification regimens should be modified to avoid oversedation.

   a. Short-acting benzodiazepines (e.g., oxazepam, lorazepam) can be used at approximately half the usual dose.

   b. Close attention should be paid to tapering over approximately 5 days (e.g., maintain initial dose for 24 to 48 hours, then decrease dose 25% per day), although detoxification may take longer than usual in older adults.

3. ***Antabuse:*** The use of disulfiram (Antabuse) has not proved useful as an adjunct to alcohol rehabilitation in older patients, and its use is generally not safe. This age group has more potential for a severe reaction to alcohol.

4. ***Depression:*** Low-dose antidepressants may be indicated and carefully prescribed if there is persistent depression after a period of sobriety. Nortriptyline at an initial dose of 25 mg has been a favorite first choice among many geriatricians.

B. Treatment Approaches

1. ***Inpatient treatment:*** Inpatient treatment is preferred when the patient is suffering the effects of poor nutrition, poor overall health status, a history of delirium tremens or seizures, or other conditions that complicate withdrawal (e.g., infection, heart disease). Inpatient treatment also is needed when the patient has no obvious community support systems (e.g., family, caretakers, services for aging). Only 8% of existing alcohol and drug treatment programs have specialized services for older adults (Institute of Medicine, 1990). Many believe that older substance abuse patients do better in age-specific programs or groups. However, evidence is equivocal as to whether age-specific or mixed-aged programs are more beneficial for these patients.

2. ***Social support:*** All treatment approaches in older patients must have a strong social support component. Group socialization experiences can help the patient overcome some of the isolation often accompanying substance abuse in this age group. Social intervention appears to benefit both early- and late-onset disorders. In some communities, Alcoholics Anonymous has chapters appropriate for older adults.

   a. Physicians may keep a list of names of patients who were successful in getting help through these programs. These patients can be enlisted (with their consent) as a resource to other patients who could benefit from self-groups or a treatment program. Sometimes this is enough to motivate an uncertain patient to seek help.

   b. Older patients tend to be more faithful than younger patients in attending support group meetings, but they prefer and receive greater benefit from *smaller groups*. They tend to complain about the high noise level, rough language, and cigarette smoke in larger groups. Hearing and visual impairment affect the types of groups that provide the most comfort.

3. ***Long-term follow-up:*** All treatment approaches need to provide for long-term follow-up. Practical follow-up concerns include transportation to support meetings, counseling sessions, and the physician's office. Follow-up phone calls and peer counseling have been effective. Visiting nurse services can help home-bound patients.

IV. Steps for Lowering the Risk of Substance Abuse

A. Psychoactive medication can be helpful when there is a clear indication for use and a time-limited contract is established and understood by the patient and family members. Guidelines (Jenike, 1988) for prescribing psychotropic medication in older adults include the following:

1. *Careful history:* It is necessary to know what concomitant illnesses the patient has and what medications have been taken.

2. *Diagnose prior to treatment:* This is imperative to avoid the inappropriate use of psychotropic medication. For example, if severe insomnia is secondary to depression, benzodiazepines may worsen the overall clinical situation, whereas a sedative antidepressant will treat the underlying disorder.

3. *Evaluate patient for noncompliance:* Make the therapeutic regimen as simple as possible. Explain which medications are to be taken, the dosage, and the timing, to both the patient and the family. Write down the dosing schedule. Choose the most appropriate dosage form; liquids may be more suitable for a patient with trouble swallowing. Encourage patients to destroy or return discontinued medication. In patients who are confused or demented, be sure adequate supervision is present.

4. *Do not avoid use of psychotropic agents because of age:* These drugs can be used safely in the elderly, and older patients deserve relief of symptoms of depression, psychosis, and severe anxiety.

5. *Use low dose initially:* Because of individual differences in the elderly, the clinician should start with very low doses and gradually adjust upward. Try to identify signs and symptoms that can be followed up, such as sleep disturbance, anorexia, hallucinations, or aggressive behavior.

6. *Know pharmacology of drug prescribed:* It is best to be familiar with the use of a few drugs in each class. The clinician needs to be aware of altered dosing schedules in the elderly and changes in half-life, elimination, and protein binding. Potential interactions with other drugs, as well as the toxicity and side effects of individual drugs are important considerations.

7. *Monitor drugs on a regular basis:* This is extremely important, especially when more than one physician may be prescribing medication or when neuroleptics are being used. It is not uncommon for medications to be continued for many months after the indication has resolved.

8. *Avoid polypharmacy:* Frequently patients receive two or more drugs of the same type or which have similar and additive side effects, perhaps prescribed by the same or different clinicians.

9. *Optimize the patient's environment:* Environmental manipulation may alleviate anxiety, loneliness, depression, and even psychosis. Optimize the patient's physical condition and encourage social activities and exercise whenever possible. Provide supportive individual and family psychotherapy when needed.

10. *Watch for adverse drug side effects:* Most psychotropic agents have side effects that can be of major significance. Because many of these may not be present when the drug is started, frequent monitoring is necessary.

B. ***Nonpharmacologic treatment for insomnia and anxiety should be emphasized:*** These are common conditions in older adults, and reliance on medication could foster dependence. The following are guidelines for these commonly occurring problems.

1. Anxiety:
   a. Rule out medical causes (e.g., chronic obstructive pulmonary disease, congestive heart failure).
   b. If there is a clear precipitating event (e.g., recent loss), social support may be adequate.
   c. If an anxiolytic medication is required, use short-acting agents for a limited time (e.g., contract with the patient to use the medication for a set time; try to wean).
   d. Oxazepam (Serax) and lorazepam (Ativan) and temazepam (Restoril) have short half-lives. They are unaffected by the age of the patient or by the use of other medication (see Table 15–1). Unlike other benzodiazepines, lorazepam has the additional advantage of excellent intramuscular or subcutaneous absorption if oral use is not possible.
   e. Titrate the dose. "Start low and go slow." Use less often (some use the dictum, "Use half as much half as often."

2. Insomnia:
   a. Nonpharmacologic approaches are primary tactics to be emphasized, and include education, reassurance, avoidance of daytime napping, avoidance of caffeine, regular bedtime.
   b. If drugs are to be used, try to limit duration of use and apply the same principles as above when using benzodiazepines.
   c. Avoid antihistamines (e.g., Benadryl), because of their anticholinergic effects.
   d. Avoid long-acting agents such as diazepam (Valium) and chlordiazepoxide (Librium); their half-lives extend with age (see Table 15–1).

C. ***Attention to OTC drug abuse:*** The use or abuse of nonprescription medication is an often unsuspected contributor to unwanted side effects and for unwanted drug interactions. This potential can be minimized by education and periodic review.

1. Avoid the common problem of polypharmacy, and warn the patient of the danger of too many medications.

2. Have the patient or family bring *all* prescription and OTC medications to the office in a "brown bag." This technique should be repeated periodically to review and update what the patient is taking.

3. Avoid the use of sleep aides, and minimize the use of Sominex and Benadryl.

4. Watch for inadvertent use of alcohol in syrups, tonics, and elixirs.

D. ***Guidelines for safer alcohol use:*** Educate the older patient and the family about strategies they can use to decrease the risk of alcohol problems in an older adult who chooses to drink alcoholic beverages.

1. Recognize the lower tolerance for alcohol in this age group, and watch for signs of impairment even at low doses (e.g., one to two standard drinks a day).

2. Recognize that some older adults should not drink at all, because of medical conditions, medications, or history of abuse.

3. Avoid daily use of alcohol as a means to relax, get to sleep, or deal with stress.

4. Watch for interactions with other drugs containing sedative properties, including OTC medications (e.g., antihistamines).

E. ***Early intervention:*** The patient and family may respond to relatively brief intervention techniques if the intervention is early in the course of problems and if the clinician educates, intervenes, and follows up.

1. Educate the patient and family about the warning signs of impairment.

2. The patient and family may respond to simple education and brief office counseling if the problem is one of misuse rather than abuse or dependence.

3. Follow-up with the patient and family. It is important to look at both the presenting problem and for more persistent hidden problems.

F. **Nursing Home Issues**

1. ***Nursing home patients are particularly susceptible to psychotropic overuse!*** Studies have noted that anywhere from 35% to 90% of nursing home patients regularly receive psychotropic medications.

2. ***Nonpsychiatric physicians provide care:*** In the United States 80% of the mental health visits and 95% of all psychotropic prescriptions for elderly nursing home patients are prescribed by primary care providers (Smith, 1990). Neuropsychiatric illness in the nursing home has therefore become a primary care responsibility.

3. ***Omnibus Budget Reconciliation Act of 1987:*** To address concerns about the recognition, diagnosis, and treatment of these illnesses, policy makers developed regulations for the care of neuropsychiatric disease in nursing facilities. The Omnibus Budget

Reconciliation Act of 1987 (OBRA), which became effective in October 1990, dictated diagnoses for which antipsychotics are indicated and behaviors that occur in the nursing home for which antipsychotics are inappropriate. Failure to comply with these regulations potentially could lead to discontinuation of Medicaid funding to a particular nursing home. These indications for drug use are a major step forward in reducing the problem of prescription drug abuse among a large portion of our older population (Smith, 1990).

a. Antipsychotics can be used for the following conditions:
   (1) DSM-III-R Axis 1 psychotic disorders, except delirium and dementia.
   (2) Tourette syndrome.
   (3) Huntington disease.
   (4) Organic mental syndromes (including dementia) with associated psychotic and/or agitated features, as defined by the following:
       (a) Hallucination, delusion, paranoia.
       (b) Psychomotor agitation interfering with provision of basic care and activities of daily living.
       (c) Hiccups, nausea, vomiting, pruritus.

b. Antipsychotics should *not* be used for the following conditions:
   (1) Simple pacing.
   (2) Wandering.
   (3) Poor self-care.
   (4) Uncooperation.
   (5) Crying out, yelling, screaming.
   (6) Impaired memory.
   (7) Anxiety.
   (8) Depression.
   (9) Insomnia.
   (10) Unsociability.
   (11) Indifference to surroundings.
   (12) Nervousness.

BIBLIOGRAPHY

Bloom PJ: Alcoholism after sixty. *Am Fam Physician* 1983; 28:111–113.

Broadening the base of treatment for alcohol problems. Report of a study by a committee of the Institute of Medicine. Washington DC, National Academy Press, 1990, pp 364–365.

Carty MA, Everitt DE: Basic principles of prescribing for geriatric outpatients. *Geriatrics* 1989; 44:85–98.

Chandler JD, Chandler JE: The prevalence of neuropsychiatric disorders in a nursing home population. *J Geriatr Psychiatry Neurol* 1988; 1:71–76.

Finlayson RE, et al: Alcoholism in elderly persons: A study of psychiatric and psychosocial features of 216 inpatients. *Mayo Clin Proc* 1988; 63:761–768.

Glynn RJ, Bouchard GR, LaCastro JS, et al: Aging and generational effects on drinking behaviors in men: Results from the normative aging study. *Am J Public Health* 1985; 75:1413–1419.

Gould L, Zahir M, DeMartino A, et al: Cardiac effects of a cocktail. *JAMA* 1971; 218:1799–1802.

Haugland S: Alcoholism and other drug dependencies. *Primary Care* 1989; 16:411–429.

The health benefits of smoking cessation: A report of the Surgeon General. Rockville, Md, Department of Health and Human Services, DHHS Publ. No. (CDC)90–8416, 1990.

Hurt RD, et al: Alcoholism in elderly persons: Medical aspects and prognosis of 216 inpatients. *Mayo Clin Proc* 1988; 63:753–760.

Jenike MA: Psychoactive drugs in the elderly: Antipsychotics and anxiolytics. *Geriatrics* 1988; 43:53–65.

Knopman DS, Sawyer-DeMaris S: Practical approach to managing behavioral problems in dementia patients. *Geriatrics* 1990; 45:27–35.

Olsen-Noll C, Bosworth M: Alcohol abuse in the elderly. *Am Fam Physician* 1989; 39:173–179.

Pfeiffer E: A short portable mental status questionnaire of an organic brain deficit in elderly patients. *J Am Geriatr Soc* 1975; 23:433–441.

Rovner BW, et al: Prevalence of mental illness in a community nursing home. *Am J Psychiatry* 1986; 143:1446–1449.

Schuckit MA: A clinical review of alcohol, alcoholism, and the elderly patient. *J Clin Psychiatry* 1982; 43:396–399.

Sheikh JI, Yesavage JA: Geriatric depression scale (GDS): Recent evidence and development of a shorter version. *Clin Gerontol* 1986; 5:165–173.

Smith DA: New rules for prescribing psychotropics in nursing homes. *Geriatrics* 1990; 45:44–56.

Sumnicht G: *Sailing White Horses: Adventures With Older Substance Abusers.* Madison, Wis, Prevention and Intervention Center for Alcohol and Other Drug Abuse (PICADA), 1991.

Willenbring M, Christensen K, Spring W, et al: Alcoholism screening in the elderly. *J Am Geriatr Soc* 1987; 35:864–869.

Willenbring M, Spring W: Evaluating alcohol use in elders. *Generations: Alcohol Drug Use* 1988, summer, 27–31.

CHAPTER 16

Substance Abuse in Patients With Physical and Cognitive Disabilities

William Schwab, M.D.

Thirty-five to 40 million Americans have a physical or cognitive disability. As a result of changes in the health care system since the 1970s, the number of people with major disabilities living in community rather than in institutional settings has increased dramatically. This change has increased the access of patients with disabilities to alcohol and other drugs and increased the prevalence of addictive disorders in this population. Health care providers and the alcohol and drug treatment system will need to develop innovative approaches to accommodate the specialized needs of this population. This chapter reviews the distinct problems encountered by clinicians when treating alcohol and drug disorders in patients with physical or cognitive disabilities.

I. Overview

This section reviews the different types of disabilities and presents the estimated prevalence of problematic alcohol and drug use in this population. Many of the problems encountered by clinicians when managing these patients are introduced using case examples.

A. World Health Association Definitions

Precise classification of disabilities is difficult because patients often have multiple problems. In addition, this is a diverse group whose disabilities range from severe mental retardation to vision or hearing impairments. The following section defines the types of disabilities and gives case examples of issues arising from the treatment of disabled patients with alcohol and drug problems.

1. ***Impairment:*** Impairment is loss or abnormality of a psychologic, physiologic, or anatomic structure or function, independent of cause.

2. ***Disability:*** A disability is a restriction or lack of ability (resulting from impairment) to perform an activity in the manner or within the range considered normal for a person of the same age, culture, and education. This usually refers to "activities of daily living" in the areas of self-care, mobility, recreation, communication, vocation, financial matters, and social interaction.

3. ***Handicap:*** A handicap is a disadvantage resulting from an impairment or disability that limits or prevents the fulfillment of a role that is normal for the individual. Handicaps are characterized by a difference in group and personal expectations and/or opportunities.

B. **Types of Disabilities**

Disabilities can be physical, sensory, or developmental. Challenges to care are increased, both for health care providers and families, by psychoactive substance use.

1. ***Physical disabilities:*** Physical disabilities are conditions resulting from injury, disease, or congenital impairment that significantly limit the ability to perform activities of daily living without the assistance of human or mechanical aid. Injuries include spinal cord trauma and amputations. Diseases include neuromuscular conditions such as multiple sclerosis, musculoskeletal conditions such as arthritis, and cardiopulmonary conditions such as congestive heart failure and emphysema. Congenital impairments include spina bifida and limb deformities.

2. ***Family issues of enabling:*** Enabling and codependence are major barriers health care providers need to address before they can convince the patient and family members that abstinence and formal treatment are in the best interests of everyone. The case example that follows exhibits a common response of family members when someone with a disability has an alcohol problem. This case clearly illustrates the importance of treating the family rather than just the patient.

a. *Case example:*

> Barbara is a 41-year-old woman with multiple sclerosis first diagnosed 7 years ago. She now must use a wheelchair for mobility and requires assistance for many other activities of daily living. She had to quit her job as a high school teacher 4 years ago, and is no longer able to care for her three children. She has a history of heavy drinking while in college, but had reduced her consumption to one to two drinks per night once she became employed. Over the past few years she has been drinking steadily throughout the day and has sustained a number of injuries while intoxicated. Although she did not experience serious depression before the development of her physical disability, her loss of physical functioning has left her depressed. Her family and friends have discussed her alcohol use with her, but in the words of her husband, they are all "reluctant to deny her the one thing she seems to enjoy in life."

3. ***Sensory disabilities:*** Sensory disabilities are conditions in which there is substantial impairment of sensory function such that adaptation is required to perform activities of daily living. Vision impairment includes legal blindness (>20/200 corrected) and low vision (between 20//70 and 20/200 corrected) due to an acquired or con-

genital cause. Hearing impairment includes profound deafness (>85 dB loss) and severe hearing loss (60–85 dB) due to an acquired or congenital cause.

4. ***Barriers to treatment:*** This case example illustrates the difficulty health care providers and patients encounter when trying to obtain treatment of alcohol and drug disorders for patients with disabilities. Patients who have mental retardation, severe physical disabilities, or impaired communication ability may face even greater barriers than in the case presented here.

   a. *Case example:*

   > Vernon is a 59-year-old man who has a long history of alcohol and tobacco abuse. His liver enzyme levels are moderately elevated, and he also has alcohol-related skin changes. He has been blind in his left eye since childhood, because of amblyopia, and 2 years ago had nearly total loss of vision in his right eye due to a spontaneous venous occlusion. He subsequently lost his job as a lumber salesman, and his application for vocational rehabilitation was turned down by the state. His functional accommodation to the disability has been limited. His alcohol intake has substantially increased over the past 18 months, and he has physically abused his wife twice in the past month while he was drunk. She has threatened to leave him unless he stops drinking. None of the treatment programs in the area believe they can accommodate a blind participant.

5. ***Developmental disabilities*** (based on federal code): Developmental disabilities include mental retardation, cerebral palsy, Down syndrome, autism, and similar conditions. Traumatic brain injury, although it may occur after age 22 years, often results in similar functional limitations and support requirements. The following are the characteristics of developmental disabilities as defined by federal code.

   a. Attributable to mental and/or physical impairment.
   b. Manifests itself before age 22 years.
   c. Likely to continue indefinitely.
   d. Results in functional limitations in three or more areas of major life activities.
   e. Requires specialized services throughout the life span.

6. ***Use of alcohol to feel normal:*** Patients with disabilities may have limited opportunities to develop friendships and establish a peer group with whom they can relate and enjoy. Some use alcohol in social situations to deal with their feelings of inadequacy and inferiority. However, they can become dependent on alcohol or marijuana and develop serious adverse effects from their use. The following is a case example of a patient with a developmental disability who became alcohol dependent in part because of his need to belong and feel normal.

a. *Case example:*

> Mark is a 26-year-old man with mild mental retardation. He lives with his parents in a rural community, and works part time doing janitorial work. He often drinks at home alone in his room, but every weekend he either rides his bicycle or hitches a ride to a local tavern. He says, "At the bar people like me. I can get drunk just like everyone else." His parents know that he goes to the bar on weekends, but have not been aware that he keeps alcohol in his room and drinks to intoxication each night. His use escalated to the point where he began to miss work, and his boss threatened to fire him unless he got some help for his drinking.

C. Epidemiology

1. ***Limitations of studies:*** In the population of individuals with disabilities, obtaining precise estimates of problematic alcohol and drug use has been difficult. Studies have applied different definitions of disability, targeted different subpopulations, or quantified substance use in different ways. Studies of drug use and abuse also are complicated by the frequent therapeutic use of prescription psychoactive medications in this population. Reporting may be inaccurate because of fear of stigma, impact on benefit status, limited self-awareness, or reliance on family or support personnel for information.

2. ***Estimating size of problem:*** The following studies have examined the prevalence of alcohol and drug problems in persons with various categories of disability.

   a. *Spinal cord injuries:* Forty percent to 60% of individuals with spinal cord injury have been found to be moderate to heavy drinkers in studies conducted in many states over the past 10 years (Anderson, 1980–1981; Department of Health and Social Services, 1989).

   b. *Patients with sensory handicaps:* Studies of individuals with significant hearing and vision impairment have demonstrated alcohol use patterns at least comparable to and probably slightly greater than those in the general population (Boros, 1980–1981; Glass, 1980–1981).

   c. *Patients with mental retardation:* Alcohol use among people who are mentally retarded varies based on several factors, including age, sex, degree of retardation, and residential arrangement. Young men and women who are mildly retarded and who live semi-independently are experiencing increasing abuse problems. This group often drinks alone at home rather than in bars (Edgerton, 1986; Krishef, 1986; Krishef and DiNitto, 1981).

   d. *Michigan study:* A study of 273 residents of a rehabilitation center in Michigan who had a variety of disabilities suggested that more than 60% had "some problems" related to alcohol use and categorized more than 30% as "clearly alcoholic" (Rassmussen and De-Boer, 1980–1981).

    e. *Berkeley study:* Twenty-five percent of clients in a county independent living program in Berkeley, California, were thought to be "problem drinkers" (Hepner et al., 1980–1981).

    f. *Wisconsin study:* The most comprehensive and recent population survey of alcohol use patterns was published in 1989 (Department of Health and Social Services, 1989). The study was based on self-report questionnaires sent to 8,000 persons whose names were taken from mailing lists of the Division of Vocational Rehabilitation and the Centers for Independent Living in Wisconsin. Although the response rate was 42%, the survey provides a conservative estimate of use. Figure 16–1 presents the results of this survey by type of disability. The prevalence of heavy to moderate use is striking, and is at least twice the prevalence in the general population in Wisconsin.

II. Clinical Issues

A. Medical Complications Associated with Substance Use

1. ***Use of psychoactive medications:*** Treatment with psychoactive prescription drugs for specific clinical indications is more common in this population, resulting in increased risk for dependence and addiction. Examples include benzodiazepines for spasticity in cerebral palsy and spinal cord injury, opioids for pain in arthritis and posttraumatic conditions, barbiturates for seizures in epilepsy, and phenothiazines for behavioral management in mental retardation.

2. ***Adverse drug interaction with other prescription medications:*** Treatment with medications of all types also is more common in this population, so the potential for adverse interactions or unsatis-

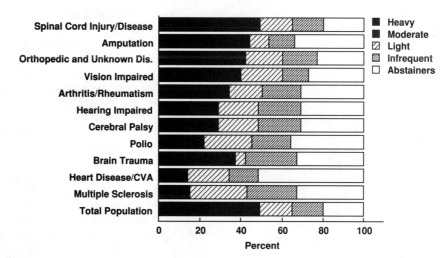

FIG 16–1.
The Wisconsin Department of Health and Social Services conducted a survey of 8,000 Wisconsin residents with disabilities. This figure summarizes alcohol use patterns in this population in 1988.

factory therapeutic responses is increased when alcohol and drug use is present.

3. ***Impairment of senses and balance:*** When intoxicated, people with preexisting conditions that impair their sensory abilities, mobility, coordination, or judgment are at even greater risk for trauma from injuries due to motor vehicle accidents, falls, or burns. There are many reports of rapid development of major decubitis ulcers in patients with spinal cord injuries who remain immobile in suboptimal positions for extended periods while intoxicated.

4. ***Tobacco use:*** Smoking exacerbates the restrictive lung disease that occurs in quadriplegia, cerebral palsy, and other disabilities that affect respiratory capacity.

5. ***Seizure disorders:*** Seizure disorders occur in more than a third of persons with developmental disabilities and more than half of those with traumatic brain injury. Use of alcohol or illicit drugs may result in onset of clinical epilepsy in patients with no previous history of seizures or in worsening of control in patients with known seizure disorders. Mechanisms include:

   a. Poor compliance with medication regimens.
   b. Altering therapeutic blood levels of antiseizure medication.
   c. Lowering the seizure threshold.
   d. Direct effects of alcohol and illicit drugs both during heavy use and withdrawal.

   The following case example illustrates problems in the management of seizure disorders complicated by alcohol abuse in patients with traumatic brain injury.

   e. *Case example:*

   > Tina is a 24-year-old woman who sustained a severe closed head injury in a motor vehicle accident 18 months ago. She was injured when she drove off the road while intoxicated. Prior to the accident she had a long history of polydrug use, including alcohol and marijuana use on a daily basis since she was 16 years old and frequent use of cocaine in recent years. During her nearly 9 months of acute care and rehabilitation hospitalization, her alcohol and drug disorders were never addressed. When she was discharged she went to live with her parents because her difficulties with poor concentration and extreme emotional lability made her unable to manage independently. During her hospitalization anticoagulation therapy had been started because of two episodes of pulmonary embolus. As an outpatient, her prothrombin time has been extremely variable, despite being stable in the hospital. Five months after discharge she had her first seizure, with increased but variable seizures over subsequent months. Anticonvulsant levels also have been erratic. She has generally been accompanied to medical appointments by her mother. On one occasion, however, her sister accompanied her and asked if drinking six to 10 beers a night might be a factor in Tina's current medical problems.

B. Psychological Issues that Increase Likelihood of Substance Use

1. *Effects of stress:* Alcohol and drug use may, in part, result from a variety of stressors that can occur as a consequence of disability.

   a. *Unemployment and underemployment* are common due to limited vocational opportunities.

   b. *Isolation* occurs because of restricted social networks and limited access to adapted leisure time activities.

   c. *Low self-esteem* can be present in persons who have not successfully worked through their feelings about their disability and may use alcohol, drugs, or tobacco to modify unpleasant emotions or to feel more "normal."

   d. *Interpreting media* and commercial images of substance use is difficult for individuals with cognitive impairment.

2. *Use patterns reflect previous use:* Use patterns in people with acquired disabilities generally reflect premorbid behavior. Alcohol and drug use is involved in more than two thirds of motor vehicle accidents and other trauma that result in spinal cord and brain injuries.

3. *Higher prevalence of use in personal care attendants:* There is some evidence that suggests that persons who choose to be employed as personal care attendants have an increased rate of substance abuse and of enabling behavior.

   This case example illustrates how drug use by a personal care attendant can increase illicit drug use by the identified patient.

   a. *Case example:*

   > Ronald is a 27-year-old man who has cerebral palsy with spastic quadriplegia. He has taken diazepam for many years to reduce spasticity. Over time, because of apparent accommodation of his neuromuscular response to the medication, the dosage has been increased gradually. A few years ago Ronald moved into a community-based living arrangement in which he shares an apartment with one other person with disabilities and a paid support person. There has been frequent turnover in staff, and major problems in his vocational programming have resulted in a cut in his work hours. Four months ago a new caregiver, Bryan, moved in with him. Bryan has been reporting that Ronald has developed markedly increased spasticity, especially in the morning when he first wakes up and at night before going to bed. For this reason, additional diazepam has been prescribed. Yesterday Bryan called in to request that the dosage again be increased. The county case manager was asked to assess the situation, and discovered that Bryan has been using Ronald's diazepam and that he has also been supplying Ronald with marijuana.

C. Family Issues

1. *Roles of family members:* Families sometimes encourage use and abuse as a way of dealing with their own feelings about the person

with the disability. While allowing a person with a disability to become drunk or stoned may provide some short-term relief for the family and may make the family members feel they are at least allowing one source of pleasure to the patient, the long-term adverse effects on the individual and the family are clear.

2. ***Patterns of alcohol and drug use in family members:*** Data are conflicting as to whether parents, siblings, and spouses of persons with disabilities are more likely to develop substance abuse problems as a result of the development of a severe disability in another family member.

3. ***Interpreting family attitudes:*** People with cognitive impairment may have difficulty interpreting family attitudes in a number of areas, including alcohol and other drug use.

D. Health Care System Issues

1. ***Barriers to treatment:***

   a. *Inaccessibility problems:* Substance abuse treatment programs are frequently inaccessible to people with disabilities, because of physical, logistical, or attitudinal barriers.

   b. *Medical insurance limitations:* People with disabilities typically are covered by Medicaid or Medicare policies that may limit treatment for substance abuse.

   c. *Attitudes of health care professionals:* Because of societal stereotypes, alcohol and drug use in people with disabilities may not be acknowledged.

2. ***Legal issues:*** People with disabilities have often retained their own guardianship and cannot be forced to submit to drug screening or treatment without their consent unless court ordered. When another person serves as the legal guardian, his or her approval must be obtained, as with any other medical intervention. However, if the patient disagrees with the plan further legal clarification should be obtained.

3. ***Fragmentation of medical care:*** Physicians may focus exclusively on medical problems and not look comprehensively at issues such as substance abuse, especially when care is fragmented among many specialists. In addition, the staff who provide most of the direct care for persons with disabilities often have no specific training in prevention, recognition, and intervention for addictive disorders. This case example examines a complication of the fragmentation of medical care.

   a. *Case example:*

   > Willie is a 24-year-old man who became quadriplegic after being thrown from the motorcycle he was driving when it skidded off the road. His blood alcohol level was three times the legal limit at the time of his injury. After an extensive rehabilitation hospitalization, he returned to his home community, where a friend was trained to become his paid attendant. To facilitate his continuing rehabilitation, he is seen

by a physical medicine specialist, an orthopedic surgeon, a urologist, a physical therapist, an occupational therapist, a rehabilitation engineer, a dietician, a vocational specialist, and a county social worker who serves as care coordinator. Two years after returning to the community he sustained a severe fracture of the right hip when he fell while being transferred from his wheelchair to his bed. At the time both he and his attendant were drunk. During the hospitalization a care conference was held that was attended by all of the professionals who work with him. At the meeting it was clear that each of the participants had been aware of Willie's drinking problem, but they had never discussed it among themselves nor had anyone ever confronted him about it.

III. Assessment, Intervention, and Treatment
A. Taking an Alcohol and Drug History

1. ***Lifetime history of alcohol and psychoactive drug use:*** A complete history of substance use patterns prior to the onset of the disability should be obtained from patients with acquired conditions. Additional history, with the patient's consent, should be sought from family members, community professionals, and support staff (see Chapter 2 for screening and assessment techniques). Particular attention to abuse issues should occur in cases of injury, because of the high frequency of alcohol and drug involvement. People with chronically painful conditions may have been self-medicating with alcohol, over-the-counter drugs, or illicit drugs prior to or concurrent with medical treatment.

2. ***Change in patient's condition:*** Alcohol and other drug problems should be considered whenever there is an unexplained change in clinical or emotional status or an increase in accidental injuries.

3. ***Family history:*** Awareness of a family history of substance abuse is essential, especially for populations at higher risk.

4. ***Use by residential care providers:*** Questioning about substance use habits of residential care providers or other key support personnel also may be relevant.

5. ***Modifying standardized screening questions:*** Health care professionals should be aware that standard screening instruments such as Alcohol Use Disorders Identification Test (AUDIT; see appendix C–2) and CAGE (see Chapter 2) may need to be modified. For example, questions about motor vehicle use may not be relevant. The method of questioning will need to accommodate specialized communication such as braille, sign language, augmentative methods, or simplified language.

B. Intervention

1. ***Negative health consequences:*** Interventions initiated by health care providers should begin with a very clear statement of the negative health consequences of substance abuse for the individual patient.

2. ***Assessment of intercurrent mental health problems,*** such as

depression and personality disorders, should be undertaken, as well as identification of emotional, interpersonal, and environmental stresses.

3. ***Team effort:*** For intervention to be successful, it is imperative that *all* of the people who work with the disabled person be involved in promoting and supporting abstinence. This includes family, close friends, other health care providers, agency professionals, and residential and vocational staff.

 a. Involvement of these people can be done only with patient consent.

 b. Community professionals often are willing to take responsibility for organizing and coordinating this type of intervention.

 c. Failure to reach consensus on the definition of the problem and on the strategy for dealing with it is the single greatest cause of the failure of treatment efforts.

 The following case presentation illustrates a creative team solution to the problem of alcohol treatment for a patient with special needs.

 d. *Case example:*

> Kwamme is a 28-year-old man who is hemiplegic and dysarthric from a cerebrovascular accident that occurred 12 years ago during an episode of sickle cell crisis. He uses a wheelchair for mobility and requires assistance for many activities of daily living. In addition, he requires clean, intermittent catheterization because of recurrent urinary tract infections that result from neurogenic bladder. He lives with his mother, sisters, and nephew, who provide his care. In the past he drank a quart of wine daily and periodically binged on vodka. These episodes often precipitated sickle crises. His hospitalizations for pain control were always complicated by alcohol withdrawal. On one occasion he was thought to have had delirium tremens, although his hallucinations may have been due to the pain medication he was receiving. His discharge instructions always included abstinence from alcohol, but no active treatment efforts were attempted until during one admission the resident assigned to his case directly confronted Kwamme about his alcoholism. He ultimately arranged a meeting that included Kwamme's family, therapists, and social worker. At the meeting, Kwamme agreed to enter an inpatient treatment program, but the family was unable to find a facility that had adequate staff to provide his daily care, perform his catheterization, and interpret his speech. Undaunted, his county caseworker was successful in securing special funding to pay Kwamme's sister to serve as his attendant during his time in the program. He has since continued in an aftercare program at this center and no longer needs special assistance, because the staff is able to understand him and has learned to do his physical care. He has maintained sobriety for 2 years, and has required hospitalization only once because of sickle crisis in that time.

C. Treatment of Alcohol or Drug Disorder

1. ***Medical care issues:*** A number of medical care issues complicate the treatment of an alcohol or drug disorder in patients with disabilities. Inpatient detoxification of patients with some disabilities may be preferable or even essential, because of intercurrent medical problems that may increase the likelihood of complications, such as seizures. Treatment staff are seldom fluent in sign language or other alternative communication methods. They may be uncomfortable relating to people who are mentally retarded or have other disabilities, especially when these patients have substantial personal care needs.

2. ***Barriers to treatment*** include the following.

   a. Treatment programs, aftercare programs, and Alcoholics Anonymous groups usually present the same problems as those described for detoxification facilities in terms of accessibility, communication, staff and client comfort, and the ability to assist with personal care.

   b. Participation in therapeutic groups may be a barrier for people with conditions that have an impact on communication or for those who have a cognitive impairment.

   c. Physical care requirements, stamina, and discomfort may additionally limit the ability to participate fully.

   d. Specialized transportation to outpatient centers on a daily basis may not be available or may be restricted in terms of hours or day of the week.

   e. Coordination with family, friends, and community support personnel during treatment and aftercare may be difficult.

   f. Third-party payment coverage, usually by Medicaid or Medicare, may be inadequate.

   g. The basic stresses associated with having a disability are not easily ameliorated.

3. ***Resources:***

   a. Some excellent specialized treatment programs do exist that can provide either direct service to patients or advice to local programs that are interested in providing care to people with disabilities (see Appendix B, General Resources)

   b. Technical assistance to adapt materials and make other modifications may be available from disability service organizations in many communities.

   c. The passage of the federal Americans with Disabilities Act in 1990 has created a legal mandate for improved access to community-based services.

   d. There is increasing awareness of this problem among both disability service providers and professionals who work with alcohol and drug disorders.

e. The presence of an already structured community system of support that may include a service coordination component can be a powerful force in assisting an individual to maintain sobriety. The following case portrays the use of community resources to achieve a good outcome for a patient with special needs in the treatment of a drug disorder.

f. *Case example:*

> Grace is a 32-year-old woman who has been deaf since birth. She is college educated, and after initially finding only clerical work, got a job as a claims reviewer in a large insurance company 2 years ago. She was extremely fearful of not doing well enough to maintain this job and so began working extensive overtime hours. To deal with her fatigue, she began to use amphetamines that were supplied by an acquaintance. Although she became alarmed about the amount she was using, she was unsuccessful in her efforts to quit on her own. She felt extremely isolated, and was certain that there were no treatment programs available that could serve a deaf client. A local advocacy group for people with hearing impairments developed a well-publicized outreach and peer support program for people with hearing impairments who have alcohol and other drug problems. Grace turned to this resource and was successful in entering a treatment program assisted by a volunteer American Sign Language interpreter.

BIBLIOGRAPHY

Anderson P: Alcoholism and the spinal cord disabled: A model program. *Alcohol Health Res World,* Winter 1980–1981; 5:37–41.

Boros A: Alcoholism intervention for the deaf. *Alcohol Health Res World* Winter 1980–1981; 5:26–29.

Dean JC, Fox AM, Jensen W: Drug and alcohol use by disabled and nondisabled persons: A comparative study. *Int J Addict* 1985; 20:629–641.

Department of Health and Social Services: Incidence of alcohol use by people with disabilities: A Wisconsin survey of persons with a disability. Madison, Wis, Division of Community Services, Aug 1989.

Edgerton RR: Alcohol and drug use by mentally retarded adults. *Am J Ment Defic* 1986; 90:602–608.

Glass EJ: Problem drinking among the blind and visually impaired. *Alcohol Health Res World.* Winter 1980–1981; 5:20–25.

Hepner R, Kirshbaum H, Landes D: Counseling substance abusers with additional disabilities: The center for independent living. *Alcohol Health Res World* Winter 1980–1981; 5:11–15.

Hindman M, Widein P: The multidisabled: Emerging responses. *Alcohol Health Res World* Winter 1980–1981; 5:4–10.

Krishef CH: Do the mentally retarded drink? A study of their alcohol usage. *J Alcohol Drug Educ* 1986; 3:64–69.

Krishef CH, DiNitto DM: Alcohol abuse among mentally retarded individuals. *Ment Retard* 1981; 19:151–155.

Little RE, Gayle JL: Epilepsy and alcoholism. *Alcohol Health Res World* Winter 1980–1981; 5:31–36.

Lowenthal A, Anderson P: Network development: Linking the disabled community to alcoholism and drug abuse programs. *Alcohol Health Res World* Winter 1980–1981; 5:16–19.

Rasmussen GA, DeBoer RP: Alcohol and drug use among clients at a residential vocational rehabilitation facility. *Alcohol Health Res World* Winter 1980–1981; 5:48–56.

Sengstock WL, Vergason GA, Sullivan MM: Considerations and issues in a drug abuse program for the mentally retarded. *Educ Training Ment Retard* 1975; 10:138–141.

Wenc F: The developmentally disabled substance abuser. *Alcohol Health Res World* Winter 1980–1981; 5:42–46.

PART FIVE

Related Medical Problems

CHAPTER 17

Eating Disorders

Kristen Lawton Barry, Ph.D.

Anorexia nervosa and bulimia have become increasingly important clinical problems. These disorders were initially characterized as psychologic, with no somatic features. With improved reporting, both the somatic and psychosomatic aspects of anorexia nervosa and bulimia have been recognized. It is estimated the incidence of anorexia nervosa has doubled in the past 20 years. Bulimia nervosa has been classified as a distinct disorder only since 1980.

Eating disorders have much in common with alcohol and drug disorders. Individuals with eating disorders experience denial, secretiveness, inability to discontinue the behavior, depression, and a range of physical symptoms also common in alcohol and drug addictions. Chemically dependent individuals may have concomitant bulimia or anorexia. Recognition of eating disorders calls for many of the same skills necessary for the recognition of alcohol and drug disorders.

I. Overview of Anorexia Nervosa

  A. The following overview of anorexia nervosa is from the *Diagnostic and Statistical Manual,* third edition—Revised (DSM-III-R), published in 1987 by the American Psychiatric Association.

  1. ***Age at onset:*** Age at onset usually is early to late adolescence.
  2. ***Sex ratio:*** The disorder occurs mainly in females (90% to 95%).
  3. ***Prevalence:*** Studies of samples from different populations have reported a range from 1 in 800 to as many as 1 in 100 females between the ages of 12 and 18 years. Estimates for other age groups and for males are less well documented.
  4. ***Course:*** The course may be unremitting until death, or episodic, or *most commonly, may consist of a single episode,* followed by return to normal weight.
  5. ***Impairment:*** The severe weight loss often necessitates hospitalization to prevent death by starvation.
  6. ***Complications:*** Follow-up studies indicate a mortality rate between 5% and 18%.
  7. ***Familial pattern:*** The disorder is more common among sisters and mothers of those with the disorder than among the general pop-

ulation. Higher than expected rates of major depression and bipolar disorder among first-degree relatives have been found.

8. ***Predisposing factors:*** In some, onset is associated with a stressful life situation. Many patients are described as overly perfectionistic ("model children"). About one third were slightly overweight prior to onset of the illness.

9. ***Differential diagnosis:*** Weight loss also can occur in depressive disorders and certain physical disorders, but *there is no disturbance of body image or intense fear of obesity* in these other disorders.

B. Recognizing and Diagnosing Anorexia Nervosa

1. ***Pronounced weight loss:*** The anorectic person usually comes to medical attention when weight loss (or failure to gain expected weight) is pronounced. By the time a person is profoundly underweight (less than 85% of expected weight), there are other signs. Common symptoms, physical signs, and laboratory abnormalities include the following:

   a. *Symptoms:*
      (1) Amenorrhea.
      (2) Compulsive behavior.
      (3) Cold sensitivity.
      (4) Emesis.

   b. *Physical signs:*
      (1) Bradycardia.
      (2) Ketotic breath.
      (3) Hypotension.
      (4) Lanugo hair.

   c. *Laboratory abnormalities:*
      (1) Decreased monoamine oxidase level.
      (2) Decreased urinary MHPG (3-methoxy-4-hydroxyphenyl-glycol).
      (3) Hypercarotenemia.

2. ***Making the diagnosis:***

   a. Diagnostic criteria for anorexia appear in the revised edition of DSM-III-R, and include:
      (1) *Refusal to maintain body weight* over a minimal normal weight for age and height; e.g., weight loss leading to maintenance of body weight 15% below the expected, or failure to make expected weight gain during a period of growth, leading to body weight 15% below the expected.
      (2) *Intense fear of gaining weight* or becoming fat, even though underweight.
      (3) *Disturbance in the way one's body weight, size, or shape is experienced;* e.g., the person claims to "feel fat" even when emaciated, believes that one area of the body is "too fat" even when obviously underweight.
      (4) In females, *absence of at least three consecutive menstrual cycles* when otherwise expected to occur (primary or secondary amenorrhea). (A woman is considered to have amenor-

rhea if her periods occur only after hormone [e.g., estrogen] administration).

   b. Additional features of anorexia nervosa are not explained by diagnostic criteria.

   c. Anorectic individuals may prepare elaborate meals for others, but tend to limit themselves to a narrow selection of low-calorie foods. They also hoard, conceal, crumble, or throw away food.

   d. As with alcohol and drug addictions, *denial* is a strong component of the illness. People with anorexia deny or minimize the severity of their illness and are *resistant* to therapy.

   e. Many anorectic adolescents have delayed psychosexual development.

   f. Many anorectic adults have a decreased interest in sex.

   g. Compulsive behavior, such as hand washing, may be present and may represent an additional illness, obsessive compulsive disorder.

3. ***Differential diagnosis:*** In evaluating a person for anorexia nervosa, it is important to consider other possible causes of the symptoms, for example:

   a. Depression.
   b. Hyperthyroidism.
   c. Crohn disease.
   d. Addison disease.
   e. Polyarthritis nodosa.

II. Bulimia

  A. The following overview of bulimia is from DSM-III-R:

1. ***Age of onset:*** The disorder usually begins in adolescence or early adulthood.

2. ***Prevalence and sex ratio:*** There is little data on this, but a recent study of college freshmen found that 4.5% of the females and 0.4% of the males had a history of bulimia.

3. ***Course:*** The usual course, in clinic samples, is *chronic and intermittent* over many years. Usually binges alternate with periods of normal eating.

4. ***Familial pattern:*** Often the parents of the bulemic are obese. A higher than expected frequency of major depression has been reported in first-degree biologic relatives.

5. ***Impairment and complications:*** Bulimia is seldom incapacitating, except in a few people who spend the whole day binge eating and vomiting. Dental erosion is a common complication of vomiting. Electrolyte imbalance and dehydration may cause serious physical complications (e.g., cardiac arrhythmias). Rare complications include esophageal tears and gastric ruptures.

6. ***Predisposing factors:*** There is some evidence that obesity in adolescents may be one of the predisposing factors in the development of the illness in adulthood.

7. ***Differential diagnosis:*** The weight fluctuations are rarely so ex-

treme as to be life-threatening. A person can have both bulimia and anorexia. Schizophrenics may have an unusual eating behavior, but generally not bulimia. Some neurologic diseases (e.g., epileptic equivalent seizures, central nervous system tumors, Klüver-Bucy–like syndrome, Kleine-Levin syndrome) have associated abnormal eating patterns, but bulimia is not often part of the diagnosis. Binge eating sometimes accompanies borderline personality disorder in females.

B. **Recognizing and Diagnosing Bulimia**

1. ***Markers of bulimia:*** Specific symptoms, physical signs, and laboratory abnormalities serve as markers of bulimia.

   a. *Symptoms:*
      (1) Binge eating.
      (2) Emesis.
      (3) Diuretic abuse.
      (4) Laxative abuse.

   b. *Physical signs:*
      (1) Abdominal distention.
      (2) Abdominal striae.
      (3) Anal tears and fissure.
      (4) Teeth etched or rotting on inner aspects.
      (5) Scarring of dorsum of a hand.
      (6) Weight fluctuation by ≥10 lb in 1 month.

   c. *Laboratory abnormalities:*
      (1) Elevated serum cholecystokinin level.

2. ***Making the diagnosis:*** To qualify for a DSM-III-R diagnosis, the person must have had, on average, a minimum of *two eating binge episodes per week for at least 3 months.*

   a. Diagnostic criteria include:
      (1) Recurrent episodes of binge eating (rapid consumption of a large amount of food in a discrete period of time).
      (2) Feeling of lack of control over eating behavior during the eating binge.
      (3) The person regularly engages in either self-induced vomiting, use of laxatives or diuretics, strict dieting or fasting, or vigorous exercise to prevent weight gain.
      (4) A minimum average of two binge eating episodes a week for at least 3 months.
      (5) Persistent overconcern with body shape and weight.

3. ***Differential diagnosis:*** In evaluating a person for bulimia nervosa, it is important to consider other possible causes of the symptoms, for example:
   a. Migraine.
   b. Opiate withdrawal.
   c. Postconcussive syndrome.
   d. Posterior fossa tumor.
   e. Mesenteric artery syndrome.
   f. Mechanical obstruction of pylorus.

TABLE 17–1.

Comparison of Anorexia Nervosa and Bulimia*

Anorexia Nervosa	Bulimia
Similarities	
Goal of weight loss	
Goal of weight loss	
Fear of fatness	Fear of losing control of eating
Increased family history of affective disorders	Distortion of body image
Differences	
Food intake severely restricted	Recurrent binge eating
Less vomiting, diuretic, or laxative abuse	Vomiting (self-induced), abuse of laxatives, diuretics
Younger (often early to middle adolescence)	Older (often later adolescence to early adulthood)
Denies hunger	Has hunger
Severe weight loss	Less severe but variable weight loss
More introverted	Often more extroverted
Takes pride in eating behavior	Views eating behavior as shameful
Amenorrhea and/or loss of sexual drive	Variable amenorrhea and change in sexual drive
Often "model" child, "perfectionist"	May have behavioral problems

*From Anderson AE: Anorexia nervosa and bulimia: Biological, psychological, and sociocultural aspects, in Galler JR (ed): *Nutrition and Behavior.* New York, Plenum Publishing, 1984. Used by permission.

III. Similarities and Differences Between Anorexia Nervosa and Bulimia

   A. Anorexia and bulimia share the following similarities and differences:

   1. *Similarities:* Anorexia and bulimia are probably best seen as disorders that share a spectrum of similar features. Both syndromes are characterized by a fear of fatness, varying degrees of body image distortion, and pursuit of weight loss. There are, however, contrasting features. Among other characteristics, anorectic patients are generally younger, deny hunger, experience severe weight loss, and are more perfectionistic than bulemic patients (Table 17–1).

   2. *Concurrence:* The concurrence of anorexia and bulimia is well-documented. In a large 1980 study, 47% of anorectic patients also were bulemic (had periods of binge eating). Of these patients who had both disorders, 57% followed binge eating with self-induced vomiting to control weight. Although there is an overlap in the disorders of anorexia nervosa and bulimia, they are distinct syndromes. There is no proof of a unitary psychologic or physiologic cause.

   3. *Cause of anorexia:* Anorexia nervosa is associated with abnormalities in hypothalamic function. While it is difficult to document hypothalamic function before the onset of anorexia nervosa, many animal and clinical studies support the hypothesis that hypothalamic dysfunction is central to the cause of this illness.

   4. *Cause of bulimia:* In contrast to anorexia, bulimia appears to be related to bipolar depression, alcoholism, and familial mental health problems. Studies suggest that 22% of relatives of bulemic patients have affective disorders, compared with 10% of relatives of a control group.

B. Recognizing and Diagnosing Nonspecific Eating Disorders

1. *Residual eating disorders:* DSM-III-R criteria includes a residual category for eating disorders that do not meet the criteria for a specific disorder. Examples include:

    a. An individual of average weight who does not have binge eating episodes but often engages in self-induced vomiting for fear of gaining weight.

    b. Someone with all the features of anorexia nervosa in the female *except* for the absence of menses.

    c. Someone with all the features of bulimia nervosa except for the frequency of binge eating episodes.

IV. Medical Complications of Eating Disorders

A. Cardiovascular: Cardiovascular complications comprise the majority of clinical disorders seen in anorexia and bulimia. Sixty percent of anorectic patients and 80% of bulemic patients have postural hypotension. Ninety percent of both groups have bradycardia. Atrial flutter or fibrillation may be present on electrocardiogram.

B. Electrolyte imbalances: Electrolyte imbalances are found in 40% of anorectics and 60% of bulimics. Potassium deficiencies are found in about 25% of bulemic patients and in most patients with end-stage anorexia. In about 20% to 30% of bulemic patients chloride deficiencies develop, associated with hypochloremic alkalosis. Metabolic acidosis occurs as the result of starvation ketosis. Calcium and sodium deficiencies are rare.

C. Endocrine system abnormalities: Abnormalities in the endocrine system occur in both female and male patients with eating disorders, but most consistently are observed in females. Decreased fertility and amenorrhea are associated with lowered levels of luteinizing hormone (LH) and follicle-stimulating hormone (FSH). Thirty percent of all anorectic girls do not menstruate, and puberty often is delayed. Testosterone levels can fluctuate in anorectic males. Potency and sperm production also are reversibly diminished. Libido, penile erection, and testicular size all may diminish, and return to normal only on return to normal weight.

D. Gastrointestinal problems: Because of decreased gastrointestinal activity, constipation and obstipation occur. Bulemic patients can experience tearing, scarring, and fissures of the anus.

E. Bone structure: The effects of anorexia on the bone structure can be pronounced. Chronic anorexia with associated amenorrhea has been shown to be related to osteopenia, with risk factors being related to amenorrhea for 3 years or longer, onset of amenorrhea before the age of 13 years, and delayed pubertal development. Osteopenia is thought to be secondary to the low estrogen levels associated with significantly diminished weight, as well as vertebral fractures and chronic back pain in later years.

F. Related problems: Other problems include intolerance to cold temperature, susceptibility to viral and bacterial infections, herpes simplex blisters, and chronic headache.

V. Medical Assessment and Treatment

  A. Initial Screening for Eating Disorders

    1. *Using diagnostic criteria:* Since primary care physicians are often the first to see a patient with an eating disorder, available information regarding the diagnostic criteria for anorexia and bulimia is critical. Screening and diagnosis can be difficult because patients do not often come to the office explicitly seeking treatment for an eating disorder. The initial contact with these patients may be disguised as an appointment to discuss amenorrhea, digestive problems, fatigue, or even weight loss.

    2. *Denial:* The single most difficult problem in the recognition, diagnosis, and management of eating disorders is that patients often deny the illness and may be unwilling to seek treatment. Anorectic patients, in particular, may be brought to the physician against their will, often by a family member. These patients may believe that their ability to exist on small amounts of food makes them special or that maintenance of low weight indicates control over their lives.

    3. *Education:* Educating the patient about the disorder is essential. The family physician is in a strong position with both the patient and the family to emphasize the medical seriousness of the disorder. The extent to which the eating disorder disrupts daily life can be pointed out. Short-term effects (e.g., concentration, cold intolerance) and long-term effects (e.g., osteopenia with increased risk for bone fracture) should be discussed. Patients are sometimes willing to acknowledge problems with concentration on school or work, depression, isolation from friends, sleep disorders, and physical problems (e.g., hair loss, cold intolerance), even when they still believe they need to maintain a low weight.

    4. *Initial questions:* Figure 17–1 lists some initial questions that may be useful in screening for an eating disorder in a primary care setting. The questions have been compiled from questionnaires and clinical experiences. A positive response to any of the sets of questions listed below indicates the need for further assessment.

      a. Question 1 assesses weight fluctuations/loss in the last 5 years. Large fluctuations or significant weight loss can lead to additional questions to determine the reason for these changes.

      b. Questions 2 and 3 help to assess the patient's concerns with weight and body image. Patients who warrant further questions often check weight frequently (multiple times per day) and have a distorted body image.

      c. Question 4, assessing loss of regular menses, is a DSM-III-R criterion for anorexia.

      d. Question 5 asks if others who may know the patient well have ever been concerned about his or her weight. Weight loss or fluc-

SCREENING QUESTIONS ABOUT WEIGHT AND EATING

		YES	NO
1.	Has your weight changed in the last year? _____	❑	❑
	If yes, how much? Gained? Lost? _____	❑	❑
	_____		
2.	How often do you weigh yourself?_____	❑	❑
3.	Have you been satisfied with your weight and body?_____	❑	❑
	If no, what has dissatisfied you? _____	❑	❑
	_____		
4.	(Female patient) Do you have regular periods?	❑	❑
	If no, explain: _____		
	_____		
5.	Have your family, friends, or doctor ever been concerned about your weight?	❑	❑
	If yes, explain: _____		
	_____		
6.	Do you ever make yourself vomit to keep your weight down?		
	If yes, when was the last time? _____	❑	❑
	_____		

7. Family history: ❑ Eating disorder ❑ Drug abuse ❑ Alcohol abuse
   ❑ Obesity ❑ Depression

FIG 17–1.
Some initial questions that may be useful in screening for an eating disorder in a primary care setting.

tuations that have caused concern in persons who know the patient well are excellent markers.

e. Question 6 addresses purging, one of the DSM-III-R criteria for bulimia.

f. Question 7 explores family history, because there is some evidence that patients with eating disorders may have a family history of eating disorders, obesity, alcohol or drug abuse, or affective disorders, particularly depression.

g. Meeting DSM-III-R criteria, while important, is not the only criteria to determine a problem. Specific eating and purging habits are as important as diagnostic labels.

B. Screening and Diagnostic Pitfalls

1. ***Challenges to diagnosis:*** Establishing the diagnosis of an eating disorder may be difficult, especially in the earlier stage. It requires involving the patient, who is indifferent to treatment, and the family in crisis, who may feel ambivalent about the therapeutic process. Diagnostic pitfalls include failing to recognize anorexia or bulimia in a patient with another complaint. For example:

   a. *Delay of puberty and primary or secondary amenorrhea* associated with thinness are indications to ask questions about daily caloric intake, recent changes in weight, and perception of body image. All women receiving fertility workups should be screened for eating disorders.

   b. *Chronic diarrhea* may be self-induced and related to laxative use.

   c. *Enamel erosion or caries* on the inner aspects of upper incisors generally does not appear in the early stages of bulimia, and should lead to questions about vomiting.

   d. *An adolescent to young adult diabetic patient* whose disease is extremely difficult to control may be omitting insulin as part of an attempt to avoid weight gain.

C. When and Where to Refer for Assessment

1. ***Using resources:*** Referral generally occurs when other causes of symptoms have been ruled out or information gathered by the physician from the patient and the family indicates further assessment is necessary. The clinician *does not need to be alone in this process.* In recent years there has been a trend toward multidisciplinary evaluation and treatment of eating disorders involving several specialties and professional groups. Most larger communities have access to one or more eating disorders programs. Practitioners in smaller communities may need to determine if larger community medical facilities in their area have specific programs to work with patients with eating disorders.

2. ***Multidisciplinary treatment teams:*** The staff of most multidisciplinary treatment programs varies, but often includes an attending physician, clinical psychologists, consulting psychiatrists, skilled nursing staff, social workers, clinical dieticians, and occupational therapists. Goals of these programs include:

   a. Establish acceptable healthy body weight and medical and nutritional status.

   b. Decrease, and eventually eliminate, all unhealthy eating and dieting patterns.

   c. Achieve at least enough psychologic change in the patient and family to allow symptom remission without someone else in the family developing problems.

   d. Help the family to function better to withstand internal and outside stresses.

3. ***Evaluation process:*** Initial evaluations by treatment teams vary, but generally include the following:
   a. Nurse evaluation.
   b. Nutritional assessment.
   c. Physical evaluation, performed either by the treatment team physician or by the referring physician.
   d. Individual and family psychologic evaluations.
   e. A treatment team conference to discuss initial impressions and recommendations.
   f. A treatment team meeting with the patient and family to discuss the diagnosis and their treatment recommendations and options.
4. ***Role of referring practitioner:*** Initial evaluations by the multidisciplinary treatment team will include the referring practitioner and will recommend either inpatient hospitalization or outpatient treatment, depending on the severity of the illness.

D. Treatment Options
1. ***Inpatient Hospitalization***
   a. *Conditions for inpatient hospitalization:* Although outpatient treatment is the most common form of management for patients with eating disorders, inpatient treatment is necessary in certain conditions:
      (1) Breaking the starvation cycle and restoring nutritional status. For anorectic patients who have lost 25% of body weight, this may mean a stay of several months for nutritional stabilization and rehabilitation.
      (2) Interrupting a bulemic patient's binge-purge cycle and remedying associated medical complications. Bulimic patients usually require briefer admissions to correct fluid and electrolyte imbalances that occur after out-of-control binging and purging.
      (3) *Brief inpatient admissions* also are used for other reasons, including diagnostic observation if the diagnosis is unclear or multiple diagnoses are a possibility, treating complications, transient crises during treatment (as with alcohol and drug addictions, *relapse* is not uncommon), confronting the patient's denial, and initiating individual and family psychotherapy.
   b. *Admission:* Entry into an inpatient eating disorders program can occur immediately after initial evaluation, after a trial of outpatient treatment, or repeatedly during a difficult course of therapy.
   c. *Program structure:* Inpatient programs are *highly structured* and include some of the following aspects.
      (1) Medical supervision of complications and progress.
      (2) Accurate weights are obtained, and the patient is assessed each day for manipulation of weight through ingestion of

large quantities of water, refusal to void, and use of hidden weighted objects directly before weight is taken.

(3) Meal supervision is needed to assure that the patient is eating the prescribed calorie level and to intervene in unusual and abnormal handling of food and rituals.

(4) Replacement of uneaten calories with nutrient supplements also is necessary.

(5) After-meal supervision to reduce the opportunity to vomit and to provide time for discussion of feelings with the patient.

(6) Bathroom supervision is used to verify that the patient does not follow through on the urge to vomit and that use of laxatives is known to the staff.

(7) Individual, group, and family therapy are used to support the patient in recovery, as emotions and reactions to problems begin to surface.

2. **Outpatient treatment**

a. *Conditions for outpatient treatment:* Eating disorder patients who are functioning at a high enough level (e.g., not in a starvation cycle, no out-of-control binging and purging, medical complications under control) can be assigned to an outpatient program. They are generally assigned to a nurse, who will meet with them as often as necessary for symptom management, initially on a weekly basis.

b. *Psychotherapy:* A psychotherapist is enlisted for individual and family therapy. This is often the responsibility of the team psychologist who provided the initial psychologic assessment. Follow-up with a clinical dietician is necessary, because although most eating disorder patients have an excellent knowledge of caloric values, they need assistance with good nutritional methods.

c. *Role of physician:* Physician assessment and follow-up can be provided by the referring physician. The physician's major responsibilities are to assess the medical condition of the patient on an ongoing basis and to discuss treatment plans and progress with the other team members. The physician also can provide initial education to the patient and family to assist in entry into the treatment system. Close contact between the physician and other members of the treatment team is essential.

BIBLIOGRAPHY

Anderson AE: Anorexia nervosa and bulimia: Biological, psychological, and sociocultural aspects, in Galler JR (ed): *Nutrition and Behavior.* New York, Plenum Publishing, 1984.

Comerci G: Eating disorders in adolescents. *Pediatr Rev* 1988; 10:1–11.

Fonseca V, Howard C: Electrolyte disturbances and cardiac failure with hypomagnesaemia in anorexia nervosa. *Br Med J Clin Res* 1985; 291:1680–1682.

Giannini A, Newman M, Gold M: Anorexia and bulimia. *Am Fam Pract* 1990; 41:1169–1176.

Giannini A, Telew N: Anorexia nervosa in geriatric patients. *Geriatr Psychiatry* 1987; 6:75–78.

Hart K, Ollendick T: Prevalence of bulimia in working and university women. *Am J Psychiatry* 1985; 142:851–854.

Hudson J, Laffer P, Pope J: Bulimia related to affective disorder by family history and response to dexamethasone suppression test. *Am J Psychiatry* 1982; 139:685–687.

Kalager T, Brubakk O, Bassoe H: Cardiac performance in patients with anorexia nervosa. *Cardiology* 1978; 63:1–4.

Levine MP: *Student Eating Disorders.* Washington, DC, National Education Association, 1987.

Moore D: Body image and eating behavior in adolescent girls. *Am J Dis Child* 1988; 142:1114–1118.

Ohlrich ES, Stephenson JN: Pitfalls in the medical and nursing care of patients with anorexia nervosa and bulimia. *Semin Adolesc Med* 1986; 2:81–88.

Ratton G: Mortality in eating disorders. *Psychol Med* 1988; 78:947.

Stephenson J, Ohlrich E: The major complications associated with eating disorders and their pathophysiology, in Clark K, Parr R, Castelli W (eds): *Evaluation and Management of Eating Disorders: Anorexia, Bulimia, and Obesity.* Champaign, Ill, Life Enhancement Publications, 1988, pp 229–260.

Stephenson J, Ohlrich E, McClintock J, et al: *The Multidiciplinary Team Approach to the Treatment of Eating Disorders in Youth.* Champaign, Ill, Life Enhancement Publications, 1988.

Szmukler G: The epidemiology of anorexia nervosa and bulimia. *J Psychiatr Res* 1985; 19:143–153.

CHAPTER 18

Mental Health Disorders and Their Impact on Treatment of Addictions

Delores Burant, M.D.

Michael R. Liepman, M.D.

Michael M. Miller, M.D.

Patients with alcohol and drug problems often have symptoms of depression or anxiety. While most of these mental health problems resolve with treatment of the primary addictive disorder, some do not. These problems may persist during periods of abstinence, and often respond to psychotropic medication. Patients who have persistent symptoms of mental illness after 3 to 6 months of abstinence are believed to have both a primary addictive disorder and a primary mental health disorder, or "dual diagnosis."

Recognizing the presence of a dual diagnosis is important. If the primary mental health disorder is untreated, traditional chemical dependency treatment methods may be neither appropriate nor successful in restoring the patient with dual diagnosis to full functioning. Sorting out which symptoms are due to the addictive disease process and which to a mental health dysfunction is crucial to the diagnosis.

The goal of this chapter is to provide clinicians with a framework to assess and manage patients with both an addictive disorder and symptoms of a psychiatric disorder. The major psychiatric disorders associated with addictive disorders include affective illnesses, anxiety and panic attacks, acute psychotic disorders, and antisocial and borderline personality disorders. This chapter addresses two clinical situations, those in which patients come to health care professionals with urgent or acute symptoms and those that occur when a health care professional gradually becomes aware that a patient with an addictive disorder also has a psychiatric illness.

I. Assessment and Management in Urgent Situations

In urgent situations the focus is on managing the symptoms rather than on establishing a diagnosis. The physician is presented with an acutely distressed patient in need of immediate care to ensure the safety of self or others. The final diagnoses may not be determined for several weeks. The differential diagnosis often is complex, and clinicians may want to consider the following clinical situations once the patient's condition is stabilized.

- Symptoms of mental illness due to acute drug or alcohol effects.
- Temporary or permanent damage to the brain due to drug or alcohol use.
- Effects of drug withdrawal with symptoms that mimic mental illness.
- Symptoms of mental illness as a reaction to severe environmental stress.
- Concurrent mental illness, the true "dual diagnosis."
- Organic problem not related to alcohol, drugs, or a mental health disorder.

A. General Management Guidelines

General management guidelines that apply to all patients in the urgent situation include:

1. ***Conduct a thorough clinical examination*** to determine the presence of non-drug- and non-psychiatric-related disease.
2. ***Laboratory tests*** should include urine, breath, and/or blood samples for toxicology screening for psychoactive substances.
3. ***Obtain a consultation*** from a physician with expertise in both addictive disorders and psychiatric illness. If such a consultant is not available in the community, a consultation with both a psychiatrist and an addiction medicine specialist is advised.

B. The Suicidal Person

The primary disorder of addiction may lead to despondency, frustration, and hopelessness, all of which become more painful in the face of confrontation. When denial is overcome and the patient becomes aware of how much his or her life has deteriorated, hopelessness can lead to suicidal behavior. Fifteen percent of alcohol-dependent patients commit suicide, and most deaths occur in the absence of a primary depression. *Do not underestimate the potential for a successful suicide attempt.* Although an intoxicated person may have threatened suicide repeatedly without attempting it, this does not decrease the likelihood of a successful attempt on *this* occasion. The intoxicated suicidal person is like a time bomb. The combination of impairment of judgment and the disinhibiting effects of alcohol, and other drugs, with psychotoxicity that can cause depressive symptoms, leads to a high risk for suicide.

Case example:

> The wife of a 30-year-old man calls you at 10:00 PM to say that her husband is threatening to shoot himself. They have just had an argument. He has said that life is not worth living anyway, so he may as well die. He does have guns in the house, and is searching for bullets. His wife is your patient, and you recall that she has recently been concerned about his depression. On further inquiry you discover that he has threatened, but never attempted, suicide in the past. She says he has been drinking and has already refused to talk with anyone.

1. ***Differential diagnosis:***
    a. *Sedatives:* Intoxication with sedatives such as alcohol, benzodiazepines, and barbiturates often leads to emotional lability, disinhibition, and impairment of judgment. Overdose with a combination of these drugs is a common method used to commit suicide. Suicide by overdose, however, may also occur by accident.
    b. *Opioids:* Patients using opioids do not usually present with suicidal ideation in the intoxicated state. During withdrawal, the person may become suicidal in an effort to escape the intense dysphoria. An accidental overdose, which may appear to be a suicide attempt, can occur with intravenous use, particularly when drugs are purchased from a new supplier. A further dangerous situation occurs when a person resumes use after a period of prolonged abstinence when tolerance is diminished.
    c. *Stimulants:* Suicidal ideation and attempts are common during amphetamine and cocaine withdrawal, particularly when large amounts of the drug were ingested by intravenous or inhalant routes. After cessation of use, there is an intense "crash" characterized by severe depression and dysphoria. Sedatives taken during drug withdrawal to promote sleep may also contribute to suicidal risk.
    d. *Intoxication-withdrawal states:* An individual can experience an acute state of intoxication or a withdrawal syndrome with suicidal thoughts and behaviors. Suicide is a phenomenon of a variety of psychiatric disorders, including substance abuse disorders.
    e. *Depression:* Individuals with the dual diagnosis of depressive illness and addiction are at risk for suicide from either condition. Paradoxically, this is particularly true during the early recovery stages from depression, when the patient's energy and motivation increase. During severe psychomotor retarded depression the patient can feel so hopeless as to be incapable of attempting suicide. As competence returns, the patient may attempt to harm himself or herself in response to the remaining dysphoria. Use of alcohol or other drugs leads to additional risk, as a result of the availability of means and interference with impulse control and judgment. It is not unusual for an abstinent person with an alcohol or drug disorder in addition to a depressive illness or bipolar disorder to attempt suicide during a relapse. This is especially true if despondency and hopelessness remain following completion of the recovery program. (See appendix E for the diagnostic criteria for major depressive illness.)
    f. *Psychosis:* Individuals with acute psychosis or chronic schizophrenia who develop an exacerbation of psychotic symptoms have one of the highest rates of suicide. Hopelessness may be engendered by the chronicity of the illness. In addition, they may have *command auditory hallucinations* directing them to kill themselves or others.

In the previously well-controlled person with psychosis, return to the use of drugs and/or alcohol may cause a resurgence of hallucinations, dilusions, and paranoia..

2. *Management:*

a. *Determine imminent risk of suicide:* A "yes" answer to any of the following questions indicates a serious risk.

   (1) Is there a positive family history of suicide completion?

   (2) Has there been a recent significant interpersonal loss?

   (3) Does the person intend to kill himself or herself now?

   (4) Is the planned method likely to be lethal, or does the patient refuse to divulge the plan?

   (5) Are there means available to carry out the plan?

   (6) Is the patient under the influence of drugs or alcohol or of command hallucinations which can lead to greater unpredictability?

   (7) Has there been a previous suicide attempt? The more lethal that previous attempt, the more dangerous is the current situation.

   (8) Does the person refuse to accept immediate help from the mental health system as an alternative to suicide?

b. *Imminent danger:* In situations where the suicidal person is not in a protective environment, immediate solicitation of help from law enforcement agencies may be vital. Those who are not trained law enforcement officers should remove themselves from the vicinity of the patient, because of the risk of violence directed toward them. They should not attempt to interfere with the patient. This may be difficult for family and friends if they have become accustomed to rescuing the patient from the consequences of his or her drinking or drug use.

c. *Involuntary commitment to a safe facility:* The primary care provider may need to help the family and friends procure an involuntary commitment designed to remove the person to safety. Providers should have copies of the necessary forms handy in the office and be familiar with how to complete them.

d. *Hospitalization:* Arrange for hospitalization on a locked unit with nursing staff trained to minimize suicidal risk. When a locked psychiatric unit is not available, placement in a locked room with 24-hour one-on-one observation and the use of chemical or physical restraints may be necessary.

e. *Referral:* Obtaining a psychiatric consultation may be helpful for three reasons:

   (1) It will reinforce the seriousness of the problem to the patient. When the effects of the alcohol or drug have abated, it is not unusual for a patient to deny suicidal ideation or to be horrified to have placed oneself in serious danger. The suicidal statements or behavior may have occurred during a blackout,

and the patient may have no memory of the event.

(2) A second opinion may uncover problems not detected by the patient's primary provider.

(3) The current medicolegal climate suggests conservative care in patients at risk for suicide.

C. The Violent Patient

Case example:

> You receive a call from the local emergency room physician. One of your patients, a 35-year-old man, has just been brought in by the local police. He had been at a local bar when he became violent and threatening. The police brought him to the emergency room because he was acting "crazy." The ER physician says they have him in five-point restraint and he is still trying to bite anyone who approaches him. He is yelling obscenities and cannot be quieted. He smells of alcohol. They notified you because he had a prescription in his wallet for penicillin written by you that was dated yesterday. You remember him as a person who had come in with an infection in his great toe that appeared to be due to a neglected sliver.

1. *Differential Diagnosis:*

a. *Alcohol:* Heavy alcohol ingestion in susceptible individuals is associated with a pathologic intoxication syndrome characterized by violent, uncontrolled behavior, often called a "mad drunk." The person strikes out indiscriminately with more power than usual. Although the patient's blood alcohol level is frequently >200 mg/dL, he or she is not sedated or ataxic. There is usually complete amnesia of the episode. This is more common in alcohol-dependent persons and occurs more frequently as the disorder progresses. A rare variant of this condition occurs at low blood alcohol levels each time the affected individual uses alcohol.

b. *Sedatives:* Sedative intoxication (e.g., methaqualone, barbiturates, benzodiazepines) can be disinhibiting. This situation occasionally occurs in the operating or recovery room when a person has been given a sedative for anesthesia. Withdrawal from alcohol and other sedatives can lead to violent behavior.

c. *Stimulants:* Cocaine and amphetamine use is associated with an acute psychosis characterized by abrupt onset of agitation and violent behavior, accompanied by hallucinations and paranoid delusions. Violent behavior is usually associated with protracted use by the intravenous or inhalant route during a "binge." Behavioral overreaction in response to hallucinated threats may precipitate a violent reaction. For example, a patient may have an intense startle response to an objectively neutral event in the environment. Patients under amphetamine intoxication sometimes develop fugue-like states in which they are disoriented. They can engage in violent behavior of which they have no recollection after the fugue-like state clears.

d. *Phencyclidine (PCP):* This drug may cause behavioral symptoms similar to those with stimulants. The clinical features include insensitivity to pain, markedly elevated blood pressure, and rapid oscillation from sedation to agitation. Phencyclidine intoxication produces vertical and circular nystagmus. The patient may report that the limbs feel distorted, exceptionally elongated, or detached from the body as though floating around the room.

e. *Schizophrenia:* Contrary to popular depiction in the media, schizophrenia alone is not a common cause of violent behavior. However, patients with paranoid schizophrenia who are actively psychotic and are using alcohol or other drugs have an increased likelihood of violent, uncontrolled behavior, especially when they have command auditory hallucinations. (See appendix E for the criteria for schizophrenia.)

f. *Other medical conditions:* Though unusual, the patient may be agitated secondary to an acute delirium associated with an infectious disease. The alcohol- or drug-dependent person is more likely to present with sepsis or encephalitis. The possibility of acquired immune deficiency syndrome with a central nervous system infection is increasingly common and should be assessed. Head trauma, subdural hematoma, CNS tumor, medication, or metabolic abnormalities (e.g., adrenal or thyroid problems) also can be associated with agitated behavior, especially in the presence of psychoactive drugs.

2. ***Management:***

a. *Protection:* Protect the patient and those around him or her, including yourself. Admit the patient to a locked room and consider using physical restraints. Staff should approach cautiously, because of the unusual strength exhibited. A calm, respectful, and empathetic manner when speaking to the patient may be helpful. Because of intense paranoid reactions and sudden shifts from calmness to violence, PCP intoxication presents special problems to emergency department staff.

b. *Pharmacologic treatment:* This varies greatly depending on the pharmacology of the intoxicating drug. In the case of hallucinogens or cannabis, reassurance and "talking down" is the approach of choice, with avoidance of chemical restraints. In the ideal situation, chemical restraints would never be used until the diagnosis is known, but this ideal is rarely possible. Obtaining a history from the patient about which drug was ingested is not always a reliable method, because of the impurities in street drug samples and the misrepresentation of products by drug dealers to their customers. For the severely agitated, threatening, and violent patient, the treatment of choice is a high-potency neuroleptic, such as haloperidol 5 mg IM or thioridazine 5 mg IM. The use of benztropine 1 to 2 mg IM may be necessary to abort extrapyramidal symptoms; however, the anticholinergic effects of this medication can worsen a delirious state. Lorazepam 2 mg IM can be an effective sedative in the highly agitated patient. Chlorpromazine is contraindicated with PCP.

c. *Time course:* The person with alcohol intoxication generally will settle down within 4 hours. Most of the violent reactions due to cocaine and amphetamines will subside within 24 hours. PCP may present an oscillating picture over days, with vacillation between sedation and agitation.

d. *Referral:* Unless the provider is familiar with the management of violent behavior, consultation with a psychiatrist or a physician with expertise in addiction medicine is indicated.

D. The Hallucinating and Delusional Patient

A family history of psychosis increases the likelihood of a psychotic disorder. The use of alcohol or drugs can precipitate an acute psychotic episode in a person who has the genetic susceptibility. Schizophrenia often begins in the late teens or early twenties, when heavy alcohol and drug use is common. Mania usually begins in the thirties, although cases have been reported even in adolescence.

Case example:

> One of your patients calls you to tell you that she is very concerned about her 23-year-old daughter and believes that she needs admission to the hospital because she is acting "crazy." She is behaving like her aunt used to act. She has been shutting herself up in her room and talking to someone or herself. When asked what is going on, she has become angry and accused the mother of wanting to lock her up. She has stopped seeing friends and going to work. Today her daughter has been closing all the drapes, saying that people are after her. She is very angry and aggressive when questioned. She was expelled from college a year ago because of problems with alcohol and drugs.

1. *Differential diagnosis:*

a. *Sedatives:* Alcohol or other sedative withdrawal can produce psychotic symptoms during delirium. Sedative withdrawal delirium (delirium tremens) is characterized by disorientation, misperception, or hallucination with tremor.

b. *Stimulants:* Cocaine and amphetamines may cause a paranoid psychotic disorder that can mimic schizophrenia. Subtle changes in behavior over the past several months could denote either a return to drug or alcohol use or the more gradual onset of a psychosis. A urine drug screen can be useful. Once a patient has developed cocaine- or amphetamine-induced paranoid psychosis, he or she may be hypersensitive to future recurrence of psychotic symptoms after exposure to relatively low doses of cocaine and amphetamines, even if the reexposure to the psychostimulants occurs years after the original psychotic episode.

c. *Other drugs:* A psychotic episode can also occur with the use of cannabinoids. Hallucinogenic drugs such as LSD, psychedelic mushrooms and mescaline produce hallucinosis requiring talking down. The methylated amphetamines—"designer drugs" such as "ecstasy" (MDMA)—are classified as hallucinogens and produce the effect of both intense psychostimulants and hallucinogenic agents. Their use can be associated with violent reactions.

d. *Acute psychosis:* The major symptom complex in acute psychosis involves loss of contact with reality, hyperalertness, measured speech and agitation. In patients who develop acute reactive psychosis in response to sleep deprivation or severe stress, symptoms should abate within a few days. Patients who have posttraumatic stress disorder (PTSD) can also develop an acute psychosis; however, these episodes typically last only seconds to minutes and are followed by a sudden return to normality. High doses of corticosteroids have been associated with the development of temporary psychotic symptoms. (See appendix E)

e. *Schizophrenia:* Hallucinations and delusions may herald the onset of chronic schizophrenia. Patients in early adulthood who develop chronic symptoms are likely to have a primary diagnosis of schizophrenia rather than a drug-induced or acute reactive psychosis.

2. ***Management:***

a. *History:* Interview relatives, friends, and health care professionals who have had contact with the patient, to obtain history of previous episodes, family history, alcohol and drug history, and behavior over the past several months. Because of the presence of paranoia, the patient's personal health care provider may want to conduct the initial interview with the patient. This may be better tolerated than an interview with an unfamiliar psychiatrist.

b. *Voluntary admission:* Hallucinations and paranoia usually indicate the need for hospitalization. If the patient cannot be admitted voluntarily, a decision needs to be made as to whether an involuntary commitment is warranted.

c. *Psychiatric referral:* Obtain a psychiatric consultation as soon as possible. Select a psychiatrist who is knowledgeable about alcohol and drug effects. If the provider has a good relationship with the patient, he or she may introduce the patient to the psychiatrist.

E. **Anxious and Agitated Patient**

Case example:

> A 42-year-old female patient entered the office at 5:00 PM on Friday. She appeared to be acutely anxious, jumpy, and was wringing her hands. Over the past 12 months you have seen her three or four times for a variety of nonspecific complaints. She had been taking diazepam for a number of years, and at the last visit the dosage was tapered. It was difficult to get a history from her because she could not concentrate. She paced continually, and asked for something to calm her down.

1. ***Differential diagnosis:***
   a. *Sedative withdrawal:* Any of the sedative hypnotic drugs are capable of producing a picture of acute anxiety, tremulousness, insomnia, and dysphoria during withdrawal. Patients may be receiving drugs from other physicians or using friends' prescriptions. In addition, they may increase their use of alcohol when drugs such as diazepam are withdrawn. Drug switching is common. Withdrawal syndrome should be suspected if there is an elevated pulse, blood pressure, flushing, diaphoresis, or tremors. Benzodiazepine withdrawal syndrome can present primarily with anxiety, without any changes in vital signs.
   b. *Stimulants:* Patients using stimulant drugs to control weight can have all of the signs of an acute anxiety episode. Sometimes urine drug screens for phenylpropanolamine, amphetamines, or cocaine can be helpful in establishing a diagnosis. Caffeine can also produce significant anxiety, including panic symptoms. Any patient with what appears to be panic disorder or generalized anxiety disorder should be questioned carefully regarding caffeine intake.
   c. *Acute anxiety reactions:* While panic disorder and other acute anxiety disorders may be overdiagnosed, there may be patients who are incapacitated by these syndromes. Some have learned to use alcohol and drugs to cope with anxiety. Identifying acute or chronic environmental situations (e.g., spouse abuse) is important. It may be impossible to determine the presence of a primary anxiety disorder until the patient has been abstinent from all psychoactive medication for at least 6 months; however, this may be difficult for an anxious patient to tolerate.

2. ***Management:***
   a. *Obtain further history:* Spend a few minutes listening quietly to allow the patient to calm down and answer questions. Questions about drug and alcohol use or spouse abuse can be difficult for the patient. A useful statement by the care provider is, "Sometimes people who have been taken off sedatives find life so difficult that they go back on a drug just to survive. Has this happened to you?" Usually, when there is a psychologic reason for anxiety it has to do with anticipation of some event in the future. Try asking, "Is there something in particular that worries you?"
   b. *Inpatient treatment:* In sedative withdrawal, seizures are common and the patient may have difficulty managing his or her own medication. If the patient has an acute anxiety disorder complicated by drug dependence, outpatient treatment with a sedative could lead to relapse. If such an approach were used, gradual tapering (e.g., giving prescriptions once a week) might reduce the risk of worsening drug dependence.
   c. *Outpatient management:* Non-hospital-based treatment is indicated if the patient has a supportive social network and no evidence of

current drug abuse. Treatment should include assistance with problem solving in a calm atmosphere away from chaos. Buspirone for chronic anxiety, combined with counseling, is a safe alternative to addictive drugs. However, drug-effect-seeking patients may be initially dissatisfied with its slow onset of action (2 to 3 weeks). The usual course of treatment is approximately 6 months. Imipramine and other tricyclic antidepressants are often effective in the treatment of panic disorders. They are prescribed at lower doses than are typically used for depressions (e.g., 75 to 150 mg/day) and begin to work in 1 to 2 days. Diphenhydramine, hydroxyzine, or low-dose neuroleptics may be helpful. If acute treatment with sedatives is prescribed to someone with a history of substance abuse, this should be only until the acute situation passes or until the buspirone or other nonsedative drug begins to be effective. Remember to taper the sedative gradually.

d. *Role of self-help groups:* Attending 12-Step self-help group meetings is sometimes effective in alleviation of anxiety and panic attacks in patients who are substance dependent. However, those with social anxiety may not tolerate groups of strangers. Likewise, those whose anxiety is based on a stigmatizing secret (e.g., sexual trauma, commission of a crime, fears of being "crazy") may not be comfortable revealing this at self-help meetings.

e. *Referral:* Differential diagnoses may be difficult to determine and require the services of an addictionist. In addition, enlisting a community mental health therapist to work with the patient can be beneficial.

F. Involuntary Commitment

All states allow for the involuntary confinement of a patient who is "gravely disabled" as a result of mental illness and is a threat of immediate harm to self or others. In most jurisdictions, a proven record of repeated threats to self or others is needed to support involuntary commitment of a person who is currently not behaving dangerously. If a patient can contract for safety, is coherent and sober, and has adequate support, he or she may be able to avert commitment. However, a person who makes overt or veiled threats to harm self or others usually can be committed. Some states make a distinction between those who are dangerous due to mental illness vs. due to substance abuse. The patient may display an inordinate amount of anger toward the physician who has instituted the confinement, and may threaten legal action. The patient may claim overreaction on the part of others and display paranoid accusations. Primary care providers are frequently called on by the family to aid with involuntary commitment. All primary care providers should become familiar with the commitment criteria and procedures in their state.

II. Diagnosis and Management in Nonurgent Situations

In the nonurgent situation, management is dictated by the diagnosis rather than by acute symptoms and signs. Patients commonly are either mentally ill or substance abusers. It is only on further assessment that the presence of a combined problem is detected.

A. General Management Guidelines

1. ***Diagnosis and abstinence:*** Diagnosis of a mental health disorder in the presence of active alcohol and drug use is fraught with error. While opinions vary on the duration of abstinence required, there is universal agreement that at least 3 months must elapse before a definitive DSM-III-R (*Diagnostic and Statistical Manual,* ed. 3, revised) psychiatric diagnosis can be established.

2. ***Delay use of medications:*** As soon as medication such as lithium, antidepressants, or neuroleptics is begun, the diagnostic issue is clouded. Resolution of the suspect symptoms may be due either to disappearance of toxic drug effects or to the action of the medication. Diagnoses may not be established with certainty until the medication is withdrawn and the patient is observed for a period extending over months.

3. ***If treatment is not going the way it should, think dual diagnosis:*** In the patient with a dual diagnosis the clinical course typically is erratic and plagued by frequent relapses, oscillations of symptoms, and bizarre occurrences. Whenever treatment and recovery are not progressing as expected with either a mental illness or chemical dependence, two primary disorders are likely.

4. ***Know referral sources:*** Referral sources should believe the following:

   a. Addiction is a primary disease, not just a symptom of another mental disorder.

   b. It is possible for a mental illness and a substance use disorder to coexist.

   c. The patient should attempt to remain abstinent from all mind-altering abusable drugs.

   d. Attendance at treatment sessions for both disorders is essential.

   e. The person with a mental illness may need to continue to take an antidepressant, neuroleptic, or lithium to remain sane and sober.

B. Depression

1. ***Common signs and symptoms:***

   a. *Depressed patient:* Initially, primary depression may be diagnosed and treated. Substance use and dependence may not be detected, because of denial and minimization. Poor response to therapeutic levels of antidepressant medication may signal an underlying condition. Alternatively, there may be appropriate lifting of depression, followed by a return of the symptoms. A history of many years of depression that has been treated by a number of physicians with unsatisfactory results also should raise questions regarding the diagnosis.

   b. *Active substance abuser:* The patient may have frequent suicidal attempts while intoxicated, relapse after short periods of abstinence, or report a history of repeated chemical dependency treatment episodes. The spouse or children may complain about the patient's persistent despondency.

   c. *Depressed chemically dependent person who is abstinent:* The patient may continue to feel depressed and despondent in spite of actively working on a solid recovery program. The patient may have vague physical complaints or insomnia.

2. ***Establishment of diagnosis:*** Initial onset of a major depressive illness most commonly occurs in patients in their late thirties and forties, and is sometimes preceded by a major trauma. The patient may show some or all of the following characteristics; with a chemically dependent or abusing person, the following features are especially important:

   a. Vegetative signs and symptoms consisting of constipation, early morning fatigue, insomnia, reduced energy and libido, appetite suppression and weight loss, and psychomotor retardation.

   b. History of occurrence of depressive episodes with vegetative signs and symptoms during abstinent intervals lasting a year or more, or onset of depression prior to the onset of chemical use.

   c. Family history of a major depressive or bipolar illness.

   d. Presence of guilt, severe despondency, and hopelessness long after successful withdrawal from all chemicals.

3. ***Types of depression:*** It may be helpful to identify the types of depression before deciding on a form of treatment.

   a. *Grief/reactive depression/adjustment disorder* expressed in response to a loss (e.g., relative or friend dies, moves away, or ceases contact; patient loses or is about to lose a job, role, or function). Time is limited usually to 6 months, with greatest severity in early stages. One may traverse the five Kübler-Ross stages: denial, anger, bargaining, depression, acceptance. The trigger usually is discrete and understandable.

   b. *Major depressive episodes* with vegetative signs plus guilt, crying spells, hopelessness, and possibly urges to die or harm self may occur without an apparent trigger. Family history is often positive. Certain organic states can precipitate the condition (e.g., hypothyroidism, corticosteroid treatment, stimulant withdrawal, sedative dependence). Episodes are steady for weeks at a time. May be recurrent. May occur along with manic or hypomanic episodes (see Bipolar affective disorder, below).

   c. *Depressed mood as part of a personality disorder* is common. The trigger usually is apparent. Episodes often tend to be transient (hours to days) and reflect self-defeating behavior. Typical are passive-aggressive, dependent, borderline, obsessive-compulsive, multiple, schizoid, narcissistic, and antisocial personality disorders.

   d. *Dysthymia* is a chronic unremitting mood disorder best described as being constant depression. There are no periods of relief, because the patient appears to be trapped in a state of helpless, hopeless, self-pity.

4. *Management:*
   a. *Abstinence:* Outpatient treatment in the presence of severe depression is difficult. The patient must be adequately detoxified from all mind-altering drugs, including those used to moderate sedative withdrawal. Disulfiram (Antabuse) may help the patient maintain abstinence from alcohol.
   b. *Use of antidepressants:* With persistence of severe depression, especially with suicidal ideation after 3 weeks of abstinence, a trial of an antidepressant may be necessary. In this situation it is paramount to make a "provisional diagnosis" of depression. A trial of desipramine beginning in the fourth week of addiction rehabilitation may increase the patient's ability to participate in the treatment program. If a patient responds to the antidepressants, the medication should be continued for 6 to 9 months. It is probably a good idea that such patients be observed by a psychiatrist.
   c. *Counseling:* Follow-up clinical visits should include discussions of craving episodes, identification of cue stimuli, and recovery activities such as attending self-help groups, readings, and having sponsor support. Helping the depressed patient to shift attention from the past and toward the present is often a successful strategy (i.e., take life one day at a time). The tendency to dwell on the past can diminish a person's sense of hope and self-efficacy. Teach the patient to refocus on today and to find things that he or she can do *now* to improve the situation. Listen to how the patient deals with the past and present, then suggest alternatives and give "homework assignments." If this strategy fails, seek a referral.
   d. *Referral:* Referral is indicated when the diagnosis is not clear, patients are experiencing drug side effects that limit adequate doses of tricyclics, or if the use of lithium, fluoxitine, or monoamine oxidase inhibitors appears necessary. Note that alprazolam (Xanax) and clonazepam (Klonopin) are *not* antidepressants.

C. **Bipolar Affective Disorder**
   1. *Common signs and symptoms:*
      a. *Addictive disorder with recurrent manic and depressive episodes:* A patient who is chemically dependent and who continually relapses after a period of abstinence because of the stress induced by recurring symptoms of mania or depression needs to be assessed for a bipolar affective disorder.
      b. *Bipolar illness followed by dependence:* Conversely, a patient with a known bipolar illness may begin to use alcohol or other drugs during relapses of the mental illness and may develop dependency.
      c. *Bipolar illness exacerbated by substance use:* A person with a known bipolar disorder may be difficult to manage because of drug or alcohol use and noncompliance with a medication regime.

2. ***Establishment of diagnosis:***
   a. *Definition:* The patient has recurrent episodes of hyperactivity or mania, often alternating with periods of severe depression and of normal mood. (See appendix E for the diagnostic criteria for manic episodes.) The onset of first illness often is seen in the late twenties and early thirties, with a manic episode usually seen first. In the manic-depressed extremes the psychotic delusions are most prominent yet orientation remains intact.
   b. *Clinical characteristics:* Manic episodes are characterized by symptoms including increasing periods of sleeplessness, elation, irritability, hostility, distractibility, and progressive psychotic delusions of persecution or grandeur. Commitments often are made that cannot be fulfilled. The periods of depression show all the characteristics of a unipolar depression, often are severe, and may be accompanied by suicidal ideation. Hypomania is a milder form than mania, which lacks the psychotic delusions and unreasonable commitments.

3. ***Differential diagnosis:***
   a. *Sedative withdrawal:* The person withdrawing from sedatives may suffer emotional lability with alternating periods of depression and irritability. The intensity of the symptoms in early recovery may mimic bipolar disease; however, the temporal pattern usually establishes the diagnosis. The person in sedative withdrawal may exhibit rapid vacillation from irritability to depression occurring over hours. However, a manic or hypomanic episode typically lasts days to weeks. The manic episode often involves psychotic delusions. The symptoms ease toward gradual improvement, rather than becoming worse as in bipolar disease.
   b. *Drug cycling:* Chemically dependent persons commonly medicate the distressing symptoms caused by their drug use. This leads to using "downers" to moderate the effects of "uppers," and vice versa, producing a pattern of alternating elation and depression. Symptoms generally become worse over time. Disorientation may accompany the extremes.

4. ***Management:*** Management of bipolar affective disorder in the patient who is also abusing substances is particularly difficult.
   a. *Medication:* Lithium is the drug of choice for preventing manic and depressive episodes. The most frequently occurring side effects are due to such factors as doubling doses, fluid shifts, and hydration. Lithium should be used only in patients who are alcohol and drug free. In particularly difficult cases, a combination of lithium, neuroleptics, and antidepressants may be used. Often neuroleptics are used for a short time while awaiting the establishment of a therapeutic lithium level. Lithium is effective in 85% of patients, but may take several days to begin to be effective. Patients who do not respond to lithium may require the addition of carbamazepine, ve-

rapamil, or nifedipine. When antidepressants are used to treat the depressive phase, caution should be exercised as mania may result.

b. *Early treatment:* Prompt treatment of a relapse into the manic or depressive phase is essential. Patients who have been abstinent may begin drinking and using drugs during mania.

D. Anxiety-Panic

While many treatment methods (e.g., counseling, self-hypnosis, desensitization, relaxation techniques) are effective, most patients are treated by nonpsychiatrists with benzodiazepines. Persons with anxiety and panic disorder are more likely to have problems with alcohol and drug dependence, and may develop sedative dependence when using benzodiazepines. For the purpose of this section, *comments are restricted to those persons with anxiety disorders who also have evidence of chemical dependence.*

1. *Common signs and symptoms:*

   a. *Anxiety with no previous addictive disorder:* The patient may have been started on benzodiazepine therapy for a well-defined panic or anxiety disorder with no previous history of alcohol or drug dependence. Over time, the patient may have begun to increase the dosage beyond that prescribed (tolerance) and begun to request extra refills.

   b. *History of alcohol or drug problem:* The patient may have a previous history of alcohol or drug abuse, which appears to be in remission. Excessive caffeine intake may be a factor. Benzodiazepine therapy is then started for an anxiety or sleep disorder that has developed during a period of abstinence. The patient who already has cross-tolerance rapidly becomes dependent and displays drug-seeking behavior and loss of control over the medication.

2. *Establishment of diagnosis:* To make a diagnosis of both anxiety-panic disorder and substance use disorder, there must be current or past evidence of the anxiety disorder during prolonged periods of abstinence.

3. *Differential diagnosis:*

   a. *Alcohol and sedatives:* As many as 90% of persons who are alcohol or sedative dependent will have symptoms of anxiety at the time of seeking treatment. The alcohol-dependent patient who drinks daily may have daily withdrawal, particularly in the morning. Withdrawal can include anxiety, restlessness, tremulousness, and hypervigilance. These symptoms may persist for weeks after cessation of use, and it can be virtually impossible to distinguish sedative withdrawal from the recurrence of an anxiety disorder.

   b. *Stimulants:* Cocaine use is characterized by anxiety and panic after the immediate euphoria and elation subside. This may occur within minutes with cocaine, or hours with amphetamines. Patients dependent on cocaine characteristically use a sedative or narcotic to attenuate these unpleasant symptoms. Caffeine or phenypropanola-mine overuse also may present in this way.

c. *Hallucinogens or cannabis* may produce or enhance anxiety through flashbacks or "bad trips."

d. *Posttraumatic stress disorder:* The result of having experienced one or more traumatic events (e.g., incest, child abuse, near-death, violence, natural disaster), this disorder leads to the frequent reexperiencing (through flashbacks) of emotions that are triggered by reminders in a manner not unlike the phobias or panic disorder. This is a common disorder in adults who were raised in homes with parental alcohol or drug disorder. However, the original traumatic events may not be available to the patient's conscious awareness when therapy begins.

e. *Anxiety disorders:* Three types of anxiety disorder may complicate the management of addictive disorders: phobias, panic disorder, and generalized anxiety disorder. (See appendix E for criteria for generalized anxiety, panic disorders, and simple phobias.)

(1) Patients with *phobias* may have focal or widespread fears about objects or situations (e.g., fear of spiders, fear of public speaking, social phobia, fear of expressing anger, fear of heights, agoraphobia [fear of leaving one's home]). When the trigger or near-trigger is encountered, the person experiences and expresses terror, and attempts to escape despite the consequences. Widespread avoidance is common with phobias.

(2) Somatic manifestations of *panic disorder* may include palpitations, tachycardia, and hyperventilation. These symptoms may further frighten the victim, creating a self-escalating vicious cycle that incorporates fear of the somatic manifestations. Panic triggers are usually unknown or unconscious. Attacks occur without warning or apparent pattern.

(3) With more vague and free-floating anxiety symptoms than the other disorders, *generalized anxiety disorder* (GAD) probably forms the diagnostic catch-all for those who do not meet criteria for the above disorders. The main feature of generalized anxiety disorder is the patients' seeming inability to calm themselves to stop worrying. Frequent use of pharmacologic or psychologic strategies to avoid resolving these fears, among these strategies being substance abuse and repression, ultimately leads to the situation where the patient feels the anxiety without knowing why he or she is anxious (free-floating anxiety). Obsession with the future rather than focusing on today is a good clue that a patient suffers from an anxiety disorder.

4. *Management:*
The patient with significant anxiety and dysphoria during withdrawal is less likely to remain abstinent with outpatient treatment.

a. *Nondrug treatment:* Use nondrug methods to decrease the symptoms of anxiety and panic if they persist in the sober interval after withdrawal is complete. Nondrug treatment approaches include behavioral therapy, desensitization, deep muscle relaxation, hypnosis, biofeedback, family therapy, and individual counseling.

b. *Use of nonaddictive drugs:* Use of tricyclic antidepressants, β-blockers, and buspirone can diminish the physiologic signs of anxiety. Fluoxitine (Prozac) should be used with caution, because it may increase the frequency of panic attacks or produce a state of general agitation or hypomania. Some experts believe the monoamine oxidase inhibitors are particularly effective, but their safety profile is low.

   (1) Therapeutic approaches to panic disorders in alcohol-dependent patients:

   (a) Begin with abstinence from ethanol and other sedatives, caffeine, and all other stimulants.

   (b) Look for a primary panic disorder (antedating substance abuse).

   (c) Look for a panic disorder that is persistent during prolonged abstinence from sedatives and stimulants.

   (d) With input from a psychiatrist, use imipramine, β-blockers, or a monoamine oxidase inhibitor.

   (e) Consider alprazolam (Xanax) or clonazepam (Klonopin) only as a last resort, because of their real dependence potential.

c. *Use of benzodiazepines in recovering persons* can lead to sedative dependence and a return to use of the drug of choice. Treatment of phobias and other anxiety disorders by psychotherapeutic techniques will be inhibited by benzodiazepines, alcohol, or other sedatives. While initial efficacy of benzodiazepines in anxiety disorders is rapid and dramatic, the long-term risks of tolerance and dependence with symptom reemergence outweigh the benefit in most instances. If used, they should only be given initially while other drugs are starting to work; then they should be discontinued.

d. *Counseling:* Patients with anxiety disorders may respond to counseling and/or exposure techniques. One exposure technique includes:

   (1) Identification of triggers, with numerical ranking of the subjective potency (e.g., no spider = 0, thought of spider = 20, see spider in magazine = 35, see spider across room = 55, see spider at arm's length = 80, spider on body = 90, spider on face = 100).

   (2) Progressive exposure (usually with a supportive person present) until the trigger loses potency.

   (3) Reestablishment of full function by reducing avoidance.

Empowering anxious patients to retake control of their lives may require educating them that they *only* control their own present behaviors and attitudes. They must learn to:
(1) Accept the past and future.
(2) Accept their own feelings and those of others.
(3) Accept the behavior and attitudes of others as out of the realm of their own control (they might be able to influence, but not control, some of these).

E. Chronic Psychoses

Chronic psychotic symptoms associated with alcohol and drug disorders may be secondary to schizophrenia, mania, organic brain disease, or other metabolic abnormalities. This section focuses on chronic schizophrenia. Management of psychotic symptoms secondary to organic brain disease or metabolic abnormalities are not discussed; readers may wish to refer to a standard neurology or psychiatry text.

1. *Common signs and symptoms:*
   a. *Primary schizophrenia affected by secondary use of substances:* Commonly the patient with known schizophrenia relapses because of alcohol or drug use. The patient clearly uses alcohol and drugs to deal with psychotic symptoms and life stresses. Heavy use can lead to exacerbation of psychotic symptoms and hospitalization.
   b. *Primary addiction with secondary symptoms of psychosis:* The patient develops psychosis after prolonged use of alcohol or drugs. Psychotic symptoms resolve within 2 months of onset of abstinence. Psychotic symptoms that last more than 2 months during abstinence may suggest a dual diagnosis.
   c. *Dual diagnosis:* The patient who continues to have symptoms of psychosis after 2 months of abstinence likely has both a primary psychosis and a primary addictive disorder. These patients are at much higher risk for relapse of psychiatric illness and the alcohol or drug disorder.

2. *Establishing diagnosis:* Schizophrenia is characterized by intermittent inability to distinguish thoughts, ideas, feelings, and emotions that are coming from within oneself from those stimuli arising from outside oneself, that is, inability to "test reality." The age at onset varies from childhood to adulthood, most frequently beginning in late adolescence or early adulthood. The disease is progressive, with symptoms worsening over time. Symptoms include social withdrawal, difficulty in concentrating, inappropriate or bizarre behavior, delusions, and auditory hallucinations. Ambivalence is often profound, interfering with decision making. Autism (tendency to isolate oneself at the feeling level) is also a cardinal symptom. While the symptoms are easy to spot in advanced stages, the early symptoms may be confused with adolescent behavior. Use of alcohol and drugs is common in this age group and by itself leads to inappropriate behavior, paranoid delusions, and social withdrawal.

3. ***Differential diagnosis:*** The following must be included in the differential diagnosis for schizophrenia:

   a. *Stimulant intoxication:* Cocaine and amphetamine use may precipitate psychotic symptoms. Initially the patient may experience paranoia, followed by auditory, visual, and tactile hallucinations and delusions of persecution. A psychotic reaction to stimulants may resemble an acute schizophrenic episode. The patient's behavior may include agitation characterized by violence and repetitive actions. The symptoms generally resolve within hours or once drug use ceases. Differentiation from schizophrenia usually is determined by the time course of the symptoms and toxicology results.

   b. *Sedative withdrawal:* An organic psychosis (a psychotic delirium) may occur during the course of sedative (including alcohol) withdrawal. Onset occurs several days (e.g., alcohol, alprazolam) to several weeks (e.g., diazepam) after cessation of use. Special features of a psychotic delirium with sedative withdrawal include the predominance of visual hallucinations and the variability in symptoms. A differential diagnosis is established by the time course of the symptoms and history of sedative abuse.

   c. *Hallucinogen intoxication:* Persons who ingest LSD, mescaline, PCP, psychedelic mushrooms, or cannabinoids can develop acute psychotic symptoms. These drugs, however, *do not* produce chronic psychosis or schizophrenia. Scopolamine toxicity from abuse of over-the-counter sleeping pills can produce psychotic symptoms.

   d. *Delirium:* Patients with organic brain syndrome may exhibit delusions and bizarre behavior. Delirium may be caused by drug intoxication or withdrawal, brain infection, tumor, electrolyte imbalance, hormonal abnormality, fever, intracranial hemorrhage, or seizures. However, this may be distinguished from schizophrenia by the disorientation that *does not occur* in schizophrenia.

   e. *Temporal lobe epilepsy:* Psychomotor epilepsy may present with episodic stereotyped nonpurposeful behavior. When limited to the sensory realm, partial complex seizures may present with visual, auditory, olfactory, or tactile hallucinations.

   f. *Multiple personality disorder:* Auditory hallucinations in the form of voices heard is extremely common in this disorder. Substance abuse is common in patients with multiple personality disorder.

   g. *Mania:* Paranoid schizophrenia may present in a form that is similar to manic episodes. Ultimately the two may be distinguished by time course, drug response, and presence or absence of depressive episodes.

4. ***Management:*** A mental health team in the community is often responsible for the management of patients with chronic psychoses. Primary care providers, as part of the team, can provide the following:

   a. *General medical care:* Diagnosis and treatment of medical conditions must be done in a way that considers the drug interactions and side effects of medications used to treat psychotic disorders.

b. *Care of the family:* Living with a person with a psychosis, an alcohol or drug disorder, or both can be difficult. Family members need both medical and psychologic support, including education about the mental and substance use disorders of their relatives. Many communities have support groups for family members of seriously mentally ill clients, and Al-Anon family groups including ACOA (Adult Children of Alcoholics) and Alateen may be helpful too.

F. Personality Disorders

There has been controversy over the prevalence of personality disorders in persons who are dependent on psychoactive substances, because symptoms of substance abuse often overlap with symptoms of personality disorders. While many patients with addictive disorders do not have concurrent personality disorders, two common disorders—antisocial personality disorder (ASPD) and borderline personality disorder (BPD)—often coexist with alcohol and drug dependence. The presence of either of these disorders complicates treatment of alcohol and drug problems. Alcoholics who also have ASPD have much higher rates of early alcohol- and drug-related morbidity and mortality.

1. *Common signs and symptoms:*

   a. *Alcohol and drug problems with ASP:* Affected patients often have a history of both conduct disorder and alcohol or drug problems in childhood and/or adolescence. (See appendix E for diagnostic criteria of ASPD.) They are fearless thrill seekers and may have had learning difficulties and/or hyperactivity. They generally experience numerous difficulties with authorities in school and the legal system. Pediatricians and primary care physicians may first be alerted to the problems by concerned parents. The combination of ASPD and alcohol or drug dependence has been classified as type II alcoholism by Cloninger (1981), a more malignant, early-onset variety of the disorder.

   b. *BPD with alcohol and drug disorders:* A person with a substance use disorder who demonstrates frequent psychiatric hospitalizations, self-mutilation, rapidly shifting extreme moods, and intense, poor relationships may have BPD. Symptoms will remain despite abstinence from alcohol and drugs, but are exacerbated by the use of these substances.

2. *Establishment of diagnosis:*

   a. Establishment of the diagnosis of a personality disorder may require psychologic testing, psychiatric consultation, and observation of behavior over time. Primary care providers are in a unique position to become alerted to the diagnosis because of contact with the family over time.

   b. The diagnosis includes the demonstration of inflexible and maladaptive responses to stress over years, with little insight into the problem. This lack of insight may be reflected in a tendency to blame others for problems and to act out rather than discuss feelings.

3. ***Differential diagnosis:***"*Pseudo-personality disorder*": The person who uses alcohol and/or drugs can exhibit many of the signs of a personality disorder. A patient with an alcohol or drug problem may appear to meet criteria for one of the many personality disorders because of shared symptoms, including deterioration in personal responsibility, deterioration in work and social relationships, denial and blaming others for problems, and low self-esteem. The differentiating characteristic is rapid disappearance of the symptoms with abstinence.

4. ***Management:*** The management of personality disorders is difficult and requires a variety of health care professionals and community resources. Community-based crisis teams that are available to providers, the patient, and family members may prove useful; and for the patient who makes frequent threats of harm or self-mutilation, such crisis services are essential. A psychologist or psychiatrist with expertise and interest in the care of patients with personality disorders is also a critical component of an overall treatment plan. Periodic meetings of this community-based treatment team is often necessary to provide optimum care for patients with BPD or ASP. Long-term psychotherapy (over several years) or intensive residential or outpatient treatment is the only remedy for personality disorders. This is effective only if done while the patient remains abstinent.

G. Attention Deficit Disorder

Attention deficit disorder (ADD) may extend into adulthood. Several studies have indicated that there is a clustering of families with both ADD and alcoholism, and 2% to 5% of cocaine addicts have ADD. These persons characteristically have persistence of problems with poor concentration, poor impulse control, short attention span, erratic reaction times, deficiencies in mental computation, reversals of letters or syllables, and poor reading skills. Primary care providers may be particularly well suited to identifying patients with both alcohol or drug problems and persistent ADD, because of a history of childhood treatment for the disorder. However, while methylphenidate may be effective as a treatment for persistent ADD in adults, there is a danger that it may lead to compulsive use and relapse to other drugs.

H. Chronic Psychiatric Sequelae

Like acute physical illness, addictive disorders can have chronic sequelae after the acute condition is resolved. For example, recovering persons who remain abstinent may continue to have liver failure from alcohol-induced cirrhosis even after rehabilitation. Chronic psychiatric sequelae of addiction include the following conditions:

1. ***Dementia associated with alcohol dependence:*** There has been some controversy about whether ethanol or its primary metabolite, acetaldehyde, produces a state of dementia. The characteristics of

this dementia are nonspecific and due to the alcohol itself rather than to secondary effects such as chronic subdural hematoma. There may be a reduction in brain size on CT scan, which may show signs of reversal (as do cognitive deficits) over the first 6 months of abstinence.

2. ***Alcohol amnestic syndrome*** (Korsakoff syndrome) is a chronic neuropsychiatric illness produced by exposure to a low level of thiamine during a 1- to 2-day alcohol-free interval. This typically occurs during intravenous therapy, when low levels of thiamine are not replenished. A low magnesium level, even in the presence of adequate thiamine, may cause this syndrome. It may also occur in patients with no alcohol abuse. It is more common in those with Mediterranean ethnicity, due to an inherited aberrant form of transketolase. The frontal lobes and the mammillary bodies at the base of the brain are damaged. Anatomic disease has been correlated with neuropsychologic deficits. Clinical features include severe impaired short-term memory storage, with preservation of long-term memory and absence of generalized dementia. It can be prevented by thiamine in the presence of adequate magnesium and the absence of alcohol, because alcohol prevents oral absorption of thiamine.

3. ***Hallucinogen-induced hallucinosis:*** While there has been controversy about whether hallucinogens produce chronic psychosis, it is now thought that psychosis that follows hallucinogen abuse was in the latent phase of expression. While symptoms of perceptual disturbance can persist chronically after hallucinogen exposure, these symptoms are usually benign and do not proceed to a psychotic state. A similar set of perceptual disturbances also may be observed with the more potent cannabinoids (hashish). Anxiety or situational disturbances can exacerbate hallucinogen hallucinosis such that the patient can reexperience misperceptions (usually visual) in response to those exogenous stimuli. Management includes reassurance or even short-term use of anxiolytics (if the patient's history is one of hallucinogen abuse only with no polysubstance dependence or sedative dependence). However, use of antipsychotic agents sometimes is required for chronic recurrent episodes of hallucinogen hallucinosis.

BIBLIOGRAPHY

Allen JP, Eckardt MJ, Wallen J: Screening for alcoholism: Techniques and issues. *Publ Health Rep* 1988; 103:586–592.

Allen JP, Faden V, Rawlings R, et al: Subtypes of substance abusers: Personality differences associated with MacAndrew scores. *Psychol Rep* 1990; 66:691–698.

Bean-Bayog M: Inpatient treatment of the psychiatric patient with alcoholism. *Gen Hosp Psychiatry* 1987; 9:203–209.

Brown SA, Irwin M, Schuckit MA: Changes in anxiety among abstinent male alcoholics. *J Stud Alcohol* 1991; 52:55–61.

Cloninger CR, Bohman M, Sigvardsson S: Inheritance of alcohol abuse. *Arch Gen Psychiatry* 1981; 38:861–868.

Collins JJ, Schlenger WE: Acute and chronic effects of alcohol use on violence. *J Stud Alcohol* 1988; 49:516–521.

DeSoto CB, O'Donnell WE, DeSoto JL: Long-term recovery in alcoholics. *Alcoholism: Clin Exp Res* 1989; 13:693–697.

Dixon L, Haas G, Weiden P, et al: Acute effects of drug abuse in schizophrenic patients: Clinical observations and patients' self-report. *Schizophren Bull* 1990; 16:69–79.

Drugs for psychiatric disorders. *Med Lett* 1991; 33:43–50.

Estroff T, Dackis C, Gold M, et al: Drug abuse and bipolar disorders. *Int J Psychiatry Med* 1985–1986; 15:37–40.

Jaffe JH, Babor TF, Fishbein DH: Alcoholics, aggression and antisocial personality. *J Stud Alcohol* 1988; 49:211–218.

Landry MJ, Smith DE, McDuff D, et al: Anxiety and substance use disorders: A primer for primary care physicians. *J Am Board Fam Pract* 1991; 4:47–53.

Liepman MR, Nirenberg TD, Porges R, et al: Depression associated with substance abuse, in Cameron OG (ed): *Presentations of Depression: Depression in Medical and Other Psychiatric Disorders.* New York, Wiley, 1987, pp 131–167.

Minkoff K: An integrated treatment model for dual diagnosis of psychosis and addiction. *Hosp Commun Psychiatry* 1989; 40:1031–1036.

Mirin SM, Weiss RD, Michael J, et al: Psychopathology in substance abusers: Diagnosis and treatment. *Am J Drug Alcohol Abuse* 1988; 14:139–157.

Murphy GE, Wetzel RD: The lifetime risk of suicide in alcoholism. *Arch Gen Psychiatry* 1990; 47:383–392.

Murphy GE: Suicide and substance abuse. *Arch Gen Psychiatry* 1988; 45:593–594.

Nace EP, Saxon JJ, Shore N: Borderline personality disorder and alcoholism treatment: A one-year follow-up study. *J Stud Alcohol,* 1986; 47:196–200.

Nace EP, Saxon JJ Jr, Shore N: A comparison of borderline and nonborderline alcoholic patients. *Arch Gen Psychiatry* 1983; 40:54–56.

Regier D, Farmer M, Rae D, et al: Comorbidity of mental disorders with alcohol and other drug abuse. *JAMA* 1990; 264:2511–2518.

Schuckit MA: Primary men alcoholics with histories of suicide attempts. *J Stud Alcohol.* 1986; 47:78–81.

Winokur G, Black DW, Nasrallah A: Depressions secondary to other psychiatric disorders and medical illnesses. *Am J Psychiatry* 1988; 145:233–237.

Winokur G, Coryell W: Familial alcoholism in primary unipolar major depressive disorder. *Am J Psychiatry* 1991; 148:184–188.

CHAPTER 19

HIV/AIDS and Substance Use

Peter Katsufrakis, M.D.

Maureen Strohm, M.D.

There is a direct relationship between the acquisition of human immunodeficiency virus (HIV) infection and intravenous (IV) drug use. Most acquired immune deficiency syndrome (AIDS) is seen in among homosexual and bisexual men, yet nearly a third of all new cases of AIDS are found in heterosexuals with a history of IV drug abuse. Most children with AIDS have contracted the disease as a result of maternal IV drug use. There is also the supposition that persons who are alcohol dependent are at higher risk for AIDS secondary to risk-taking behavior while intoxicated. This chapter provides health care providers with a brief review of HIV infection as it relates to persons affected by alcohol and drug disorders.

I. Risk Factors Associated With Development of HIV Infections
A. Epidemiology of HIV/AIDS

Statistics regarding HIV infection are reported separately from statistics on the development of the clinical disease process called AIDS. While it appears that most persons who test positive for HIV eventually will develop AIDS, the process may take more than 10 years.

1. ***AIDS mortality/reported deaths:*** National AIDS surveillance data from the Centers for Disease Control enable us to examine AIDS mortality from the perspective of HIV risk category, ethnicity, age, and gender (Table 19–1).

   a. Most AIDS deaths (59.1%) have occurred among homosexual/bisexual men; an additional 6.8% of AIDS deaths occurred among homosexual/bisexual men who were also intravenous drug users. However, IV drug use constitutes the second major risk factor, with 27.8% of deaths in this group.

   b. African-American and Hispanic persons are represented disproportionately in the mortality statistics when compared with overall population statistics. In fact, AIDS surveillance data from New York State revealed that by 1988 HIV infection/AIDS was the leading cause of death among Hispanic children under 5 years of age and the second leading cause of death for African-American children. If

TABLE 19–1.

Characteristics of Persons Who Died of AIDS: United States, 1981–1990*

Characteristics	n	%
Total	100,777	100
HIV exposure group		
Homosexual/bisexual men	59,586	59.1
Intravenous drug users (IVDUs)		
Women/heterosexual men	21,126	21.0
Homosexual/bisexual men	6,894	6.8
Persons with hemophilia		
Adult/adolescent	945	0.9
Child	74	0.1
Transfusion recipient		
Adult/adolescent	2,793	2.8
Child	150	0.1
Heterosexual contact	3,587	3.6
Perinatal (children)	1,186	1.2
No identified risk	3,276	3.3
Race/ethnicity		
White, non-Hispanic	55,494	55.1
Black, non-Hispanic	28,575	28.4
Hispanic	15,805	15.7
Age at death (yr)		
<5	1,141	1.1
5–14	308	0.3
15–24	3,266	3.2
25–34	36,418	36.1
35–44	37,634	37.3
45–54	14,256	14.1
≥55	7,405	7.3
Gender		
Male	90,715	90.0
Female	10,056	10.0

*From National AIDS surveillance. *MMWR* 1991; 40:43.

we examine regional data, the East Coast demonstrates a different profile, with IV drug use representing the highest risk category.

2. ***Other seroprevalence studies:*** Since HIV seropositivity is not uniformly reportable in all states, limited data are available regarding individuals at this level. Three studies present interesting, and disturbing, data:

    a. *Sentinel hospitals (26 hospitals in 21 cities):* Anonymous testing (excluding patients with HIV-related diagnoses), revealed median seroprevalence rate of 0.7%, male-female ratio of 7, and in the hospital with the highest seroprevalence rates, 3.8% of adolescents

TABLE 19–2.

Ethnic Shift in AIDS Cases 1990

Ethnicity	US Population (%)	AIDS Deaths (%)	New AIDS Cases (%)
White	80	55.1	11.7
Black	12	18.4	42.3
Hispanic	6	15.7	31.6

(ages 15 to 19 years) and 22% of all men (ages 25 to 44 years) were seropositive.

b. *College students* (19 universities/student health centers): HIV seroprevalence surveys using blood collected for routine medical purposes revealed that the overall seroprevalence rate was 0.2%, and men were more often positive (0.5%) than women (0.02%).

c. *Other groups:* Military recruits have an expected lower seroprevalence rate, given the active exclusion of individuals with a history of IV drug use and discouragement of homosexual men from applying for military service. Current population estimates from the CDC indicate that approximately one million people in the United States are HIV infected, yielding a population-based seroprevalence rate of 0.4%.

3. Ethnic shift is most dramatic when examining U.S. population statistics, AIDS deaths to date, and new AIDS cases reported in 1990 (Table 19–2).

B. **Spectrum of Behavioral Risk Factors**

1. *Definite risk of virus transmission:*

   a. *IV drug use* (and other parenteral use, e.g., "skin-popping"): Shared needles, unsterile needle-cleaning procedures.

   b. *Other exposures to infected blood:* Transfusions, tattooing, and blood rituals.

   c. *Sexual practices:* Vaginal or anal intercourse without a condom, intercourse during menses (infected female partner), cunnilingus, fellatio, analingus.

2. *Probably safe:*

   a. *IV drug use:* Sterilize needles in bleach, rinsing several times; then rinse several times with boiled water. The inside of needles need to be thoroughly cleaned to remove old blood.

   b. *Sexual practices:* Kissing with exchange of saliva, fellatio without exposure to pre-ejaculate, urine contact with unbroken skin.

3. *Definitely safe:*

   a. *IV drug use:* New needles with each use, never sharing.

   b. *Blood transfusions:* Autologous transfusion.

   c. *Sexual practices:* Kissing socially (dry), frottage (rubbing bodies together), massage, mutual masturbation (if no contact between bodily fluids and cuts, sores, or abrasions).

C. Alcohol and Drug Abuse

1. ***Intravenous drug use:*** The most common method of infection is by direct transmission or inoculation. This occurs via contaminated needle and/or syringe shared by users or "loaned" to the user by the dealer.

   a. *Intravenous cocaine users:* This group injects more frequently than opioid users, because of the shorter half-life of cocaine (10 to 20 times/day vs 3 to 4 times/day). They are also more likely to frequent *"shooting galleries,"* where contaminated needles and/or syringes are offered as part of the drug deal or where sharing is viewed as an expression of trust in fellow users.

   b. *Sexual activity:* Cocaine users, with their need for more frequent doses of drug, are more likely to trade sex for drugs, putting them at risk for sexual transmission.

   c. *Ethnic differences:* Most disturbing, these differences may be more important when ethnicity is considered. Frequency of cocaine injection was strongly related to seroprevalence in African-Americans and Hispanics, as identified in one study in San Francisco (Table 19–3).

   d. *Impact on immune function:* There is no consistent evidence of impairment of immune function by parenteral drugs, particularly heroin and cocaine. The impact of parenteral drugs themselves is difficult to separate from the effects of possible contaminants (chemical or infectious) and the life-style of the user. Often the IV drug user also is malnourished, likely to be living or spending extended periods of time in crowded conditions, and exposed to multiple infectious diseases that may tax the immune system even in the absence of HIV infection. Such a scenario has been suggested as a possible basis for increased susceptibility to HIV infection, but also is compounded by unsafe sexual practices, which pose a separate and critical risk.

   e. *Progression of AIDS:* In the multicenter AIDS cohort study of seropositive homosexual men who were IV drug users, the use of parenteral drugs did not result in acceleration in the progression of HIV disease compared with nonusers (Kaslow et al., 1989).

TABLE 19–3.

Ethnic Factors in Cocaine Use (San Francisco Study)

Frequency of IV Cocaine Use	HIV Positive (%)		
	White	Black	Hispanic
None	5	18	3
Monthly	11	24	12
Weekly	8	30	17
Daily	6	60	36

2. *Non-IV drug use:*
   a. *Non-IV cocaine use:* Cocaine use, whether parenteral, nasal, or inhaled, seems to pose a significant risk for acquiring HIV infection, although the mechanisms remain unclear. The most likely explanation, given the findings of the multicenter AIDS cohort study, centers on the behavioral and sexual practices of cocaine users. Cocaine users are more likely to trade sex for drugs, and in that setting are more likely to disregard the necessary precautions of "safer sex" and engage in high-risk sexual practices.
   b. *Possible mechanism:* Recent animal studies and in vitro studies suggest direct immunosuppression by certain drugs, such as marijuana and heroin, and indirect immunomodulation via impact on the neuroendocrine system. Data regarding cocaine are inconclusive. This is currently under significant study through the National Institute of Drug Abuse.

3. *Alcohol:*
   a. *Direct transmission of HIV:* To date there are no data to suggest enhanced transmission of HIV infection related to alcohol use alone. Anecdotal information from patient interviews supports the concept that these patients are less likely to follow safer sex practices when under the influence, increasing their risk through behavioral practices rather than as an effect of alcohol alone.
   b. *Immune system impairment:* Increased susceptibility to infection, particularly bacterial infections and tuberculosis, is well accepted in alcohol-dependent patients.

D. **Risk of HIV Infection Via Blood Transfusion Since 1985**
   1. *Contamination of blood products:* Approximately 5 to 25 of every 1,000,000 units screened as negative actually are HIV-infected.
   2. *Risk of infection from blood products:* The risk of acquiring HIV via transfusion of a screened unit of blood ranges from $1:40,000$ to $1:200,000$. Therefore, although risk of HIV infection via blood transfusion essentially is negligible, it is possible for a donor unit to test negative in the initial period after infection (i.e., "window period").

E. **Perinatal Transmission of HIV Infection**
   Women with AIDS who are IV drug users appear to have the same risk of infecting their fetuses as women with AIDS who are not IV drug users.
   1. *Method and time of transmission:* HIV infection in a pregnant women carries clear risks for the fetus.
      a. Transplacental transmission can occur at any time during pregnancy.
      b. Intrapartum transmission is possible during labor and delivery.
      c. Infection can occur through breast-feeding, either via the breast milk itself or via infected blood from small abrasions of tissues of the nipple.

2. ***Risk of infection:*** The risk of transmission to the infant of an infected mother is close to 30%, with a reported range of 20% to 60%. However, because antibodies to HIV cross the placental barrier, virtually 100% of newborns of infected mothers will test HIV positive on usual antibody testing. HIV positivity may persist for up to 18 months *without* signifying true HIV infection of the newborn.

II. Identification of High-Risk Behaviors, Preventive Counseling, and HIV Testing

A. Screening Questions

Screening questions are useful in the identification of high-risk behaviors associated with exposure to HIV. Primary care providers may want to assess risk of development of an HIV infection either by interview or by self-administered questionnaire.

1. ***General health factors that may indicate increased risk:***
   a. Did you receive a transfusion of blood or blood products between 1978 and 1985?
   b. Have you ever had tuberculosis, hepatitis, or "shingles?"
   c. Have you ever had syphilis, herpes, gonorrhea, *chlamydia* infection, pelvic inflammatory disease, or other sexually transmitted disease?

2. ***Alcohol and drug-related risk factors:***
   Any use of alcohol or other drugs should prompt use of CAGE questions, as discussed elsewhere in this volume. Addition questions should include the following:
   a. Do you use or have you ever used cocaine, heroin, or any other drugs?
   b. Have you ever used a needle to use drugs?
   c. Have you ever shared needles with anyone?
   d. Did you ever have a blackout?
   e. Do you have sex when you are drunk, stoned, or high?

3. ***Sexual practices:***
   a. Do you have sex with men, women, or both?
   b. From 1978 until now have you ever had sex with a gay or bisexual male?
   c. Have you ever exchanged money or drugs for sex?
   d. Are you presently active with more than one partner?
   e. How many partners have you had (estimate) during the past 10 years?
   f. Were any of your partners IV drug users, prostitutes, or infected with HIV?
   g. Do you use condoms? Always, usually, or occasionally? What type of lubricant?
   h. Do you ever use sex toys? If so, (how) are they cleaned between each person?

B. Guidelines for Risk Reduction Counseling

Discuss risk reduction in the context of other health behaviors, such as safety issues (e.g., driving and drinking; use of seat belts, bike helmets, and reducing the risk of exposure to violence).

1. ***Patients at low risk*** (light drinkers, those in a monogamous relationship, recreational users of mood-altering drugs): Preventive counseling should include general information on three major risk categories: IV drug use, blood transfusions, and sexual activities and use of condoms.

2. ***Drug- and alcohol-dependent patients who deny use of IV drugs:*** Treatment of the underlying substance use disorder is the most important aspect of prevention. In addition, preventive counseling for this group may include general information plus a more extensive discussion of high-risk sexual activities. It is important to emphasize risk of blackouts and avoidance of high-risk situations when using drugs (e.g., partying with infected persons, visiting shooting galleries).

3. ***Persons who inject drugs intravenously:*** Performing preventive counseling in this group should first focus on treatment of the primary addictive disorder. Helping patients participate in abstinence-based treatment programs or methadone maintenance programs is the first step. Patients who are unwilling to enter treatment for primary addiction need to be counseled on methods they can use to minimize their risk of exposure:

   a. *Methods to Minimize Risk of Exposure from IV drug use:*
      (1) Do not share needles.
      (2) If using, enroll in a needle/syringe exchange program, if available.
      (3) If sharing, sterilize equipment between each user with 10% bleach solution.
      (4) If sharing, limit partners.

   b. Methods to minimize exposure from sexual activities:
      (1) Limit number of sexual partners, preferable to one mutually monogamous relationship.
      (2) Safest sexual practices include abstinence, mutual masturbation, other contact not involving bodily fluids.
      (3) Use latex condoms for all acts of intercourse.
      (4) Use only water-based lubricants with latex condoms.
      (5) Spermicides containing nonoxonyl-9 may provide virucidal activity and may be preferable to other lubricants.
      (6) Withdraw erect penis before erection subsides. Safest to withdraw before ejaculation.
      (7) Orogenital sex should not involve contact with vaginal secretions, ejaculate, or pre-ejaculatory fluid.

C. **Testing in Alcohol- and Drug-Dependent Patients at Risk for Exposure to HIV**

   1. **Pretest counseling** ("PRE," *P*rivacy, *R*isk reduction, *E*ducation):
      a. *Privacy:* Conduct counseling in private. Discuss measures used to keep results confidential.

    b. *Risk reduction:* Take the opportunity to review safer sex practices and reinforce the need for safer sex *regardless* of the outcome of the test.

    c. *Education:* Use the model of informed consent.

       (1) Discuss the indications for HIV testing in persons who use IV drugs or abuse mood-altering drugs, and review the nature of the test focusing on the patient's understanding of HIV infection and AIDS.

       (2) Explain that testing determines the presence or absence of antibodies, and discuss the concept of false positive and false negative results, as well as the meaning of indeterminate results.

       (3) Present the risk of having the HIV test by discussing the potential risk of discrimination if a positive result should be revealed.

       (4) Explore the psychologic impact a positive test might have. It may be better to defer testing until the patient can be counseled further.

       (5) Review the potential benefits.

       (6) For pregnant women, explain that a positive test implies a strong possibility (30% is a good estimate, based on several series of patients) that her unborn child will become infected. Explain also that pregnancy may hasten the progression of HIV disease.

       (7) Reinforce the decision for testing, because early diagnosis can lead to appropriate medical care.

2. ***If patient agrees to the test, conduct the following procedure:***

    a. Document informed consent by signed consent form (or by progress note in the medical record).

    b. Schedule a follow-up appointment to discuss test results.

    c. Disclosure of test results via telephone is strongly discouraged.

3. **Post-test, negative result:** Reinforce safe sex guidelines and recommend repeat testing in 6 months if patient continues with IV drug use and at-risk sexual practices.

4. **Post-test, positive result** ("POSST,"*P*rivacy, *o*ptimism, *s*uicide, *s*upport, *t*ransmission):

    a. *Privacy:* Answer questions regarding how family, friends, coworkers, and health care providers should be informed of the positive results.

    b. *Optimism:* Reassure patient that his or her life is not over. Offer hope that HIV does not progress to AIDS in everyone and that life-prolonging treatments are available. Reiterate that in addition to medical evaluation and treatment, the patient can promote health via exercise, adequate rest, diet, and smoking cessation.

    c. *Suicide:* Assess emotional impact, including risk of suicide. Because of emotional distress, much of the following information on support and transmission may need to be repeated at a later time.

d. *Support:* Discuss potential need for counseling. Facilitate the process by suggesting a specific counselor or making an appointment with a mental health care professional. Consider sociocultural and sexual preference factors when selecting a counselor.

e. *Transmission:* Review safe sex guidelines and need for adherence to protect self and others. Encourage the patient to inform others who may be at risk (i.e., sex partners or persons with whom they Answer questions regarding the need for infection precautions in the home and work place. Explain that persons testing positive are prohibited by law from donating blood, body organs, other tissue, semen, or breast milk, and that to do so is a felony.

5. ***Other issues:*** Explain next step(s) in medical evaluation, initiating this during the visit in order to demonstrate to the patient that action is being taken to control this infection. Address denial, if present, to remove obstacles to seeking further care.

D. Special and Controversial Issues

The American Society of Addiction Medicine developed and adopted the following public policy statement on the treatment of patients with alcoholism or other drug dependencies and who have or are at risk for AIDS:

1. ***Needle exchange program:***

a. May reduce transmission of HIV among IV drug users by limiting needle and syringe sharing.

b. While there is a theoretical risk that greater availability of needles and syringes will increase drug use, in countries such as Australia and in western Europe there is no evidence to support this concern.

c. In countries where needle exchange has been tried, it seems to have found adequate levels of acceptance among IV drug users.

d. Its efficacy at reducing transmission of HIV is difficult to measure.

E. Risk to Health Care Professionals Who Care for Patients with Alcohol and Drug Disorders Who are Infected With HIV

Physicians and other health care professionals frequently care for persons who are alcohol or drug dependent, some of whom are either HIV positive or are at significant risk. While the risk to health care providers is low, we need to be aware of methods we can use to minimize our exposure risk.

1. ***General information on risk of occupational exposure:*** Current evidence suggests that the risk of HIV infection following a single percutaneous exposure to HIV-infected blood is approximately 1 in 250.

a. The risk of HIV infection following mucous membrane or skin exposure is less than that after percutaneous exposure.

b. The risk of infection seems to be relatively less with smaller amounts of blood than with larger amounts.

c. It also seems to be less when the HIV source patient is asymptomatic, as compared with exposure to blood from a patient with severe symptoms or AIDS.

2. ***What is a significant exposure?***
   a. Percutaneous injury (e.g., a needle stick or cut with a sharp object).
   b. Contact with mucous membranes.
   c. Contact of nonintact skin with blood tissues or fluids to which Universal Precautions apply.
   d. Fluids to which Universal Precautions apply include blood, semen, cerebrospinal fluid, vaginal secretions, synovial fluid, peritoneal fluid, pericardial fluid, pleural fluid, amniotic fluid, breast milk.
   e. Fluids to which Universal Precautions do not apply include tears, saliva, sweat, urine, feces, nasal secretions, sputum, vomitus. If these fluids have visible contamination with blood, they should be handled using Universal Precautions.

3. ***Health care professionals exposure:*** Does prophylactic treatment with zidovudine reduce the risk of infection?
   a. As shown by animal studies, zidovudine may prevent the development of HIV infection in persons exposed to the virus if treatment is begun after exposure.
   b. No benefit from zidovudine was found in animals who received zidovudine more than 1 week after exposure.
   c. Various regimens have been proposed, ranging from 100 mg every 4 hours five times daily to 200 mg every 4 hours six times daily. Treatment for 4 to 6 weeks is common.
   d. As data are inadequate to support or refute efficacy. Data are lacking to suggest the optimal therapeutic regimen.
   e. Although generally fairly well tolerated for short-term therapy, zidovudine has been reported to cause fever, myalgia, fatigue, nausea, vomiting, anemia, reversible peripheral neuropathy, and transient clinical hepatitis. The long-term toxicity and possible teratogenicity or carcinogenicity of a short course of zidovudine are unknown.

4. ***Management of an occupational exposure within chemical dependency treatment unit:***
   a. Record date and time of exposure.
   b. Describe job being performed by worker.
   c. Summarize details of exposure, including amount of fluid or material, type of fluid or material, and severity of exposure (e.g., depth of injury and whether fluid was injected, extent and duration of skin contract, condition of exposed skin).
   d. Document counseling performed, post-exposure management, and follow-up.

5. ***Overview of issues surrounding HIV testing and results:*** The best source for answers to the following issues is the local public health department.
   a. Reporting of HIV positivity is variable from state to state.

b. All states require reporting of AIDS.

c. Must informed consent be obtained before testing?

d. If reportable, is this anonymous or confidential?

e. May sexual or needle-sharing contacts be notified?

f. Is it mandatory that sexual or needle-sharing contact be notified?

III. **Pertinent Clinical Information in Patient with Alcohol or Drug Disorder and HIV**

Providers who care for alcohol- and drug-dependent patients need to be able to conduct a comprehensive history and physical in those patients who are also infected with the AIDS virus. It is important for providers to be able to recognize and deal with medical issues associated with HIV infection.

A. **Patient Interview**

1. *Present illness:* Symptoms followed by an asterisk may require urgent evaluation:

a. *General:* Fever*, night sweats, unexplained weight loss, fatigue.

b. *Dermatologic:* New rashes or lesions on skin or in mouth.

c. *Nodes:* Location, duration, pain.

d. *Pulmonary:* cough*, dyspnea*.

e. *GI:* Odynophagia or diarrhea, and if present, frequency and characteristics.

f. *Heme:* Easy bleeding or bruising.

g. *Neurologic:* Headache*, altered vision*, altered cognition*, paresthesias*.

2. *Past medical history:* Problems that predated the alcohol or drug dependence and HIV infection may have important consequences both in determining the length of time for asymptomatic infection and in the course of the AIDS disease itself. Important information includes a past history of:

a. *Infectious diseases,* such as tuberculosis, positive PPD, hepatitis, syphilis and other sexually transmitted disease, herpes simplex or zoster.

b. *Neurologic disease,* such as seizures, memory or cognitive impairment, peripheral nerve damage.

c. *Pulmonary disease,* such as asthma, emphysema, chronic bronchitis.

3. *Social history:*

a. *Support network:* Does patient have family or friends who are aware of the diagnosis (and life-style, if pertinent) who can help with care?

b. *Legal concerns,* such as power of attorney.

c. *Practicing safe sex* should reduce risk of other infections that could hasten progress of HIV infection.

B. **Physical Findings**

1. *Vital signs:* Changes in weight, temperature, and respiratory rate may be the first sign of AIDS. Mild tachypnea is an early sign of *Pneumocystis* pneumonia (as well as other respiratory problems).

2. **Skin:** HIV-infected patients are prone to a host of skin ailments, including the following. Questionable lesions should be biopsied.
   a. *Herpes zoster* in a young person.
   b. *Severe seborrheic dermatitis* (especially facial).
   c. *Kaposi sarcoma:* lesions characteristically are brownish purple nodules with a faint yellowish halo in surrounding skin, but vary greatly. May begin as flat, pink macules.
   d. *Coagulation disorders.*
   e. *Recurrent molluscum contagiosum,* especially facial.
   f. *Recurrent herpes simplex,* especially perianal.
   g. *Recurrent dermatomycosis.*
3. **Eyes:** Fundi should be examined initially to document preexisting lesions.
   a. *Cotton wool spots:* White patches on retina, represent local ischemia.
   b. *Hemorrhages and exudates:* May be retinitis due to CMV or other agent(s).
   c. *If patient is febrile,* examination with the pupils dilated must be done to look for evidence of retinitis, with ophthalmologic referral if hemorrhages or exudates are present.
4. **Mouth:** A common site of disease, including:
   a. *Candida:* Confluent white plaques on an erythematous base, often found on the dorsum of tongue, palate, and buccal mucosa.
   b. *Hairy leukoplakia:* White epithelium, usually found on the lateral margins of the tongue, which cannot be removed by scraping and is thought to represent Epstein-Barr virus or papillomavirus infection. This waxes and wanes and is rarely symptomatic. Acyclovir can be used to treat.
   c. *Kaposi sarcoma:* Purple raised lesions, often found on palate or along gingiva. May begin as flat, pink macule.
   d. *Aphthous ulcers:* Very common. Treatment has variable success. The most effective treatment may be the topical steroid in methylcellulose gel (e.g., triamcinolone 0.1% in Ora-Base gel).
   e. *Herpes stomatitis:* May have typical vesicles, though diagnosis rests on culture and/or Tzanck smear. Treat with acyclovir 200 mg five times/day; increase dosage or long-term suppression as needed.
   f. *Angular stomatitis:* Redness and/or fissuring at corners of mouth.
5. **Lymph nodes:** Nodes greater than 1 cm in two or more extrainguinal sites persisting 3 months or more without identifiable cause in the setting of the HIV infection is persistent generalized lymphadenopathy (PGL).
6. **Chest:** Normal auscultation is common in early *Pneumocystis* pneumonia, and in the presence of a persistent dry cough should not be taken as adequate reassurance.
7. **Central nervous system:** Subtle cognitive deficits are common,

even early in HIV infection, and may go unrecognized by the patient. A mental status examination may be indicated.

C. Laboratory Examination

1. ***Initial evaluation*** should include the following laboratory tests:
   a. Complete blood cell count with differential and platelet count.
   b. Erythrocyte sedimentation rate.
   c. Urinalysis.
   d. SMAC (including lactic dehydrogenase, aspartate and alanine transaminase values).
   e. VDRL.
   f. T cell subsets.
   g. Hepatitis B surface antigen.
   h. PPD (if no history of positive reaction).
   i. Chest x-ray examination.
   j. Consider arterial blood gas (ABG) and/or carbon monoxide diffusing capacity (DLCO) if past history of tobacco use or other pulmonary disease, as baseline for future comparison.
   k. Other tests as directed by symptoms.
   l. *Toxoplasma* titer.
2. ***Periodic laboratory surveillance*** of asymptomatic patients should be performed every 2 to 6 months. These tests should include a complete blood cell count with differential and platelet count, SMAC, and T cell subsets.
3. ***Tests of little diagnostic value in HIV-infected patients*** include CMV antibody titers and CMV stool culture.

BIBLIOGRAPHY

Morbidity and Mortality Weekly Report (MMWR), published by the CDC, provides the most current statistical information regarding HIV infection and AIDS. Much of the epidemiologic information in this chapter was taken from MMWR, (not listed in separate references).

National AIDS Clearinghouse (PO Box 6003, Rockville, MD 20850; 1-800-458-5231) is another valuable resource for up-to-date information and referral.

Chaisson RE, et al: Cocaine use and HIV infection in intravenous drug users in San Francisco. *JAMA* 1989; 261:561–565.

Cohen PT, et al (eds): *The AIDS Knowledge Base: A Textbook on HIV Disease From the University of California, San Francisco, and the San Francisco General Hospital.* Waltham, Mass, Massachusetts Medical Society, 1990.

Gayle HD, et al: Seroprevalence rates of human immunodeficiency virus among university students. *N Engl J Med* 1990; 323:1538–1541.

Hahn RA: Prevalence of HIV infection among intravenous drug users in the United States. *JAMA* 1989; 261:2677–2684.

HIV/AIDS Surveillance Report, Jan 1991.

Karan LD: Primary care for AIDS and chemical dependence. *West J Med* 1990; 152:538–542,

Kaslow RA, et al: No evidence for a role of alcohol or other psychoactive drugs in accelerating immunodeficiency in HIV-1 positive individuals: A report from the multicenter AIDS cohort study. *JAMA* 1989; 261:3424–3429.

Kirn TF: Drug abuse: More help available for addicted persons, but main problem continues unabated. *JAMA* 1988; 260:2170–2171.

MacGregor RR: Alcohol and immune defense. *JAMA* 1986; 256:1474–1478.

Raymond CA: Combating a deadly combination: Intravenous drug abuse, acquired immunodeficiency syndrome. *JAMA* 1988; 259:329–332.

Raymond CA: Study of IV drug users and AIDS finds differing infection rate, risk behaviors. *JAMA* 1988; 260:3105.

St Louis ME, et al: Seroprevalence rates of human immunodeficiency virus infection at sentinel hospitals in the United States. *N Engl J Med* 1990; 323:213–218.

Ward JW, Holmberg DS, Allen JR, et al: Transmission of human immunodeficiency virus (HIV) by blood transfusions screened as negative for HIV antibody. *N Engl J Med* 1988; 318:473–478.

Weiss SH: Links between cocaine and retroviral infection (editorial). *JAMA* 1989; 261:607–608.

Wilford BB (ed): *Syllabus for the Review Course in Addiction Medicine*. Washington, DC, American Society of Addiction Medicine, 1990.

CHAPTER 20

Gambling Disorders

Robert M. Politzer, M.S., Sc.D

Clark J. Hudak, M.S.W., Ph.D.

Gambling, or wagering on the outcome of an event of which we have little or no control has become a mainstay of American culture. Gambling behavior ranges from young persons playing monopoly and substituting pennies for play money to persons wagering on sports outcomes through bookies with money borrowed from the underworld. People who gamble range from those who experience innocent pleasures from a few hours of playing poker with the boys to those who gamble in the face of great harm to themselves and their families. This chapter focuses on those gamblers who are considered problem gamblers. What distinguishes problem gamblers from others who wager on outcomes beyond their control and skill is that wagering is harmful to the problem gambler. Problem gamblers can be people who are highly mature, well organized, and successful as well as in those who have had legal, social, and emotional problems all their adult lives.

I. Understanding the Problem
A. Pathologic Gambling
1. *Definition:* A gambling disorder is defined as progressive inability to control gambling in spite of serious adverse consequences.
2. *Problem gambling:* The dynamic and developmental formulation of problem gambling is reflected in the new DSM-IV (Diagnostic and Statistical Manual, ed 4) criteria, which provide an expanded set of criteria for diagnostic assessment. We encourage the reader to think of this pathologic behavior on a gradient of severity with many underlying causes producing a range of gambling disorders.

B. Role of Primary Care Provider
It is important for the primary care provider to become familiar with pathologic gambling disorders for at least two reasons.
1. *Secondary illness:* There is high probability that afflicted individuals and their significant others frequently seek medical assistance for illnesses secondary to the gambling disorder. These medical prob-

lems are usually in the form of stress-related illnesses, further discussed later in this chapter.

2. *Referral sources:* Providers are often contacted for gambling treatment referral sources. In this regard, a significant other typically initiates the treatment process and views the primary care physician as a medical expert in whom to confide.

C. Prevalence

1. *Prevalence study:* The National Institute of Mental Health sponsored a prevalence study of pathologic gambling in New York, New Jersey, Maryland, and Iowa. The results of the telephone interviews using the South Oaks Gambling Screen (Fig 20–1) produced reliable and comparable estimates of prevalence for these states. Of the adult population, 1.5% were classified as pathologic gamblers, and an additional 2.5% were considered problem gamblers (Volberg and Steadman, 1989).

2. *Increase in prevalence:* A review of the literature produces evidence that the prevalence of pathologic gambling has increased in the last 15 years, along with the proliferation of legalized gambling.

   a. In 1974, 61% of the US adult population gambled, wagering more than $17 billion legally (Commission on the Review of the National Policy Toward Gambling, 1976). In 1986, $166.7 billion was wagered (Christiansen, 1987), an increase of almost 950%.

   b. Conservative estimates by law enforcement officials suggest that three to five times as much is bet illegally on sports events and betting with bookmakers (Lorenz, 1988).

3. *Magnitude of problem:* Except for alcohol, the prevalence of pathologic gambling exceeds that of any abused substance. The nation has witnessed a dramatic increase in various types of legalized gambling in recent years with the advent of state lotteries and casinos. It should be mentioned that the proliferation of illegal gambling contributes to the growing number of addicted gamblers, although this component is difficult to measure.

4. *Precision of telephone studies:* Assessing pathologic gambling prevalence over the telephone, particularly when illegal activities are present, is far less precise than assessment of the prevalence of other disorders. The lack of corroborating information from family members enhances the probability of denial.

D. Economic and Social Costs

1. *Direct and indirect costs:* Economic costs of illness and disease are classified as direct and indirect (Rice et al., 1985).

   a. Direct costs are those dollars lost to gambling as well as those spent by society for prevention (both primary and secondary), detection, and treatment.

   b. Indirect costs are defined as those resulting from lost productivity, measured as income foregone, and are divided into productivity lost due to morbidity and to mortality. The costs of pathologic gambling have been estimated earlier (Politzer et al., 1981). Since

---

South Oaks Gambling Screen*

Name _____   **Date** _____

1. Please indicate which of the following types of gambling you have done in your lifetime.
   For each type, mark one answer: Not at all, "Less than once a week, "Once a week or more."

		Not At All	Less Than Once a Week	Once a Week or More
a.	Play cards for money...............................	❏	❏	❏
b.	Bet on horses, dogs, or other animals (at .... the track or with bookie)	❏	❏	❏
c.	Bet on sports (parlay cards, with bookie, or............. Jai Alai)	❏	❏	❏
d.	Played dice games (including craps, over and........... under, or other dice games) for money	❏	❏	❏
e.	Went to casino (legal or otherwise)..................	❏	❏	❏
f.	Played the numbers or bet on lotteries................	❏	❏	❏
g.	Played bingo.......................................	❏	❏	❏
h.	Played the stock and/or commodities market............	❏	❏	❏
i.	Played slot machines, poker machines, or other gambling machines			
j.	Bowled, shot pool, played golf or some other............. game of skill for money	❏	❏	❏

2. What is the largest amount of money you have ever gambled with on any one day?

   ❏ Never have gambled.   ❏ More than $100 up to $1,000.
   ❏ $1 or less.   ❏ More than $1,000 up to $10,000.
   ❏ More than $10 up to $100.   ❏ More than $10,000.

3. Do (did) your parents have gambling problem?

   ❏ Both my father and mother gamble(d) too much.
   ❏ My father gambles (gambled) too much.
   ❏ My mother gambles (gambled) too much.

FIG 20–1.
Self-administered screening and diagnostic instrument. As noted on the scoring sheet, patients with a score of 5 or more likely are pathologic gamblers.

4. When you gamble, how often do you go back another day to win back money you lost?
   - ❏ Never.
   - ❏ Some of the time (less than half the times I lose).
   - ❏ Most of the times I lose.
   - ❏ Every time I lose.

5. Have you ever claimed to be winning money gambling but weren't really? In fact, you lost?
   - ❏ Never (or never gamble).
   - ❏ Yes, less than half the times I lost.
   - ❏ Yes, most of the time.

6. Do you feel you ever had a problem with gambling?
   - ❏ No.
   - ❏ Yes in the past but not now.
   - ❏ Yes.

7. Did you ever gamble more than you intended to? . . . . ❏ Yes ❏ No

8. Have people criticized your gambling?. . . . . ❏ Yes ❏ No

9. Have you ever felt guilty about the way you gamble or what. . . . .❏ Yes ❏ No
   happens when you gamble?

10. Have you ever felt like you would like to stop gambling but. . . . . ❏ Yes ❏ No
    didn't think you could?

11. Have you ever hidden betting slips, lottery tickets gambling . . . .❏ Yes ❏ No
    money, or other signs of gambling from your spouse, children,
    or other important people in your life?

12. Have you ever argued with people you live with over how you . . . .❏ Yes ❏ No
    handle money?

13. (If you answered yes to question 12): Have money arguments . . . .❏ Yes ❏ No
    ever centered on your gambling?

14. Have you ever borrowed from someone and not paid them. . . . . ❏ Yes ❏ No
    back as a result of your gambling?

15. Have you ever lost time from work (or school) due to gambling? . . . .❏ Yes ❏ No

16. If you borrowed money to gamble or to pay gambling debts, who or where did you borrow
    from? (check "yes" or "no" for each):
a.	From household money	❏ Yes	❏ No
b.	From spouse	❏ Yes	❏ No
c.	From other relatives or in-laws	❏ Yes	❏ No
d.	From banks, loan companies, or credit unions	❏ Yes	❏ No
e.	From credit card	❏ Yes	❏ No
f.	From loan sharks	❏ Yes	❏ No
g.	Cashed stocks, bonds, or other securities	❏ Yes	❏ No
h.	Sold personal or family property	❏ Yes	❏ No
i.	Borrowed on checking account (passed bad checks)	❏ Yes	❏ No
j.	Have (had) a credit line with bookie	❏ Yes	❏ No
k.	Have (had) a credit line with a casino	❏ Yes	❏ No

FIG 20–1 (cont.).

South Oaks Gambling Score Sheet

Scores are determined by adding up the number of questions with an "at risk " response.

Questions 1, 2, & 3 not counted.

❏ Question 4: Most of the times I lose or every time I lose.

❏ Question 5: Yes, less than half the times I lost, or Yes, most of the time.

❏ Question 6: Yes, in the past but not now, or Yes.

❏ Question 7: Yes.

❏ Question 8: Yes.

❏ Question 9: Yes.

❏ Question 10: Yes.

❏ Question 11: Yes.

Question 12 not counted.

❏ Question 13: Yes.

❏ Question 14: Yes.

❏ Question 15: Yes.

❏ Question 16a: Yes.

❏ Question 16b: Yes.

❏ Question 16c: Yes.

❏ Question 16d: Yes.

❏ Question 16e: Yes.

❏ Question 16f: Yes.

❏ Question 16g: Yes.

❏ Question 16h: Yes.

❏ Question 16i: Yes.

Question j and k not counted.

❏ Total (20 questions are counted)

❏ 0 = no problem; 1-4 = some problem; 5 or more = probable pathologic gambler.

*From South Oaks Foundation, Amityville, NY, 1986. Used by permission.

FIG 20−1 (cont.).

much of the pathologic gamblers' working hours are channeled toward gambling (e.g., they are either at the track, on the phone, or studying the racing forms, rather than working), lost productivity can be a serious economic cost.

2. ***Estimates of cost:*** Researchers have updated the total cost estimate from $20,000 per pathologic gambler per year in 1980 to about $30,000 in 1988 dollars. The total cost estimate is a combination of the productivity lost on the part of the gambler in 1 year and the total resources gambled in 1 year (Politzer et al., 1981). When these components are corrected for inflation, the 1988 estimate is conservatively increased to $30,000 per year. With the conservative 1.5% of the total population, or 2.7 million pathologic gamblers at an average cost of $30,000 per gambler, pathologic gambling cost society about $80 billion in 1988.

3. ***Social cost:*** This cost estimate is considered conservative, because we have not included costs such as suicide attempts, family neglect, incarceration, or other health problems resulting from pathologic gambling. Recent estimates of the costs of alcoholism, substance abuse, and mental illness (Department of Health and Human Services, 1987) account for such social costs as crime, social welfare programs, and property damage from motor vehicle accidents. We have maintained a conservative approach to estimating the cost of pathologic gambling to facilitate cost comparisons *by component* with physical illnesses and diseases.

4. ***Financial cost:*** Obtaining alcohol is relatively inexpensive compared with obtaining money to gamble. Pathologic gamblers tap their own resources and deplete those available to their families, then con money from many different sources. From 10 to 17 individuals may be affected by a single pathologic gambler (Lesieur, 1984). Their addictive behavior requires that they get money from any and all available sources. Therefore pathologic gambling becomes a cost borne by the victims and employers of the addicted gamblers.

5. ***Family costs:*** The damage inflicted on the institution of the family and the obligations of parenthood may be overwhelming, as shown by research in recent years.
   a. Shame, concealment, and guilt were followed by breakdown in communication, trust, and support.
   b. Anger and resentment were among the negative emotions on the part of the gambler's spouse.
   c. Sexual relationship between the couples suffered.
   d. Parenting obligations were neglected.
   e. Fifty-nine percent of couples had considered separating. Thirty-three percent of couples separated but have since reconciled. The series of stressful events was associated with depression and psychosomatic symptoms. The institution of the family and its sociopsychologic health were found to have been seriously impaired (Lorenz and Yaffee, 1986, 1988, 1989).

II. Diagnosis
A. Classification of Gamblers

Four types of gamblers commonly are described: social, professional, criminal, and pathologic gamblers.

1. *Social or recreational gamblers:*
   a. Players who gamble with friends, mainly on special occasions and with predetermined acceptable losses, are categorized as social gamblers. While they may gamble heavily or often, they define a fixed limit to their losses.
   b. The primary difference between social and pathologic gamblers is that social gamblers stop when losses become too painful. The fact that they realize gambling is a recreation gives them the understanding that the escape is temporary and that life's responsibilities must be resumed. Social gamblers do not allow gambling to interfere with their lives.

2. *Professional gamblers:*
   a. The primary income is from gambling. Gambling is their business, their livelihood. Like social gamblers, professional gamblers know their limits. They get satisfaction from winning, not from the action.
   b. They study the game, the odds. Thus, while their talent is their ability to estimate probabilities in games (e.g., card counter), they are also able to "fold" accordingly. Their homework is to study their losses, not be destroyed by them. Their level of self-esteem is high and does not depend on gambling.

3. *Criminal gamblers:*
   a. Criminal gamblers are people with antisocial personality characteristics. In contrast to pathologic gamblers, they do not intend to repay money obtained illegally.
   b. Criminal gamblers have a sociopathic lifestyle and will go to any extreme to win. When they lose, they often feel victimized and resort to blaming and even violence. The rarely feel remorse or guilt, therefore rarely experience depression, as do pathologic gamblers.

4. *Pathological gamblers:* The antisocial criminal gambler can be differentiated from the pathologic gambler by the associated features of antisocial behavior.
   a. This differentiation is particularly important to treatment and to the judicial process. In the criminal gambler, sociopathy represents the true character of the individual. With pathologic gambling, antisocial behavior typically occurs as a means of obtaining funds to gamble. Such crimes as forgery, theft, fraud, and embezzlement are atypical of the pathologic gambler's true character.
   b. Pathologic gamblers intend to repay the illegally obtained money. The criminal gambler feels a sense of entitlement and has no such intention.

    c. A detailed and accurate psychosocial history, focusing on the chronology of symptomatic antisocial behavior, is necessary to make the distinction between pathologic and criminal gambling. To make a diagnosis of antisocial personality disorder, the existence of adolescent sociopathy that continues into adulthood is paramount. Antisocial behavior that appeared after the onset of the gambling behavior can be considered a corollary of the disorder rather than a primary disorder.

    d. Other psychiatric symptoms, such as anxiety and depression, may be either corollary manifestations of the gambling disorder or components of primary affective disorders.

B. Diagnostic Criteria for a Pathologic Gambling Disorder

Pathologic gambling has been classified in the DSM-III-R manual as an impulse control disorder. The following criteria must be met for a diagnosis of a pathologic gambling disorder. Maladaptive gambling behavior is indicated by at least four of the following (American Psychiatric Association, 1987):

1. Frequent preoccupation with gambling or with obtaining money to gamble.
2. Frequent gambling of larger amounts of money or over a longer time than intended.
3. Need to increase the size or frequency of bets to achieve the desired excitement.
4. Restlessness or irritability if unable to gamble.
5. Repeated loss of money by gambling and returning another day to win back losses ("chasing").
6. Repeated efforts to reduce or stop gambling.
7. Frequent gambling when expected to meet social or occupational obligations.
8. Sacrifice of some important social, occupational, or recreational activity to gamble.
9. Continuation of gambling despite inability to pay mounting debts or despite other important social, occupational, or legal problems that the person knows to be exacerbated by gambling.

C. Chronicity and Progression

Essential features in diagnosing pathologic gambling are chronicity and progressiveness. More closely defined, this means that gambling persists over a long time, with increased amounts of money wagered and with psychologic dependency on the game.

1. ***Quantity and frequency:*** These are relative terms in that the absolute and cumulative amounts of money wagered and lost do not solely determine the presence of the disorder. Rather, the amounts relative to what the individual can "afford," along with the priority of, preoccupation with, and dependence on gambling are the diagnostic criteria.
2. ***Desperation:*** Typically, pathologic gamblers will gamble until their

last dollar is gone, and even beyond. They will exhaust all possible lending options, and often resort to loan sharks and other illegal sources to obtain money to gamble. In their most desperate phase, they may commit criminal acts, such as forgery, fraud, or embezzlement. Pathologic gamblers chronically default on debts and other financial responsibilities and are unable to account for losses of money or produce evidence of winning money, if claimed. They lose time from work due to gambling bouts, and they usually have diminished work productivity. Family life and spouse relationships are severely impaired because of the chronic indebtedness and the pervasive dishonesty.

3. ***Complications and associated features*** include:
   a. Anxiety, depression, psychosomatic illnesses, suicidal behavior, substance abuse, and other symptoms of personal stress.
   b. Many pathologic gamblers have reported some form of sexual dysfunction, such as inhibited sexual desire and inhibited sexual response.

4. ***Characteristics*** of pathologic gamblers:
   a. They are generally friendly, gregarious, and engaging persons who are usually self-serving. They are frequently intellectually bright, successful, and hard working.
   b. They may be highly competitive (often having a history of athletic involvement), easily bored, and constantly in search of stimulation, appearing overconfident and even abrasive. When their drives for immediate gratification are not met they become demanding, volatile, restless, and irritable.
   c. Their high energy levels, low tolerance for frustration and boredom, and need for psychologic escape predispose them to crave the action, challenge, and competition for gambling.

D. Sociodemographics

Pathologic gambling affects persons at all socioeconomic levels. Based on data of those having sought treatment, the disorder has affected more men than women (about 80% of cases are male). However, a significant increase in female addiction has been reported in recent years. This change may be attributed to the increased accessibility of legal gambling and the larger numbers of women in the work force, with more access to money and credit. There do not appear to be any racial differences in the prevalence of gambling disorders.

E. Forms of Gambling

While all forms of gambling are abused, pathologic gamblers tend to choose games over which they think they have some control, such as sports betting, where the odds can be studied. Lotteries and illegal numbers are games that allow the least amount of predictability and therefore are the least prevalent.

III. Etiology
  #### A. Family Background
  Clinically, most pathologic gamblers are reported to be products of childhood family dysfunction. More often than not, they have lost a parent, either through death, separation, divorce, or desertion, especially before the age 15 years. Inappropriate parental discipline also is common, often manifested by inconsistency and harshness.

  1. *Role model:* Exposure to gambling by a significant adult role model during adolescence usually precedes early onset of the disorder.
  2. *Value of materialism:* Of particular importance is a high family value on materialistic and financial symbols. This focus is often coupled with a lack of family emphasis on saving, planning, and budgeting.
  3. *Family patterns:* Research shows the predominance of either pathologic gambling or alcoholism in the fathers of male gamblers and the mothers of female gamblers, supporting the etiologic perspective of role modeling (Maryland Task Force on Gambling Addiction, 1991).

  #### B. Addiction Theory
  1. *Similarities to alcohol and drug disorders:* The more accepted notion among contemporary research is that pathologic gambling is an addiction with similar psychologic underpinnings as those associated with alcohol and drug disorders (Blume, 1987; Custer and Milt, 1984; Jacobs, 1986). Of interest, though, is that the DSM-III-R lists pathologic gambling under the category of "Impulse Control Disorders." Close scrutiny of the diagnostic criteria for pathologic gambling, however, reflects strong similarities to those of alcohol and drug abuse and dependence categorized elsewhere in the DSM-III-R. These similarities include:
     a. Preoccupation with the behavior and increasing "doses" (amounts and frequency of betting).
     b. Tolerance (the need for increased betting to achieve the desired psychologic effect).
     c. Withdrawal (discomfort if unable to gamble).
     d. Loss of control; unsuccessful efforts to cut down or stop gambling.
     e. Social or personal irresponsibility: gambling despite conflicting social expectations, important activities, or negative consequences (Blume, 1987; Jacobs, 1986).
  2. *Specific characteristics:* Unlike chemical addiction, pathologic gambling is considered the purest form of a psychologic addiction, because no external substances are ingested (Custer et al., 1975). Most clinicians and researchers agree that the gambler's addiction is to the action of the game (the time preoccupied with, anticipating, and actually gambling). Custer, for example, believes that the pathologic gambler's motive is to minimize psychologic discomfort, that is, anxiety or depression. The action therefore provides emotional and

psychologic relief. Eventually, winning and losing (the outcome) become secondary to the action, and winning is only a means for continuance.

IV. Management
A. Screening and Diagnosis
1. *Suggested screening questions:* Health care providers may want to use the following five questions for initial screening:
   a. Do you bet on horses, dogs, or other animals, either at a track or through a bookie?
   b. What is the largest amount of money you have ever gambled with on any given day?
   c. Do your parents have a gambling problem?
   d. Do you ever gamble more than you intend to?
   e. Have you ever felt like you would like to stop gambling but didn't think you could?
2. *Assessment instrument:* The South Oaks gambling test (see Fig. 20–1) was developed by Dr. Sheila Blume, and is an effective instrument to detect a gambling problem. It is considered a reliable and valid instrument used for both screening and diagnosis.

B. Patient Resistance to Treatment
1. *Denial:* Whether the approach is professional or self-help, the gambler's resistance to treatment is the foremost obstacle to overcome. Similar in other addictions, this is the dynamic of denial. The motivation for treatment usually stems from severe financial crises, legal complications, and pressures from family, friends, or significant others. The treatment process therefore often begins with crisis intervention, usually by telephone and most often with a third party.
2. *Engaging gambler in treatment:* A critical aspect of the early treatment phase is to educate those involved or affected, including the gambler, about the chronic and progressive nature of the disorder and therefore the need for help. Once this difficult task is accomplished and the gambler is engaged, clinical intervention can follow.

C. Initial Treatment
1. *Once a patient is willing to accept help,* treatment is directed at:
   a. Alleviating any further psychiatric crises.
   b. Further educating the individual about the disorder.
   c. Reconstruction of the characteristic disease underlying the impulsivity and nature of the disorder.
      (1) Psychopharmacologic treatment could prove effective in stabilizing the patient in crisis.
      (2) Fast-acting antianxiety agents or antidepressants are useful in the early phases of treatment, but should be used only in severe psychiatric emergencies.
      (3) Suicidal precautions should be taken in this early treatment phase.

(4) Once treatment is under way, medication should be reevaluated, particularly in regard to a clinical picture of a primary affective disorder or anxiety state.

2. ***Early education:***
   a. Emphasize that the gambling compulsion can be placed in remission, that impending urges will persist, and that abstinence is necessary. Hence the real "cure" will come from learning how to control the urges.
   b. For a permanent arrest of the gambling behavior, treatment of the characteristic pathology is essential.

3. ***Interpersonal conflicts:***
   a. With the devastating effects on the marriage and family, intervention with marital, family, or group therapy is necessary. Marital and family intervention should focus on rebuilding the trust that has been destroyed.
   b. Various communication techniques should be stressed, including assertiveness training.

4. ***Financial counseling*** is instrumental in the recovery process. Since the dollar is the "substance" abused, most gamblers who come for treatment have some degree of indebtedness. If ignored, indebtedness creates additional anxiety and perpetuates the disorder. Therefore a solid and realistic financial and budgetary plan is necessary to teach the gambler responsibility, organization, control, and limit setting.
   a. Recommend that a spouse or significant other assume responsibility for family checking and savings accounts.
   b. *Most important in financial counseling is the prerequisite that the gambler make restitution of incurred debts.* The aim is to teach gamblers to assume responsibility for their action (indebtedness) and to avoid any further bailouts (i.e., money gamblers receive from a third party to either stake their continued gambling or cover a prior debt).

5. ***Occupational counseling:*** Most pathologic gamblers who have sought treatment have experienced some degree of job dissatisfaction or conflict. Often their jobs are in jeopardy because of lost time and diminished productivity related to bouts of gambling. Direct intervention with supervisors or employers is helpful to educate them about the disorder. If an individual is occupationally dissatisfied, career counseling and placement can be helpful.

D. Treatment Programs

To realize treatment, inpatient or residential care is critical. This intervention is hindered because either treatment is not available or it is financially unfeasible. In these instances, Gamblers Anonymous (GA) is appropriately referred, and is a proved treatment method. Ideally, GA plus professional care is the preferred approach.

1. ***Gamblers Anonymous:***

The most available treatment option is GA. Started in 1957, GA has grown to more than 700 chapters in the United States, also is located in nearly 20 foreign countries, including Australia, Israel, and Argentina.

2. ***GamAnon*** is a fellowship for the families and friends of compulsive gamblers. It was founded on spiritual principles, and has a 12-Step recovery program. GamAnon members learn to cope with the problems created by compulsive gambling.

3. ***National Council on Problem Gambling*** is a national clearinghouse for treatment programs that disperses information about the problem. The National Council is located in New York, and state chapters are beginning to emerge.

4. ***Inpatient treatment:*** Professional help is a second option, and differs from GA in its treatment strategies. Inpatient programs are more often integrated in alcohol and drug addiction units of psychiatric hospital. This option should be considered when a patient is suicidally depressed or so out of control that 24-hour medical supervision is necessary.

5. ***State-sponsored gambling treatment programs:*** Most often these programs are limited to outpatient counseling for the gambler and family members. New York, New Jersey, Connecticut, Massachusetts, Delaware, Ohio, and Iowa have allocated funds for gambling education and treatment. Iowa spent more than $1.5 million of its lottery proceeds for assistance to compulsive gamblers and the training of mental health professionals in 1989; New York spent $750,000. Maryland, the first state to grant such funds ($100,000 in 1978), has withdrawn its support for treatment. However, Maryland houses three private treatment programs: the Washington Center for Pathological Gambling in College Park, The National Center for Pathological Gambling in Baltimore, and Taylor Manor Hospital in Ellicott City.

BIBLIOGRAPHY

American Psychiatric Association: *Diagnostic and Statistical Manual of Mental Disorders,* ed 3, rev. Washington DC, American Psychiatric Association, 1987, pp 324–325.

Blume S: Compulsive gambling and the medical model. *J Gambling Behav* 1987; 3:237–247.

Christiansen EM: US gaming revenue tops $22 billion in '86: Up 8%. *Gaming Wagering Business* 1987; 8:1–20.

Commission on the Review of the National Policy Toward Gambling: Gambling in America: Final report 1976. Washington, DC, US Government Printing Office, 1976.

Custer RL, Glen A, Burns R: Characteristics of compulsive gambling. Paper presented at the 2nd Annual Conference on Gambling, Lake Tahoe, Nev, June 1975.

Custer RL, Milt H: *When Luck Runs Out.* New York, Facts on File Publications, 1984.

Department of Health and Human Services: Sixth special report to the US Congress on alcohol and health. DHHS Publ No (ADM)87-1519. Washington, DC, Jan 1987.

Jacobs D: A general theory of addictions: A new theoretical model. *J Gambling Behav* 1986; 2:15–31.

Lesieur HR: *The Chase: Career of the Compulsive Gambler.* Cambridge, Mass, Schenkman Books, 1984.

Lorenz VC, Yaffee RA: Compulsive gamblers and their spouses: A profile of interaction. *J Gambling Behav* 1989; 5:113–126.

Lorenz VC, Yaffee RA: Pathological gambling: Psychosomatic, emotional, and marital difficulties as reported by the spouse. *J Gambling Behav* 1988; 4:13–26.

Lorenz VC, Yaffee RA: Pathological gambling: Psychosomatic, emotional, and marital difficulties as reported by the gambler. *J Gambling Behav* 1986; 2:40–49.

Lorenz VC: An overview of pathological gambling. Draft paper prepared for testimony. National Center for Pathological Gambling, May 1988.

Maryland Task Force on Gambling Addiction 1991: Final report to the Secretary, 1991.

Politzer R, Morrow J: The Johns Hopkins compulsive gambling counseling center. Paper presented at the American Psychological Association, Montreal, Nov 1989.

Politzer RM, Morrow JS: Report on cost effectiveness of the compulsive gambling center. Presented to the Subcommittees on Health and the Environment, Appropriations Committee, House of Delegates, Maryland State Assembly, Feb 24, 1981.

Politzer R, Morrow J, Leavy S: Report on the societal cost of pathological gambling and the cost-benefit/effectiveness of treatment. The gambling papers: Proceedings of the 1981 Conference on Gambling, University of Nevada, Reno, 1981.

Rice D, Hodgson TA, Kopstein AN: The economic costs of illness: A replication and update. *Health Care Financ Rev* 1985; 7:61–80.

Volberg R, Steadman H: Developing an accurate profile of pathological gamblers. Interim Report to the National Institute of Mental Health, April 1989.

Appendixes

Terminology*

abstinence Nonuse of a specific substance. In recovery, nonuse of any addictive psychoactive substance. May also denote cessation of addictive or compulsive behavior (e.g., gambling, overeating).

abuse Harmful use of a specific psychoactive substance. The term also applies to one category of psychoactive substance use disorder. While recognizing that "abuse is part of present diagnostic terminology," the American Society of Addictive Medicine (ASAM) recommends that an alternative term be found for this purpose, because of the pejorative connotations of the word "abuse."

addiction Disease process characterized by continued use of a specific psychoactive substance despite physical, psychologic, or social harm.

addictionist Physician who specializes in addiction medicine.

Adult Children of Alcoholics (ACOA) Lay self-help groups intended to provide support and guidance to adults whose parents were alcohol or drug dependent. Most follow a specific set of beliefs popularized by a group of authors who suggest that growing up in alcoholic households predisposes children to grow into adults with specific problems in self-esteem and difficulty with interpersonal relationships. They do not necessarily cover the same topics or present ideas that are similar to Alanon and Alateen.

Alanon Lay self-help organizations intended to provide support and guidance for family members of alcohol- and drug-dependent persons or anyone else whose life has been affected by someone's alcohol or drug problem. The meetings are patterned after the 12-Step process of Alcoholics Anonymous, and often involve mutual sharing of experiences and feelings. Some meetings offer special educational presentations by guest speakers; some are explicitly open to special groups such as nonsmokers, women, or men; and some follow the specific steps toward recovery. Meetings are often held in churches, schools, hospitals, or private businesses after hours. There is no formal charge to attend, but small donations are encouraged to cover costs of food and beverages.

Alateen Lay self-help organizations intended to provide support and guidance to adolescent family members of alcohol- and drug-dependent persons. Many are lead by young people who have had some experience in recovery pro-

*Reprinted in part from *ASAM News* 1990; Nov-Dec, p 9. Used by permission.

grams. Some have sponsoring organizations that provide support to the group. Frequently Alateen groups meet in schools or churches, with some participation by trained counselors.

alcohol and drug disorder   Term used to describe the whole spectrum of problems and illness associated with the adverse effects of mood-altering chemicals. Drug problems include illicit drug use and prescription drug addiction. The clinical syndromes of dependence and problematic use are considered alcohol and drug disorders.

alcoholism   Primary, chronic disease with genetic, psychosocial, and environmental factors influencing its development and manifestations. The disease often is progressive and fatal. It is characterized by continuous or periodic impaired control over drinking, preoccupation with the drug alcohol, use of alcohol despite adverse consequences, and distortions in thinking, most notably denial. (This definition was conceived by a joint ASAM/NCAdd committee; it was first published in *ASAM News* 1990; March-April p 1.)

blackout   Acute anterograde amnesia with no formation of long-term memory, resulting from the ingestion of alcohol or other drugs (i.e., period of memory loss for which there is no recall of activities).

co-dependence   Emotional, psychologic, and behavioral condition that develops as the result of prolonged exposure to and practice of a set of oppressive rules, rules that prevent the open expression of feeling as well as the direct discussion of personal and interpersonal problems

decriminalization   Removal of criminal penalties for the possession and use of illicit psychoactive substances.

dependence

physical dependence   Physiologic state of adaptation to a specific psychoactive substance, characterized by emergence of a withdrawal syndrome during abstinence, which may be relieved in total or in part by readministration of the substance;

psychologic dependence   Subjective sense of need for a specific psychoactive substance, either for its positive effects or to avoid negative effects associated with its absence. One category of psychoactive substance use disorder.

detoxification   Process of withdrawing a specific psychoactive substance in a safe and effective manner.

dual diagnosis   Diagnosis in patients who have persistant symptoms of mental illness after 3 to 6 months of abstinence and who are believed to have both a primary addictive disorder and a primary mental health disorder.

enabling   Any action by another person or institution that intentionally or unintentionally has the effect of facilitating the continuation of an individual's addictive process.

impairment   Dysfunctional state resulting from use of psychoactive substances.

intervention   Planned interaction with an individual who may be dependent on one or more psychoactive substances, with the aim of making a full assessment, overcoming denial, interrupting drug-taking behavior, or inducing the individual to initiate treatment. The preferred technique is to present facts regarding psychoactive substance use in a caring, believable, and understandable manner.

legalization Legal restriction of the cultivation, manufacture, distribution, possession, and/or use of a psychoactive substance.

loss of control Inability to consistently limit the self-administration of psychoactive substances.

problem drinking Informal term describing a pattern of drinking associated with life problems prior to establishing a definitive diagnosis of alcoholism. Also, umbrella term for any harmful use of alcohol, including alcoholism. ASAM recommends that the term not be used in this latter sense.

recovery Process of overcoming both physical and psychologic dependence on a psychoactive substance with a commitment to sobriety.

relapse Recurrence of psychoactive substance-dependent behavior in an individual who has previously achieved and maintained abstinence for a significant period of time beyond withdrawal.

sobriety State of complete abstinence from psychoactive substances by an addicted individual in conjunction with a satisfactory quality of life.

tolerance State in which an increased dosage of a psychoactive substance is needed to produce a desired effect.

user

light to moderate users consume between 1 and 12 drinks per week, less than 4 drinks per occasion, and/or use other drugs one to two times per week in small quantities.

heavy users drink ≥ 2 drinks per day, ≥ 4 drinks three or more times per week, exhibit binge patterns of use, and/or use illicit drugs more than twice per week.

problematic users have experienced one or more alcohol- or drug-related problems, such as being arrested for "driving under the influence of alcohol" (DUI), medical complications, family problems, or other behavioral consequences.

withdrawal syndrome Onset of a predictable constellation of signs and symptoms following the abrupt discontinuation of, or rapid decrease in dosage of, a psychoactive substance.

Resources

I. General Resources

    A. Groups and Organizations

        1. ***National Clearinghouse for Alcohol and Drug Abuse Information*** (NCADI)

        The Clearinghouse is a service of the Office for Substance Abuse Prevention (OSAP) and the Alcohol, Drug Abuse, and Mental Health Administration (ADAMHA). The Clearinghouse maintains a list of hundreds of articles and publications about alcohol and drug abuse. The majority are written for the lay public, but some are oriented to health professionals. Single copies are generally available free of charge. NCADI also does literature searches on specific alcohol and drug topics. They will search MEDLARS and other data bases and send a bibliography and abstracts at no charge. For a list of publications, order forms, and to get on their mailing list, contact:

            Office for Substance Abuse Prevention
            PO Box 2345
            Rockville, MD 20852
            (301)468-2600

          a. One publication worth requesting is the *NCADI Resources Update: Medical Education and Substance Abuse* (August 1987). This annotated list of curriculum guides and other resources pertaining to medical education in substance abuse originally was prepared by Brown University Center for Alcohol and Addiction Studies.

          b. Another worthwhile publication is *Alcohol Resources Directory: Self-Help Groups for Professionals and Special Populations* (August 1986).

        2. ***Substance Abuse Librarians and Information Specialists*** (SALIS)

        SALIS is an organization of 160 substance abuse information centers in the United States. Some of these centers are in hospitals, medical schools, and other institutional libraries that provide special information services in the area of substance abuse. For the name of information centers near you, contact:

Ms. Nancy Sutherland
Alcohol and Drug Abuse Institute
University of Washington
Seattle, WA 98195
(206)543-0937

3. *Center of Alcohol Studies, Rutgers University*

The Center of Alcohol Studies at Rutgers maintains several data bases about alcohol use. Of particular interest is the Ralph G. Connor Alcohol Research Reference File (CARF), an archive of instruments that have been used in studies of various aspects of drinking behavior and alcoholism. For more information, contact:

Center of Alcohol Studies
Smithers Hall
Rutgers University
Allison Road
Piscataway, NY 08854
(201)932-2190

4. *Quick Facts*

Quick Facts is an electronic bulletin board system operated by the Alcohol Epidemiologic Data System, under contract to the Division of Biometry and Epidemiology of the National Institute of Alcohol Abuse and Alcoholism (NIAAA). Quick Facts provides access to tables containing the latest alcohol-related data (e.g., alcohol use by age, race, sex). Files are added to and updated as new data become available. This might be a good source of information when preparing a lecture. Quick Facts also includes a public messages section to provide a forum for discussion. The system is free to users. Contact the Quick Facts System Operator:

Mr. Fred Stinson
Alcohol Epidemiologic Data System
CSR, Inc.
1400 I St. NW, Suite 600
Washington, DC 20005
(202)842-7600

5. *Drug Abuse & Alcoholism Newsletter*

This brief and practical newsletter is available free from:

Vista Hill Foundation
3420 Camino del Rio North, Suite 100
San Diego, CA 92108
(619)563-1770

B. **Teaching Resources**

1. *NCADI Resource Update: Medical Education and Substance Abuse*

This is an updated, annotated bibliography of articles pertaining to clinical and educational aspects about alcohol and alcoholism. Available free from:

> National Clearinghouse for Alcohol and Drug Information
> PO Box 2345
> Rockville, MD 20852
> (301)468-2600

2. *Interactive Computer-Simulated Cases*

Dr. Richard Brown created three computer software programs for teaching medical students and residents about primary care management of substance abuse. These programs focus on early diagnosis of alcoholism, physician attitudes, and screening questionnaires. Dr. Brown is developing additional modules on the diagnostic interview, discussing the diagnosis of substance abuse with the patient, and alcohol withdrawal. In addition, he has funding from the Pew Trusts to construct an interactive video curriculum on the same topics. For more information, contact:

> Richard L. Brown, M.D.
> Department of Family Practice
> University of Wisconsin Medical School
> 777 South Mills St.
> Madison, WI 53715
> (608)262-6349

II. Adolescent Resources

A. Groups and Organizations

1. *Families Anonymous* (FA)

A national network of more than 2,000 regional groups similar to Al-Anon, following the Alcoholics Anonymous (AA) program. FA groups are open to parents, relatives and friends concerned about drug abuse. Contact:

> Families Anonymous
> PO Box 528,
> Van Nuys, CA 91408
> (818)989-7841

2. *National Federation of Parents for Drug Free-Youth* (NFP)

A national umbrella organization of more than 8,000 parent groups, NFP is involved in public policy promotion and drug-related education for parents and other interested community members. Contact:

> National Federation of Parents for Drug-Free Youth
> 8730 Georgia Ave., #200
> Silver Spring, MD 20910
> (301)585-5437

3. *Parent Resources and Information for Drug Education* (PRIDE)

PRIDE is an information resource, and sponsors a library of materials related to drug abuse, and conferences, and publishes a newsletter. Contact:

PRIDE
Robert Woodruff Building
Volunteer Service Center, Suite 1012
100 Edgewood Ave. NE
Atlanta, GA 30303
(800)241-9746

4. ***Toughlove***

A national network of local self-help programs for families of teen-agers with behavioral and drug problems, Toughlove espouses a philosophy of firm parental action. A newsletter and educational materials are available. Contact:

Toughlove
PO Box 1069l
Doylestown, PA 18901
(215)348-7090

5. ***Mothers Against Drunk Driving*** (MADD)

Established by the mothers of victims of drunk drivers, this national organization with over 400 local chapters is open to all parents. MADD promotes public policy against drunk driving, provides vic-tim assistance, and conducts community education. Contact:

MADD
669 Airport Freeway, Suite 310
Hurst, TX 76053
(817)268-MADD

6. ***Students Against Drunk Drivingmain*** (SADD)

A national organization with thousands of local chapters in high schools, junior high schools, and colleges, SADD promotes educa-tional programs about the dangers of drunk driving in schools and communities. Contact:

SADD
PO Box 800
Marlboro, MA 01752
(617)481-3568

7. ***Doctors Ought to Care*** (DOC)

DOC is a coalition of health professionals who are helping to edu-cate the public, especially adolescents, about the dangers of to-bacco, alcohol, and other preventable causes of poor health. DOC takes a unique health promotion approach by focusing on the image-based advertising used by the tobacco and alcohol industries to sell their products. DOC has pioneered a variety of strategies to counteradvertise, and offers materials that can be used in commu-nity and office health education programs. For more information, contact:

DOC
1423 Harper St.
Augusta, GA 30912

III. AIDS Resources
A. Groups and Organizations
1. *National AIDS Hotline*

English   (800)342-AIDS or (800)342-2437; 24 hours, 7 days a week
Spanish   (800)344-SIDA or (800)344-7432, 8:00 AM–2:00 AM Eastern Time, 7 days a week
Deaf   (800)AIDS-TTY or (800)243–7889), 8:00 AM–10:00 PM Eastern Time, 7 days a week

Referral information on testing and counseling centers, treatment centers, and support groups. Sponsored by the Centers for Disease Control, the hotline provides patients and consumers with direct access to trained information specialists and counselors. They can answer questions about routes of transmission, prevention techniques, and sources of additional information. They can send single copies of free government publications and posters including:

Surgeon General's Report on Acquired Immune Deficiency Syndrome
Understanding AIDS
How You Won't Get AIDS
AIDS and You
AIDS Prevention Guide (for parents and other adults concerned about youth)
Condoms and Sexually Transmitted Disease—Especially AIDS
Eating Defensively: Food Safety Advice for Persons with AIDS

2. *National AIDS Information Clearinghouse*

(800)458-5231, 9:00 AM–7:00 PM Eastern Time, Monday–Friday

Sponsored by the Centers for Disease Control, the Clearinghouse is a comprehensive information source for those involved in AIDS education.

Information is available on more than 6,000 programs, projects, and organizations providing AIDS-related services.

The Clearinghouse takes orders for large quantities of free materials that are otherwise available in single copy from the National AIDS Hotline. Single copies of scientific and technical reports from the CDC are available through this center, including the following prevention documents:

Order Code	Report
18	Guidelines for Effective School Health Education to Prevent the Spread of AIDS (Supplement), 1/29/88, vol 37, no S-2
30	Recommendations for Prevention of HIV Infection in Health Care Settings (Supplement), 8/21/87, vol 36, no 2S
31	Update: Universal Precautions for Prevention of Transmission of Human Immunodeficiency Virus, Hepatitis B Virus and Other Bloodborne Pathogens in Health Care Settings (Supplement), 6/24/88, vol 37, no 24

127	Condoms for Prevention of Sexually Transmitted Diseases, 3/11/88, vol 37, no 9
128	HIV-Related Beliefs, Knowledge, and Behaviors Among High School Students, 12/2/88, vol 37, no 47
466	Eating Defensively: Food Safety Advice for Persons with AIDS, 9/89, videotape

3. *American Academy of Family Physicians*

(800)274-2237 or (816)333-9700

AIDS: A Guide for Survival

Eighty-eight page book for patients and public, covering routes of transmission, risky behavior, prevention, and treatment. Produced by the Harris County Medical Society and the Houston County Medical Society. AAFP offers a special printing with the Academy name and message. A project of the Committee on Health Education. Contact: Order Department, ext 1132.

AIDS: WHAT YOU SHOULD KNOW. A Sunday Morning Message about Health

SIDA: Que Debe Usted Saber: Mensaje Dominical Sobre La Salud

Four-page brochure on AIDS risks and prevention, available in English or Spanish. A project of the Committee on Minority Health. Contact Cheryl Denslow, ext 5430.

4. *American Foundation AIDS Research* (AmFAR)

Learning AIDS: An Information Resource Directory, ed 2, 1989; 270 pages, $24.95 plus shipping and handling. Evaluated education materials for general and targeted groups, including ethnic and sexual minorities, sexually active persons, drug users, health care professionals, service providers, counselors, and others. Contact: R.R. Bowker, (800)521-8110; in New York, (212)337-6934; in Canada, (800)537-8416.

5. *AIDS Education Training Centers*

AIDS Clinical Trials (through the National Institute for Allergic and Infectious Diseases), (800)TRIALS-A or (800)874-2572

B. **Books/Journals/Tapes/Films**

1. Ward JW, Holmberg DS, Allen JR, et al: Transmission of human immunodeficiency virus (HIV) by blood transfusions screened as negative for HIV antibody. *N Engl J Med* 318:473-478.

2. Oral manifestations of AIDS: Diagnosis and management of HIV associated infections.

Denver Office of Asterilization and Asephix Procedures Research Foundation, (303)243-1233

3. HIV Disease Patient Health Care

Blue Cross/Blue Shield Association

676 N. St. Claire St.

Chicago, IL 60611

IV. **Drugs in Sports Resources**

A. **Groups and Organizations**

1. US Olympic Committee on Drug Education Hotline (800)233-0393

B. Books/Journals/Tapes/Films

1. Bartimole J: *Drugs and the Athlete—A Losing Combination* (1988) National Collegiate Athletic Association
   PO Box 1906
   Mission, KS 66201
   (913)384-3220.

2. Landry GL, Wagner LL: *Anabolic Steroids: What's the Hype?* Patient information pamphlet available from the Wisconsin Clearinghouse.
   University of Wisconsin—Madison
   PO Box 1468
   Madison, WI 53701
   (608)263-2797

3. Newsom MM (ed): *Drug Free:* US Olympic Committee Drug Education Handbook, 1989–1992.

V. Drug Testing in the Workplace
A. Groups and Organizations

1. American Academy of Forensic Scientists
   PO Box 669
   Colorado Springs, CO 80901-0669
   (719)636-1100

VI. Eating Disorder Resources
A. Groups and Organizations

1. American Anorexia/Bulimia Association, Inc. (AA/BA)
   133 Cedar Lane
   Teaneck, NJ 07666
   (201)836-1800

2. Anorexia/Bulimia Treatment and Education Center (ABTEC)
   621 S. New Ballas Road, Suite 7019B
   St. Louis, MO 63141
   (800)22ABTEC

3. Help Anorexia, Inc.
   5143 Overland Ave.
   Culver City, CA 90230
   (213)837-5445

4. National Association of Anorexia Nervosa and Associated Disorders, Inc. (ANRED)
   Box 5102
   Eugene, OR 97405
   (503)344-1144

5. National Anorexia Aid Society, Inc. (NAAS)
   5796 Karl Road
   Columbus, OH 43229
   (614)436-1112

6. Bulimia and Anorexia Nervosa Association (BANA)
   University of Windsor
   401 Sunset Ave.

Windsor, Ontario, Canada N9B 3P4
(519)253-7545

B. Books/Journals/Tapes/Films

1. *Bulimia: The Binge-Purge Obsession*
   Carle Medical Communications
   510 W. Main St.
   Urbana, IL 61801
   (217)384-4838

2. "Dieting—The Danger Point"
   CRM/McGraw-Hill Films
   100 Fifteenth St.
   San Francisco, CA 94114
   (619)453-5000

3. "The Hunger Artist: A Portrait of Anorexia Nervosa"
   Fat Chance Films
   390 Elizabeth St.
   San Francisco, CA 94114
   (415)821-6217

4. "Killing Us Softly" (impact of advertising on women's body image)
   Cambridge Documentary Films
   PO Box 385
   Cambridge, MA 02139
   (617)354-3677

5. "The Waist Land: Eating Disorders"
   Coronet/MTI Film and Video, Distributors of Learning Corporation
   of America
   108 Wilmot Road
   Deerfield, IL 60015

6. "A Season in Hell" (documentary on eating disorders)
   Walter Brock
   PO Box 1275
   Lexington, KY 40590
   (606)266-1969

VII. Family Resources

A. Groups and Organizations

1. *Al-Anon*
   Al-Anon Family Group, Inc.
   PO Box 862, Midtown Station
   New York, NY 10018-0862
   (800)356-9996).

2. *Families Anonymous* (FA)
   A national network of more than 2,000 regional groups similar to
   Al-Anon, following the AA program. FA groups are open to parents,
   relatives, and friends concerned about drug abuse. Contact:
   Families Anonymous
   PO Box 528

Van Nuys, CA 91408

(818)989-7841

B. Books/Journals/Tapes/Films

1. Johnson VE: *I'll Quit Tomorrow.* New York, Harper & Row, 1973, 165 pp. Directed at alcoholics, their families, and friends. Includes materials used in both training and treatment. A detailed account of the treatment program at the Johnson Institute, which approaches the disease with multidisciplinary action at various levels: physical, mental, psychological, and spiritual.

2. Sculpturing: An Update, 1988 (videotape)

   Onsite

   2820 W. Main

   Rapid City, SD 57702

VIII. Gambling Resources

A. Groups and Organizations

1. Gambler's Anonymous International Service Office

   PO Box 17173

   Los Angeles, CA 90017

   (213)386-8789

2. GamAnon International Service Office

   PO Box 157

   Whitestone, NY 11357

   (718)352-1671

3. South Oaks Hospital

   400 Sunrise Highway

   Amityville, NY 11701

   (516)264-4000

4. The National Council on Problem Gambling

   445 W. 59th St.

   New York, NY 10019

   (212)765-3833

5. State Sponsored Gambling Treatment Programs

   Iowa, Massachusetts, New York, New Jersey, Ohio

6. Maryland houses three private treatment programs, the Washington Center for Pathological Gambling in College Park, The National Center for Pathological Gambling in Baltimore, and Taylor Manor Hospital in Ellicott City.

7. Brecksville Veterans Administration Medical Center (other VA sponsored programs) Brecksville, OH 44141

   (216)526-3030

IX. Perinatal Substance Use

A. Groups and Organizations

1. National Council on Alcoholism and Drug Dependence, Inc. Coalition on Alcohol & Drug Dependent Women and Their Children

   Washington Office

1511 K St. NW, Suite 926
Washington, DC 20005
(202)737-8122

2. National Association for Perinatal Addiction Research and Education
11 E. Hubbard St., Suite 200
Chicago, IL 60611
(312)629-4321

3. Healthy Mothers, Healthy Babies Coalition
409 12th St. SW
Washington, DC 20024
(202)863-2458

B. Books/Journals/Tapes/Films

1. "A Pregnant Woman Never Drinks Alone"
Eight-minute videotape that addresses key aspects of the risks to fetal development taken by a pregnant woman when she drinks alcohol. The video uses a gentle yet firm tone to explain the nature of the risks, and offers suggestions for women who may find it difficult to stop drinking. $95.00 or $25.00/1-week preview.

   Universal Health Association, Inc.
   1701 K St. NW, Suite 600
   Washington, DC 20035-5465
   (202)429-9506

2. "Drugs, Smoking and Alcohol During Pregnancy"
Twenty-minute videotape discusses the confusion many pregnant women face about what may be harmful to their unborn babies. Facts about smoking and alcohol and drug use during pregnancy are provided, and the effects of over-the-counter medications, such as cold and headache remedies, are discussed. $250.00.

   Milner-Fenwick, Inc.
   2125 Greespring Dr.
   Timonium, MD 21093
   (800)638-8652

3. "Substance Abuse and Pregnancy: A Health Professional's Guide"
Thirty-minute videotape aimed at obstetrical nurses, counselors, and others working with pregnant women. Contents include harmful affects of alcohol, cigarettes, and prescription and illicit drugs, and an overview of the professional's role in assessment and intervention with the substance-abusing patient. Pregnancy is presented as an opportunity to change a patient's long-term behavior, and effective therapeutic approaches are shown. Includes a study guide; $295.00, rental $50.00.

   Polymorph Films, Inc.
   118 South St.
   Boston, MA 02111
   (617)542-2004

X. Physical and Cognitive Disability Resources
A. Groups and Organizations

1. Addiction Intervention with the Disabled (AID)
   Sociology Department
   Kent State University
   Kent, OH 44242
   (216)672-2440

2. Abbott Northwestern Hospital/Sister Kenny Institute
   Chemical Dependency/Physical Disability Program
   1800 First Ave. South
   Minneapolis, MN 55403
   (612)863-1500

3. Congress on Chemical Dependency and Disability, Inc.
   15519 Crenshaw Blvd., Suite 209
   Gardena, CA 90249
   (213)679-6523

4. National Rehabilitation Information Center
   8455 Colesville Road, Suite 935
   Silver Spring, MD 20910
   (800)346-2742

XI. Smoking Cessation Resources
A. Groups and Organizations

1. American Lung Association
   1330 N. 113th St.
   Milwaukee, WI 53226-3285
   (800)242-5160.

2. American Cancer Society
   (800)249-0487

3. National Cancer Institute
   (800)4CANCER

4. Cancer Care Line
   (800)622-8922

B. Office System Materials

1. *Doctors Helping Smokers:* The authors of this system developed and tested it in one clinic, and subsequently worked with many private practices to establish and maintain such a system, with comparable success. The office manual and sample materials are available for $10.50 from:
   Dr. Leif Solberg
   Blue Plus
   PO Box 64179
   St. Paul, MN 55164

2. *AAFP Stop Smoking Kit:* Contains an office manual describing how to use the kit and set up an effective office system. Includes Smoke Cards similar to those described in Chapter XX, chart labels, and self-help booklets. In addition, there are signs and booklets for the

waiting and examining rooms, quit contracts and certificates, counseling guides, and audiotapes for patients or staff. The cost is $50 for members, $80 for nonmembers.

Whitehead Enterprise
1210 Brighton
Newport, KY 41071
(606)491-4127.

3. *How to Help Your Patients Stop Smoking*

A National Cancer Institute Manual for Physicians; available free.

National Cancer Institute
Office of Cancer Communications
Bldg. 31, Rm. 10A24
Bethesda, MD 20892
(800)638-6694

4. *Clean Air Health Care:*

A practical step-by-step guide to making a health care institution smoke-free; $11.75.

Minnesota Coalition for a Smoke-Free Society 2000
Ford Center, Suite 525,
420 North Fifth St.
Minneapolis, MN 55404.

C. Self-Help Materials

1. *Clearing the Air*

Quitting tips. Available free in quantities of 200.

National Cancer Institute
Office of Cancer Communications
Bldg. 31, Rm. 10A24
Bethesda, MD 20892
(800)638-6694.

2. *A Patient Guide to Nicotine Reduction Therapy*
Available free.

Department of Public Health and Preventive Medicine
Oregon Health Sciences University
3181 S.W. Sam Jackson Park Road, L352
Portland, OR 97201

3. *Stop Smoking, Stay Trim*

Low cost guide to weight control when quitting.

American Lung Association
1740 Broadway
New York, NY 10271

4. *Freedom From Smoking*

Excellent; easily readable and accessible.

American Lung Association
1330 N. 113th St.
Milwaukee, WI 53226-3285
(800)242-5160

5. *Stop Smoking—A Guide for Patients*
Part of the AAFP Stop Smoking Kit, available in quantities at $1.00 each.

XII. Women and Substance Abuse

A. Groups and Organizations

1. Coalition on Alcohol and Drug Dependent Women and Their Children
1511 K St. NW
Washington, DC 20005
(202)737-8122

2. Office of Substance Abuse Prevention (OSAP)
5600 Fishers Lane
Rockwall II
Rockville, MD 20857
(301)443-0373

B. Books/Journals/Tapes/Films

1. Finkelstein N, et al: *Getting Sober, Getting Well: A Treatment Guide for Caregivers Who Work With Women.* The Women's Alcoholism Program of CASPAR, 6 Camelia Ave., Cambridge, MA 02139, 1990.

2. Sandmeier M: *The Invisible Alcoholics: Women and Alcohol Abuse in America.* New York, McGraw-Hill Book Co, 1980.

3. Wilsnack S, Beckman L: *Alcohol Problems in Women.* New York, Guilford Press, 1984.

Screening Instruments

APPENDIX C–1.

Adolescent Alcohol Involvement Scale and Scoring Instructions*

1. How often to you drink?
   a. Never
   b. Once or twice a year
   c. Once or twice a month
   d. Every weekend
   e. Several times a week
   f. Every day
2. When did you have your last drink?
   a. Never drank
   b. Not for over a year
   c. Between 6 months and 1 year ago
   d. Several weeks ago
   e. Last week
   f. Yesterday
   g. Today
3. I usually start to drink because:
   a. I like the taste
   b. To be like my friends
   c. To feel like an adult
   d. I feel nervous, tense, full of worries or problems
   e. I feel sad, lonely, sorry for myself
4. What do you drink?
   a. Wine
   b. Beer
   c. Mixed drinks
   d. Hard liquor
   e. Substitute for alcohol (e.g., paint thinner, Sterno, cough medicine, mouthwash, hair tonic)
5. How do you get your drinks?
   a. Supervised by parents or relatives
   b. From brothers or sisters
   c. From home without parents' knowledge
   d. From friends
   e. Buy it with false identification
6. When did you take your first drink?
   a. Never
   b. Recently
   c. After age 15
   d. At age 14 or 15
   e. Between ages 10 and 13
   f. Before age 10

7. What time of day do you usually drink?
   a. With meals
   b. At night
   c. Afternoon
   d. Mostly in the morning or when I first awake
   e. I often get up during my sleep and drink
8. Why did you take your first drink?
   a. Curiosity
   b. Parents or relatives offered
   c. Friends encouraged me
   d. To feel more like an adult
   e. To get drunk or high
9. How much do you drink when you do drink?
   a. 1 drink
   b. 2 drinks
   c. 3 to 6 drinks
   d. 6 or more drinks
   e. Until "high" or drunk
10. Whom do you drink with?
    a. Parents or relatives only
    b. With brothers or sisters only
    c. With friends own age
    d. With older friends
    e. Alone
11. What is the greatest effect you have had from alcohol?
    a. Loose, easy feeling
    b. Moderately "high"
    c. Drunk
    d. Became ill
    e. Passed out
    f. Was drinking heavily, and the next day didn't remember what happened
12. What is the greatest effect drinking has had on your life?
    a. None, no effect
    b. Has interfered with talking to someone
    c. Has prevented me from having a good time
    d. Has interfered with my school work
    e. Have lost friends because of drinking
    f. Has gotten me into trouble at home

(Continued.)

g. Was in a fight or destroyed property
h. Has resulted in an accident, an injury, arrest, or being punished at school for drinking

13. How do you feel about your drinking?
   a. No problem at all
   b. I can control it and set limits on myself
   c. I can control myself, but my friends easily influence me
   d. I often feel bad about my drinking
   e. I need help to control myself
   f. I have had professional help to control my drinking

14. How do others see you?
   a. Can't say, or a normal drinker for my age
   b. When I drink I tend to neglect my family or friends
   c. My family or friends advise me to control or cut down on my drinking
   d. My family or friends tell me to get help for my drinking
   e. My family or friends have already gone for help for my drinking

Scoring Instructions

The highest total score is 79. An *a* response is scored 1 (except on questions 1, 2, 6, 12, 13, and 14, on which $a = 0$, $b = 2$, $c = 3$, and so on, to $h = 8$. When more than one response is made, the one with the highest score is used. An unanswered question is scored 0.

Score	Involvement
41–57	Alcohol misuse
58–79	Alcoholic-like

*From Mayer J, Filstead WJ: *J Stud Alcohol* 1979; 40:291–300. Used by permission.

APPENDIX C-2.

Alcohol Use Disorders Identification Test (AUDIT)*

AUDIT is a brief structured interview, developed by the World Health Organization, that can be incorporated into a medical history. It contains questions about recent alcohol consumption, dependence symptoms, and alcohol-related problems.

Begin AUDIT by saying, "Now I am going to ask you some questions about your use of alcoholic beverages *during the past year*. Explain what is meant by alcoholic beverages (e.g., beer, wine, liquor [vodka, whiskey, brandy.]).

Record the score for each question in the box on the right side of the question [ ]

1. How often do you have a drink containing alcohol?
   - ☐ Never   (0)   [ ]
   - ☐ Monthly or less   (1)
   - ☐ 2 to 4 times a month   (2)
   - ☒ 2 to 3 times a week   (3)
   - ☒ 4 or more times a week   (4)

2. How many drinks containing alcohol do you have on a typical day when you are drinking?
   - ☐ None   (0)   [ ]
   - ☐ 1 or 2   (1)
   - ☒ 3 or 4   (2)
   - ☒ 5 or 6   (3)
   - ☒ 7 to 9   (4)
   - ☐ 10 or more   (5)

3. How often do you have six or more drinks on one occasion?
   - ☐ Never   (0)   [ ]
   - ☐ Less than monthly   (1)
   - ☒ Monthly   (2)
   - ☒ Weekly   (3)
   - ☐ Daily or almost daily   (4)

4. How often during the last year have you found that you were unable to stop drinking once you had started?
   - ☒ Never   (0)   [ ]
   - ☐ Less than monthly   (1)
   - ☐ Monthly   (2)
   - ☐ Weekly   (3)
   - ☐ Daily or almost daily   (4)

5. How often during the last year have you failed to do what was normally expected from you because of drinking?
   - ☒ Never   (0)   [ ]
   - ☐ Less than monthly   (1)
   - ☐ Monthly   (2)
   - ☐ Weekly   (3)
   - ☐ Daily or almost daily   (4)

6. How often during the last year have you needed a first drink in the morning to get yourself going after a heavy drinking session?
   - ☒ Never   (0)   [ ]
   - ☐ Less than monthly   (1)
   - ☐ Monthly   (2)
   - ☐ Weekly   (3)
   - ☐ Daily or almost daily   (4)

(Continued.)

7. How often during the last year have you had a feeling of guilt or remorse after drinking?

    ☒ Never   (0)   [   ]
    ☐ Less than monthly   (1)
    ☐ Monthly   (2)
    ☐ Weekly   (3)
    ☐ Daily or almost daily   (4)

8. How often during the last year have you been unable to remember what happened the night before because you had been drinking?

    ☒ Never   (0)   [   ]
    ☐ Less than monthly   (1)
    ☐ Monthly   (2)
    ☐ Weekly   (3)
    ☐ Daily or almost daily   (4)

9. Have you or someone else been injured as the result of your drinking?

    ☒ Never   (0)   [   ]
    ☐ Less than monthly   (1)
    ☐ Monthly   (2)
    ☐ Weekly   (3)
    ☐ Daily or almost daily   (4)

10. Has a relative, friend, or a doctor or other health worker been concerned about your drinking or suggested you cut down?

    ☒ Never   (0)   [   ]
    ☐ Less than monthly   (1)
    ☐ Monthly   (2)
    ☐ Weekly   (3)
    ☐ Daily or almost daily   (4)

Record the total of the specific items. A score of *11 or greater* may indicate the need for a more in-depth assessment.   [   ]

*From Babor TF, Ramon de la Fuente J, Saunders J, et al: AUDIT: Guidelines for Use in Primary Health Care. Developed by the World Health Organization, AMETHYST Project, 1987. Used by permission.

APPENDIX C–3.

Alcohol Use Disorders Identification Test (AUDIT) (Revised to include drugs)*

This questionnaire asks you some questions about your use of alcohol and drugs during the past year. Alcoholic beverages include beer, wine, and liquor (vodka, whiskey, brandy, etc). Drugs include cocaine, marijuana, narcotics, and tranquilizers.

1. How often do you have a drink containing alcohol or use other drugs (e.g., marijuana, cocaine, narcotics)?

☐ Never (0) [ ]
☐ Less than monthly (1)

If *more than once a month:*

(Alcohol)
☐ Monthly (2) [ ]
☒ Weekly (3) [3]
☒ Daily or almost daily (4) [ ]

Cocaine
☐ Monthly (2) [ ]
☐ Weekly (3) [ ]
☐ Daily or almost daily (4) [ ]

(Marijuana)
☐ Monthly (2) [2]
☐ Weekly (3) [ ]
☐ Daily or almost daily (4) [ ]

Tranquilizers
☐ Monthly (2) [ ]
☐ Weekly (3) [ ]
☐ Daily or almost daily (4) [ ]

Other Ritalin
☐ Monthly (2) [ ]
☐ Weekly (3) [ ]
☐ Daily or almost daily (4) [ ]

2. On a day when you drink alcohol or use other drugs, how many drinks (alcohol), lines (cocaine), joints (marijuana), or tranquilizer pills do you use?

Alcohol ☐ None (0) ☐ 1 or 2 (1) ☒ 3 or 4 (2) ☒ 5 or 6 (3) ☒ 7 to 9 (4) ☐ 10 or more (5) [4]
Cocaine ☒ None (0) ☐ 1 or 2 (1) ☐ 3 or 4 (2) ☐ 5 or 6 (3) ☐ 7 to 9 (4) ☐ 10 or more (5) [0]
Marijuana ☒ None (0) ☒ 1 or 2 (1) ☐ 3 or 4 (2) ☐ 5 or 6 (3) ☐ 7 to 9 (4) ☐ 10 or more (5) [1]
Tranquilizers ☒ None (0) ☐ 1 or 2 (1) ☐ 3 or 4 (2) ☐ 5 or 6 (3) ☐ 7 to 9 (4) ☐ 10 or more (5) [0]
Other ☐ None (0) ☒ 1 or 2 (1) ☐ 3 or 4 (2) ☐ 5 or 6 (3) ☐ 7 to 9 (4) ☐ 10 or more (5) [1]

3. How often do you have 6 or more drinks, 1 or more joints, 10 or more lines, or 3 or more tranquilizer pills on one occasion?

Alcohol
☐ Never (0) [3]
☐ Less than monthly (1)
☒ Monthly (2)
☒ Weekly (3)
☐ Daily or almost daily (4)

Other drugs
☒ Never (0) [2]
☐ Less than monthly (1)
☒ Monthly (2)
☐ Weekly (3)
☐ Daily or almost daily (4)

4. How often during the last year have you found that you were unable to stop drinking or using other drugs once you had started?

Alcohol
☒ Never (0) [1]
☒ Less than monthly (1)
☐ Monthly (2)
☐ Weekly (3)
☐ Daily or almost daily (4)

Other drugs
☒ Never (0) [0]
☐ Less than monthly (1)
☐ Monthly (2)
☐ Weekly (3)
☐ Daily or almost daily (4)

(Continued.)

5. How often during the last year have you failed to do what was normally expected from you because of drinking or using other drugs?

Alcohol

☒ Never	(0)	[Ø]
☐ Less than monthly	(1)	
☐ Monthly	(2)	
☐ Weekly	(3)	
☐ Daily or almost daily	(4)	

Other drugs

☒ Never	(0)	[Ø]
☐ Less than monthly	(1)	
☐ Monthly	(2)	
☐ Weekly	(3)	
☐ Daily or almost daily	(4)	

6. How often during the last year have you needed a first drink or drug in the morning to get your self going after a heavy drinking or drug using session?

Alcohol

☒ Never	(0)	[Ø]
☐ Less than monthly	(1)	
☐ Monthly	(2)	
☐ Weekly	(3)	
☐ Daily or almost daily	(4)	

Other drugs

☒ Never	(0)	[Ø]
☐ Less than monthly	(1)	
☐ Monthly	(2)	
☐ Weekly	(3)	
☐ Daily or almost daily	(4)	

7. How often during the last year have you had a feeling of guilt or remorse after drinking or using other drugs?

Alcohol

☒ Never	(0)	[Ø]
☐ Less than monthly	(1)	
☐ Monthly	(2)	
☐ Weekly	(3)	
☐ Daily or almost daily	(4)	

Other drugs

☒ Never	(0)	[Ø]
☐ Less than monthly	(1)	
☐ Monthly	(2)	
☐ Weekly	(3)	
☐ Daily or almost daily	(4)	

8. How often during the last year have you been unable to remember what happened the night before because you had been drinking or using other drugs?

Alcohol

☒ Never	(0)	[2]
☐ Less than monthly	(1)	
☐ Monthly	(2)	
☐ Weekly	(3)	
☐ Daily or almost daily	(4)	

Other drugs

☒ Never	(0)	[Ø]
☐ Less than monthly	(1)	
☐ Monthly	(2)	
☐ Weekly	(3)	
☐ Daily or almost daily	(4)	

9. Have you or someone else been injured as the result of your drinking or drug use?

Alcohol

☒ Never	(0)	[Ø]
☐ Less than monthly	(1)	
☐ Monthly	(2)	
☐ Weekly	(3)	
☐ Daily or almost daily	(4)	

Other drugs

☒ Never	(0)	[Ø]
☐ Less than monthly	(1)	
☐ Monthly	(2)	
☐ Weekly	(3)	
☐ Daily or almost daily	(4)	

10. Has a relative, friend, or a doctor or other health worker been concerned about your drinking or drug use or suggested you cut down?

Alcohol

☒ Never	(0)	[√]
☐ Less than monthly	(1)	
☐ Monthly	(2)	
☐ Weekly	(3)	
☐ Daily or almost daily	(4)	

Other drugs

☒ Never	(0)	[Ø]
☐ Less than monthly	(1)	
☐ Monthly	(2)	
☐ Weekly	(3)	
☐ Daily or almost daily	(4)	

Record the total of the specific items. In a general population, a score of *11 or greater* may indicate the need for a more in-depth assessment.

*Developed by the World Health Organization, AMETHYST Project, 1987; adapted by Fleming, Barry, 1990.

APPENDIX C–4.

Diagnostic Interview Schedule—IIIR: Alcohol Abuse/Dependence Subscale*

The following questions are about your lifetime alcohol use. Please answer to the best of your ability. *All of your answers are confidential.*

1. Have you ever been drunk in your life?
   _____ NO   __X__ YES
   a. If *no*, you are finished with this section of the questionnaire. Go to the section on other drugs.
   b. If *yes:* Do you think it was before or after you were 15 years old?
   __✓__ BEFORE   __X__ AFTER

2. What is the largest number of drinks you've had in a day?
   __X__ Less than 5 (You are finished with this section of the questionnaire. Go to section on other drugs.)
   __X__ Less than 7 (go to question 4)   __X__ 8–15   _____ 16–19   _____ 20 or more
   a. When did you have as many as 20 drinks in a day?
   _____ Within the last 2 weeks   _____ Within the last month   _____ Within the last 6 months
   _____ Within the last year   _____ More than 1 year ago

3. Has there ever been a *couple of months* when every day you were drinking 7 *or more drinks or bottles of beer or glasses of wine?*
   __X__ NO (Skip to question 4.)   __X__ YES
   a. If *yes:* How long has it been since you drank at least 7 drinks a day?
   __X__ Within the last 2 weeks   __X__ Within the last month   _____ Within the last 6 months
   _____ Within the last year   _____ More than 1 year ago

4. Have you ever gone on binges or benders where you kept drinking for a couple of days or more without sobering up?
   __X__ NO (Skip to question 5.)   __X__ YES (Answer A and B.)
   a. Did you neglect some of your usual responsibilities then?
   __X__ NO   _____ YES
   b. Did you do that *several times* or go on a binge that lasted *a month or more?*
   __X__ NO   _____ YES

5. a. Did you ever get tolerant of alcohol so that you needed to *drink a lot more in order to get an effect* or found that you could *no longer get high on the amount you used to drink?*
   __X__ NO   __X__ YES
   b. Some months or years after you started drinking, did you begin to be *able to drink a lot more before you would get drunk* (that is, your speech would get thick or you would get unsteady on your feet)?
   __X__ NO   __X__ YES (If yes, go to C.)
   c. Did your ability to drink more without feeling these effects last for a month or more?
   __X__ NO   _____ YES

6. Have there been many days when you *drank much more than you expected to* when you began, or have you often continued drinking for more days in a row than you intended to?
   _____ NO   __X__ YES

7. Have you more than once *wanted to quit or cut down* on your drinking?
   __X__ NO (Go to question 8.)   _____ YES
   a. If *yes:* Have you ever tried to quit or cut down on drinking?
   _____ NO   _____ YES
   Did you find you couldn't quit or cut down?
   _____ NO   _____ YES
   Were you unable to quit or cut down more than once?
   _____ NO   _____ YES

(Continued.)

8. Some people *try to control* their drinking *by making rules,* like not drinking before 5 o'clock or never drinking alone. Have you ever made rules like that for yourself?

_____ NO (Go to question 9.) __X__ YES

a. If *yes:* Did you make these rules because you were having trouble limiting the amount you were drinking?

__X__ NO _____ YES

b. Did you try to follow those rules for a month or longer or make rules for yourself several times?

_____ NO __X__ YES

9. Has there ever been a period when you *spent so much time drinking alcohol or getting over its effects* that you had little time for anything else?

__X__ NO (Go to question 10.) _____ YES

a. If *yes:* Did the period when you spent a lot of time drinking last a month or longer?

_____ NO _____ YES

10. Have you ever *given up or greatly reduced* important activities in order to drink, like sports, work, or associating with friends or relatives?

__X__ NO (Go to question 11.) _____ YES

a. If *yes:* Did you give up or cut down on activities for a month or more, or several times, in order to drink?

_____ NO _____ YES

11. Has your drinking or being hung over often *kept you from working or taking care of children?*

__X__ NO (Go to question 12.) _____ YES

a. If *yes:* Have you often worked or taken care of children at a time when you had drunk enough alcohol to make your speech thick or to make you unsteady on your feet?

_____ NO _____ YES

12. Have you ever had *trouble driving because of drinking,* like having an accident or being arrested for drunk driving?

__X__ NO (Go to question 13) _____ YES

a. If *yes:* Have you several times had trouble driving because of drinking?

_____ NO _____ YES

13. Have you ever *accidentally injured yourself* when you had been drinking, for example, had a bad fall or cut yourself badly?

__X__ NO (Go to question 14.) _____ YES

a. If *yes:* Did that happen several times?

_____ NO _____ YES

14. Have you several times been high from drinking in a situation *where it increased your chances of getting hurt,* for instance, when driving a car or boat; using knives, machinery, or guns; crossing against traffic; climbing or swimming?

__X__ NO _____ YES

15. People who cut down or stop drinking after drinking for a considerable time often have *withdrawal symptoms.* Common ones are the "shakes" (hands tremble), being unable to sleep, feeling anxious or depressed, sweating, heart beating fast, or the DTs (seeing or hearing things that aren't really there). Have you had any problems like that when you stopped or cut down on drinking?

__X__ NO (Go to question 16) _____ YES

If *yes:* Have you had withdrawal symptoms several times?

_____ NO _____ YES

(Continued.)

16. a. Did you ever *need a drink just after you woke up* (that is, before breakfast)?
    _X_ NO   ____ YES
    b. Did you ever take a drink *right after you woke up* to keep from having a hangover or the shakes?
    _X_ NO   ____ YES
    c. Have you ever taken a drink to *keep from having a hangover,* the shakes, or any withdrawal symptoms or taken a drink to make them go away?
    _X_ NO   ____ YES
    d. Have you several times taken a drink to keep from having withdrawal symptoms?
    _X_ NO   ____ YES

17. There are several *health problems* that can result from drinking. Did drinking ever cause you to have liver disease or yellow jaundice, give you stomach disease, or make you vomit blood, cause your feet to tingle or feel numb, give you memory problems even when you weren't drinking, or give you pancreatitis?
    _X_ NO (Go to question 18)   ____ YES
    If *yes:*
    a. When did you first find out drinking had given you a health problem?
    ____ Within the last 2 weeks   ____ Within the last month   ____ Within the last 6 months
    ____ Within the last year   ____ More than 1 year ago
    b. Did you continue to drink (more than once) knowing that drinking caused you to have a health problem or injury?
    ____ NO   ____ YES
    c. Have you continued to drink when you knew you had any (other) serious physical illness that might be made worse by drinking?
    ____ NO   ____ YES
    d. When was the last time you drank in spite of an illness that could be made worse by drinking?
    ____ Within the last 2 weeks   ____ Within the last month   ____ Within the last 6 months
    ____ Within the last year   ____ More than 1 year ago

18. Has alcohol ever caused you *emotional or psychological problems,* such as feeling uninterested in things, depressed, suspicious of others (paranoid), or caused you to have strange ideas?
    ____ NO   ____ YES
    a. If *yes:* Did you continue to drink (more than once) after you knew that drinking caused you psychological or emotional problems?
    ____ NO   ____ YES

*From Robins L, Helzer J, Cottler L, et al: *NIMH Diagnostic Interview Schedule,* version III revised. St Louis, Washington University, 1989. Used by permission.

APPENDIX C–5.

Diagnostic Interview Schedule—IIIR: Drug Abuse/Dependence Subscale*

The following questions ask about your experience with drugs. All of your answers are confidential.

1. Have you ever used at least one drug on this list to get high (show card) or for other mental effects, or more than was prescribed, or for longer than the doctor wanted you to? If yes, how old were you when you first tried it?

Drug	No	Yes	Age
Marijuana: hashish, bhang, ganja	X	X	16
Stimulants: Amphetamines, khat, betel nut	X	___	___
Sedatives: Barbiturates, sleeping pills, Seconal, Valium, Librium, tranquilizers, Quaaludes, Xanax	X	___	___
Cocaine, crack, coca leaves	X	___	___
Heroin	X	___	___
Opiates: Codeine, Demerol, morphine, Percodan, methadone, Darvon, opium, Dilaudid	X	___	___
PCP	X	___	___
Psychedelics: LSD, mescaline, peyote, psilocybin, DMT	X	X	16
Inhalants: Glue, toluene, gasoline	X	___	___
Other: Nitrous oxide, amyl nitrite; specify_____	X	___	___

If you answered "no" to all of the items in question 1, you are finished with this section of the questionnaire. Go to last section.

If you answered "yes" to any of the items in question 1, please continue.

2. Have you taken any of these drugs more than five times (on your own)? If yes, how old were you when you first tried those drugs you've used more than five times?

Drug	No	Yes	Age
Marijuana: hashish, bhang, ganja	___	___	___
Stimulants: Amphetamines, khat, betel nut	___	___	___
Sedatives: Barbiturates, sleeping pills, Seconal, Valium, Librium, tranquilizers, Quaaludes, Xanax	___	___	___
Cocaine, crack, coca leaves	___	___	___
Heroin	___	___	___
Opiates: Codeine, Demerol, morphine, Percodan, methadone, Darvon, opium, Dilaudid	___	___	___
PCP	___	___	___
Psychedelics: LSD, mescaline, peyote, psilocybin, DMT	___	___	___
Inhalants: Glue, toluene, gasoline	___	___	___
Other: Nitrous oxide, amyl nitrite; specify_____	___	___	___

If you answered "no" to all of the items in question 2, you are finished with this section of the questionnaire. Go to last section.

3. Have you ever used any of these drugs almost every day for 2 weeks or more? (If no, go to question 4.)

Yes____ No ____

a. If yes, indicate below how old you were when you first used that drug every day for at least 2 weeks or more and the time you last used the drug almost every day for 2 weeks or more.

Drug	First Used	Last Used
Marijuana: Hashish, bhang, ganja	___	___
Stimulants: Amphetamines, khat, betel nut	___	___
Sedatives: Barbiturates, sleeping pills, Seconal, Valium, Librium, tranquilizers, Quaaludes, Xanax	___	___
Prescribed drug		
Cocaine, crack, coca leaves	___	___

(Continued.)

Heroin	——	——
Opiates: Codeine, Demerol, morphine, Percodan, methadone, Darvon, opium, Dilaudid	——	——
PCP	——	——
Psychedelics: LSD, mescaline, peyote, psilocybin, DMT	——	——
Inhalants: Glue, toluene, gasoline	——	——
Other: Nitrous oxide, amyl nitrite; specify_____	——	——

4. Has there ever been a period when you spent a great deal of your time using drugs, getting drugs, or getting over the effects of drugs? (If no, skip to question 5.)

   Yes____ No____

   a. If yes, indicate how old you were the first and last times each drug took up a lot of your time.

Drug	First Used	Last Used
Marijuana: Hashish, bhang, ganja	——	——
Stimulants: Amphetamines, khat, betel nut	——	——
Sedatives: Barbiturates, sleeping pills, Seconal, Valium, Librium, tranquilizers, Quaaludes, Xanax	——	——
Prescribed drug	——	——
Cocaine, crack, coca leaves	——	——
Heroin	——	——
Opiates: Codeine, Demerol, morphine, Percodan, methadone, Darvon, opium, Dilaudid	——	——
PCP	——	——
Psychedelics: LSD, mescaline, peyote, psilocybin, DMT	——	——
Inhalants: Glue, toluene, gasoline	——	——
Other: Nitrous oxide, amyl nitrite; specify_____	——	——

5. Have you often used much larger amounts of a drug than you intended to, or for more days in a row than you intended to? (If no, skip to question 6.)

   Yes____ No ____

   a. If yes, indicate how old you were the first time and the last time you used larger amounts than you intended to.

Drug	First Used	Last Used
Marijuana: Hashish, bhang, ganja	——	——
Stimulants: Amphetamines, khat, betel nut	——	——
Sedatives: Barbiturates, sleeping pills, Seconal, Valium, Librium, tranquilizers, Quaaludes, Xanax	——	——
Prescribed drug	——	——
Cocaine, crack, coca leaves	——	——
Heroin	——	——
Opiates: Codeine, Demerol, morphine, Percodan, methadone, Darvon, opium, Dilaudid	——	——
PCP	——	——
Psychedelics: LSD, mescaline, peyote, psilocybin, DMT	——	——
Inhalants: Glue, toluene, gasoline	——	——
Other: Nitrous oxide, amyl nitrite; specify_____	——	——

(Continued.)

6. Have you ever felt dependent on any of these drugs or found you were unable to keep using them? (If no, skip to question 7.)

       Yes_____ No_____

a. If yes, indicate how old you were the first and last times you felt dependent on each drug.

Drug	First Used	Last Used
Marijuana: Hashish, bhang, ganja	____	____
Stimulants: Amphetamines, khat, betel nut	____	____
Sedatives: Barbiturates, sleeping pills, Seconal, Valium, Librium, tranquilizers, Quaaludes, Xanax	____	____
Prescribed drug	____	____
Cocaine, crack, coca leaves	____	____
Heroin	____	____
Opiates: Codeine, Demerol, morphine, Percodan, methadone, Darvon, opium, Dilaudid	____	____
PCP		
Psychedelics: LSD, mescaline, peyote, psilocybin, DMT	____	____
Inhalants: Glue, toluene, gasoline	____	____

7. Have you ever tried to cut down on any of these drugs but found you couldn't. (If no, skip to question 8.)

       Yes _____ No_____

a. If yes, indicate how old you were the first and last times you tried to cut down on each drug.

Drug	First Used	Last Used
Marijuana: Hashish, bhang, ganja	____	____
Stimulants: Amphetamines, khat, betel nut	____	____
Sedatives: Barbiturates, sleeping pills, Seconal, Valium, Librium, tranquilizers, Quaaludes, Xanax	____	____
Prescribed drug	____	____
Cocaine, crack, coca leaves	____	____
Heroin	____	____
Opiates: Codeine, Demerol, morphine, Percodan, methadone, Darvon, opium, Dilaudid	____	____
PCP		
Psychedelics: LSD, mescaline, peyote, psilocybin, DMT	____	____
Inhalants: Glue, toluene, gasoline	____	____
Other: Nitrous oxide, amyl nitrite; specify_____	____	____

8. Did you ever get tolerant to any of these drugs or need larger amounts of them to get an effect? (If no, skip to question 9.)

       Yes_____ No_____

a. If yes, indicate which drugs you became tolerant to and how old you were the first time you became tolerant to each drug.

Drug	Became Tolerant	First Time Tolerant
Marijuana: Hashish, bhang, ganja	____	____
Stimulants: Amphetamines, khat, betel nut	____	____
Sedatives: Barbiturates, sleeping pills, Seconal, Valium, Librium, tranquilizers, Quaaludes, Xanax	____	____
Prescribed drug	____	____
Cocaine, crack, coca leaves	____	____

(Continued.)

Drug	Became Tolerant	First Time Tolerant
Heroin	____	____
Opiates: Codeine, Demerol, morphine, Percodan, methadone, Darvon, opium, Dilaudid	____	____
PCP	____	____
Psychedelics: LSD, mescaline, peyote, psilocybin, DMT	____	____
Inhalants: Glue, toluene, gasoline	____	____
Other: Nitrous oxide, amyl nitrite; specify_____	____	____

9. Has stopping or cutting down on any of these drugs made you sick or given you withdrawal symptoms? (If no, skip to question 10.)

        Yes ____   No____

    a. If yes, indicate those drugs for which you felt sick after cutting down or stopping, if you got sick several times from cutting down on a drug, if you used a drug several times to keep from getting sick, and the ages you were when these things happened.

Drug	Sick	Sick Several Times	Used to Keep From Getting Sick	Age First Got Sick/Used to Not Feel Sick	Age Last Got Sick/Used to Not Feel Sick
Marijuana	____	____	____	____	____
Stimulants	____	____	____	____	____
Sedatives	____	____	____	____	____
Prescribed	____	____	____	____	____
Cocaine	____	____	____	____	____
Heroin	____	____	____	____	____
Opiates	____	____	____	____	____
PCP	____	____	____	____	____
Psychedelics	____	____	____	____	____
Inhalants	____	____	____	____	____
Other	____	____	____	____	____

10. Have you had any health problems, like accidental overdose, persistent cough, seizure (fit), infection, cut, sprain, burn, or other injury, as a result of taking any of these drugs? (If no, skip to question 11.)

        Yes____   No____

    a. If yes, indicate how old you were the first and last times a drug caused you a health problem and whether you used a drug on more than one occasion after you knew it caused a health problem.

Drug	Yes	First Time Drug Caused Health Problem	Last Time Drug Caused Health Problem	Continued to Use Despite Health Problem
Marijuana	____	____	____	____
Stimulants	____	____	____	____
Prescribed	____	____	____	____
Sedatives	____	____	____	____
Cocaine	____	____	____	____
Heroin	____	____	____	____
Opiates	____	____	____	____
PCP	____	____	____	____
Psychedelics	____	____	____	____
Inhalants	____	____	____	____
Other	____	____	____	____

(Continued.)

11. Did any of these drugs cause you considerable problems with your family, friends, on the job, at school, or with the police? (If no, skip to question 12.)

   Yes_____ No_____

   a. If yes, indicate how old you were the first and last times you had a problem and whether you used the drug more than once after realizing it was causing you problems.

Drug	Yes	First Time Drug Caused Health Problem	Last Time Drug Caused Health Problem	Continued to Use Despite Problem
Marijuana	_____	_____	_____	_____
Stimulants	_____	_____	_____	_____
Sedatives	_____	_____	_____	_____
Prescribed	_____	_____	_____	_____
Cocaine	_____	_____	_____	_____
Heroin	_____	_____	_____	_____
Opiates	_____	_____	_____	_____
PCP	_____	_____	_____	_____
Psychedelics	_____	_____	_____	_____
Inhalants	_____	_____	_____	_____
Other	_____	_____	_____	_____

12. Did you have any emotional or psychologic problems from using drugs, such as feeling uninterested in things, depressed, suspicious of people (paranoid), or having strange ideas? (If no, skip to question 13.)

   Yes_____ No_____

   a. If yes, indicate how old you were the first and last times you had this problem and if you used each drug on more than one occasion after you found out it was causing you emotional problems.

Drug	Yes	First Time Drug Caused Health Problem	Last Time Drug Caused Health Problem	Continued to Use Despite Problem
Marijuana	_____	_____	_____	_____
Stimulants	_____	_____	_____	_____
Sedatives	_____	_____	_____	_____
Prescribed	_____	_____	_____	_____
Cocaine	_____	_____	_____	_____
Heroin	_____	_____	_____	_____
Opiates	_____	_____	_____	_____
PCP	_____	_____	_____	_____
Psychedelics	_____	_____	_____	_____
Inhalants	_____	_____	_____	_____
Other	_____	_____	_____	_____

13. Have you ever given up or greatly reduced important activities in order to use a drug, activities like sports, work, or associating with friends or relatives? (If no, skip to question 14.)

   Yes_____ No_____

   a. If yes, indicate how old you were the first and last times and if you ever gave up any important activities for a period of a month or more (or several times) because of the drug.

Drug	Yes	First Time	Last Time	Month Several Times
Marijuana	_____	_____	_____	_____
Stimulants	_____	_____	_____	_____
Sedatives	_____	_____	_____	_____
Prescribed	_____	_____	_____	_____
Cocaine	_____	_____	_____	_____

(Continued.)

Heroin	____	____	____	____
Opiates	____	____	____	____
PCP	____	____	____	____
Psychedelics	____	____	____	____
Inhalants	____	____	____	____
Other	____	____	____	____

14. Have you several times been high from a drug in a situation where it increased your chances of getting hurt, for instance, when driving a car or boat; using knives, machinery, or guns; crossing against traffic; climbing or swimming?

    ____ Yes   ____ No

    a. If yes, indicate how old you were the first and last times you were high in situations where it increased your chances of getting hurt because of the drug. Did this happen over a period of time or several times?

Drug	Yes	First Time	Last Time	Month Several Times
Marijuana	____	____	____	____
Stimulants	____	____	____	____
Sedatives	____	____	____	____
Prescribed	____	____	____	____
Cocaine	____	____	____	____
Heroin	____	____	____	____
Opiates	____	____	____	____
PCP	____	____	____	____
Psychedelics	____	____	____	____
Inhalants	____	____	____	____
Other	____	____	____	____

*From Robins L, Helzer J, Cottler L, et al: *NIMH Diagnostic Interview Schedule,* version III revised. St Louis, Washington University, 1989. Used by permission.

Scoring DIS-R (DSM-IIIR Criteria)

Alcohol or drug dependence

Criteria A. — Subjects must meet ***three*** or more of the following:

1. Used the substance in larger amounts over longer periods of time than intended
2. Unsuccessful efforts to cut down or control use
3. Large amount of time spent in activities to get the substance or to recover from use
4. Frequent intoxication or withdrawal when expected to fulfill major obligations
5. Given up social, occupational, or recreational activities because of substance use
6. Continued use despite social, psychologic, or physical problems caused by use
7. Marked tolerance: need for increased amounts of the substance to achieve desired effect, or diminished effect with same use

8. Withdrawal symptoms
9. Substance taken to avoid withdrawal symptoms

and

Criteria B. — The subject must have persisted in these symptoms for more than *1 month* or experienced *recurrent episodes* of these symptoms.

Alcohol or drug abuse
Criteria A. — DSM III-R criteria for *alcohol or drug abuse* include at least one of the following:

1. Continued use despite social, psychologic, or physical problems caused by use
2. Recurrent use in situations in which use is physically hazardous (e.g., driving while intoxicated).

Criteria B. — The subject must have persistence of these symptoms for more than *1 month* or *recurrence* of these symptoms over time.

For further information contact:

Michael Fleming, M.D., or Kristen Barry, Ph.D.
Department of Family Medicine and Practice
University of Wisconsin
777 South Mills St.
Madison, WI 53715
(608)263-9953

APPENDIX C–6.

Prenatal Health Questionnaire: Kaiser Permanente

This questionnaire is confidential and will not remain in your chart. Please **do not** put your name or medical record number on this form.

We are asking your help. There is increasing evidence that use of alcohol, nicotine (cigarettes), or other drugs during pregnancy can put the mother and developing baby at risk for harmful outcomes. We therefore are trying to identify such "at risk" pregnant women as early as possible. There are many confidential and effective services to help women stay free of alcohol and other drugs during pregnancy. Women who gave up alcohol, drugs, and cigarettes in the early months of pregnancy are having healthy infants!

1. In the past year have you smoked, consumed any alcoholic beverages, or used other drugs?
   - ☒ Yes. Please answer the rest of your questions below.
   - ☐ No. Thank you. You may stop here.

   If yes, complete the following items.

	Used in Last 7 days	Used Since Last Period	Used Since Knew of Pregnancy	How Much	Never Used
Alcohol (wine, beer, liquor)	☐	☒	☐	_____	☐
Nicotine (cigarettes, smokeless tobacco, etc.)	☐	☐	☐	_____	☒
Speed, Crank, ice	☐	☐	☐	_____	☒
Pain medication (codeine, Darvon, etc.)	☐	☐	☐	_____	☒
Anxiety medicine (Valium, Xanax, etc.)	☐	☐	☐	_____	☒
Sleep medicine (Dalmane, Halcion)	☐	☐	☐	_____	☒
Marijuana	☐	☐	☐	_____	☒
Cocaine or crack	☐	☐	☐	_____	☒
Heroin or methadone	☐	☐	☐	_____	☒

2. In the past, have you occasionally drunk more alcohol or used more drugs than you intended? ☒ Yes ☐ No
3. Have you ever thought you ought to cut down on your drinking or drug use? ☐ Yes ☒ No
4. Have people annoyed you by criticizing your drinking or drug use? ☐ Yes ☒ No
5. Have you ever felt bad or guilty about your drinking or drug use? ☐ Yes ☒ No
6. Have you ever had a drink first thing in the morning to steady your nerves or get rid of a hangover (eye opener)? ☐ Yes ☒ No
7. Would you like counseling or group support to help you stay off alcohol, cigarettes and other drugs during this pregnancy? ☒ Yes ☐ No

Completed by: Patient/Nurse/MD. Doctor comments:_____

APPENDIX C–7.

Prenatal Health Questionnaire*

Please mark an X in the box representing your answer for each of the following questions.	1	2	3	4	5	6	7
Prescribed Medications							
1. Have you taken any prescription medicines since you became pregnant?							
Yes					☐		
No							☑
If yes, which ones (pills for acne, antibiotics, allergy medicines, etc.)?							
If yes, does your doctor know you are taking these medicines?							
Yes							☐
No				☐			
Over-the-Counter Medicines and Drugs							
2. Have you taken over-the-counter (nonprescription) medicines since you became pregnant?							
Yes					☐		
No							☑
If yes, which ones (aspirin, Tylenol, diet pills, cold medicines, etc.)?							
Tobacco							
3. In the 3 months before you found out you were pregnant, how many cigarettes did you usually smoke per day?							
More than 1 ½ packs	☐						
½ to 1 ½ packs		☐					
½ pack			☐				
About ¼ pack				☐			
Less than 1 per day					☐		
I didn't smoke						☐	
I have never smoked							☐
4. How many cigarettes do you usually smoke a day now?							
More than 1 ½ packs	☐						
½ to 1 ½ packs		☐					
½ pack			☐				
About ¼ pack				☐			
Less than 1 per day					☐		
I don't smoke						☐	
I have never smoked							☐

Alcohol	1	2	3	4	5	6	7
5. How many drinks does it take to make you feel high?							
More than 6		☑					
Between 4 and 6			☑				
Between 2 and 4				☐			
Between 1 and 2					☐		
Less than 1						☐	
I never drink							☐
6. Have people annoyed you by criticizing your drinking?							
Yes				☐			
No						☑	
7. Have you felt you ought to cut down on your drinking?							
Yes				☐			
No							☑

(Continued.)

8. Have you ever had a drink first thing in the morning to steady your nerves or get rid of a hangover?
   Yes ☐
   No ☑ ✓
9. Since you became pregnant, how often do you have 3 or more drinks at one time?
   Most weeks ☐
   A few times a month ☐
   About once a month ☐
   Less than once a month ☐
   Never ☐
   I don't drink at all ☑ ✓

Other Drugs

10. Which of the following drugs did you use in the 3 months before you became pregnant?
    Marijuana or hash ☐
    Cocaine or crack ☐
    Amphetamines (ice, etc.) ☐
    Narcotics ☐
    Psychedelics (PCP, LSD, etc.) ☐
    Inhalants ☐
11. Which of the following drugs have you used since you became pregnant?
    Marijuana or hash ☐
    Cocaine or crack ☐
    Amphetamines (ice, etc.) ☐
    Narcotics ☐
    Psychedelics (PCP, LSD, etc.) ☐
    Inhalants ☐

SCORING

The following responses suggest the need for an assessment interview to determine level of substance abuse risk. All of these responses fall in the center (column 4) or to the left of center.

1. Have you taken any prescription medicines since you became pregnant?   NO
      If yes, does your doctor know you are taking these medicines?   No
2. Have you taken over-the-counter (nonprescription) medicines since you became pregnant?   No
3. In the 3 months before you found out you were pregnant, how many cigarettes did you usually smoke per day?
   More than 1 ½ packs
   ½ to 1 ½ packs
   ½ pack
   About ¼ pack
4. How many cigarettes do you usually smoke a day now?
   More than 1 ½ packs
   ½ to 1 ½ packs
   ½ pack
   About ¼ pack
5. How many drinks does it take to make you feel high?
   More than 6
   Between 4 and 6
   Between 2 and 4
6. Have people annoyed you by criticizing your drinking?   Yes
7. Have you felt you ought to cut down on your drinking?   Yes

(Continued.)

8. Have you ever had a drink first thing in the morning to steady your nerves or get rid of a hangover?

Yes No

9. Since you became pregnant, how often do you have 3 or more drinks at one time?

None

Most weeks
A few times a month
About once a month

10. Which of the following drugs did you use in the 3 months before you became pregnant?

Marijuana or hash
Cocaine or crack
Amphetamines
Narcotics
Psychedelics
Inhalants

11. Which of the following drugs have you used since you became pregnant?

Marijuana or hash
Cocaine or crack
Amphetamines
Narcotics
Psychedelics
Inhalants

RATIONALE FOR SCORING
Prescription and Over-the-Counter Medications
A "yes" response to questions 1 and 2 requires a follow-up question about the particular medications used by the patient, but a "yes" response does not necessarily warrant an assessment interview. However, if a patient is taking a prescription medicine without her physician's knowledge, an assessment is required to determine reasons for this.
Tobacco
Smoking ¼ pack of cigarettes or more per day indicates the need for further assessment and probable intervention.
Alcohol
Use of any alcohol during pregnancy warrants further assessment. Included in this questionnaire are the T-ACE questions, a screening test validated for use in obstetric-gynecologic practice to determine risk-drinking (Sokol et al., 1989). On the Sokol T-ACE instrument, the *Tolerance* question is scored positive if it takes more than two drinks to make a woman feel "high." This question is particularly important because the question does not seem to trigger a denial response. The Tolerance question is scored as 2 points; a positive response to each of the other questions (*Annoyed*, *Cut down*, and *Eye-opener*) is scored as 1 point. Sokol and colleagues use a total score greater or equal to 2 on these four questions as a positive indicator of risk drinking by pregnant women.

As used in the Prenatal Health Questionnaire and the Women's Health Questionnaire, a positive response to any of the four questions is indicative of the need for an assessment.

Question 9 on the Prenatal Health Questionnaire and question 8 on the Woman's Health Questionnaire ask about binge drinking. Any binge drinking is considered risk drinking and indicates the need for an assessment. For pregnant women, the definition of binge drinking set at three or more drinks on one occasion is based on the work by Fleming et al. (1989) and by Little and Streissguth (1978). For nonpregnant women (Women's Health Questionnaire), binge drinking is defined as five or more drinks on one occasion.
Other Drugs
Use of any illicit drugs warrants further assessment.

*From Cox NS, Fleming MF, 1991. Developed for Rural South Central Wisconsin Perinatal Substance Abuse Grant, University of Wisconsin Funding Agency Office for Substance Abuse Prevention, Grant #5-H6-SP01641-02; 0491. Used by permission.

APPENDIX C–8.

Women's Health Questionnaire*

Please mark an X in the box representing your answer for each of the following questions.

	1	2	3	4	5	6	7

Prescribed Medications

1. Do you take any prescription medicines?
   - Yes — column 5
   - No — column 7
   - If yes, which ones (pills for acne, antibiotics, allergy medicines, etc.)?

   _____

   If yes, does your doctor know you are taking these medicines?
   - Yes — column 7
   - No — column 4

Over-the-Counter Medicines and Drugs

2. Do you take over-the-counter (nonprescription) medicines?
   - Yes — column 5
   - No — column 7
   - If Yes, which ones (aspirin, Tylenol, diet pills, cold medicines, etc.)?

   _____

Tobacco

3. How many cigarettes do you usually smoke per day?
   - More than 1 ½ packs — column 1
   - ½ to 1 ½ packs — column 2
   - ½ pack — column 3
   - About ¼ pack — column 4
   - Less than 1 per day — column 5
   - I didn't smoke — column 6
   - I have never smoked — column 7

Alcohol

4. How many drinks does it take to make you feel high?
   - More than 6 — column 2
   - Between 4 and 6 — column 3
   - Between 2 and 4 — column 4
   - Between 1 and 2 — column 5
   - Less than 1 — column 6
   - I never drink — column 7

5. Have people annoyed you by criticizing your drinking?
   - Yes — column 4
   - No — column 6

6. Have you felt you ought to cut down on your drinking?
   - Yes — column 4
   - No — column 6

7. Have you ever had a drink first thing in the morning to steady your nerves or get rid of a hangover?
   - Yes — column 4
   - No — column 6

(Continued.)

8. How often do you have five or more drinks at one time?

Most weeks ☐

A few times a month ☐

About once a month ☐

Less than once a month ☐

Never ☐

I don't drink at all ☐

Other Drugs

9. Which of the following drugs did you use in the past 6 months?

Marijuana or hash ☐

Cocaine or crack ☐

Amphetamines (ice, etc.) ☐

Narcotics ☐

Psychedelics (PCP, LSD, etc.) ☐

Inhalants ☐

10. When was the most recent time you used one of these drugs?

_____

SCORING

The following responses suggest the need for an assessment interview to determine level of substance abuse risk. All of these responses fall in the center (column 4) or to the left of center.

1. Do you take any prescription medicines?   ____

   If yes, does your doctor know you are taking these medicines?   No

2. Do you take over-the-counter (nonprescription) medicines?

3. How many cigarettes do you usually smoke per day?   More than 1 ½ packs

   ½ to 1 ½ packs

   ½ pack

   About ¼ pack

4. How many drinks does it take to make you feel high?   More than 6

   Between 4 and 6

   Between 2 and 4

5. Have people annoyed you by criticizing your drinking?   Yes

6. Have you felt you ought to cut down on your drinking?   Yes

7. Have you ever had a drink first thing in the morning to steady your nerves or   Yes
   get rid of a hangover?

(Continued.)

8. How often do you have five or more drinks at one time?	Most weeks A few times a month About once a month
9. Which of the following drugs did you use in the past 6 months?	Marijuana or hash Cocaine or crack Amphetamines Narcotics Psychedelics Inhalants

RATIONALE FOR SCORING

Prescription and Over-the-Counter Medications

A "yes" response to the first two questions requires a follow-up question about the particular medications used by the patient, but a "yes" response does not necessarily warrant an assessment interview. However, if a patient is taking a prescription medicine without her physician's knowledge, an assessment is required to determine reasons for this.

Tobacco

Smoking ¼ pack of cigarettes or more per day indicates the need for further assessment and probable intervention.

Alcohol

Use of any alcohol during pregnancy warrants further assessment. Included in this questionnaire are the T-ACE questions, a screening test validated for use in obstetric-gynecologic practice to determine risk drinking (Sokol et al., 1989). On the Sokol T-ACE instrument, the *Tolerance* question is scored positive if it takes more than two drinks to make a woman feel "high." This question is particularly important because the question does not seem to trigger a denial response. The Tolerance question is scored as 2 points, a positive response to each of the other questions (*Annoyed, Cut* down, and *Eye*-opener) is scored as 1 point. Sokol and colleagues use a total score greater or equal to 2 on these four questions as a positive indicator of risk drinking by pregnant women.

As used in the Prenatal Health Questionnaire and the Women's Health Questionnaire, a positive response to any of the four questions is indicative of the need for an assessment.

Question 9 on the Prenatal Health Questionnaire and question 8 on the Woman's Health Questionnaire ask about binge drinking. Any binge drinking is considered risk drinking and indicates the need for an assessment. For pregnant women, the definition of binge drinking set at three or more drinks on one occasion is based on the work by Fleming et al. (1989) and by Little and Streissguth (1978). For nonpregnant women (Women's Health Questionnaire), binge drinking is defined as five or more drinks on one occasion.

Other Drugs

Use of any illicit drugs warrants further assessment.

*From Cox NS, Fleming MF, 1991. Developed for Rural South Central Wisconsin Perinatal Substance Abuse Grant, University of Wisconsin Funding Agency Office for Substance Abuse Prevention, Grant #5-H6-SP01641-02; 0491

Street Names of Common Drugs: Partial Compendium*

A

A	Amphetamines
A Stick	Marijuana
Abbots	Pentobarbital
Acapulco Gold	Marijuana
Acballo	Heroin
Ace	Marijuana cigarette
Acid	LSD
Afghani	Hash oil
Aimes	Amyl nitrate
All-Star	Multiple drug user
Amoeba	Phencyclidine (PCP)
Amys	Amyl nitrate
Angel Dust	Phencyclidine (PCP)
Angel Hair	Phencyclidine (PCP)
Angel Mist	Phencyclidine (PCP)
Anhalonium	Amescaline, peyote
Animal	LSD
Animal Tranquilizer	Phencyclidine (PCP)
Areca Nut	Betel nut
Ashes	Marijuana

B

Baby	Marijuana; small drug habit
Bad Seed	Peyote buttons
Badoh Negro	Morning Glory seeds
Bam	Amphetamine
Benewort	Belladonna
Barbs	Barbiturates
Barrels	LSD
Beans	Amphetamine, barbiturates, mescaline
Beast	LSD
Beautiful Lady	Belladonna
Belly Habit	Opiate addiction
Bennies	Amphetamine
Benny Jag	High on amphetamines
Benzies	Amphetamines
Bernice	Cocaine

Bernies	Cocaine
Betel Morsel	Betel nut
Bhang	Marijuana
Big C	Cocaine
Big Chief	Mescaline
Big D	Dilaudid, LSD
Big H	Heroin
Big Harry	Heroin
Biscuits	Methadone
Black and Whites	Diet Pills
Black Beauties	Amphetamines
Black Cadillacs	Biphetamine
Black Dex	Biphetamine
Black Mollies	Amphetamines
Black Oil	Hash oil
Black Russian	Hashish (potent hashish, possibly with opium)
Blackbirds	Amphetamines
Blanco	Heroin
Blanks	Heroin
Blockbusters	Barbiturates
Blotter	LSD
Blotter Acid	LSD
Blow	Cocaine
Bluebirds	Amobarbital
Blue Acid	LSD
Blue Berkley	LSD on blue blotters
Blue Cap	LSD
Blue Cheer	LSD
Blue Devils	Amobarbital
Blue Dragon	LSD
Blue Heaven	Barbiturates, LSD
Blue Mist	LSD
Blue Star	Morning Glory seeds
Blues	Amobarbital
Bo	Marijuana

Bomber	Large marijuana cigarette
Bombita	Amphetamines or cocaine for injection
Bombito	Amphetamines or cocaine for injection
Boo	Marijuana
Bottle	Amphetamines
Boy	Heroin
Broccoli	Marijuana
Brother	Heroin
Brown	Mexican heroin
Brown Dots	LSD
Brown Sugar	Heroin
Brownstuff	Opium
Buddha Sticks	Marijuana
Bumblebees	Amphetamines
Burese	Cocaine
Bush	Marijuana
Businessman's Special	DMT (dimethyltryptamine)
Business Trip	Amphetamines
Businessman's Trip	DMT (dimethyltryptamine)
Busy Bee	Phencyclidine (PCP)
Butter Flower	Marijuana
Buttons	Mescaline

C

C	Cocaine
Caballo	Heroin
Ca-ca	Heroin
Cactus	Mescaline
Cadillac	Phencyclidine (PCP)
California Sunshine	LSD
California Poppy	Poppy with marijuana-like effects
Camel	LSD
Candles	LSD
Candy	Barbiturates; term often used for any drug
Cannabis	Marijuana
Carrie	Cocaine
Cartwheels	Amphetamines
Cecil	Cocaine
Chalk	Amphetamines
Channel	Vein used for injection
Charas	Marijuana
Cherry Leb	Hash oil
Cherry Top	LSD
Chicago Green	Marijuana mixed with opium
Chicken Powder	Amphetamines
Chief	LSD
China White	Heroin, fentanyl
Chinese Red	Heroin
Chiva	Heroin
Chocolate Chips	LSD
Cholly	Cocaine
Christmas Trees	Tuinal (amytal + seconal), dextroamphetamine
CJ	Phencyclidine (PCP)
Clear Light	LSD

Copilots	Dextroamphetamine
Coast-to-Coasts	Amphetamines
Cobics	Heroin
Cobies	Morphine
Coca	Cocaine
Coffee	LSD
Coke	Cocaine
Cola	Cocaine
Colombo	Marijuana
Colombian	Marijuana
Colombian Red	Marijuana
Contact Reds	LSD
Corine	Cocaine
Cotton Habit	Irregular heroin habit
Courage Pills	Barbiturates
Crack	Cocaine
Crank	Methamphetamine
Crap	Heroin
Cross	Amphetamines
Crossroads	Amphetamines
Crosstops	Amphetamines
Crystal	Amphetamines, phencyclidine (PCP)
Crystal Meth	Methamphetamine
Crystal Joints	Phencyclidine (PCP)
Cube	LSD, meperidine, morphine
Cupcakes	LSD
Cyclones	Phencyclidine (PCP)

D

D	Dilaudid
Dava	Iranian heroin
Deadly Nightshade	Belladonna
Death's Head	Amanita muscaria (hallucinogenic mushroom)
Death's Herb	Belladonna
Demis	Demoral
Devil's Apple	Jimson Weed
Devil's Testicle	Mandrake
Devil's Trumpet	Jimson Weed
Devil's Weed	Jimson Weed
Dexies	Dextroamphetamine
Dice	Methamphetamine (possibly Desoxyn)
Dillies	Dilaudid
Dirt	Heroin
DOA	Phencyclidine (PCP)
Do-Jee	Heroin
Dollies	Methadone
DOM	Methylamphetamine
Domes	LSD
Dope	Heroin, marijuana, morphine
Dors and Fours	Doriden and Tylenol no. 4
Dots	LSD
Double Trouble	Barbiturates
Doublecross	Amphetamines
Downers	Amytal, other barbiturates, glutethimide

Downs	Dalmane, benzodiazepines
Dream	Cocaine
Drivers	Amphetamines
Dry High	Marijuana
Dummy Dust	Phencyclidine (PCP)
Dust	Cocaine, heroin, morphine, phencyclidine (PCP)
Dust of Angels	Phencyclidine (PCP)
Dusting	Mixing heroin, PCP with marijuana
Dynamite	Cocaine

E

Electric Kool Aid	LSD mixed with punch
Elephant	Phencyclidine (PCP)
Embalming Fluid	Phencyclidine (PCP)
Emsel	Morphine
Endurets	Phenmetrazine
Estuffa	Heroin
Eye-Openers	Amphetamines

F

F-40s	Secobarbital
F-66	Amobarbital, secobarbital
Fifty	LSD
Fit	Drug injecting equipment
First Line	Hydromorphone, morphine
Fives	Amphetamines
Flake	Cocaine
Flats	LSD
Flea Powder	Heroin, diluted
Flower of Paradise	Khat
Flowers of the Virgin	Morning Glory seeds
Fly Agaric	Amanita muscaria (hallucinogenic mushrooms)
Flying Saucers	Morning Glory seeds
Fools Pills	Barbiturates
Footballs	Dextroamphetamine, hydromorphone
Forwards	Amphetamines
Fur Way	LSD
Fours	Tylenol with codeine (60 mg)
Freebase	Cocaine
French Quaalude	Methaqualone
Fuel	Marijuana with insecticide, smoked
Funny Stuff	Marijuana

G

Gage	Marijuana
Gainesville Green	Marijuana
Gangster Pills	Barbiturates
Ganja	Marijuana
Gas	Nitrous oxide
GB	Barbiturates
Giggles Smoke	Marijuana
Gin	Cocaine
Girl	Cocaine
Glass	Methamphetamine

Glory Seeds	Morning Glory seeds
Gold	Marijuana (potent)
Gold Dust	Cocaine
Gold Colombian	Marijuana
Goma	Morphine, oxymorphone
Goma de Mota	Hashish
Goods	Heroin, morphine
Goof Butt	Marijuana
Goofballs	Barbiturates
Goofers	Barbiturates, other sedative/hypnotics
Goon	Phencyclidine (PCP)
Goric	Paregoric
Gorilla Pills	Amobarbital, Seconal
Grass	Marijuana
Green	Dextroamphetamine/ Amobarbital, Ketamine, Marijuana
Green Dragons	Barbiturates, LSD
Greenies	Amphetamines
Griefo	Marijuana
Griffa	Marijuana
Griffo	Marijuana
Gun	Hypodermic needle
Gunk	Inhalants
Gutter	Vein used to inject drugs

H

H	Heroin
Happy Dust	Cocaine
Hard Candy	Heroin, any "hard" drug
Hard Stuff	Morphine
Hard Stuff	Heroin
Harry	Heroin
Has	Marijuana
Hash	Hashish
Hawaiian	Marijuana
Hawaiian Salt	Recrystalized methamphetamine
Hawk	LSD
Hay	Marijuana
Haze	LSD
Hearts	Amphetamines
Heaven Dust	Cocaine
Heavenly blue	LSD
Heavenly blues	Morning Glory seeds
Hemp	Marijuana
Her	Cocaine
Herb	Marijuana
Heroina	Heroin
Hikori	Mescaline, peyote
Hocus	Morphine
Hot	Chloral hydrate, phencyclidine (PCP)
Hombre	Heroin
Hombrecitos	Psilocybin
Honey Oil	Hash oil
Hootch	Marijuana
Hooter	Marijuana
Hort	To sniff a drug

Horse	Heroin
Horse Hearts	Amphetamine
Huatari	Mescaline, Peyote

I

Ice	Recrystalized methamphetamine
Ice Cream Habit	Irregular drug habit
Idiot Pills	Barbiturates
Incentive	Cocaine
Indian Oil	Hash oil
Indian hay	Marijuana
Instant Zen	LSD

J

J	Marijuana
Jamaican	Marijuana
Java	Caffeine
Jay	Marijuana
Jellies	Chloral hydrate
Jelly Babies	Amphetamines
Jelly Beans	Amphetamines
Jive	Heroin, marijuana
Joint	Marijuana cigarette
Jolly Beans	Amphetamines
Joy Juice	Chloral hydrate
Joy Powder	Cocaine, heroin
Juanita Weed	Marijuana
Jug	Amphetamines
Juice	Methadone
Junk	Demerol, Dilaudid, heroin, morphine

K

Ka-ka	Heroin
Kaif	Marijuana
Kauii	Marijuana
Kif	Hashish, marijuana, tobacco-marijuana mix
Killer Weed	Phencyclidine (PCP) with marijuana
King Kong Pills	Barbiturates
King Tut	LSD
KJ	Phencyclidine (PCP)
Krystal	Amphetamine, phencyclidine

L

Lady	Cocaine
Lady Snow	Cocaine
Laughing Gas	Nitrous oxide
Leaf	Cocaine
Leaf of God	Calea
Leaper	Amphetamine
Lidpoppers	Amphetamine
Lightening	Amphetamine
Lilly	Secobarbital
Line	Cocaine; vein used to inject drugs

Locoweed	Jimson Weed, marijuana
Love Drug	MDA
Love Week	Marijuana
LSD-25	LSD
Lucy in the Sky	LSD
Ludes	Methaqualone
Luding out	Using methaqualone, alone or with alcohol

M

M	Morphine
M and Ms	Secobarbital
Mach	Marijuana
Magic Mist	Phencyclidine (PCP)
Magic Mushroom	Psilocybin
Mandragora	Mandrake
Mandrakes	Methaqualone
Marijuana	Marijuana
Marshmallow Reds	Barbiturates
Mary	Marijuana
Mary Werner	Marijuana
Mary Jane	Marijuana
Material	Heroin
Mauii	Marijuana
MBD	Pemoline
MDA	Methylenedioxyamphetamine
Medicine	Methadone
Merck	General term for high-grade drugs
Mellow	MDA
Mellow Yellow	Banana skins
Mellow Yellows	LSD
Mesc	Mescaline
Mescal	Mescaline, peyote
Mescal Buttons	Mescaline, peyote
Meth	Methamphetamine
Methadose	Methadone
Mex	Marijuana
Mexican	Marijuana
Mexican Brown	Heroin, average strength

N

Nail	Hypodermic needle used to inject drugs
Nebbies	Pentobarbital
Nebbish	Barbiturates
Nembies	Pentobarbital
Nemmies	Barbiturates
Nimbies	Pentobarbital
Ninos	Psilocybin
Nitrous	Nitrous oxide
Noble Princess	Psilocybin
Nose	Cocaine
Nose Candy	Cocaine
Nose Powder	Cocaine
Nuggets	Amphetamines
Number	Marijuana cigarette
Number threes	Codeine 0.5 grain

Number Fours	Codeine 1.0 grain

O

O	Opium
Oil	Hash oil
Op	Opium (paregoric)
One-Hit Grass	DMT
Orange Hearts	Dextroamphetamine
Orange Mushrooms	LSD
Orange Sunshine	LSD
Orange Wedges	LSD
Oranges	Dextroamphetamine
Owsley	LSD
Ozone	Phencyclidine (PCP)

P

Pajao Rojo	Barbiturates
Panama Red	Marijuana
Paper Acid	LSD
Paradise	Cocaine
Paris 400	Methaqualone
PCE	Phencyclidine analog
PCP	Phencyclidine (PCP)
PCPy	Phencyclidine analog
Peace	Phencyclidine (PCP)
Peace Pill	Phencyclidine (PCP)
Peaches	Amphetamines
Peanuts	Barbiturates
Pearls	Amyl nitrate
Pearly Gates	LSD, Morning Glory seeds
Pearly Whites	Morning Glory seeds
Pep Pills	Amphetamines
Perks	Percodan
Perico	Cocaine
Persian	Iranian heroin
Persian Brown	Iranian heroin
Peruvian Flake	Cocaine
Peruvian Marching Powder	Cocaine
Peyote	Mescaline
Peyotyl	Peyote
Pharmaceutical Powder	Cocaine
Phennies	Barbiturates
PHP	Phencyclidine analog
Pimp	Cocaine
Ping Lang	Betel nut
Pink Ladies	Barbiturates, propoxyphene
Pink and Green Amps	Amphetamines
Pinks	Propoxyphene, Seconal
Plants	Mescaline
Pod	Marijuana
Poison	Heroin
Polvo	Heroin
Polvo Blance	Cocaine
Poppers	Amyl nitrate
Poppy	Opium (paregoric)
Pot	Marijuana

Product	Heroin
Pumpkin Seeds	Propoxyphene
Purple Haze	LSD, phencyclidine (PCP)
Purple Hearts	Phenobarbital
Purple Microdot	LSD

Q

Quaas	Methaqualone
Quacks	Methaqualone
Quads	Methaqualone
Quarter Moon	Hashish
Quartz	Recrystallized Methamphetamine
Quas	Methaqualone

R

Rainbows	Amobarbital, Tuinal, (amobarbital + Seconal)
Red	Marijuana, secobarbital
Red and Blues	Barbiturates
Red Birds	Secobarbital
Red Devils	Secobarbital
Red Dragon	LSD
Red Oil	Hash oil
Reds and Grays	Propoxyphene
Reefer	Marijuana cigarette
Rippers	Amphetamines
Roach	Marijuana cigarette
Rhythms	Amphetamines
Rock	Cocaine
Rock Candy	Cocaine
Rocket Fuel	Phencyclidine (PCP)
Rockets	Marijuana
Rope	Marijuana
Rosas	Amphetamines
Roses	Amphetamine
Royal Blue	LSD
Rufus	Iranian heroin

S

Satan's Apple	Mandrake
Sativa	Marijuana
Scag	Heroin
Scar	Heroin
Schmeck	Heroin
Schoolboy	Codeine
Scuffle	Phencyclidine (PCP)
Seccies	Secobarbital
Seeds	Morning Glory seeds
Seggies	Barbiturates
Seni	Mescaline, peyote
714s	Methaqualone
She	Cocaine
Sheets	Phencyclidine (PCP)
Sherman's	Phencyclidine cigarette
Shit	Demerol, Dilaudid, heroin, marijuana

Short Flight	Coricidin and beer
Shrooms	Psilocybin
Silly Putty	Psilocybin
Sinsemilla	Marijuana
Sister	Morphine
Skag	Heroin
Skinny	Marijuana
Skyrockets	Amphetamines
Sleepers	Barbiturates, other sedative/hypnotics
Sleeping Pills	Barbiturates
Smack	Heroin
Smash	Cannabis (acetone extract), hash oil
Smeck	Heroin
Smoke	Marijuana
Snappers	Amyl nitrate
Snop	Marijuana
Snorts	Phencyclidine (PCP)
Snow	Cocaine, heroin
Snowbird	Cocaine
Soapers	Methaqualone
Society High	Cocaine
Soles	Hashish
Soma	Phencyclidine (PCP)
Son of One	Hash oil
Sopes	Methaqualone
Sparkle Plenties	Amphetamines
Speckled Birds	Amphetamines
Speed	Amphetamine, methamphetamine
Speed Ball	Cocaine with heroin
Splash	Amphetamine
Spliff	Marijuana
Splim	Marijuana
Star Dust	Cocaine
Stick	Marijuana cigarette
Stinkweed	Jimson Weed, marijuana
Stogie	Nicotine
Stofa	Heroin
STP	Methamphetamine
Straw	Marijuana
Strawberry Fields	LSD
Strawberry Mescaline	Mescaline
Stuff	Demerol, Dilaudid, heroin, marijuana, morphine
Stumblers	Barbiturates
Sugar	Heroin, LSD
Sugar Lump	LSD
Summer Skies	Morning Glory seeds
Sunshine	LSD
Supari	Betel nut
Super Blow	Cocaine
Super Soper	Methaqualone
Supergrass	Phencyclidine (PCP)
Superjoint	Marijuana mixed with PCP
Superweek	Phencyclidine (PCP)
Surfer	Phencyclidine (PCP)

Sweet Lucy	Marijuana
Sweet Lunch	Marijuana
Sweets	Amphetamines
Synthetic Marijuana	Phencyclidine (PCP)

T

T	Phencyclidine (PCP)
TCP	Phencyclidine analog
Tea	Marijuana
Tecaba	Heroin
Tecata	Heroin
Tees and Blues	Talwin and Tripelennamine
Tens	Amphetamines
Texas Reefer	Large marijuana cigarette
Texas Tea	Marijuana
Thai Sticks	Asian marijuana with opium, tied to red
THC	Marijuana; sometimes used for phencyclidine (PCP)
The Force	LSD
The One	Hash oil
Thing	Heroin
Thorn apple	Jimson Weed
Thrusters	Amphetamines
Tic Tac	Phencyclidine (PCP)
Tie Stick	Marijuana mixed with opium, tied to stick
Tlitiltzen	Morning Glory seeds
Toke	Nicotine
Tooies	Tuinal (Amytal + Seconal)
Toot	Cocaine
TPCP	Phencyclidine analog
Tranq	Phencyclidine (PCP)
Trees	Tuinal (Amytal + Seconal)
Trips	LSD
Truck Drivers	Amphetamines
Turnabouts	Amphetamines
Turnarounds	Amphetamines
Twenty-five	LSD
Twist	Marijuana

U

Unkie	Morphine
Uppers	Amphetamines
Ups	Amphetamines

V

Vipe's Weed	Marijuana

W

Wake-ups	Amphetamines
Wakowi	Mescaline, peyote
Water	Methamphetamine
Wedding Bells	Morning Glory seeds
Wedding Bells Acid	LSD
Wedges	LSD
Wedgies	LSD
Weed	Marijuana, phencyclidine (PCP)
Weekend Habit	Irregular drug use
Weekend Warrior	Irregular drug user

Wheat	Marijuana		
Whit(s)	Amphetamines, cocaine	**Y**	
White Cross	Amphetamines	Yellow Bam	Methamphetamine, possibly desoxyn
White Dexies	Amphetamines		
White Horizon	Phencyclidine (PCP)	Yellow Footballs	Propoxyphene
		Yellow Jackets	Pentobarbital
White Horse	Cocaine	Yellows	LSD
White Stuff	Cocaine, Dilaudid, heroin, morphine	Yellows	Pentobarbital
White Girl	Cocaine	Yerba	Marijuana
White Lightning	LSD	Yerba del Diablo	Jimson Weed
White Man's Plant	Jimson Weed	**Z**	
Window Pain	LSD	Zeeters	Amphetamine
Wobble	Phencyclidine (PCP)	Zen	LSD
Woodpecker of Mars	*Amanita muscaria* (hallucinogenic mushroom)	Zip	Amphetamine
		Zig-Zag Man	LSD

*From National Council on Alcoholism and Drug Dependence, vol 1, no 2, 1990.

References:
Felter R, et al: Emergency department management of the intoxicated adolescent. *Pediatr Clin North Am* 1987; 34:399–421.
Wilford BB: *Drug Abuse: A Guide for the Primary Care Physician*. Chicago, American Medical Association, 1981.
Young LA, et al: *Recreational Drugs*. New York, Berkeley Books, 1977.

Criteria for Mental Health Disorders*

I. MAJOR DEPRESSIVE EPISODE

Major depressive syndrome is defined by criterion A, as follows:

A. At least five of the following symptoms have been present during the same 2-week period, and represent a change from previous functioning; at least one of the symptoms is either (1) depressed mood or (2) loss of interest or pleasure. (Do not include symptoms that are clearly due to a physical condition, mood-incongruent delusions or hallucinations, incoherence, or marked loosening of associations.)

1. Depressed mood (can be irritable mood in children and adolescents) most of the day, nearly every day, as indicated either by subjective account or observation by others.
2. Markedly diminished interest or pleasure in all or almost all activities most of the day, nearly every day, as indicated either by subjective account or observation by others of apathy most of the time.
3. Significant weight loss or weight gain when not dieting (e.g., more than 5% of body weight in a month), or decrease or increase in appetite nearly every day (in children, consider failure to make expected weight gains).
4. Insomnia or hypersomnia nearly every day.
5. Psychomotor agitation or retardation nearly every day (observable by others, not merely subjective feelings of restlessness or being slowed down).
6. Fatigue or loss of energy nearly every day.
7. Feelings of worthlessness or excessive or inappropriate guilt (which may be delusional) nearly every day (not merely self-reproach or guilt about being sick).
8. Diminished ability to think or concentrate, or indecisiveness, nearly every day, either by subjective account or as observed by others.
9. Recurrent thoughts of death (not just fear of dying), recurrent sui-

*From *Diagnostic and Statistical Manual,* ed 3, revised. New York, American Psychiatric Association.

cidal ideation without a specific plan, or a suicide attempt or a specific plan for committing suicide.

B. **Exclusion Criteria:**

1. It cannot be established that an organic factor initiated and maintained the disturbance.

2. The disturbance is not a normal reaction to the death of a loved one (uncomplicated bereavement).

3. At no time during the disturbance have there been delusions or hallucinations for as long as 2 weeks in the absence of prominent mood symptoms (e.g., before the mood symptoms developed or after they have remitted).

4. Not superimposed on schizophrenia, schizophreniform disorder, delusional disorder, or psychotic disorder.

C. **Severity** of current state of bipolar disorder, depressed or major depression:

1. *Mild:* Few if any symptoms in excess of those required to make the diagnosis, *and* symptoms result in only minor impairment in occupational functioning or in usual social activities or relationships with others.

2. *Moderate:* Symptoms or functional impairment between "mild" and "severe."

3. *Severe, without psychotic features:* Several symptoms in excess of those required to make the diagnosis, *and* symptoms markedly interfere with occupational functioning or with usual social activities or relationships with others.

4. *Severe with psychotic features:* Delusions or hallucinations. If possible, specify whether the psychotic features are *mood congruent* or *mood incongruent.*

a. *Mood-congruent psychotic features:* Delusions or hallucinations whose content is entirely consistent with the typical depressive themes of personal inadequacy, guilt, disease, death, nihilism, or deserved punishment.

b. *Mood-incongruent psychotic features:* Delusions or hallucinations whose content does not involve typical depressive themes of personal inadequacy, guilt, disease, death, nihilism, or deserved punishment. Included are such symptoms as persecutory delusions (not directly related to depressive themes), thought insertion, thought broadcasting, and delusions of control.

D. **Criteria for Remission:**

1. *Partial remission:* Intermediate between "full remission" and "mild" *and* no previous dysthymia. (If major depressive episode was superimposed on dysthymia, the diagnosis of dysthymia alone is given once the full criteria for a major depressive episode are no longer met.)

2. *Full remission:* During the past 6 months no significant signs or symptoms of the disturbance.

II. MANIC EPISODE

Manic syndrome is defined as including criteria A, B, and C below. Hypomanic syndrome is defined as including criteria A and B but not C (i.e., no marked impairment).

A. Distinct period of abnormally and persistently elevated, expansive, or irritable mood.

B. During the period of mood disturbance, at least three of the following symptoms have persisted (four if the mood is only irritable) and have been present to a significant degree:

1. Inflated self-esteem or grandiosity.
2. Decreased need for sleep (e.g., feels rested after only 3 hours of sleep).
3. More talkative than usual, or pressure to keep talking.
4. Flight of ideas or subjective experience that thoughts are racing.
5. Distractibility; attention too easily drawn to unimportant or irrelevant external stimuli.
6. Increase in goal-directed activity (either socially, at work or school, or sexually) or psychomotor agitation.
7. Excessive involvement in pleasurable activities that have a high potential for painful consequences (e.g., engages in unrestrained buying sprees, sexual indiscretions, or foolish business investments).

C. Mood disturbance sufficiently severe to cause marked impairment in occupational functioning or in usual social activities or relationships with others or to necessitate hospitalization to prevent harm to self or others.

D. Exclusion Criteria:

1. At no time during the disturbance have there been delusions or hallucinations for as long as 2 weeks in the absence of prominent mood symptoms (i.e., before the mood symptoms developed or after they have remitted).
2. Not superimposed on schizophrenia, schizophreniform disorder, delusional disorder, or psychotic disorder.
3. It cannot be established that an organic factor initiated and maintained the disturbance. NOTE: Somatic antidepressant treatment (e.g., drugs, electroconvulsive therapy) that apparently precipitates a mood disturbance should not be considered an etiologic organic factor.

E. Severity of Manic Episode:

1. ***Mild:*** Meets minimum symptom criteria for a manic episode (or almost meets symptom criteria if there has been a previous manic episode).
2. ***Moderate:*** Extreme increase in activity or impairment in judgment.
3. ***Severe without psychotic features:*** Almost continual supervision required to prevent physical harm to self or others.
4. ***Severe with psychotic features:*** Delusions, hallucinations, or

catatonic symptoms. If possible, specify whether the psychotic features are *mood congruent* or *mood incongruent.*

a. *Mood-congruent psychotic features:* Delusions or hallucinations whose content is entirely consistent with the typical manic themes of inflated worth, power, knowledge, identity, or special relationship to a deity or famous person.

b. *Mood-incongruent psychotic features:* Either of the following:

(1) Delusions or hallucinations whose content does not involve the typical manic themes of inflated worth, power, knowledge, identity, or special relationship to a deity or famous person. Included are such symptoms as persecutory delusions (not directly related to grandiose ideas or themes), thought insertion, and delusions of being controlled.

(2) Catatonic symptoms (e.g., stupor, mutism, negativism, posturing).

F. Criteria for Remission:

1. ***Partial remission:*** Full criteria were previously but are not currently met; some signs or symptoms of the disturbance have persisted.

2. ***Full remission:*** Full criteria were previously met, but there have been no significant signs or symptoms of the disturbance for at least 6 months.

III. GENERALIZED ANXIETY DISORDER

A. At least 6 of the following 18 symptoms often are present when anxious (do not include symptoms present only during panic attacks):

Motor tension

1. Trembling, twitching, or feeling shaky.
2. Muscle tension, aches, or soreness.
3. Restlessness.
4. Easy fatigability.

Autonomic hyperactivity

5. Shortness of breath or smothering sensation.
6. Palpitations or accelerated heart rate (tachycardia).
7. Sweating or cold clammy hands.
8. Dry mouth.
9. Dizziness or light-headedness.
10. Nausea, diarrhea, or other abdominal distress.
11. Flushes (hot flashes) or chills.
12. Frequent urination.
13. Trouble swallowing or "lump in throat."

Vigilance and scanning

14. Feeling keyed up or on edge.
15. Exaggerated startle response.
16. Difficulty concentrating or "mind going blank" because of anxiety.
17. Trouble falling asleep or staying asleep.
18. Irritability.

B. Unrealistic or excessive anxiety and worry (apprehensive expectation) about two or more life circumstances (e.g., worry about possible misfortune to one's child who is in no danger, or worry about finances for no good reason) for 6 months or longer, during which time the person has been bothered more days than not by these concerns. In children and adolescents, this may take the form of anxiety and worry about academic, athletic, or social performance.

C. Exclusion Criteria:

1. It cannot be established that an organic factor initiated and maintained the disturbance (e.g., hyperthyroidism, caffeine intoxication).
2. If another axis 1 disorder is present, the focus of the anxiety and worry in A is unrelated to it (e.g., the anxiety or worry is not about having a panic attack, as in panic disorder; being embarrassed in public, as in social phobia; being contaminated, as in obsessive compulsive disorder; or gaining weight, as in anorexia nervosa).
3. The disturbance does not occur only during the course of a mood disorder or a psychotic disorder.

IV. PANIC DISORDER

A. At least four of the following symptoms developed during at least one of the attacks:
1. Shortness of breath (dyspnea) or smother sensation.
2. Dizziness, unsteady feelings, or faintness.
3. Palpitations or accelerated heart rate (tachycardia).
4. Trembling or shaking.
5. Sweating.
6. Choking.
7. Nausea or abdominal distress.
8. Depersonalization or derealization.
9. Numbness or tingling sensation.
10. Flushes (hot flashes) or chills.
11. Chest pain or discomfort.
12. Fear of dying.
13. Fear of going crazy or of doing something uncontrolled.
    NOTE: Attacks involving four or more symptoms are panic attacks; attacks involving fewer than four symptoms are limited symptom attacks.

B. Either four attacks, as defined in criterion A, have occurred within a 4-week period or one or more attacks have been followed by a period of at least 1 month of persistent fear of having another attack.

C. During at least some of the attacks, at least four of the C symptoms developed suddenly and increased in intensity within 10 minutes of the beginning of the first C symptom noticed in the attack.

D. At some time during the disturbance, one or more panic attacks (discrete periods of intense fear or discomfort) have occurred that were (1) unexpected (i.e., did not occur immediately before or on exposure to a situation that almost always caused anxiety) and (2) not triggered by situations in which the person was the focus of others' attention.

E. Exclusion Criteria:
1. It cannot be established that an organic factor initiated and maintained the disturbance (e.g., amphetamine or caffeine intoxication, hyperthyroidism).
2. Mitral valve prolapse may be an associated condition, but does not preclude a diagnosis of panic disorder.

V. SIMPLE PHOBIA

A. Fear or avoidant behavior significantly interferes with the person's normal routine or with usual social activities or relationships with others, or there is marked distress about having the fear.

B. The object or situation is avoided or endured with intense anxiety.

C. During some phase of the disturbance, exposure to the specific phobic stimulus (stimuli) almost invariably provokes an immediate anxiety response.

D. There is persistent fear of a circumscribed stimulus (object or situation) other than fear of having a panic attack (as in panic disorder) or of humiliation or embarrassment in certain social situations (as in social phobia).

NOTE: Do not include fears that are part of panic disorder with agoraphobia or agoraphobia without history of panic disorder.

E. The person recognizes that his or her fear is excessive or unreasonable.

F. The phobic stimulus is unrelated to the content of the obsessions of obsessive compulsive disorder or the trauma of posttraumatic stress disorder.

VI. POSTTRAUMATIC STRESS DISORDER

Posttraumatic stress disorder is defined as meeting criteria from categories A, B, and C, below.

A. The traumatic event is persistently reexperienced in at least one of the following ways:

1. Recurrent and intrusive distressing recollections of the event (in young children, repetitive play in which themes or aspects of the trauma are expressed).
2. Recurrent distressing dreams of the event.
3. Sudden acting or feeling as if the traumatic event were recurring (includes a sense of reliving the experience, illusions, hallucinations, and dissociative [flashback] episodes, even those that occur on awakening or when intoxicated).
4. Intense psychologic distress at exposure to events that symbolize or resemble an aspect of the traumatic event, including anniversaries of the trauma.

B. Persistent avoidance of stimuli associated with the trauma or numbing of general responsiveness (not present before the trauma), as indicated by at least three of the following:

1. Efforts to avoid thoughts or feelings associated with the trauma.
2. Efforts to avoid activities or situations that arouse recollections of the trauma.
3. Inability to recall an important aspect of the trauma (psychogenic amnesia).
4. Markedly diminished interest in significant activities (in young children, loss of recently acquired developmental skills such as toilet training or language skills).
5. Feeling of detachment or estrangement from others.
6. Restricted range of affect (e.g., unable to have loving feelings).
7. Sense of a foreshortened future (e.g., does not expect to have a career, marriage, or children, or a long life).

C. Persistent symptoms of increased arousal (not present before the trauma), as indicated by at least two of the following:

1. Difficulty falling asleep or staying asleep.
2. Irritability or outbursts of anger.
3. Difficulty concentrating.
4. Hypervigilance.
5. Exaggerated startle response.
6. Physiologic reactivity on exposure to events that symbolize or resemble an aspect of the traumatic event (e.g., a woman who was raped in an elevator breaks out in a sweat when entering any elevator).

D. Duration of the disturbance (symptoms in A, B, and C) of at least 1 month.

NOTE: Posttraumatic stress disorder develops in persons who have experienced an event that is outside the range of usual human experience and that would be markedly distressing to almost anyone, for example, serious threat to one's life or physical integrity; serious threat or harm to one's children, spouse, or other close relatives and friends; sudden destruction of one's home or community; or seeing another person who has recently been or is being seriously injured or killed as the result of an accident or physical violence.

VII. ANTISOCIAL PERSONALITY DISORDER

Persons must meet criteria A, B, and C before a diagnosis of antisocial personality disorder can be diagnosed.

A. Current age at least 18 years.

B. Evidence of conduct disorder with onset before age 15 years, as indicated by a history of *three or more* of the following:
1. Was often truant.
2. Ran away from home overnight at least twice while living in parental or parental surrogate home (or once without returning).
3. Often initiated physical fights.
4. Used a weapon in more than one fight.
5. Forced someone into sexual activity.
6. Was physically cruel to animals.
7. Was physically cruel to other people.
8. Deliberately destroyed others' property (other than by fire-setting).
9. Deliberately engaged in fire-setting.
10. Often lied (other than to avoid physical or sexual abuse).
11. Has stolen without confrontation of a victim on more than one occasion (including forgery).
12. Has stolen with confrontation of a victim (e.g., mugging, purse snatching, extortion, armed robbery).

C. Pattern of irresponsible and antisocial behavior since the age of 15 years, as indicated by at least *four* of the following:
1. Is unable to sustain consistent work behavior, as indicated by any of the following (including similar behavior in academic settings if the person is a student):
   a. Significant unemployment for 6 months or more within 5 years when expected to work and work was available.
   b. Repeated absences from work unexplained by illness of self or family.
   c. Abandonment of several jobs without realistic plans for others.
2. Fails to conform to social norms with respect to lawful behavior, as indicated by repeatedly performing antisocial actions that are grounds for arrest (whether arrested or not), such as destroying property, harassing others, stealing, pursuing an illegal occupation.
3. Is irritable and aggressive, as indicated by repeated physical fights or assaults (not required by one's job or to defend someone or self), including spouse or child beating.
4. Repeatedly fails to honor financial obligations, as indicated by defaulting on debts or failing to provide child support or support for other dependents on a regular basis.
5. Fails to plan ahead or is impulsive, as indicated by one or both of the following:
   a. Travel from place to place without a prearranged job or clear

goal for the period of travel or clear idea about when the travel will terminate.

   b. Lack of a fixed address for a month or more.

6. Has no regard for the truth, as indicated by repeated lying, use of aliases, or "conning" others for personal profit or pleasure.

7. Is reckless regarding own or others' personal safety, as indicated by driving while intoxicated or recurrent speeding.

8. If a parent or guardian, lacks ability to function as a responsible parent, as indicated by one or more of the following:

   a. Malnutrition of child.

   b. Child's illness resulting from lack of minimal hygiene.

   c. Failure to obtain medical care for a seriously ill child.

   d. Child's dependence on neighbors or nonresident relatives for food or shelter.

   e. Failure to arrange for a caretaker for a young child when parent is away from home.

   f. Repeated squandering on personal items of money required for household necessities.

9. Has never sustained a totally monogamous relationship for more than 1 year.

10. Lacks remorse (feels justified in having hurt, mistreated, or stolen from another).

D. Occurrence of antisocial behavior not exclusively during the course of schizophrenia or manic episodes.

VIII. BRIEF REACTIVE PSYCHOSIS

A diagnosis of brief reactive psychosis is based on criteria A and B.

A. Presence of at least one of the following symptoms indicating impaired reality testing (not culturally sanctioned):

1. Incoherence or marked loosening of associations.
2. Delusions.
3. Hallucinations.
4. Catatonic or disorganized behavior.

B. Emotional turmoil (e.g., rapid shift from one intense affect to another or overwhelming perplexity or confusion).

C. Appearance of the symptoms in A and B shortly after, and apparently in response to, one or more events that singly or together would be markedly stressful to almost anyone in similar circumstances in the person's culture.

D. Duration of an episode of the disturbance of from a few hours to 1 month, with eventual full return to premorbid level of functioning. (When the diagnosis must be made without waiting for the expected recovery, it should be qualified as "provisional.")

E. Exclusion Criteria:

1. Absence of the prodromal symptoms of schizophrenia and failure to meet the criteria for schizotypal personality disorder before onset of the disturbance.
2. Not due to a psychotic mood disorder (i.e., no full mood syndrome is present), and it cannot be established that an organic factor initiated and maintained the disturbance.

IX. SCHIZOPHRENIA

A. Presence of characteristic psychotic symptoms in the active phase (either 1, 2, or 3) for at least 1 week (unless the symptoms are successfully treated):

    1. Two of the following:

        a. Delusions.

        b. Prominent hallucinations (throughout the day for several days or several times a week for several weeks, each hallucinatory experience not limited to a few brief moments).

        c. Incoherence or marked loosening of associations.

        d. Catatonic behavior.

        e. Flat or grossly inappropriate affect.

    2. Bizarre delusions involving a phenomenon that the person's culture would regard as totally implausible (e.g., thought broadcasting, being controlled by a dead person).

    3. Prominent hallucinations (as defined in 1b above) of a voice, with content having no apparent relation to depression or elation, or a voice keeping up a running commentary on the person's behavior or thoughts, or two or more voices conversing with each other.

B. During the course of the disturbance, functioning in areas such as work, social relations, and self-care is markedly below the highest level achieved before onset of the disturbance (or when the onset is in childhood or adolescence, failure to achieve expected level of social development).

C. Continuous signs of the disturbance for at least 6 months. The 6-month period must include an active phase (of at least 1 week, or less if symptoms have been successfully treated) during which there were psychotic symptoms characteristic of schizophrenia (symptoms in A) with or without a prodromal or residual phase, as defined below.

    1. ***Prodromal phase:*** Clear deterioration in functioning before the active phase of the disturbance that is not due to a disturbance in mood or to a psychoactive substance use disorder and that involves at least two of the symptoms listed in 3, below.

    2. ***Residual phase:*** Following the active phase of the disturbance, persistence of at least two of the symptoms noted in 3, below, these not being due to a disturbance in mood or to a psychoactive substance use disorder.

    3. ***Prodromal or residual symptoms:***

        a. Marked social isolation or withdrawal.

        b. Marked impairment in role functioning as wage-earner, student, or homemaker.

        c. Markedly peculiar behavior (e.g., collecting garbage, talking to self in public, hoarding food).

        d. Marked impairment in personal hygiene and grooming.

        e. Blunted or inappropriate affect.

    f. Digressive, vague, overelaborate, or circumstantial speech, or poverty of speech, or poverty of content of speech.

    g. Odd beliefs or magical thinking, influencing behavior and inconsistent with cultural norms (e.g., superstition, belief in clairvoyance, telepathy, "sixth sense," "others can feel my feelings," overvalued ideas, ideas of reference).

    h. Unusual perceptual experiences (e.g., recurrent illusions, sensing the presence of a force or person not actually present).

    i. Marked lack of initiative, interests, or energy.

4. ***Examples:*** Six months of prodromal symptoms with 1 week of symptoms from A; no prodromal symptoms with 6 months of symptoms from A; no prodromal symptoms with 1 week of symptoms from A and 6 months of residual symptoms.

D. Exclusion Criteria:

1. Schizoaffective disorder and mood disorder with psychotic features have been ruled out; that is, if a major depressive or manic syndrome has ever been present during an active phase of the disturbance, the total duration of all episodes of a mood syndrome has been brief relative to the total duration of the active and residual phases of the disturbance.

2. It cannot be established that an organic factor initiated and maintained the disturbance.

3. If there is a history of autistic disorder, the additional diagnosis of schizophrenia is made only if prominent delusions or hallucinations also are present.

E. Severity:

1. ***Subchronic:*** The time from the beginning of the disturbance, when the person first began to show signs of the disturbance (including prodromal, active, and residual phases) more or less continuously is less than 2 years but at least 6 months.

2. ***Chronic:*** Same as subchronic but for more than 2 years.

3. ***Subchronic with acute exacerbation:*** Reemergence of prominent psychotic symptoms in a person with a subchronic course that has been in the residual phase.

4. ***Chronic with acute exacerbation:*** Reemergence of prominent psychotic symptoms in a person with a chronic course that has been in the residual phase.

5. ***Remission:*** When a person with a history of schizophrenia is free of all signs of the disturbance (whether or not on medication), "in remission" should be coded. Differentiating schizophrenia in remission from no mental disorder requires consideration of overall level of functioning, time since the last episode of the disturbance, total duration of the disturbance, and whether prophylactic treatment is being given.

Index

acw- 5567

DATE DUE

MR2 6 '96			
MY - 9 '96			
JE1 7 '96			
JY 1 2 '96			
MY - 7 '97			
NO3 0 '97			
DE1 0 '98			
JAN 0 2 '01			
NOV 2 4 2001			
MAR 1 3 2002			